After Yugoslavia

Stanford Studies on Central and Eastern Europe
Edited by Norman Naimark and Larry Wolff

After Yugoslavia

The Cultural Spaces of a Vanished Land

Edited by Radmila Gorup

Stanford University Press

Stanford, California

Stanford University Press
Stanford, California

The publication of this book was made possible, in part, from the Harriman Institute.

An earlier version of Gordana P. Crnković's chapter, "Vibrant Commonalities and the Yugoslav Legacy: A Few Remarks" (Chapter 7), appeared in her book *Post-Yugoslav Literature and Film: Fires, Foundations, Flourishes* (London and New York: Continuum, 2012), 31–39. It is reprinted here with the permission of the publisher.

An earlier version of Tomislav Z. Longinović's essay, "Post-Yugoslav Emergence and the Creation of Difference" (Chapter 9), then entitled "Serbo-Croatian: Translating the Non-identical Twins," was first published in *Translation and Opposition*, ed. Dimitris Asimakoulas and Margaret Rogers (Bristol, England: Multilingual Matters, 2011), 283–95. It is reprinted here with the permission of the publisher.

An earlier version of Dubravka Ugrešić's essay, "The Spirit of the Kakanian Province" (Chapter 19), appeared in her book *Karaoke Culture* (Rochester, NY: Open Letter Books, 2011), © 2011 by Dubravka Ugrešić. It is reprinted here with the permission of the publisher.

Printed in the United States of America on acid-free, archival-quality paper

Library of Congress Cataloging-in-Publication Data

After Yugoslavia : the cultural spaces of a vanished land / edited by Radmila Gorup.
    pages cm.--(Stanford studies on Central and Eastern Europe)
  Includes bibliographical references and index.
  ISBN 978-0-8047-8402-3 (cloth : alk. paper)
  1. Former Yugoslav republics--Social life and customs. 2. Yugoslavia--Social life and customs. I. Gorup, Radmila Jovanovic, editor of compilation. II. Series: Stanford studies on Central and Eastern Europe.
  DR1317.A34 2013
  949.703--dc23   2013005094

ISBN 978-0-8047-8734-5 (electronic)

Typeset by Bruce Lundquist in 11/13.5 Adobe Garamond

For Everett, Hudson, and Lucas

Contents

Contributors

Radmila Gorup is Senior Lecturer at the Department of Slavic Languages and Literatures at Columbia University. Her fields of interest are theoretical linguistics, cultural history, and languages of the Balkans, Yugoslav literatures and sociolinguistics. She has authored one book and edited and coedited five volumes, most recently *The Slave Girl and Other Stories About Women by Ivo Andrić* (2009). Gorup was a guest editor for the summer 2000 issue of *Review of Contemporary Fiction*, dedicated to Milorad Pavić.

Venko Andonovski is a best-selling novelist, short story writer, playwright, and literary critic. He is currently Professor of Macedonian and Croatian literatures, narratology and semiotics at the University of Ss. Cyril and Methodius, Skopje (Macedonia). Andonovski has written three novels, two collections of short stories, twelve plays and six books of literary theory and cultural studies, and received the award "Balkanika" for his novel *Papokat na svetot* (2001). His works have been translated into nine languages.

Davor Beganović is Assistant Professor of South Slavic Literatures at the University of Vienna. His main research interests are contemporary literature, theory of memory in relation to cultural studies, and theory of literature. Beganović's monographs include *Pamćenje trauma: Apokaliptična proza Danila Kiša* (2007), *Poetika melankonije* (2009), *Pamćenje trauma* (2007). He coedited *Unutarnji prijevodi* (with Enver Kazaz, 2011) and *Krieg Sichten* (with Peter Braun, 2007).

Marijeta Božović is Assistant Professor in Russian and Eurasian Studies at Colgate University. She recently completed work on a monograph based on her dissertation, "From *Onegin* to *Ada*: Nabokov's Canon and the Texture of Time." Her recent publications include articles on Nabokov's *The Origin of Laura*, and the traces of English-language modernism in Ivan Goncharov's *Oblomov*.

Ranko Bugarski is Professor of English and General Linguistics at the University of Belgrade (Emeritus). He has held numerous scholarships and guest lectureships at universities throughout Europe, the United States and Australia. Among Bugarski's many publications are *Language Planning in Yugoslavia* (1992) and *Language in the Former Yugoslav Lands* (2004), both coedited with Celia Hawkesworth. He is past President of Societas Linguistica Europaea, member of Academia Scientiarum et Artium Europea (Salzburg), and a Coucil of Europe expert on minority languages (Strasbourg).

Gordana P. Crnković is Associate Professor of Slavic and Comparative Literature at the University of Washington (Seattle), where she is also a member of the Program in Theory and Criticism and Cinema Studies. In addition to numerous articles and book chapters, Crnković is the author of *Imagined Dialogues: Eastern European Literature in Conversation with American and English Literature* (2000), *Post-Yugoslav Literature and Film: Fires, Foundations, Flourishes* (2012), and coeditor of *Kazaaam! Splat! Ploof! The American Impact on European Popular Culture Since 1945* (with Sabrina P. Ramet, 2003) and of *In Contrast: Croatian Film Today* (with Aida Vidan, 2012).

Dejan Djokić is Reader in Modern and Contemporary History and Director of the Centre for the Study of the Balkans at Goldsmiths, University of London. He works on modern Balkan history, particularly the political, social and cultural history of former Yugoslavia. Djokić's books include *Nikola Pašić and Ante Trumbić: The Kingdom of Serbs, Croats, and Slovenes* (2010) and *Elusive Compromise: A History of Interwar Yugoslavia* (2007). He is coeditor of *New Perspectives on Yugoslavia: Key Issues and Controversies* (2011).

Vesna Goldsworthy is a British-based Serbian writer, broadcaster, and academic. She is the author of several widely translated books, including *Inventing Ruritania: The Imperialism of the Imagination* (1998), an influential study of the Balkans in literature and film. Her best-selling memoir, *Chernobyl Strawberries* (2005), was serialized in the *Times* and on BBC radio, and had fourteen editions in German alone. Her most recent work, a Crashaw Prize–winning poetry collection, *The Angel of Salonika*, was one of the *Times*'s Best Poetry Books in 2011. A former BBC journalist, Golds-worthy continues to produce programs for a range of broadcasters. She currently holds the post of Professor in English Literature and Creative Writing at Kingston University in London.

Andrew Horton is the Jeanne H. Smith Professor of Film and Media Studies at the University of Oklahoma. He is an award-winning screenwriter, and author of twenty-six books on film, screenwriting, and cultural studies, including his most recent *Screenwriting for a Global Market* (2004). His films include Brad Pitt's first feature *The Dark Side of the Sun* and the much-awarded *Something in Between* (1983), directed by Srđan Karanović.

Tomislav Z. Longinović is Professor of Slavic and Comparative Literature at the University of Wisconsin-Madison. His research interests include South Slavic literatures and cultures, literary theory, Central and East European literary history, comparative Slavic studies, translation studies, and cultural studies. Longinović most recent scholarly monograph is *Vampire Nation: Violence as Cultural Imaginary* (2012). He is also the author of several books of fiction, both in Serbian and English.

Meta Mazaj is a Senior Lecturer in Cinema Studies at the University of Pennsylvania. Her writing on critical theory, new European cinema, Balkan cinema, and contemporary world cinema, has appeared in edited volumes and journals such as *Cineaste, Studies in Eastern European Cinema*, and *Situations*. She is the author of *National and Cynicism in the Post 1990s Balkan Cinema* (2008) and *Critical Visions in Film Theory: Classic and Contemporary Readings* (with Timothy Corrigan and Patricia White, 2010). Mazaj is currently working on a book on new world cinema.

Zoran Milutinović is Senior Lecturer in South Slavic Literature and Culture at University College London, and the editor-in-chief of Brill's book series *Balkan Studies Library*. His publications are mostly on South Slavic Literature, twentieth-century European drama and drama theory, and the theory of comparative literature. His publications include four authored and one edited book. Milutinović's most recent monograph is *Getting Over Europe. The Construction of Europe in Serbian Culture* (2011).

Milorad Pupovac is Professor in the Department of Linguistics and head of the Department of Applied Linguistics at the University of Zagreb. He specializes in sociolinguistics, pragmatics, psycholinguistics, epistemology of linguistics, and philosophy of language and communication. His publications include *Lingvistika i ideologija* (1986) and numerous articles and book chapters. Dr. Pupovac became actively involved in politics in 1989, and has been a member of Croatian Parliament since 1995.

Tatjana Rosić is Professor of Writing and Media Studies at Singidunum University (Belgrade), Research Fellow at the Institute for Literature and arts (Belgrade), and Lecturer at the Gender Research and Women's Studies Center (Belgrade). Her fields of interests include cultural and media studies, literary theory and gender studies as well as history and theory of Serbian literature and criticism. Rosić's most recent works include the monograph *Mit o savršenoj biografiji: Danilo Kiš i figura pisca u srpskoj kulturi* (2008) and the edited volume *Teorija i politike roda: Rodni identiteti u književnostima i kulturama jugoistočne Europe* (2008).

Maria Todorova is Gutgsell Professor of History at the University of Illinois, Urbana, Champaign. She specializes in the history of Eastern Europe in the modern period, with special emphasis on the Balkans and the Ottoman empire. Her publications include *Remembering Communism: Genres of Representation* (2010), *Post-Communism Nostalgia* (2010), *Bones of Contention: The Living Archive of Vasil Levski and the Making of Bulgaria's National Hero* (2009), *Balkan Identities: Nation and Memory* (2004), *Imagining the Balkans* (1997, 2009), *Balkan Family Structure and the European Pattern* (1993, 2006), *English Travelers' Accounts on the Balkans* (1987), *England, Russia, and the Tanzimat* (1980, 1983) and other edited volumes, as well as numerous articles on social and cultural history, historical demography, and historiography of the Balkans in the nineteenth and twentieth centuries.

Dubravka Ugrešić is an acclaimed writer and cultural critic based in Amsterdam. Born and educated in Yugoslavia, Ugrešić worked at the Institute for Literary Theory at the University of Zagreb for twenty years before leaving the independent republic of Croatia for political reasons. She has written six novels and several collections of essays dwelling on themes such as nationalism and kitsch, the manipulation of memory, popular culture, and mass media as well as the status of literature in a globalized age. She is a recipient of numerous awards and her books have been translated to more than twenty languages.

Mitja Velikonja is Professor of Cultural Studies at University of Ljubljana, Slovenia. His main research interests include Central European and Balkan ethnic and cultural processes and political mythologies, subcultures, collective memory and postsocialist nostalgia. Velikonja's latest monographs are *Titonostalgia: A study of Nostalgia for Josip Broz* (2008), *Eurosis: A Critique of the New Eurocentrism* (2005), and *Religious Separation and Political Intolerance in Bosnia-Herzegovina* (2003).

Andrea Zlatar-Violić is Professor of Comparative Literature and Cultural Studies at the University of Zagreb, an essayist, and writer. She was editor-in-chief of the independent cultural magazines *Vijenac* and *Zarez*, and the literary review *Gordogan*. She has published several books on literary history and theory, as well as three collections of essays: *Istinito, lažno, izmišljeno* (1989), *Autobiografija u Hrvatskoj: Nacrt povijesti žanra i tipologija narativnih oblika* (1998), and *Tijelo, tekst, trauma* (2004). Dr. Zlatar-Violić is currently Croatia's minister of culture.

Vladimir Zorić is Lecturer at the University of Nottingham, England. He is a scholar of South Eastern European cultures with a background in comparative literature and literary theory. His research interests include comparative rhetoric of exile in the humanities and law, as well as cultural memory of Central Europe and the Habsburg Monarchy in post-Yugoslav literatures. He is the author of *Kiš, legenda i priča* (2005).

Alojzija Zupan Sosič is Associate Professor of Slovene literature at the University of Ljubljana, Slovenia. Her research interests lie in contemporary Slovene novel, Slovene literature in a comparative context, Slovene love poetry, theory of narrative, narrative genres, theory of gender and gender identity. Her books include: *Zavjetje zgodbe: Sodobni roman ob koncu stoletja* (2003), *Robovi mreže, robovi jaza: Sodobni slovenski roman* (2006), *V tebi se razraščam: Antologija slovenske erotične poezije* (2008), and *Na pomolu sodobnosti ali o kniževnosti in romanu* (2011).

Acknowledgments

I am deeply grateful to the many people who assisted in the preparation of this book.

The idea for the volume came from a conference I organized at Columbia University in 2010 (March 26–28), entitled "*Ex Uno Plures*: Post-Yugoslav Cultural Spaces and Europe." I am very grateful to the Harriman Institute and the Balkan Program of the Columbia University for their generous support of this conference.

This volume would not have been possible without the contributions of my colleagues and friends: Maria Todorova, Vesna Goldsworthy, Dejan Djokić, Zoran Milutinović, Vladimir Zorić, Mitja Velikonja, Gordana P. Crnković, Tomislav Z. Longinović, Ranko Bugarski, Milorad Pupovac, Davor Beganović, Andrea Zlatar-Violić, Tatjana Rosić, Alojzija Zupan Sosič, Venko Andonovski, Andrew Horton, Meta Mazaj, Dubravka Ugrešić, and especially Marijeta Božović, who helped with the conference and wrote the excellent introduction.

I am grateful to Kirsten Painter, Jovana Babović, Dragana Obradović, Robert Greenberg, Alan Timberlake, Roland J. Meyer, Elsie E. Martinez, and Vasa D. Mihailovich, who helped with editing or other aspects of manuscript preparation.

My special thanks to the Harriman Institute and the Department of Slavic Languages and Literatures, at Columbia University, for their generous support of this book.

I wish to thank the editors at Stanford University Press, Norris Pope, Emma Harper, Mariana Raykov, and Andrew Frisardi, for their assistance with preparation of this volume.

Last but not least, I thank my husband, Ivan, who was always there to help and encourage me.

Radmila Gorup

Notes on the Pronunciation of Proper Names and Words Given in Original Spelling

With few exceptions, the original spelling of proper names and some other words has been retained throughout this volume. The following key will help the reader in pronouncing them.

C c = *ts* as in *cats*

Č č = *ch* as in *charge*

Ć ć = softer *ch* as in Italian *ciao*

Dž dž = *j* as in *just*

Đ đ = close to *dž* but softer

J j = *y* as in *boy*

Š š = *sh* as in *shine*

Ž ž = *s* as in *pleasure*

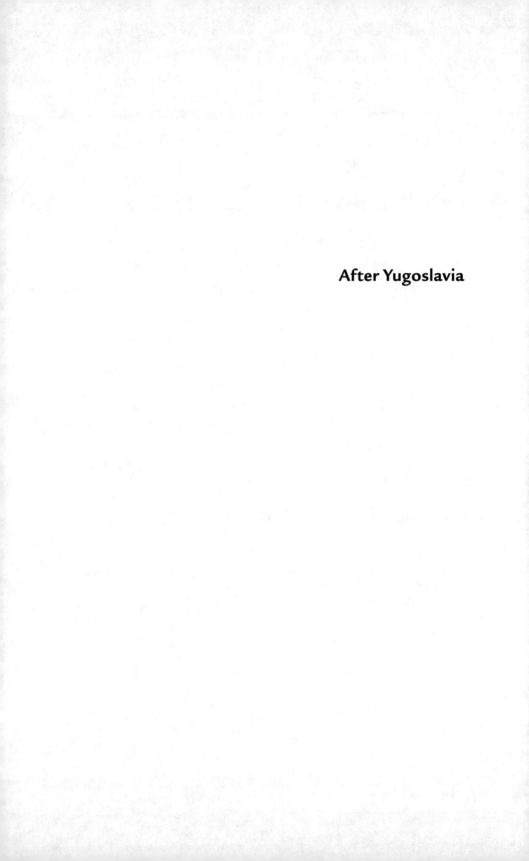

After Yugoslavia

Introduction

Marijeta Božović

A Personal Beginning

In the spring of 2010, I went no fewer than three times to see Marina Abramović's performance piece and retrospective show *The Artist Is Present* at the New York City MoMA. The first time I went with a friend and knew that I had to return; the second time I went alone, to study the fifth-floor retrospective of her work; and finally I went back very briefly near the end of her atrium performance, part superstitiously and part protectively, to check that she was still all there.

Her performance—and the entire exhibit—was intended to provoke strong reactions. In a piece for the *New York Times*, Arthur Danto described the experience of sitting with Abramović as akin to witnessing a shamanistic trance. Danto, who has sat across from Abramović in more sociable environments, was quick to mention her wit and her charming "kind of Balkan humor" outside of the performance space. But more striking is his rhetorical leap from Abramović's fairly abstract, conceptual piece of performance art to his own connections with socialist Yugoslav history. He writes:

I had put three months into the catalog essay for the MoMA show, reading about her performances and about her life. I had spent some time in Yugoslavia in the 1970s teaching philosophical seminars as a Fulbright professor at the Inter-University Center of Postgraduate Studies in Dubrovnik. It was around then that Marina was doing her first performances in Belgrade. I recalled that, years before she was born, I had, as a young soldier in Italy, sailed one dark night to the Dalmatian coast with some partisans

I had fallen in with, to bring some of their wounded comrades back to Bari for treatment. One's experience of art draws on one's total experience in life.[1]

I am struck by Danto's sudden reference to World War II because this mental backsliding mirrors my own. Our reactions are justified by the intellectual content of Abramović's work: the child of two partisan war heroes, Abramović has played with Yugoslav World War II iconography throughout her oeuvre, from the flaming five-pointed communist star that nearly killed her in the 1974 performance *Rhythm 5*, to the white horse-and-flag tribute to her father in *The Hero* (2001).

But for me, the stronger personal association has to do with the particular physicality of Abramović's art, and with the wounded female body. I too was raised in the cult and culture of World War II heroism, and my grandmothers, both partisans, were fairly spectacularly riddled with lead: one had been machine-gunned through the knees, and the other carried a rifle bullet lodged near her ninety-something shoulder until the very end, May 2012. I had some very odd ideas about the female body as a child: the bodies I knew best were scarred but evidently unstoppable by bullets, and seemed made from a different substance than fragile men. Theirs are the older, scarred figures that I continue to see, glimmering indistinctly behind Abramović's body of work.

But what I have just described is only one of so many possible memories, intellectual approaches, and rhetorical roads leading into the lingering ghostly outlines of the former Yugoslavia. Twenty years after disintegration, all of the contributors to *After Yugoslavia: The Cultural Spaces of a Vanished Land* find themselves looking back to move forward. They are united here in an unprecedented attempt to address and reshape the effects of what Andrea Zlatar-Violić, quoting the French phenomenologist Paul Ricoeur, calls "too much memory in one place, too much forgetting in the other."

The overwhelming majority of the contributing authors (I believe, all but two) has lived in, however briefly, and draws roots from the former Yugoslavia. Sixteen contribute scholarly articles; three offer personal essays; and on occasion the distinctions prove porous. For one of the central binaries interrogated throughout this volume is that of individual versus collective memory. What of this post-Yugoslavia is mine alone, and what is ours? And, perhaps as fundamental as the same question posed in the first-person singular, who are/were *we*? How do we reconcile, or comprehend contradicting memories and national narratives? How is post-Yugoslav collective memory, or rather memories, being shaped by contemporary culture and external influences? Who would we like to become? Hyphenated diaspora? Europeans?

The burning question of all the chapters in this collection remains: how do we make sense of the diverse, yet clearly interconnected post-Yugoslav cultural spaces? What combination of admittedly contradictory tools and methodologies will shed genuine light on the story of the Western Balkans, Central Europe, Southeast Europe, the former Yugoslavia, or any of these transitional spaces with contested names? The attempts offered here range from the meditative personal history, to historical inquiry, to linguistic research, to theoretically charged interventions, and even to close readings that bracket recent political history in pursuit of other categories of knowledge. In place of a dominant metanarrative, the contributors to *After Yugoslavia* attempt a polylogue, a multiplicity of communicating voices.

However, certain names and terms recur with frequency, suggesting some common ground and shared assumptions underlying the discussion. Unsurprisingly, a recurring motif involves the mapping of cultural capital. Pascale Casanova offers one model: following in the footsteps of French sociologist Pierre Bourdieu, she imagines a combative "world republic of letters," where national canons compete for prestige and cultural capital. She writes of literary frontiers "independent of political boundaries, dividing up a world that is secret and yet perceptible by all (especially its most dispossessed members); . . . a world that has its own capital, its own provinces and borders, in which languages become instruments of power."[2] Franco Moretti's *Atlas of the European Novel* and Dudley Andrew's "Atlas of World Cinema" serve comparable purposes.[3] Clearly there are centers and peripheries when it comes to the distribution of cultural capital, and evidently the experience of marginality or marginalization (Dubravka Ugrešić calls it provincialization) is painfully relevant to the post-Yugoslav cultural experience.

Likewise, hardly a single article fails to mention Sigmund Freud or to use Freudian terminology, whether quoting his famous phrase on the "narcissism of minor differences," often applied to intra-Balkan tensions, or borrowing more general notions such as trauma, melancholy, repetition compulsion, and the return of the repressed. This language appears unavoidable in descriptions of literature and film after the wars of secession; moreover, the "return of the Yugoslav repressed" emerges as one of the crucial concepts of the book. Sometimes the revenant-repressed is what lurked below the forced-idyll of the former Yugoslavia and brought about its ruin; and sometimes it resembles the borders of the country that no longer exists but that all of the contributors to this volume can redraw by heart. In either case the "living dead," as in Maria Todorova's essay, will return to haunt you.

There are many other telling areas of overlap, as I will discuss below in more depth. George Steiner's *After Babel* informs or complicates arguments over translation and language identity. Mikhail Bakhtin's works on hetero-glossia and polyphony provide a link between the experiences of reading texts on the page and encountering the cultural texts of marginal, border spaces. The Bakhtinian notion of the "carnivalesque" is used with more ambivalence to describe literary and film industries prone to self-exoticism, or as Tomislav Longinović has put it, "self-Balkanization." Finally, the Frankfurt school and its heirs provide the infrastructure to cultural-studies approaches: the words of Theodor Adorno, Max Horkheimer, Fredric Jameson, and Walter Benjamin are coded into recurring critiques of the "free market" and of globalization as the new colonialism.

This volume of essays about a region that "dare not speak its name," aims both to report and to build on shared culture. The pieces repeat the experience of so many individuals and communities: the human mind can-not but quest for models to explain, rationalize, simplify, or conceptualize what are potentially infinitely complex phenomena. Several of our authors also number among the more pertinent writers contributing to these new or revised literary traditions. But direct involvement by no means cancels out the need for continual sense-making—through memoirs, scholarly ar-ticles, literary works, or films. All of these are efforts to "map" Yugoslavia, its wars, and its cultures in transition.

It remains to ask the naïve-sounding question: to what exactly are these nations transitioning? Presumably, to membership in the European Union, but in 2011 the writers collected in this anthology express far more skepticism toward this new idyll than unproblematic unionism. Part of their reserve comes from bitter experience: we have already tried brother-hood and unity, cry the insulted and the injured. Europe might do well to skip the condescension and instead take a long hard look at the rise and fall of the South Slavic confederation: the EU has lessons to learn from YU.

Finally, for all the "progress" of transitioning to democracy and capi-talism from socialism, presumably inevitable after the fall of the Commu-nist Party and the Soviet Union, the free market does not seem so free to scholars of post-Yugoslav culture. The five chapters included in the part on national literatures after 1991, as well as the pieces on cinema and on the history of a "common culture," all speak with varying degrees of pessimism about print runs for fiction of no more than five hundred copies, the drastic decline of cinemas, and the failure of local products to compete with translated international bestsellers. The argument is familiar but remains troubling; as Tatjana Rosić puts it, cheesecake always wins over homemade local pastries.

The idea for this volume came from the conference "*Ex Uno Plures*: Post-Yugoslav Cultural Spaces and Europe," organized by Radmila Gorup at Columbia University in March 2010. The event itself was a lesson in polyphony, bringing together specialists from the regional cultural capitals, academics from the diaspora, and Western Slavists and regional studies scholars. Despite the phrase "and Europe" in the title, New York was the physical space mediating the conference, and stands in metonymically for the largely American academic culture that continues to "mediate" in this volume, conceived, compiled, and intended for publication in the United States. Several of the pieces nod to this other cultural presence, whether as further evidence of trends that they describe, or to suggest alternative transnational communities. This anthology emerged as an attempt to reflect that complexity, to encourage the counterpoint of multiple perspectives, and to avoid the semantic violence of one totalizing master narrative. Narratives and stances certainly do emerge, but one hopes that they do so out of a creative and collaborative "struggle for mutual freedom"—to conclude somewhat archly with a phrase that Stanley Cavell has used to describe the relations between men and women.

An Overview

After Yugoslavia opens with "My Yugoslavia: Personal Essays," two short chapters by Maria Todorova and Vesna Goldsworthy. The volume closes in the same vein, with a personal essay by Dubravka Ugrešić, bringing together three remarkable writers never before published under the same cover. Addressing the tension between individual and collective memory, these framing essays foreground personal, subjective experiences of the region, moving east to west from the Balkans to the republic of "Kakania," counter to the flow of the Danube.

Todorova, best known for her work on Balkan Orientalism in *Imagining the Balkans* (1997), offers "My Yugoslavia," the keynote address at the

2010 Ex Uno Plures conference. Todorova remembers Yugoslavia from the perspective of an initially disinterested neighbor: "In my Balkan map," she writes, "Turkey was western (because of a handful of fascinating intellectuals), and Yugoslavia was eastern." She traces the rise of regional comparativist studies, such as the 1934 founding of the Balkan Institute in Belgrade, in the then Kingdom of Yugoslavia. The institute's first "Balkanological" manifesto identified "two immanent trends—unification and particularism," that determined the historical evolution of the region. Today and in the wake of disintegration, Todorova suggests an approach based on the study of legacy. The region abounds with legacies: from the long shadows of the Ottoman and Hapsburg empires emerges what Todorova calls the 1990s "continued unmixings," the last throes "on the road to homogenized Europeanization." Likewise Yugo-nostalgia is but a peculiar subgenre of the postcommunist nostalgia stretching from Europe to Central Asia, China, and beyond. For one or two generations and diasporic communities, Yugoslavia will survive in memory like the "living dead."

In "Yugoslavia: A Defeated Argument?" Goldsworthy brings old documents and artifacts to ekphrastic life: her album, postcards, passport, and identity card. She speaks of the return of the Yugoslav repressed: "The familiar shape of the Socialist Federal Republic remains visible on maps of Europe, in the way that old outlines bleed through layers of new paint." An alternative space/time, the Yugoslav chronotope includes an entire ghostly calendar of nonholidays. Goldsworthy calls herself "much better versed in writing about the idyll" of Tito's Yugoslavia, although her firsthand memories have been partly supplanted by the violent "newsreel" Yugoslavia of the 1990s mediascapes. Admitting freely to her own possessive nostalgia, Goldsworthy notes the irritation we feel at others' memories, which always seem to falsify our own. Western academic industries with "professional Serbs, Croats, Albanians, or Yugoslavs" provoke extra suspicion, for "such experts love their subject fervently if only to kill it for most other people." Finally, Goldsworthy turns to the dimmed appeal of the European Union, whose byzantine bureaucracy looks suspiciously familiar to post-Yugoslavs: both "confederations" derive from the afterlife of Austria-Hungary. Perhaps more positive cultural continuity will take place online, or in the works of transnational writers like Aleksandar Hemon and Téa Obreht.

The second part, "Histories and Common Culture," includes chapters by Dejan Djokić, Zoran Milutinović, and Vladimir Zorić. In "The Past as Future: Post-Yugoslav Space in the Early Twenty-First Century,"

Djokić attempts a concise overview of Yugoslav history, and a rebuttal of the nationalist "para-histories" of the 1990s. Opening with Stojan Novaković's futuristic 1911 essay, "After One Hundred Years," Djokić charts the rise and perhaps temporary fall of the Yugoslav idea, which preceded Tito's Yugoslavia by one hundred years. Djokić compares Yugoslav nation building and language standardization to those of Germany and Italy, and finds Yugoslavia to have been something between a nation-state, with 80 percent of the population South Slavs, and a multinational state with a complex counterpoint of individual nationalisms. Ultimately the collapse of the Party and of international relevance spelled doom for socialist Yugoslavia—but why was disintegration so incomprehensibly violent? There is still no good, book-length study of the Wars of Yugoslav Secession, Djokić notes. He ends with the warning that "Europe should closely watch," for the attempt "to build a viable multinational state in the twentieth century, and their ultimate failure, could provide valuable lessons for the EU project," and with a nod to Tim Judah's concept of a "Yugosphere." Paradoxically, some form of "Yugoslavism" might continue to flourish outside of the confines of a common state.

Milutinović picks up from there with "What Common Yugoslav Culture Was, and How Everybody Benefited from It." Warning that a clear picture cannot emerge from nationalist, anticommunist agendas or from Yugo-nostalgia, he calls for a rational assessment of the benefits of a common South Slavic culture. He agrees with Pascale Casanova that "minor" cultures are poor in resources, and posits that, unlike the Hapsburg or Ottoman empires, Yugoslavia managed to create a successful supraculture in only seventy years. The Slovene Bartholomus Jernej Kopitar, the Serb Vuk Karadžić, and the Croat Ljudevit Gaj once dreamed of a common "Illyrian" culture; at the turn of the twentieth century, "many 'Illyrians' felt at home everywhere between Austria and Bulgaria, and treated it as a single cultural space." From partisan films to Ljubiša Ristić's KPGT theater troupe,[4] Milutinović runs through a list of "self-consciously supranational" Yugoslav phenomena. A shared culture was fostered through state funding, mandatory education, and translations—for culture mattered in socialist Yugoslavia. Where, he asks, are the great writers and artists today? The European Union makes no comparable effort to protect small languages and cultures: ironically, only Slavoj Žižek survives in the free market. The Yugosphere can only ever be the "pale shadow" of a once-vibrant Yugoslav culture. Milutinović demands how it is possible for a people to lose so much, to gain so little, and yet to look forward to voluntary colonization and disenfranchisement reminiscent of that under the Austro-Hungarian empire.

Zorić in turn interrogates the once powerful Central European model in "*Discordia Concors*: Central Europe in Post-Yugoslav Discourses." This semiotic concept and imagined space was born of Milan Kundera's 1986 essay "The Tragedy of Central Europe," which cast Soviets as "an anti-European totalitarian force which captured the geographical center of the continent." More appealing was Danilo Kiš's "Variations on Central European Themes," which proposed a utopian republic without center or borders. Zorić analyzes the works of Dragan Velikić, László Végel, and Drago Jančar, writers who treat Kiš as a spiritual guide. Velikić calls Serbia a temporally frozen "country on the other side of the mirror," and maps Central Europe by tracing the Danube River upstream to the West. Végel, a Vojvodina Hungarian playwright, casts the region as a Bakhtinian hybrid cultural space: "The great paradigm of Central-Eastern Europe is precisely this feeling of periphery, a traumatic meeting of cultures . . . and despite all that, an extremely volatile space of hope." Jančar focuses on the Slovenians: a Euro-skeptic, he fears that Slovenia has lost what it so recently gained, and that EU accession will "redraw the map of Europe and, for the first time, consign Slovenia to the East." Zorić suggests Trieste, a city that even James Joyce called home, as a hybrid border-city and ideal Central European capital. Zorić joins his authors in mapping Central Europe as a literary "versatile trope of pluralistic space," a metaphor rather than a political union.

Looked at as a group, these chapters map out a territory similar to the personal essays that open and close the volume, drifting west from Yugoslavia to Central Europe. Djokić suggests that Yugoslav culture will not entirely vanish; Milutinović argues that it will and that this is a tragedy; and Zorić interrogates Central Europe as an alternative utopia. All three texts are fascinated with shared culture, cultures in dialogue, and cultures as dialogic; all turn with interest to marginal, borderline, or virtual spaces such as the Yugosphere. Zorić's study offers fascinating parallels to the final essay by Ugrešić, examining the Central European alternative as a republic of letters. The Danube River runs through the literature, suggesting continuity and flow in both space and time, a powerful image of the cultural/phenomenological experience of Central Europe.[5]

The third part, "Legacies of Yugoslavia: Cultural Returns," is comprised of chapters by Mitja Velikonja, Gordana P. Crnković, and Marijeta Božović, focusing on what cultural traces remain or rise again in the post-

Yugoslav spaces. All three texts step back in time in order to move forward. Not coincidentally, all three chapters deal with culture more broadly: Yugo-music, posters, journals and avant-garde design, or the film career of Rade Šerbedžija. Nonliterary arts, or projects that include other media as well as language, have an easier time crossing and blurring borders. These chapters turn to the Frankfurt school and Western Marxist thinkers for the tools to explore leftist subversions of capitalist/neocapitalist culture. Crnković finds a great local inspiration in Krleža, the "Croatian Sartre," and Božović in the journal *Zenit*, an attempt to spark an internationally relevant Balkan avant-garde. Both chapters wonder at these radical subversions of Yugoslavia before state socialism, and at their lessons for transitional spaces in a globalized world.

In "'Something Has Survived . . .': Ambivalence in the Discourse About Socialist Yugoslavia in Present-Day Slovenia," Velikonja takes inspiration from a 2009 billboard advertising a popular radio station with the silhouette of Yugoslavia and the promise to play more "yugo" music than other stations. The silhouette is seductive; exotic "Balkan parties" are already popular with the Slovenians. Velikonja critiques the new "EUrocentrism" and Balkanophobia, and analyzes the 2003 film *Kajmak i marmelada* (*Cheese and Jam*, in the unfortunate English translation) as typical of dominant national discourses. The pretty blonde Slovenian heroine leaves her criminally macho Bosnian boyfriend: they tried, but they are just "too different"—the message is clear. And yet, iconic images borrowed from socialist Yugoslavia serve as inspiration to diverse "anti-establishment leftist groups like alterglobalists, pacifists, punks, anarchists, left-oriented students, and others who are fighting for a more just world." A 2009 survey showed Slovenians more likely to identify terms like *welfare, justice,* and *freedom* with socialism than with capitalism. Velikonja notes that even the current Slovenian ruling elite were once members of the League of Communists, a past that haunts them in the "typical Freudian situation." The old times are subversive, inspire love and hate, selective amnesia or selective nostalgia. But as we know, nostalgia always longs for a lost time more than for a lost space: a true return is impossible.

Crnković structures her "Vibrant Commonalities and the Yugoslav Legacy" in two parts: first she looks to Yugoslav and post-Yugoslav film industries for examples of an enduring common culture. Despite the efforts of the dominant political establishments, she argues that "works of art shape the fluidity of space and time." Individuals transcend national borders: the paradigmatic Rade Šerbedžija is one such voice for reason and unity, initially as a member of the KPGT theater group and now quietly reuniting Yugoslavia through his numerous local and Western films. Filmmakers still rely on collaborations across post-Yugoslav spaces. Crnković turns to the same film as Velikonja, *Kajmak i marmelada*, as an example of continued collaboration: the Slovenian film is written, directed by, and stars the Bosnian Branko Đurić. Crnković then moves back in time to Miroslav Krleža: she echoes Ugrešić that the rest of Croatian literature *should* be a footnote to Krleža, whose great interwar texts were "not about a socialist society, but about a capitalist one of control." Imitating Europe blindly never ends well. She finds hope in recent publications and reprinted works, for reappropriating Krleža "may show a way of reactivating and revitalizing other vibrant commonalities." In one moving quote, Krleža defines socialism simply as "the fight against earthly evils by earthly means." Meanwhile, recent Bosnian films betray profound anxieties over the new "rational ways of doing business," an automatized drive for profit that finds its logical conclusion in the drug trade and trafficking in women.

"*Zenit* Rising: Return to a Balkan Avant-Garde" follows a similar logic but in reverse order. I begin with the recent revival of interest in *Zenit*, an interwar journal centered around a core group of Serbs but originally printed in Zagreb, in two alphabets and usually at least five languages, including Esperanto as well as the "language" of images and visual design. The ambitious if tiny group aimed to reverse the fall of Babel, and consciously strove to evolve a radical, collective, and ephemeral new form of art. This Balkan avant-garde drew on Russian and German models, but sought to turn its double marginalization into an advantage. The *Zenit* circle, with Ljubomir Micić serving as the André Breton of the group, invented a new hero in the Balkan Barbarogenius, a near relative of Aleksandr Blok's Scythian and Nietzsche's *übermensch*. I study this movement in relation to other European avant-gardes, and to theoretical writing on the possibilities of new media and of new incarnations of print culture from the interwar period. This deeply self-conscious avant-garde practice evolved radical notions of "marginal art," anticipating debates in the Frankfurt school and ongoing today. Finally, I suggest that the ideas of *Zenit* move beyond the historical avant-garde, and interrogate the paradoxical idea of an avant-garde tradition (as Marjorie Perloff has suggested of Anglo-American poetry). I end with the suggestion that the most internationally renowned avant-garde practice stemming from the Balkans today, the performance art of Marina Abramović, is perhaps the true heir to little *Zenit*.

The fourth part, "The Story of a Language," consists of chapters by Tomislav Longinović and by the linguists Ranko Bugarski and Milorad Pupovac. All three question the demise of Serbo-Croatian, which may well prove to have a life beyond the grave. These chapters consider questions of translation, intelligibility, and the complex interpenetration of language and identity. George Steiner's broad-ranging study *After Babel: Aspects of Language and Translation* (1975) considers all human communication to be a form of translation, and the extreme plurality of human languages to stem from a desire for difference. Steiner famously interrogates the myth of Babel, common to so many languages: one might conclude that there can be—and in some sense, are—as many languages as there are models for mapping human experience. But Longinović, Bugarski, and Pupovac look closely at one particular and politicized mini-Babel, striving to understand why only certain Romantic efforts at language-standardization and nation building took root and became autoregulating (e.g., Germany, Italy).

Longinović analyzes the fate of Serbo-Croatian in "Post-Yugoslav Emergence and the Creation of Difference," merging his own experience as "a person trying to come to terms with the linguistic divisions imposed as a result of Yugoslavia's violent dismemberment" with his "scholarly interest in understanding translation as a cultural practice promoting communication and understanding." He begins with the surreal screening of the Serbian film *Wounds* (*Rane*, 1998) with added Croatian subtitles in Zagreb after the end of the war. The "translation" was nearly identical to the original, with occasional attempts to find synonymous alternatives. The already comical situation provoked audience hysteria when it came down to the "shared arsenal of obscenities." What is less humorous is that translation, supposedly a bridge between cultures, became a tool to enforce difference. Longinović recalls the collaborative efforts of Vuk and Gaj in the nineteenth century, and argues that the failure of Yugoslavia marks the end of "the Romantic notion of the nation-state, imagined as a territory based on common linguistic heritage and a shared folklore," to be replaced with "historically residual cultural formation based on religious affiliation and identification with the former imperial master." Invoking Freud's "narcissism of minor differences," Longinović critiques the Orientalization of Serbs "as genocidal *guslars*." He ends by predicting the "soft return of the hyphen in Serbo-Croatian," should cultural bonds prove stronger than political agendas.

Bugarski asks "What Happened to Serbo-Croatian?" and offers several valid but mutually contradictory answers. Linguistically, he writes, not much has happened and Serbo-Croatian is alive and well. Politically, very much has happened: the language no longer exists. Finally, "something" has happened, referring to the psychological experiences of the speakers. Outlining the history of the language, he finds that the compound term was first put into use as early as 1824 by foreign scholars. He too recalls the Pan-Slavic Illyrian movement led by Ljudevit Gaj and Vuk Karadžić: from the vantage point of 2010, the term *Serbo-Croatian* has been around for 186 years, the idea of a common literary language for 160 years, and the standard language of that name was "codified about 110 years ago." Despite the shift in politics, Bugarski concludes that there is "no inherent necessity" for the language to simply disappear with the end of Yugoslavia. He runs through the various extreme claims that have been put forward about the language/languages, and argues that linguistic considerations should take precedence over political or psychological reactions on the part of speakers. As a "native speaker of a dead language," he notices the growing use of ambiguous but telling terms such as *our language* and *the region* more or less coinciding with Serbo-Croatian and the territory of the former Yugoslavia.

In "Language Imprisoned by Identities; or, Why Language Should Be Defended," Pupovac uses the term *identitization* to describe the process by which language is used primarily as a vehicle for the standardization of identity. Language should be defended both from itself and from us, Pupovac claims. He compares identitized language with secret languages and the metalanguage of researchers and specialists: none of these languages are dialogical, whereas in practice "languages survive because they meet and combine with each other," just as do individual identities. Pupovac traces the "vernacular revolution" of the European languages and the foundations for modern linguistics put forward by Herder, von Humboldt, and others. He finds a particularly rich history of research into the language and folklores of the South Slavs, and contrasts such cumulative efforts with language policies in the 1990s that erased history and meaning through the forceful elimination of synonyms and "foreign" vocabulary. Through a "lack of continuity in language policy," the language/languages of the region failed to arrive at the stage of autoregulation. Pupovac is especially critical of the recently standardized Montenegrin, with its insistence on a language layer that "belongs to all *autochthonous* Montenegrin citizens" and on minute differences such as the phonemes ś and ź. For a welcome and practical alternative, Pupovac offers a traditional recipe for stuffed turkey from a Bosnian cookbook, a text "polyphonic through and through," which combines regional synonyms, substandard usages, neologisms, and calques—all with the goal of maximum communication with the greatest number.

The fifth part, "Post–Film," consists of two chapters. As the most internationally accessible cultural medium, Yugoslav and post-Yugoslav film has consistently met with the most, and often most favorable, critical coverage.[6] On the one hand, Balkan film often stands apart from literature and other forms of art in the public eye. On the other hand, as evidenced already in this book, no larger discussion of post-Yugoslav culture would be complete without an overview of recent films, recontextualized by the discussions of other media that earlier articles have aimed to provide. Andrew Horton and Meta Mazaj provide two very different overviews in a section that in its own way encapsulates many of the recurring motifs of Ex Uno Plures.

In "The Vibrant Cinemas in the Post-Yugoslav Space," Horton agrees with Crnković that newly international collaborations are alive and well. Despite market pressures, "the drastic decline of cinemas everywhere," and the "rise in video/DVD viewing, partly on illegal bootleg copies," film industries appear to be coping. "Until the very end of its existence," he writes, "Yugoslavia often had four or five films in the top ten [list at the box office], a phenomenon that continues today in Serbia and some of the other former Yugoslav republics." He grimly lists the local predicaments: "high unemployment, often over 50 percent; the continuous departure of young people to other countries; lack of political security; and a huge illegal trade of goods, drugs, and women, often controlled by local 'mafia.'" The movies reflect this reality, as well as the imperative to make sense of life after war—which gives contemporary projects an odd sense of continuity with the very first local industry of partisan films. Horton revisits the FAMU group of the 1960s and 1970s (Rajko Grlić, Goran Paskaljević, Emir Kusturica), then turns to a younger generation. Arsen Anton Ostojić's *A Wonderful Night in Split* (*Ta divna splitska noć*, 2003) and Srđan Vuletić's *Summer in the Golden Valley* (*Ljeto u zlatnoj dolini*, 2003) echo with familiar themes: trafficking in women, drug wars and crime culture, the neonoir of a lost generation. He closes with the somewhat more life-affirming or at least self-ironizing comedies, and Miroslav Momčilović's *Seven and a Half* (*Sedam i po*, 2006). In the finale, which sounds suspiciously like the

Soviet musical comedy *The Circus* (*Tsirk*, 1936), a multi-ethnic cast of characters sings a lullaby to a newborn Bosnian baby in a Belgrade hospital.

If Horton reflects the most prevalent themes in post-Yugoslav cinema, Meta Mazaj stages an intervention with "Marking the Trail: Balkan Women Filmmakers and the Transnational Imaginary." Balkan film has undergone a sea-change since 2000. The films of the 1990s that brought Balkan cinema international attention, Mazaj writes, were not only all by male directors but "presented, without a slight hint of ambiguity, a hyper-masculine and patriarchal image . . . that appealed to international audiences, in no small amount because it affirmed the stereotypical image of the Balkans." Balkan carnivalesque caters dangerously to the worst kind of voyeurism.[7] Mazaj counters with the "transnational imaginary" of collaborative efforts run by female directors, such as Maja Weiss's *Guardian of the Frontier* (*Varuh meje*, 2002), Jasmila Žbanić's *Grbavica* (2006), and Aida Begić's *Snow* (*Snijeg*, 2006). Most of these films are international co-productions, often with Austria, Germany, and France, and with Iran in the case of *Snow*. The intervention of women's cinema ends the Balkan decade and the "cinema of self-Balkanization." These new female filmmakers explore a poetics of normalization, putting traditional markers of realist aesthetics to uses that simultaneously engage with and reject the expectations of "world cinema" and the "palatable foreignness" of quasi-documentary and ethnographic film. *Grbavica* deals with the institutionalized mass rapes that gendered the Bosnian War and prompted the UN International Criminal Tribunal to define rape as a war crime in 1996. *Guardian of the Frontier* uses an innocent canoe trip down the Kolpa, a border river between Slovenia and Croatia, to explore internal and external borders—"landscape and mindscape"—and preoccupations with national purity. *Snow* finds a strangely idyllic and self-sufficient female world in a Bosnian village whose men have all disappeared in the war.

In the sixth part, "The New National Literatures," Davor Beganović, Andrea Zlatar-Violić, Tatjana Rosić, Alojzija Zupan Sosič, and Venko Andonovski sketch out five different flightmaps of contemporary literary developments in Bosnia, Croatia, Serbia, Slovenia, and Macedonia. Perhaps due to the very nature of the topic, all five chapters turn inward to look at cultural developments in their respective nations. The experiences of war-torn Bosnia have been very different from those of Slovenia: there can be no equivalent to the subgenre of Sarajevo siege stories in Ljubljana. One expects less antagonism toward American intervention in

Zagreb than in Belgrade after bombardment; and even for purely literary-historical reasons, different practices to emerge in the newest national literature, Macedonian. However, the literatures explored by these chapters seem more similar than divergent. The novels are preoccupied with trauma and with the noir of urban subcultures; they combine the tricks and stylistic "reveals" of postmodernism with more traditional realistic narratives.[8] The essays in turn enact as well as depict a sense of isolation; all of the pieces either critique or betray powerful anxieties over the new market for local literature, or the lack thereof. Yet, regardless of the relative pessimism or optimism of their introductory remarks, all five contributors still find much new national literature to discuss.

Beganović opens "Traumatic Experiences: War Literature in Bosnia and Herzegovina Since the 1990s" with Freud's famous essays "Beyond the Pleasure Principle" (1917) and "Mourning and Melancholy" (1920). From these he borrows the language that he and the other post-Yugoslav literary critics so inevitably use: these terms include *trauma, melancholy, repetition compulsion*, and *the return of the repressed*. Beganović notes that trauma has gone from meaning a physical wound to psychological damage in popular usage. Beganović draws a direct parallel between post–World War I Europe and Bosnia after the wars of succession: literature dealing with the Bosnian wars repeats the "classic modernism created in the aftermath of World War I." In turn, contemporary Bosnian letters veer toward either realist or modernist techniques. Essentially, the two styles come down to the competing schools of Ivo Andrić and Krleža. The former foregrounds a poetics of melancholy, claustrophobic internal spaces, and suspended time: such are the novels of Sarajevo under siege. The latter is marked by "warrior's prose," grotesque and charged with images of violence and the front, and by external spaces. In these works everything changes, including the topography: the familiar becomes unfamiliar just as bodies are disfigured beyond recognition. There are psychological risks involved in war writing, which may give the reader voyeuristic pleasure: black humor offers some release, but the challenge is to avoid self-exoticizing and the "Balkan carnivalesque" for which Emir Kusturica and other filmmakers have been so often criticized.

In "Culture of Memory or Cultural Amnesia: The Uses of the Past in the Contemporary Croatian Novel," Zlatar-Violić remarks that Croatian poetry has faded away as a viable literary form, in favor of the more readily marketable and consumable novel. In a free-market competition, bestsellers win by definition, and their lists are "invariably topped by translations of international hits, on the whole Anglo-American." The new Croatian literary market and publishing industry are not yet self-sustaining: Zlatar-Violić describes a "failure to restore the distribution network" after the 1990s. However, a relatively stable reading public continues to grow. She finds several categories and subspecies of contemporary Croatian fiction, such as women's writing, war stories, and various testimonials. Writers active before secession, such as Slavenka Drakulić, a pioneer of Croatian feminism, and Dubravka Ugrešić, from abroad, continue to produce. New voices like Maša Kolanović conjure Novi Zagreb as a complex cultural city-text with the capacity to remember. Characters are veterans of one kind or another, suffering from posttraumatic stress syndrome and experiences that cannot be represented directly. One recurring tendency in contemporary Croatian letters is to "deconstruct the existing stereotypes and to dismantle the key collective images which have dominated our fiction, nonfiction, and the media scene." Zlatar-Violić ends with a meditation on memory and amnesia. The peculiar power of the individual speech act, "I recall," is particularly evident when writers in exile defend their memories against dominant national narratives. She repeats the words of Paul Ricoeur, "Too much memory in one place, too much forgetting in the other," a summary with melancholy overtones of the irremediable human condition.

In "Cheesecakes and Bestsellers: Contemporary Serbian Literature and the Scandal of Transition," Rosić emphasizes the agonies of market pressure. More pessimistic than either Beganović or Zlatar-Violić, Rosić considers the "transitional" literary market to be neocolonial and to have "fatally impacted" Serbian literature. Gone is the highbrow "pleasure of the text," as she uses Roland Barthes' phrase, to be replaced with mass entertainment of the sort that Adorno and Horkheimer considered the end of resistance. Summarizing what remains, Rosić turns to *Cake Parlor Stories*, a collection edited by David Albahari and Vladan Mijatović Živojinović. Rather than a locale for self-indulgent nostalgia (baklava, tulumbe, chestnut purée, wheat with whipped cream—and ashtrays!) the cake parlor turns out to be the "arena for gory transition conflicts," such as abductions, mafia extortions, terrorist conspiracies, and grotesque *gastarbeiter* one-upmanship, as well as a "venue possessed since time immemorial by foreign, demonic, and colonial" forces. Rosić also notices a surge in women's writing, but marked by a tendency to trade on sex appeal. She veers tantalizingly into metacriticism with a discussion of the critical publication *Beton* and its attempts to "build a dam" of intelligent and sustained critique.[9] Most compellingly, after remarking on the fascination with the "culture and aesthetics of urban subcultural communities," she draws attention to the virtual soundtrack running through new Serbian literature. A post-1968 "spirit of freedom, individualism, and social resistance" finds its best tools of subversion in music: Rosić even suggests that these soundtracks function as a kind of symbolic unconscious, one way of struggling against the "reality" presented by the media.

Sosič opens the modestly titled "Slovene Literature Since 1990" with relative optimism: while sharing many concerns with the other contributors to this part, Sosič considers Slovenian literature to be blossoming. The bad news is that the "restructuring of capital within the global neoliberal system effectively destroyed the Slovene economy and negatively impacted the development of all genres of noncommercial literature." Print runs of local literature have dropped to five hundred from the state-supported ten thousand, while market conditions favor the fast turnover likely to come from cookbooks, travel guides, and "various New Age guides to personal growth." (Arguably, these same contradictions hold across the globe: statistically speaking, people are reading more than ever, but there is a sense that high culture is under siege.) However, Sosič emphasizes Slovenia's relatively peaceful secession from the former Yugoslavia and its cultural consequences. Working from different premises and without the direct experience of trauma, she divorces her study from post-Yugoslav or regional contexts. She writes that "it is often tempting to rely on the umbrella category 'transition literature' to understand Slovene works in the last two decades"; but her own stance is that "Slovene literature is better understood outside the confines of political demarcations." Sosič believes that high-quality novels are emerging (poetry remains nonviable) around "small themes" and personal topics such as romantic disappointment and the inability to communicate, rather than "great themes" like national identity. Sosič divides the new literary phenomena into "literary eclecticism," "new emotionality," and "transrealism." Many of these post-postmodern works rely on traditional literary formulae and approaches, modified in subtle ways. The category of "transrealism" sounds especially tempting. The Russian-American theorist Mikhail Epstein coined the term *transculture* to describe traditions that cross and challenge national borders. Sosič seems to use transrealism to suggest the crossing of temporal rather than spatial boundaries—but perhaps this too is something that will evolve in time.

Finally in this part of the book, Andonovski turns to Macedonian literature in "The Palimpsests of Nostalgia." Macedonian literature as such was founded in 1945; the end of Yugoslavia in 1991 marked its second critical hour. In between, literary currents have swept from socialist realism to "truth as construct," a phrase Andonovski borrows from the philosopher Richard Rorty. Beginning with the late 1960s, exposure to new literary theory, such as the works of Bakhtin, immediately sparked or coincided with experiments in the novel. Macedonian literature has gone on to produce highly polyphonic novels that portray history as subjective experience. Complex allegories borrow from the Bible, and a certain species of neo-neo-Romantic irony and palimpsestic structures are prevalent. Andonovski insists that these are not just postmodernist games "revealing the codes" of literature, but stylistic tricks with ethical and political implications. Just as an early modernist novel drew allegorically on the subversive religious practices of the Bogomils (Georgi Abadjiev's *Desert*, 1961), now stories of false prophets prevail, such as in *The Prophet of Diskantrija* (*Pustina and prorokot od diskantrija*, 2001; *diskantrija* = "this country," Slavicized), by leading Macedonian postmodernist Dragi Mihajlovski. Andonovski suggests that contemporary Macedonian literature seeks to deconstruct the binary of local and global settings, in awareness of the "'cursed' Balkan area as a geopolitical projection of Western political discourses." Finally, he insists that today's identity is only temporary for Macedonia, caught post-YU and pre-EU. If nostalgia is ever the key word, in the Macedonian case it seems to extend forward as well as back.

Lastly, *After Yugoslavia* ends as it began, with a personal essay. In "The Spirit of the Kakanian Province," Dubravka Ugrešić muses that the Austro-Hungarian empire "stamped a watermark on the souls of its subjects, an internal landscape, the coordinates of periphery and center." Her thumbnail sketches of Kakanian novels uncover a requisite melancholy male protagonist, a local Werther or Byronic hero who returns to the provinces after an education in the West. Deprived of either context or audience, this country cousin to the superfluous men of Russian letters inevitably goes mad or commits suicide. The reader, Ugrešić quips, might conclude that Croats "used the sea for nothing but drowning," but in reality sea tourism was already booming. The subgenre of the tragic return culminates in Krleža: "In an ideal literary republic, all other Croatian writers . . . would be nothing but a footnote to—Miroslav Krleža." Herself a kind of female incarnation of the Kakanian exile, the Amsterdam-based Ugrešić mourns for the brief deprovincialization of socialist Yugoslavia. We had passports, she writes, and now we have the philosophy of the *palanka* and a cult of death. "Foreign media exercise their almost knee-jerk colonialism"; the crowds follows false prophets; "the five-hundred-year-old Gutenberg galaxy is dying while the new, young, omnipresent Digital galaxy is ascendant." Culture has become a brand: culture is the "ideological Euro." Unfortunately, the "Kakanian" republic of letters is too utopian a project to attract many citizens.

. . .

This volume hardly presents the final word on the cultures of the former Yugoslavia and the post-Yugoslav spaces, but it strives to create an alternative space for discussion, one that might not have been possible at the turn of the new century. These essays, inquiries, articles, and interventions seek both to describe and to shape possibilities for extended regional communication. I find it beautifully fitting that the book begins and ends with the work of female writers: in fact, the entire structure of *After Yugoslavia* has something in common with the argument presented by Mazaj's chapter. Ultimately and partly through fortuitous accident, the project is framed by a chorus of women's voices; by collaboration and the promise of a sea-change in the discourse on post-Yugoslavia. Perhaps in criticism as well as in film, the era of self-Balkanization is fading: the increasing presence of female voices seems to me a very good sign.

Part I

My Yugoslavia: Personal Essays

1

My Yugoslavia
Maria Todorova

"My Yugoslavia" is my way of sharing with the ones for whom Yugoslavia was an existential reality, their home for good or for bad, how a view from the outside was shaped. While it is an external view, it is not necessarily foreign: I would dare to say it is the view of an intimate stranger (or, less poetically, of a neighbor). This is not a research essay that pretends to add new knowledge or novel analysis. What it does do is illustrate my scholarly and personal engagements with Yugoslavia; it is a kind of *Bildungs* essay.

When I was a little girl, of the four borders of my country my favorite was the one on the right side of the map: the eastern border, the Black Sea, where we went every summer on vacation. But I knew that on the left side of the map there was a country called Yugoslavia, and I was positively disposed to it, because from there came the chocolates called Kraš, which *tetkica* Božena would bring ever so often. She was a close family friend, born in Zagreb; she had moved to Sarajevo during the Second World War because she could not stand the Germans, and there she met and married a Bulgarian. We grew up with her daughter, who now lives in Canada with her Bulgarian husband. But that was pretty much all. Like most Balkan people at the time (and I think this pattern is very gradually beginning to be broken only in the past two decades), I was least of all interested in my neighbors. I had started school in Austria, then spent time in Germany, and later attended an English school; this is where my cultural interests lay. The one exception was Greece. I had been weaned, like many of my contemporaries, on Greek mythology, and I came from a mixed Greek-Bulgarian background, so sometime in high school I started learning

Greek. My interest in the country almost vanished, however, when I began dating Bulgarian boys, and my Greek grandmother told me solemnly that I should never forget that I was a "daughter of Pericles." I don't remember myself ever understanding the appeal of nationalism, but if ever there was a potential for my developing some national pride, this was the dire end of it. On top of it came my interest in the Ottoman empire, and when I entered university, I began studying Ottoman Turkish. My interests thus gravitated in a southeastern direction. When I first visited Istanbul, I instantly fell in love with the city. I was aware that the people I was meeting there, who were all wonderfully educated and cultivated, were not your average Turks, but this gave me enough ammunition to fight all the profound anti-Turkish prejudices at home.

When the first Congress of Balkan Studies was convened, in Sofia in 1966, I was still in high school. Coming from a historian's household, I had already encountered such silver-haired scholars, who came to our house from all over the world. I would regularly fall in love with one or more of them. Two in particular held my fancy for many years, both of them in their seventies: One, Anatolii Filipovich Miller, a prominent Russian Ottomanist, who sported a watch that had been given him by Atatürk, was like my third grandfather. The other one, an Albanian, I saw in a more romantic light: Alex Buda, a historian and president of the Albanian Academy of Sciences, who had studied in Vienna in his youth and could recite Goethe by heart. As a result, Albania was for me the epitome of real intellectuals, and the few contacts I had later with Albanian academics only confirmed this belief. This is significant, as it inadvertently influenced my first impressions of Serbian academics. At one of my earliest scholarly conferences, when I was a kind of debutante, nervous at presenting my work and at having left behind a husband with two tiny children for a few days, my colleague at the panel was a young Serbian academic. I had clashed with him in the corridors, when he enlightened me with regard to my naïveté about Albanians, all of whom he believed were savage and backward. Of course, my measure of Albania was Alex Buda. But it became worse when, unsatisfied with my continuing naïveté, he asked me how my husband and children were faring without their mother? What were they eating? Canned food? No, I replied, I had actually prepared cooked meals that I had put in boxes in the deep freezer with a different menu for every day. That was already a crime. I heard a lecture about organic and freshly prepared food, and how he refused to eat anything but what his mother prepared for him from the farmer's market. We parted, both of us firm in our negative impressions. For him, I was a naïve person (part of the postwar feminization of scholarship), and a failure as a mother, and my verdict of him was no less generous: he was a racist and a macho. To me this meant "Oriental." So, I nested Orientalism in Serbia (*avant la lettre*) many years before I came to know Milica Bakić-Hayden, and many years before she had conceived of her felicitous and evocative concept. In my Balkan map, Turkey was Western (because of the handful of fascinating intellectuals there), and Yugoslavia was Eastern. Even one of my earliest positive encounters with Yugoslavia was mediated through Turkey. I must have been nineteen, when, browsing in an antiquarian bookshop in Istanbul, I stumbled upon Milovan Đilas's *Conversations with Stalin* (*Stalinle konuşmalar*, 1964), in Turkish, and bought it. It did not much improve my Turkish, but it certainly whetted my appetite to learn more about Tito and why a broader Balkan federation had not materialized.

My subsequent encounters with Serbian colleagues did not entirely disabuse me of my first negative impression until quite later, although I excluded women from my harsh judgment. And even there, the beginning was thorny. Olga Zirojević, the great Ottomanist, whose book *Carigradski drum od Beograda do Budima u XVI i XVII veku* (The Constantinople Road from Belgrade to Buda in the Sixteenth and Seventeenth Centuries, 1976) I had long admired, approached me after one of my comments at a conference and told me that I was *vrlo vredna*. I was deeply mortified. The literal translation of *vrlo vredna* in Bulgarian is "exceedingly harmful"—in a word, a huge pest. Luckily, Olga saw me blush and gasp for air, and the misunderstanding was dispersed with lots of laughter, but it taught me never to arrogantly assume that I knew a language simply because it was the closest to my own. So when I did my next purchase of Yugoslav books, I made sure that it was in the original. But it was still mediated: I bought Ivo Andrić's *Na Drini ćuprija* (*The Bridge on the Drina*) in the foreign-language bookshop in Moscow. My real-life introduction to inflation I also owe to another remarkable Serbian historian: the Ottomanist Bojanka Desanić-Lukać. We were in Hungary for a conference in the 1980s, and we had to pay our registration fee "in currency"—three dollars, no national equivalent. So Bojanka opened her large purse and started rummaging through a pile of banknotes, which turned out to be dinars, until at the very bottom of her purse she fished out the three precious green banknotes, exclaiming: "Ovo su pare [Here is the money]."

Nor were my impressions of Yugoslav males, especially Serbian ones, entirely negative. One of the finest (of the *very few* fine Bulgarian feature movies) of the 1960s was a film adaptation of a novella by the great Bulgarian writer Emilian Stanev, *Kradetsît na praskovi* (The Peach Thief). The story—set in the First World War—is about a POW camp in Tîrnovo, in which a Serbian officer and the wife of the Bulgarian chief-of-garrison fall in love with each other. At the end, when the camp has to be relocated, he decides to say a last farewell, sneaking into the garden of his beloved trying to bring her peaches. He is shot by the guards as a mere peach thief. It was a wonderful role—of the sophisticated, disillusioned, peace-loving, internationalist, and cosmopolitan Serb, contrasted with the priggish, disciplined, and boring Bulgarian military husband. The beautiful Nevena Kokanova was in the leading female role, and the Serbian officer was played by Rade Marković, who for a brief time became the dream of many Bulgarian women. Maybe because this, my first encounter with Serbs, was artsy, my first real-life one was very disappointing. It felt like a betrayal. I have to say, though, and this is my way of paying homage to one of the sweetest human beings I have ever encountered, that when I was already in the United State and came to know closely the late and much missed Mita Đorđević, his warm and soft nature reminded me of the peach thief.

All of this is the stuff out of which stereotypes are made. Why am I telling these unimportant stories without any seeming connection or purpose? Because they all shaped a perception or, rather, a stereotype, and because this is how stereotypes are formed. They revolve around true occurrences, but it is the blanket generalization that elevates them to a seemingly coherent and, most often, dangerously sweeping and oversimplified picture. Later, I learned that such stereotypes are shared. In the mid-1990s, when I was writing *Imagining the Balkans* at the Woodrow Wilson Center in Washington, D.C., the journalist Liljana Smajlović, a cofellow, told me that at one point she had lived in Algeria, where her mother, a doctor, was posted for a period of time. When rambunctious Yugoslavs would go to the beach with wine and beer, and were accosted there by the local police, they maintained that they were Bulgarians. Recently, I read Vesna Goldsworthy's wonderfully moving memoir *Chernobyl Strawberries*, in which she describes going to a bookstore near St. Paul's Cathedral in London. I remember this very same bookstore from before 1989: it gave out free books to Eastern Europeans—mostly forbidden literature, but also useful dictionaries, textbooks, and guides—and all you had to do was sign up in a pro forma book with your name and provenance, without being obliged to provide an identity. Vesna, upon picking up her volume of Solzhenitsyn (I believe), signed up as Bulgarian, just to be on the safe side. But this was not necessarily malicious. It displayed a certain kind of "cultural intimacy," to use Michael Herzfeld's notion, where you partake in the dirty linen of your group or a group you consider sufficiently close or well known.

Yugoslavia was the last Balkan country (outside of Albania, where I have never been) that I visited while still living in the Balkans. As a child, I had actually passed through it once with my family en route to Hungary, but I did not remember anything. But Yugoslavia was a favorite choice for many Bulgarians. The language was similar, there were often open border meetings (even in the days of the Cold War), and then there was Macedonia, the bleeding Bulgarian irredenta until the Second World War. To conclude my section on personal reminiscences, I recall how recently I almost lost a good Serbian friend with my potentially hurtful comments. Countering the bitter complaint about the fate of the Kosovo monasteries and what was the sacred symbolic center of Serbian national consciousness, I pointed out (obviously tactlessly): "You'll get over it. The Bulgarians got over Macedonia, but most importantly the Greeks got over Constantinople, and Constantinople is worth a couple of hundred Serbian monasteries and Macedonia on top, and even I would not be able to get over the city." We are, however, still friends.

It was mostly because of Macedonia that I was demonstrably not interested in Yugoslavia, since for many Bulgarians, and certainly for most of my historian colleagues, Macedonia was an obsession. I was sick of it and did not want to have anything to do with it (in fact, Macedonia is the only one of the former Yugoslav republics that I have not been to). But apart from Macedonia (and that primarily in unofficial conversations), university courses actually gave me a fairly solid grounding in the history of the neighboring South Slavs. As undergraduates conforming to a curriculum still owing a lot to the Humboldtian system we were drilled with an inordinate amount of ancient and medieval history. Apart from Bulgarian medieval history, I have passed exams in ancient Greece and Rome, Byzantine, Serbian medieval history, Russian medieval history, and Western European medieval history. All these courses were remarkably devoid of any nationalist zeal. The same was true, more or less, for the modern period, but it depended on the instructor. I happened to be exposed to professors of both kinds. For example, the professor who gave the lecture course on modern

Balkan history went against every cliché that would have been instilled in school. Explaining the Treaty of San Stefano, for example, the cornerstone of the idea of the modern Bulgarian state, he did not necessarily challenge the idea that it resurrected a Bulgarian state in its ethnic boundaries, since it actually did follow the borders of the Bulgarian Exarchate recognized by the Sublime Porte. However, the professor accompanied this with a map showing that this new Bulgaria of 1878 was larger than the territories of the new kingdoms of Serbia and Greece combined. Here was a wonderful illustration not only of clashing perspectives but of the conflict between the principles of balance of power and self-determination. On the other hand, his young assistant, who was writing a dissertation on the Comintern policy toward Macedonia, was of the opinion that Yugoslavia was an "artificial formation" that would inevitably disintegrate. I thought this was silly at the time and I still think so, even as he seems to have been vindicated by the latest developments. What is natural as opposed to artificial in the world of politics, after all?

One of the most valuable graduate seminars I had at the University of Sofia was a seminar devoted to the history of the discipline. It was not exhaustive and there was little written on this subject at the time, but it provided a sound framework that remained intact over the years, to be filled in with detail and nuance. It is here that I first learned about Jovan Cvijić and his major work *La Péninsule balkanique* (1918). This grand regional survey was a paradigmatic work of geopolitical theory, drawing on the conjunction of geomorphologic and geophysical analysis with human geography and migrations, which bestowed a central political and strategic role to "Greater Serbia" as ordained by geography and in the best interests of the West. Thus history was subordinated to a geopolitical and ethno-cultural framework and the regional narrative was meant to buttress Yugoslav nation building, where common racial characteristics overwrote divergent historical and religious experiences.

While the turn of the twentieth century was generally characterized by the radicalization of national discourses, it also saw the rise of nonnational historical comparative methodologies, primarily among linguists, literary scholars, and ethnographers. Historiography, to the extent that it ventured beyond the national framework, later followed suit. The interwar period saw the institutionalization of Southeastern European studies in the whole region, and in this respect what was happening in Yugoslavia was crucial. In 1934, a Balkan Institute was founded in Belgrade under the auspices of the

King of Yugoslavia. Alongside its research program, it had a regional geopolitical agenda envisaged on the basis of Balkan solidarity. "Our patriotism, if it wants to be real, should be a Balkan patriotism," was the programmatic pronouncement of the founders of the Belgrade Balkan Institute.[1] Two scholars were pivotal in defining the new discipline of Balkanology: the linguists Petar Skok, a Croat, and the Serb Milan Budimir. As editors of the Belgrade-based *Revue internationale des études balkaniques*, of which only three volumes were published between 1934 and 1938, they aimed at demonstrating the commonality of Balkan societies through the comparative method of the nineteenth century. They related the new discipline to Byzantinology, Egyptology, or to classical philology which studies together and in a comparative way Greek and Roman antiquity.[2]

In their first editorial, a sui generis Balkanological manifesto, Skok and Budimir observed that Balkan studies "divided into national compartments, such as were constituted after the fall of the Ottoman Empire, researched, in fact, solely the parts of an organic whole."[3] Thus, "state particularism has been duplicated with a scientific particularism." They lamented that at present no scholar studies the common Balkan reality and pleaded that "the time has come to contemplate the coordinating of national academic Balkan studies, to give them cohesion, and, above all, to orient them towards the study of a Balkan organism that had constituted one whole since the most distanced times of classical and pre-classical antiquity. This is the principal goal of the science that we have called Balkanology and to which our journal is devoted."[4]

The Yugoslav scholars posited for the Balkans "a unique law guiding the vicissitudes of the totality of their history." This law manifested itself in two alternating historical trends—cohesion and particularism—from antiquity to the present.[5]

The major forces of "Balkan aggregation," whether locally engendered or imposed from the outside, were the Hellenistic, the Roman, the Byzantine, and the Ottoman empires. The particularism of the Greek city-states was overcome by "the first Balkan aggregation" under Philip and Alexander the Great, which "issued from the proper forces of the peninsula and thanks to which the basis of the European civilization were laid." Irrespective of the linguistic divide between the Greek and the Latin worlds, the region preserved its political unity and internal cohesion under Roman and, subsequently, Byzantine domination. The tribal particularisms of the Slavs eventually succumbed to the same "Balkan law of aggregation": the prime ambition of two Bulgarian empires and of the empire of Stefan Dušan was the unification of the peninsula.[6]

Where they really went against the grain was in their assessment of the Ottoman empire. Budimir and Skok attributed the present degree of social and cultural cohesion of the Balkan region primarily to the aggregation achieved and imposed by the empire of the "Turks." Modern scholarship, however, had misinterpreted, according to them, the productive results of this aggregation; moreover, it had not duly recognized that the imperial regime had never pursued policies of denationalization typical of many other European states. The roots of this skewed interpretation lay in the ideology of nineteenth century Balkan romanticism. Balkan intellectuals, imbued with the desire to deliver their peoples from Ottoman oppression, saw the long centuries of Ottoman rule only as a continuous degradation of a formerly illustrious independent national past. This view was widely shared by practitioners in the new national disciplines, who focused accordingly on the study of the periods preceding the coming of the Turks, especially antiquity and the medieval states. Research on aspects of national life during the Ottoman period was almost completely ignored, with the exception of the anti-Turkish resistance.[7]

The Ottomans, according to Skok and Budimir, exerted their most significant impact by having imposed identical political and social conditions on the Balkan peoples. They had introduced "oriental urbanism": the Balkan city originating with the Turks was "totally different from the ancient and the European" one and it exerted a strong impact on everyday life as well as on language. By tolerating and even favoring the mixture of Balkan races, the Turks had obliterated to a great extent the differences in mentality induced by the previous exclusivist medieval states. Skok and Budimir even attributed folklore and popular literature to the stimulus coming from Turkish rule insofar as the period of Turkish domination had encouraged the creation of national epics that became major sources of national pride for the Balkan peoples. The fact that popular poetry could travel freely across the space of the Ottoman empire allowed for the creation of common themes and vocabularies among the different Balkan folklores. Even the Romantic literary movement, known as "Balkan romanticism," equally owed its unique characteristics that set it apart from the other European romanticisms, to Turkish rule. Finally—and this was the most powerful contention—it was utterly wrong to consider the Turks hostile to the civilization created in the Balkans before them since their empire had embraced and maintained a number of Byzantine institutions.[8] All of this had a singular appeal to me, legitimizing, as it were, my scholarly interests in a period that was not held in high esteem.

In the manifesto "But et signification des études balkaniques," Balkanology is defined as a "science based on inter-Balkan comparison."[9] It was also an interdisciplinary science, encompassing history, linguistics, folklore, economics, the study of religion, literature, jurisdiction, and so on.[10] It also formulated the methodology of a the inter-Balkan science that was to "to define and explain the parallel facts that make themselves manifest in the different domains of human activity in the Balkans."[11] A Balkanologist should be looking for analogies among the neighboring Balkan peoples. For any given question, at least two Balkan peoples should be compared, but the analysis should never be confined to a single case.[12] Only a perspective of this kind was capable of explicating major historical processes and circumventing the strictly national frameworks. This advocacy of a comparativist framework within the region even prompted them to transcend the confines of the region itself. For example, they advocated a cross-regional comparison between the Balkans under Ottoman rule and the Iberian peninsula, stressing parallels between the impact of Arabs and Turks on traditional Christian societies.[13]

All in all, Balkanology had two objectives—theoretical and practical: "As a theoretical science it is expected to deepen our knowledge about the mutual relations between the Balkan peoples and to throw light on the intrinsic laws which have governed and continue to govern their development and their life." As a practical science, it had a singular moral importance "to influence the Balkan mentality by offering Balkan statesmen knowledge of the Balkan man, his natural and social environment, his way of thinking and feeling, and at the same time by teaching the Balkan communities the necessity to know, understand, and cooperate with each other."[14]

This interwar conceptualization of Balkan history, which was shared across the peninsula—already in 1920 a Balkan Near Eastern Institute was inaugurated in Sofia, and in Romania the first Institute of Southeast European Studies in 1913 continued with the Nicolae Iorga–established Institute of Byzantine Studies and then the Victor Papacostea Institute of Balkan Studies and Research in 1937—had much to do with the political conjuncture, especially adding a scholarly facet to Balkan cooperation following the establishment of the Balkan Pact (1934). The Second World War put an end to this, and only the thaw in East-West relations in the early 1960s made possible a renewed regional dialogue. The present institutional organization of Balkan studies institutes in Greece, Turkey, the countries of the former Yugoslavia, Bulgaria, Romania, and Albania, as well as the ongoing system of Balkan congresses, has its immediate roots in the 1960s, but the fundamental principles and conceptualizations as they were formulated especially clearly by the influential Belgrade-based *Revue internationale des études balkaniques* (6 volumes, 1935–38) stood the test of time and structures research in the area to this day.

This is the bookish baggage with which I came to the United States in the late 1980s, exactly at a time when the geopolitical reconfiguration produced a concomitant boom of interest in the region (catalyzed mainly by the dramatic events of the dissolution of Yugoslavia). On the one hand, it internationalized even further the scholarship on this region; on the other hand, it opened up gates for the revival of ethno-nationalist and exclusivist constructions. I began to read more closely in the history of Serbia and Croatia while I was working on my historical demography project, trying to make sense of the phenomenon that had been posited as Balkan par excellence, or rather typical of the South Slavs: the existence of the large communal family, the *zadruga*. This put me in touch with the works of a host of great pre-Yugoslav and Yugoslav scholars: Vuk Karadžić who coined the word, Baltasar Bogišić, Milenko Filipović, Rudolf Bićanić, Milovan Gavazzi, Vera Erlich, and Wayne Vucinich. I read most of them in the serene surroundings of Dumbarton Oaks under the wonderful care of the librarian of the Byzantine and Slavic collection—the late Seka Allen. Using rigorous statistical methods and data on population structure, marriage patterns, fertility and mortality rates, family and household size and structure, and inheritance patterns, I could show the great diversity in the Balkan region but, at the same time, its similarity to Western and Central European patterns. Above all, I reassessed the traditional stereotype of the complex Balkan family, showing that even in the periods where the *zadruga* was documented (only from the late eighteenth to the early twentieth centuries), it was never statistically predominant. Its appearance (or recurrence) and decline could be due to different factors; I hypothesized that the most plausible explanation was the link between pastoral economy and multiple households.[15] My work on this problematic cemented contacts and friendships with younger scholars, of whom the historical demographer and anthropologist Jasna Čapo-Žmegač is the most prominent. With her, we had to fight for the acceptance of our theses against a wall of prejudice—my first real scholarly encounter with Balkanism.

Technically, I would not have written *Imagining the Balkans* had it not been for the events of the 1990s, yet I have to confess that my very first irritant was not so much *what* was said about Yugoslavia but that what was said was generalized to the whole of the Balkans when it was a distinctly internal Yugoslav affair, and on top of that it was often said by people who did not want to be described as Balkan. Very soon, however, I realized that I was getting inordinately more emotionally involved than I would have done had this been somebody else's affair, and not simply with what was being said but with what was going on. I realized that I was thinking and feeling Balkan. As an aside, when I was given a *doctor honoris causa* by my alma mater, the University of Sofia, I was told that there had been only one voice against conferring the honor on me, the accusation being that "she does not love Bulgaria; she loves the Balkans." But the bigger surprise was that I was not thinking only "Balkan." My mind did understand, but my heart could not share any of the separate national arguments, even when they were articulated in a relatively moderate fashion: the Croatian ebullience over newly acquired independence, the Serbian wounded pride, the Bosnian newly found spirituality, the Slovenian sigh of relief. The Macedonians, as the saying in Bulgaria went, finally proved they were Bulgarian; they were the only ones that did not fight. But, as I was later enlightened, the Macedonians too were unhappy with their provenance: as good Darwinians, they knew that all people stemmed from apes, only the poor Macedonians from Bulgarians. I was feeling sorry for Yugoslavia, and the only people with whom I could calmly speak were the ones who described (and continue to describe) themselves as Yugoslav.

But, by then, Yugoslavia was no more and the issue on the agenda was how to think of it now. There were numerous options on the table: a failed state doomed from the outset by the incompatibility between the principles of centralization and federalism, or between the constituent principles of the contending nationalisms (one based on ethnic self-determination, the other on historical rights); or because none of the constituent elements was strong enough to dominate over the others and serve as the magnetic center (the Bismarckian model—Pašić's hesitancy in 1917 may have been vindicated); or because it was not sufficiently democratic and so turned into a Serbian dictatorship; or, on the contrary, because it was excessively democratic and its constitution provided the logical blueprint for the ensuing conflict; or, it was thought of as a mini-empire after the general demise of empires in the wake of the First World War, and Tito as the last Habsburg; or as one of the most successful federative experiments, or as one of the most successful socialist experiments, one that maneuvered deftly during the Cold War and made its citizens proud of its policy of nonalignment; or as a state that was not doomed at all, had it not been for the international conjuncture and the premature recognition of secession, and on and on. There is probably truth in all these contradictory assessments, when we take into account who pronounces them and why.

Personally I am not interested in any of these verdicts but rather in the question of what is left of Yugoslavia. And I propose that the best way to approach this issue is in terms of historical legacies. Earlier, for the sake of making sense of the Ottoman empire, I developed the framework of historical legacies and then argued that it is the most appropriate approach to analyzing historical regions. Any region or other geographical entity (in this case, a nation-state) can be approached as the complex result of the interplay of numerous historical periods, traditions, and legacies. For purely cognitive purposes, I distinguish between legacy as continuity and legacy as perception. Legacy as continuity is the survival but also gradual waning of some of the characteristics of the entity immediately before its collapse. Legacy as perception, on the other hand, is the articulation and rearticulation of how the entity is seen at different time periods by different individuals or groups. These should not be interpreted, as perhaps is implied by the use of the terms *continuity* and *perception*, as "real" versus "imagined" characteristics. The characteristics of the continuity are themselves often perceptual, and perceptions are no less a matter of continuous real social facts. The better way to define the distinction is to say that in both cases the categories designate social facts but that these are at different removes from experience. In the instance of perception, the social fact is removed yet a further step from immediate reality and one can perhaps juxtapose the natural versus the cultural or textual status of the social interaction. Thinking in terms of historical legacies—with their simultaneity and overlap as well as their gradually waning effects—allows us to emphasize the complexity and plasticity of the historical process.[16]

I will now turn to a couple of concrete examples to show how the category can be applied. When political entities disintegrate, the first casualty is the institutional structure. When they disintegrate through a bloody war, as was the case of Yugoslavia, it is accompanied by major demographical discontinuities. Indeed, one of the most significant breaks has been the final ethnic unmixing of populations that had lived side by side for centuries if not for millennia. Of course, here we see lurking the vestiges of two imperial legacies, the Ottoman and the Habsburg, and this already involves the territories of the former Yugoslavia in spaces that are larger than the entity we analyze. In fact, it was the demographic complexity that I once described as one of the two persisting Ottoman legacies as continuity (the other being popular culture) that were still apparent in the Balkans. One can even posit that the present continuing unmixings are the last throes of an imperial legacy on the road to homogenized Europeanization just at the time when a fairly homogenized Europe raises the banner of cultural diversity.

The institutions linked to the federal structure have been all dismissed, earlier in the secessionist republics, last in Serbia which sported the name Yugoslavia until the very end. The existing or nascent national institutions, however, are mostly in place, as are the generations who served in them, although since the beginning of the new century there surely has been some significant generational turnover. As long as the generations with institutional memories are in place, however, the legacy as continuity in this sphere will also be alive. I assume that the most drastic break in the institutional sphere will have occurred in education, with the conscious coining of vernaculars as far removed from each other as possible (either in terms of vocabulary, grammar, or phonetics). But again, this would be true only for the republics that had to disengage themselves from the common Serbo-Croatian, not for Slovenia or Macedonia.

Like all of Eastern Europe, Yugoslavia is afflicted by the curious phenomenon of postcommunist nostalgia, and again this links it to a larger space and legacy: the space and legacy of "really lived socialism" with a thousand faces, stretching through the Eurasian landmass to Central Asia (and including China by some counts, not to speak of Cuba in others). In the Yugoslav case, just as in the Soviet case, and to a negligible extent the East German one, this is complicated because of a double loss: the political loss (of a state structure), in conjunction with a host of social losses (economic security, employment, educational opportunities, a break in distinct patterns of sociability). We still live within the realm of legacy as continuity, and this is secured, among other ways, by the presence of people with immediate experiences of living in Yugoslavia. It is like the Swahili saying that the deceased who remain alive in people's memory are called "the living dead." It is only when the last to have known them passed away that they are pronounced completely dead. So Yugoslavia's legacy as continuity needs at least one or two more generations before one can expect its final waning.

It seems to me too early to prognosticate what shape the continuity as perception will take. In the Ottoman case, it was firmly built in the discourse of Balkan nationalism as one of its most important pillars, and displayed striking similarities in all Balkan countries. Precisely because it was at the center of securing present social arrangements, and above all legitimizing the state, it was reproduced for a long time. Only in the decades since the 1980s, a century and a half after the separate Balkan countries seceded from the Ottoman empire, and with the new geopolitical configuration that gradually incorporated (or will do so) the Balkans in the European framework, is this particular perception also gradually receding, to take on new forms but as a whole losing its central significance.

Whether the perception of Yugoslavia will serve some legitimizing function (either positive or negative) is yet to be seen. I do believe, however, that for historians it will always be an attractive realm for research, especially for those seeking to analyze historical alternatives. Lately scholars have begun to recoil from "finalism" and have become aware of the historical importance of "failed" projects (the "failure" being measured in terms of how they were realized as a political reality). But these "failed" projects can teach us quite a lot if we care to analyze them in all their richness and their promise throughout their whole existence, not only at the moment of their demise.

Then there is memory. One of the most complex issues today in sciences and humanities alike is how memory operates on the individual as well as on the collective level. How are communities of memory created? This concept was coined to describe how communities create "constitutive narratives" and how group narratives form collective identities (like personal narratives—individual ones). Usually they are defined as small-scale groups who share common experiences and shape their memories through daily face-to-face interaction and acts of remembrance (so-called experiential communities of memory). On a broader level, they can be political communities of memory (structured by ideologies mediated through the public arena—commemorations, conferences, electronic lists, and websites). Not all of them are defined exclusively through a relationship to a single place, nor are they shaped by shared experience alone; they can be linked through transnational bonds, by a community of interests and thoughts or shared feelings. Some speak of "communities of sentiment" beyond the nation-state, and the formation of "diasporic public spheres." More and more, they are transformed from experiential to textual communities. Recently, Tomislav Longinović has movingly paid tribute to the cultural promise of Yugoslavism by promoting Cyber Yugoslavia (www.juga.com) as the promising, ironic, and all too human heart of the complex labyrinth.[17]

Perceptions often shape geopolitical nomenclature. In 1989, Europe, which until then had only an East and a West, suddenly acquired a center, which caused Eastern Europe to officially disappear from the map. In due time, Central Europe died, having played out its function, and now we only have Europe, with Russia and its "near abroad" just beyond. The Balkans also disappeared (and I trace this to the unintended consequences of the bombing of Yugoslavia in 1999). Now that the real geographic Balkan mountains are part of Europe, the area has been elevated (especially in American writing) to Southeastern Europe, and what is left is a tilted Western Balkans, ironically designating the space of the former Yugoslavia that was usually not brandished as "Balkan" until the end of the Cold War, and was certainly not part of the self-perception of Yugoslavs. In due time, the Western Balkans will also disappear, becoming just a curious item and food for intellectual historians.

But toponymy is not only created in the corridors of the State Department or the Pentagon, or NATO, or the CIA. I live in Urbana-Champaign next to a lake. We chose our house because of the lovely view of the water. From late May and into the first week of October, you can swim in the lake. But very few of our neighbors do. In fact, when we started swimming, we thought we were the only ones. And then, one day, we saw an elderly couple from the other shore swim their way into the center of the lake where they greeted us with "Welcome to the neighborhood" and "At long last, people with good taste and good sports." The swimming brotherhood engendered a (mild-)drinking friendship. The charming couple were retirees from the University of Illinois, in their late seventies and early eighties. He was Harry Triandis, a psychology professor with an impeccable Greek genealogy. His wife, Pola Triandis, née Fokić, was the daughter of the last royal ambassador of Yugoslavia to the United States. The lake united us, and we have named it the Balkan Lake and, if this is objectionable, we can still call it "Jugoslovensko more"—a genuine, not virtual, post-Yugoslav and real South Slavic space.

2

Yugoslavia
A Defeated Argument?
Vesna Goldsworthy

Yugoslavia no longer exists, not even as a name, but in a kind of
Rorschach test I still see the land of the South Slavs on every map of
Europe. It is a vision which dates me: the way in which my eye still
arranges its constituent parts into a country on the salty palm of the
Balkans, the way in which I still call myself Yugoslav, and my mother
tongue Serbo-Croat, without thinking, as though the very act of
leaving, paradoxically, makes it impossible to let go.

> Vesna Goldsworthy, *Chernobyl Strawberries* (2005)

We have to take note not only of the opinions that won—or allegedly
won—in the debates, but also of the other points of view that were
presented and are recorded or remembered. A defeated argument that
refuses to be obliterated can remain very alive.

> Amartya Sen, *The Argumentative Indian* (2006)

The Family Album:
How Does One Remember Yugoslavia?

With pleasure. With pain. With pride. With shame. Silently. Often
reluctantly.

The memory of it returns, whether or not I choose to dwell on it.
Not because it was Yugoslavia, but because it is half of my life. I neither
mourn nor celebrate it. I hesitate when I need to write anything about
it down. Writing gives a momentary thought an unsettling permanence.
Some days, I feel incredibly lucky to have been born Yugoslav in 1961. And
yet, I also thought—and wrote—that I wished I were Danish.

Contemplating Yugoslavia reminds me of a game of smoke and mirrors. Most frequently, it is the remembered fragments of sensory pleasure
which float uninvited to the surface: the azure of Lake Ohrid, the stones

of Studenica monastery bleached by eight centuries of sun and rain, the arches of Ottoman bridges in Višegrad and Mostar floating above emerald waters, the scent of lavender in the heat which rises over the Adriatic Sea, the screams of swifts plummeting toward the walls of Dubrovnik at sundown, the taste of sour cherries and peaches from my Serbian grandfather's orchard, the pale ribbon of road unfurling from the Montenegrin mountains downward into the fjord of Boka, like a tress of Rapunzel's hair.

It is easy to paint one's mother country in such watercolor hues of sentimental recollection. Yugoslav life did indeed seem idyllic to me. I was born into what became a reasonably affluent Belgrade family. I grew up in one of Yugoslavia's glitziest square miles, an area synonymous with wealth and power, halfway between the royal palaces of the Karađorđević dynasty and Tito's official residence. Admittedly, ours was a modest, one-bedroom apartment, but it was surrounded by lush parkland full of jasmine and lilac. It had a long balcony and, from it, glorious views of the domes and spires of central Belgrade in the distance.

The brighter side of my family history tells a tale of progress through education rather than business acumen, determination rather than entitlement. When my paternal grandfather arrived in Belgrade with a group of young Herzegovinian Serbs soon after World War One—forced only a year or two beforehand into the Habsburg army—he worked as a porter in the city's railway station while living in what was literally a dugout at the edge of town. The arc which connects him and the present generation of my family, with comfortable professional careers in London and Toronto, can easily corroborate any optimistic narrative of the twentieth century.

Like any other Yugoslav family, however, mine has its dark tales too: the Second World War and its divided loyalties; violent deaths both at the frontline and on the doorstep; prisoners of war and labor camps; then the communist appropriations of swaths of property, further imprisonments, political defeats, and a myriad of compromises. Homes were abandoned under threat or falling bombs, babies born to dead fathers (my mother tongue must be the only language in the world to have a word for "posthumous child"), heirlooms exchanged for half a dozen eggs. Much of the time, hunger and deprivation lurked just below the surface. When times were good, the dark stories were willingly suppressed and hidden. They surfaced in unreliable fragments, and only if fresh traumas forced them into the light of day; otherwise, we were happier to let bygones be bygones.

Like most of those born into Tito's socialist Yugoslavia I am much better versed in writing about the idyll. Throughout our school days, we were expected to compose essays and poems dedicated to our country's glories, the variant takes on "This Land Is Your Land," which will be familiar to the Yugoslavs of my generation, where the Vardar River in Macedonia and the Triglav Peak in Slovenia stand in lieu of Woody Guthrie's California and New York Island. I enjoyed literary composition and regularly claimed school prizes by finding original ways to describe the perfection of my fatherland.

It was not until the 1970s and my midteens that cynicism began to fight the earnest patriotic muse. The worm of suspicion fed on subversive limericks and political jokes which proliferated and—so long as they were not nationalist or openly insulting toward Tito—went largely unpunished. (When a high school classmate, for example, inserted a line claiming that Coca-Cola refreshes the parts other drinks do not reach into an otherwise moving poem about a mother searching for the body of her son, a partisan fighter, the teacher told him to "put the piece away immediately and not show it again.") My doubts grew during foreign travels which revealed that achievements of our unique brand of self-managed socialism had been surpassed by states which had not bothered to embrace it, in whispered stories of Yugoslav political prisoners such as Milovan Đilas, and in books by Eastern European dissidents such as Solzhenitsyn, Shalamov, Škvorecký, Kołakowski, and Kundera.

Banned in the Eastern Bloc proper, "dangerous" books by dissident writers, together with Western totalitarian dystopias created by authors such as George Orwell, Aldous Huxley, or Anthony Burgess, were translated into Serbo-Croatian, made freely available in Yugoslav bookshops, and their ideas disseminated further by popular film adaptations. Since there were no age restrictions in Yugoslav cinemas, I was about twelve when I first saw Kubrick's *Clockwork Orange*. I assumed that the film—and Burgess's book—used Serbo-Croatian words in its dialogue and that the author must have had Yugoslavia in mind when he created his horrifying vision of teenage "droogs." Cultural products which attacked communism were fine. It was Yugoslavia's own variant, and of course Tito, which was protected. Paradoxically, while the easy availability of such potentially subversive works testified loud and clear that Yugoslavia was a different and freer place, those who bothered to read or see them also realized that it might not be entirely different, nor entirely free.

However, I am no longer sure what kind of country I would like to say Yugoslavia really was. Are those who think that, in the 1970s and the early 1980s, Yugoslavia was one of the hotsprings of cultural innovation and excitement, any more correct than those who claim that it was a provincial backwater which punished thought crimes while stifling economic growth with its ridiculous charade of self-management that acted as a smoke-screen for nepotism and corruption? Both lines of argument are defensible.

My adolescence in Belgrade coincided with the era when the performance artist Marina Abramović carved a five-pointed communist scar into her own skin at the Student Cultural Centre, while New York's La Mamma and the Living Theatre alternated on Belgrade's stages, with the Russian actor Vladimir Vysotsky performing one of the best Hamlets I have ever seen, alongside Václav Havel's plays that were banned in his own country. All of them were rivaled by the explosive productions of the pan-Yugoslav KGPT theater group, which kicked off its tour in 1978 with Dušan Jovanović's *Liberation of Skopje*, with Rade Šerbedžija in the title role. In the same two decades, Emir Kusturica made his best early films, Danilo Kiš wrote his novels, and rock bands and gypsy musicians started playing "world music" two decades *avant la lettre*.

Meanwhile, the country was led by an aging and increasingly capricious "president for life," who at one stage put even his own wife under house arrest, and—after his death in May 1980—by the ridiculous "rotating presidency," comprised of one president from each republic, each succeeding one more forgettable than the last. When the apparent boom fuelled by preferential Western loans came to an end in the 1980s, there were shortages of basic goods, power blackouts and petrol rationing, creeping inflation, and all-pervasive corruption. You could not get a job, have a telephone line installed, nor have your teeth fixed without calling on the favors of a *veza*, a familiar person in the right position.

Even then, Yugoslavia still enjoyed the centrality afforded by being "the East in the West and the West in the East." It was (unlike any of its successor states today) a prestigious diplomatic posting for both NATO and Eastern Bloc countries, the kind of place where people who would one day end up very high in the hierarchies in Washington and Moscow learned the tricks of international politics, a country upon whom attention was lavished because it was a useful listening post and an important player rather than a potentially explosive basket case. One need look no further than Tito's obsequies in May 1980. Where else could one have found Margaret Thatcher and Kim Il Sung united in grief?

In the 1990s, this Yugoslavia which I remembered firsthand was partly supplanted in my mind by the "newsreel" Yugoslavia. This was the stuff of nightmare: pavements pockmarked by detonations, streetscapes dotted with the gangrenous cavities of bombed-out buildings, public parks turned into cemeteries, green slopes yielding shallow graves, columns of people being marched away in slow motion while staring at the camera with mournful, familiar eyes. A Yugoslav friend summed it up succinctly when he sent me a postcard showing a 1970s roundabout and on it a few Yugo model cars in the primary colors of Lego bricks. "Greetings from hell," he wrote, "Have we not turned ourselves into a bloody spectacle?"

I bristled with irritation at the British news correspondents who reported in front of flaming backdrops of familiar buildings, and I got upset at every shadow of glee or excitement they showed, at every unfeeling turn of phrase, and every "gross oversimplification"—as though anyone could do the Yugoslav story justice in three minutes. My anger was directed at them mainly because they were the bearers of bad news: anger was easier to deal with than the overarching sadness of it all.

In common with so many expatriate Yugoslavs who followed the disintegration of their country through such nightly spoonfuls of televised horror, I now carry memories which feel both more powerful than the lived recollection and at the same time unreal, like something recovered after a trauma. Instead of an essay, I would rather offer a blank page. Draw a line here, reader. Draw Yugoslavia as you remember it, and let me guess where you are coming from.

Postcards from a Federation: Wish You Were Here?

So they come out, week after week, these tales from the borderlands,
murders followed by bland denials. He reads the reports and feels soiled.
So this is what he has come back to! Yet where in the world can one hide
where one will not feel soiled? Would he feel any cleaner in the snows of
Sweden, reading at a distance about his people and their latest pranks?
How to escape the filth: not a new question. An old rat-question that will
not let go, that leaves its nasty, suppurating wound.

J. M. Coetzee, *Summertime* (2010)

My mind contains a detailed atlas of the ultimately tragic experiment that was Yugoslavia. To those of my generation, the familiar shape of the Socialist Federal Republic remains visible on maps of Europe, in the way that old outlines bleed through layers of new paint. Lists of phrases, numbers, and rhymes, memorized long ago, pop up in my head and refuse to leave, lingering and persistent like chords of an infectious tune. Place names trigger a Proustian game of associations. A shadow Yugoslav calendar runs like a palimpsest through the year: March 8, May 25, July 7, October 20, November 29, December 22—each an important communist anniversary. My address book is full of redundant dialing codes, streets, and towns named in honor of now discredited heroes, places which one can no longer find on the maps. I can still identify the tallest Yugoslav mountain, the largest island, the deepest lake, and the longest river. I know the total length of a rugged coastline now divided between four different states. I can recite outdated population statistics, list the languages, dialects, and alphabets used, and distances between places no one connects any more. Whenever I talk of politics, and whether the talk is of Europe, America, Middle East, or China, my knowledge of Yugoslavia runs like shadow software in the background, a *memento mori*.

I have written a book-length memoir in English of my Yugoslav life, published in 2005 as *Chernobyl Strawberries*. This project brought me much pleasure, yet even the book's title reflected ambivalence about naming Yugoslavia as one its main themes. Instead, with its reference to Chernobyl, it harked back to the explosion of a Soviet nuclear reactor, which I saw, even more than the fall of the Berlin Wall, as a symbol of a wider Eastern European world that could no longer be contained in its concrete straitjacket. It was, in many ways, easier to contemplate the broad shifts in European history which have marked my life than my disintegrating country. Writing about Yugoslavia was clearly, and still is, an emotive issue. I did not wish to adjust my memories of the country only to make them fit the newly constructed "grand narratives" of national self-realization, yet insofar as *Chernobyl Strawberries* was my version of "I remember," an inventory of everyday recollections such as that Georges Perec created in *Je me souviens* (1976), it felt a bit like dispatching a gift of a wooden horse into a walled city. Who or what was to be found inside such an offering? It has been and gone. What can possibly be gained by going on about it?

When *Chernobyl Strawberries* was serialized on BBC and in *The Times*, for a while I seemed to have become one of Yugoslavia's self-appointed yet reluctant ambassadors, a member of the phantom crew of its posthumous foreign service. I became a recipient of memories. British readers offered snippets of their own from "before all this happened": a 1970s holiday on the Adriatic coast; a boring journey across the Pannonian flatlands on the way to somewhere more exciting in Greece or the Middle East; the garbled name of a tennis player; or a Yugoslav neighbor, mentioned on an off chance that I might happen to know them. They rehearsed odd Serbo-Croatian phrases, most often *nema problema*, uttered with the kind of mirth which implied that the context in which the phrase was acquired was far from unproblematic.

The writing of a literary memoir is in some ways peculiarly ill-suited to historiographical tasks, yet being "a stranger in a strange land" (to paraphrase the Old Testament by way of Count Dracula) one is often expected to perform them, to act as an intermediary between the country of origin and the new domicile. I have qualms about those who feel elect to speak for the collective in any capacity, and perhaps because this strikes so very close to home, I am particularly watchful of those who become professional Serbs, Croats, Albanians, or Yugoslavs, specializing in their country of origin (or their mother's or father's origin), in any one of the Western academic and related industries dedicated to regional subjects. If, as in Oscar Wilde's verse, each man kills the thing he loves, then such experts often love their subject fervently only to kill it for most other people. We, former Yugoslavs abroad, easily become locked in our own echo chamber, and sometimes—because what we say still resonates "back home"—we do not even notice that we compensate for a lack of external interest by talking to each other instead of to the world.

Unsurprisingly, although *Chernobyl Strawberries* managed to reach a constituency of readers well outside such South Slav spheres of interest, ex-Yugoslav compatriots were particularly keen to offer their impressions, to let me know how well—or badly—I performed my act of literary mediation. Scattered by the winds of war, members of the ex-Yugoslav diaspora are now found in the most unlikely corners of the globe. Letters and emails were forwarded by my U.K. publisher who was unaware of their content but impressed by the range of places they came from. Most were glad to read in English what they called a "normal" book (shorthand for not writing a history of the Yugoslav wars). Given the prolonged trauma of the disintegration, surprisingly few among the four hundred letters and messages I received before I stopped counting, were hostile or abusive, although—because of my Serbian background—

one or two did take me to task about Slobodan Milošević in ways which suggested a suspicion that I failed to declare an intimate connection with the man. This achieved as much as writing to any small-time American writer about the doings of George W. Bush, but I am sure it felt cathartic for the senders.

Others were more polite while nonetheless irritated. Their messages sometimes started with a courteous line or two, only to proceed to disabuse me of my views on "matters Yugoslav." When Serbs go on about Yugoslavia, they are, it would appear, most annoying to other Serbs. Perhaps because I am so young (or so old) I am completely wrong about x, such correspondents would say. How could I write about z and keep silent about y? They did not "recognize" my Yugoslavia, my Serbia, my Belgrade, even though they knew "exactly where I was coming from."

I have a lot of sympathy for these readers. Other people's recollections of Yugoslavia frequently irritate me too, more often than they touch me. Whether they are lyrical or stark, they can seem counterfeited. They are like old wedding photographs in which someone is missing, a wedding guest airbrushed so clumsily that you can still see an errant finger on a shoulder, an unexplained shadow falling across the tablecloth. Although I had never felt bold enough to do it, I too have often wished to write to an author of an article or a book about Yugoslavia and to say: "You fraud. That is not it at all."

Habitually, we ex-Yugoslavs seek books and articles about Yugoslavia, particularly those written for external consumption in languages such as English, German, or French, in order to detect their ideological underpinnings. We scan them with the gentle masochism of someone who anticipates imminent annoyance at yet another display of blatant self-interest. Blind-love Titoists. Ardent royalists. Seekers of western funding. PC-brigades with their prepacked judgments, running on NGO software. Dreamers of pan-Slavonic or pan-European dreams. Deniers of war crimes and fabricators of war crimes. Yugo-philiacs. Euroslavs. Serbian and Croatian Yugo-phobes with their own variants on the same grievances. Slovenes who need someone to take notice of how well they have done. Bosnians and Macedonians who believe in brotherhood and unity so long as they are in the majority. Choose a flag of convenience and there is a bundle of Yugoslav memories to go with it. I can tell the banner as soon as the boat appears on the horizon. I am no different—except, possibly, that I mistrust myself. Of course I am biased. How could I not be?

The Passport:
Six Torches Burning in a Common Flame

It would be useful, for the sake of a memorable line, to be able to give the exact date in the 1980s when I left Yugoslavia for good. Unlike Eastern Europeans who moved to the West in the years before the 1989 thaw, there is no symbolic moment of defection, no date when I slipped under the wire in some border zone of Central Europe, deliberately failed to make the connecting flight to my Cuban holiday at a western airport, or climbed over the wall in Berlin. Although I swam in the Danube a few times, I have never had to swim across it in a bid for freedom. The Czechs who escaped the Soviets in the boot of a German car; the Romanians smuggled away from Ceauşescu's horrors in the loudspeakers of a visiting rock band; the East Germans who flew over barbed wire on precarious hang gliders: these are the mythical stories of Eastern European courage from the time when Europe was divided by an Iron Curtain which ran, in Churchill's phrase, from Stettin in the north to Trieste in the south.

Instead of a clean break, I can produce dozens of smeared stamps for entrances and exits, imprinted on the crowded pages of the passport which I keep as a souvenir of the beginnings of an expatriate life. When I am referred to as an exiled writer, I politely refuse the tag. I feel no entitlement to the poetry of exile because I have suffered no share of an exile's hardship. I am not so much a *sans-papier* as someone with too many papers.

I hold the passport of a vanished state in front of me as I write, and marvel at its solidity against the fragile nature of the country which produced it. On the dark red background of faux morocco grain, above the double inscription of the Socialist Federal Republic of Yugoslavia in Latin and Cyrillic alphabets, the passport cover carries a coat of arms. It is a wreath made of golden sheaves of wheat joined on top by a five-pointed communist star, and—inside it—the torches of the six constituent South Slav republics, six flames coming together in a common fire. A ribbon below carries the birth date of this second, communist, Yugoslavia—November 29, 1943. The hindsight gives the torches a new, tragic meaning.

My sense of myself as Yugoslav was primarily shaped on travels abroad. When Yugoslavs of my generation remember Yugoslavia, the freedom to travel is often high on the list of what we mention most fondly. Unlike Westerners, however, we felt that travel was a privilege rather than an entitlement. The freedom felt so precious because in this respect, as in so many other things, we looked Eastward rather than Westward for comparisons although we did not automatically feel inferior to Westerners. Travelling abroad from Yugoslavia in the 1970s and 1980s, I felt luckier than Hungarians, Bulgarians, and Russians, but I did not particularly envy Italians or the Greeks. I recollect distinctly—whatever the more reliable economic indicators might say—that in the early 1980s, Lisbon seemed much poorer than Belgrade, while Madrid appeared more or less the same in terms of visible wealth. Always ready to tell and enjoy the cruelest anti-Tito joke back home, I defended his record when a Spanish acquaintance argued that Franco was much better for Spain than Tito was for Yugoslavia, yet I reacted against those well-meaning British and American people who would say in the 1990s: "Was Tito not much better than this lot? He kept Yugoslavia together for so long." I could tell a patronizing tone in such questioning. It seemed to imply that Tito was the best we could ever hope for.

Although I cannot be sure about this, I think the last time I used my Yugoslav passport for anything other than entering Yugoslavia was in February 1989 on a trip to Kenya. I breezed through the Non-Aligned visitors' channel, leaving behind a long queue of tourists with blue British passports. Things changed soon enough. By the early 1990s, the Yugoslav travel document had become less of a *laisser passez* and more a sign of trouble to weary border officials. In the intervening years, even the colors of British and Yugoslav passports have symbolically swapped over a few times. The British royal blue was replaced by a European red, while the red Yugoslav turned blue for the last, truncated Yugoslavia of Serbia and Montenegro. The Yugoslav successor states now mainly opt for the European red, and they wave European flags enthusiastically, most in hope rather than entitlement.

The appeal of Europe has dimmed in the recent years of economic woes, but in former Yugoslavia, Europe still inspires dreams of new jobs, investment, and all manner of gravy trains leading to Brussels. The way the European Union operates, with equitable national quotas of numerous well-paid officials, its teams of translators engaged in building "unity in diversity," its complex and easily misused subsidies, its bland supranational symbols calculated neither to offend nor delight anyone, is often described by the British as "byzantine," but it is so inherently "Yugoslav" that it seems like a natural home to all of us who have lived in Yugoslavia. We may have fought to leave the Yugoslav federation in the name of Europe, but in Europe we will, as Tito urged, once again protect brotherhood and unity like the apple of our eye.

The Identity Card

My Yugoslav identity card expired more than twenty years ago. I have never bothered to replace it. I have a phobia of filling out forms and the Yugoslavs had perfected bureaucracy into an art rarely seen elsewhere in the world. The less competent the service was, the more impressive and extensive the forms, the longer the queues to submit them, the more elaborate the stamps, and the more officious the clerks who wielded them. Law graduates to the last person—Yugoslavia produced them each year by the thousand—they sat behind thick glass panes with narrow horizontal openings positioned so low that one had to bow just to speak to them. A supplicant was put in his place before any words were uttered. *Službenici*— Yugoslav bureaucrats—took unpredictable breakfast and lunch breaks, received applications at highly capricious but invariably extremely short stretches of time, and inspected them at length and in a way that suggested that one was guilty of something distasteful. A couple of hours at a Yugoslav registry office was enough to reduce anyone to slobbering nervous exhaustion or heightened aggression. At the end of a long day, one rarely had anything to show, for an application was invariably returned for amendments. The duty paid was not right, the details were not filled in the way requested, or one found out that one was queuing in the wrong office altogether. Only a naive fool would start the process unnecessarily.

In 1985, I made some preliminary enquiries about organizing my wedding ceremony in Yugoslavia. A meeting with a Belgrade registrar soon put that plan to rest. Marrying a foreigner was an extremely serious business. The official listed innumerable documents my foreign groom and I would have to present before the ceremony could take place. Some seemed moderately logical, if difficult to obtain: a passport, a certificate of citizenship, confirmation of domicile, proof that he was not already married, and an identity card, for example. The British have no identity cards, strongly oppose their introduction on the grounds that such a document would limit civil liberties, and do not register their place of residence. Others were completely unexpected. My future husband was to produce medical evidence confirming that he was of sound mind and therefore aware what he was entering into. As I interpreted this back to him, he laughed at the notion of a "sound mind" like someone who was not entirely above suspicion. Neither of us had any idea where such a document could be obtained, even less how one would go about having it officially stamped as stipulated. Stamps are a rare sight in Britain, and are not seen, of themselves, to confer credibility to any document.

A memory of this conversation returned recently in some dealings I had with the Austrian tax office. The sum I was trying to claim back was modest, but the procedure was lavish. A thick envelope landed on my doormat bearing a black eagle in its top left corner, with the name Finance Ministry and the words *Finanzamt Wien* covered by an elaborate circular black-ink stamp, and further down, a smaller stamp with a handwritten date and a long number. Inside it was a long form. My German was not nearly good enough to grasp every detail of what I was required to do, but the presentation of the document was so uncannily familiar that understanding it seemed almost to be part of my DNA. I felt the palpitations of a long-dormant Yugoslav anxiety. It was not so much like home, as *unheimlich*. There was that recognizable Kafkaesque disquiet at being unexpectedly put in the situation of having to prove something self-evident in ways which were anything but. In tax affairs, as in so many other things, Austria is the ur-bureaucracy from which all our baby bureaucracies spring.

We, former Yugoslavs, like to speak of our Mediterranean temperament, our Slavic soul, our French manners, and our Italian sense of elegance. Vienna is mentioned more rarely, perhaps because its influence is so much more all-pervasive in so many parts of former Yugoslavia, or because the memory of it is so conflicted, tainted by the subjugation to its power and a historical trauma even when "we" were the victorious side. I feel this connection with much more pleasure in Viennese cake shops and haberdasheries, its bookshops and in the hotels where one dreams of childhood because of the aroma of long-forgotten breakfast foods which wafts from somewhere downstairs before waking up to the familiar rattling noise of tramways. The sense of "at-homeness" extends, in a much more complex way, to delicatessens and tearooms of Manhattan, those islands on an island which might be called not New York, but New Vienna, except for the enormity of Austria's sins toward its Jewish population. That I have this sense of being "at home" painfully and ambivalently is characteristic of all those Central European places where, to borrow Danilo Kiš's phrase, "it gets dark very quickly."

The afterlife of Austria-Hungary is worth dwelling upon as one contemplates not the former but the future "Yugoslavia"—not some new re-creation, of course, but that Yugoslavia which is a defeated argument that refuses to go away. I talk about Austria-Hungary not in order to ignore Yugoslavia's Ottoman heritage, which is considerable and equally pervasive—I have written about it in my book *Inventing Ruritania* (1998) and elsewhere—but to commune briefly with the Habsburg ghosts haunting the second, the Titoist Yugoslavia. They are there in most aspects of our everyday life—from the shape of lampposts, mailboxes and park benches, to our gymnasiums and technical schools, the way our university syllabi were structured and our hospitals were run. In that sense, Franz Joseph handed over to one of his NCOs (Tito was one). Tito remained in many ways a true Habsburg Ruritanian, and as a ruler he was a worthy descendant of his namesake and erstwhile commander-in-chief and emperor. His tailored uniforms with rows of medals and complex frogging, his weakness for opera singers, his predilection to tinkle the ivories of a piano, even his choice of holiday homes, bear outward aesthetic witness to deeper influences. Yugoslavia responded to a monarchical figure just as Franz Joseph provided Austria with a raison d'être.

Just as New Delhi echoed London and Rabat preserved the memory of France, Tito's Yugoslavia was a left-field heir of Austria-Hungary under its layer of communism, particularly in its ever more complex and ill-fated constitutional arrangements. When these arrangements cracked, both Joseph Broz and Franz Joseph were prone to authoritarian measures, yet neither was ever fully totalitarian. They both attempted to steer a path somewhere "between East and West," and though relatively popular as leaders, their edifices did not long survive their deaths.

If Yugoslavia in some ways represented a South Slav "Austria-Hungary" which grew out of the disintegration of the Habsburg empire, then it is fitting that Bosnia-Herzegovina, which sees itself as a "Yugoslavia after Yugoslavia," should also be the latest version of Austria-Hungary, and—like Russian dolls or Chinese boxes—possibly the final shrunken version of the Austro-Hungarian model. Bosnia was the last Austrian colony and the last outpost of its "civilizing" mission. I use the word *colony* deliberately, for there are clearer parallels with the British and French nineteenth-century colonialism in Africa and Asia than with the pre-enlightenment land-grab of medieval territorial empires. They are to be found both in the chronology and in the way the colonizer set about running its newly acquired protectorate.

Occupied in 1878, and annexed in 1909, Bosnia was enthusiastically dotted with Orientalist fantasy architecture similar to the edifices the French built in the Middle East and Morocco, which acted both as a symbol of Austria's projection of its power in the East and a reminder of the way the rulers saw their new dominion. It was slowly integrated into the empire and connected to the metropolis by the new railways, with familiar neoclassical railway stations some way outside the center of town. Bosnia is yet again a protectorate, now European rather than Habsburg, but the Habsburg spirit is still there. Just as the Habsburgs used to send their Czechs and Slovaks to manage Bosnia, not only because of linguistic affinity but also because such far-flung postings were seldom prestigious enough for the Viennese, so the Slovak Miroslav Lajčak arguably felt much more at home in Sarajevo than did the British Lord Ashdown.

Looking further East, Belgrade—like post-1918 Vienna—is now an outsized capital of a small country, still adjusting to its changed circumstances and uncertain what to do with the legacy of a dismantled federation, including the financial drain of maintaining vast federal buildings built in an expensive international modernist style that was former Yugoslavia's signature architecture just as much as neoclassicism was Vienna's. Meanwhile Vienna has become one of the largest Serbian cities in the region, showing optimistically that, with prosperity, a new vibrancy can come from outside the reduced frontiers, including from the ranks of an erstwhile enemy.

If there are legitimate parallels to be made here, then what happened to the cultural heritage of Austria-Hungary after 1918 may also hold clues relevant to any discussion of a post-Yugoslav cultural future. A shared culture still connects the vast area between Kracow and Brasov, even as the linguistic unity of a Germanic commonwealth fades, and even as it—tragically—still hums with the absence of its Jews. The Jewish diaspora, in its turn, translated the memories of Vienna, Kracow, and Czernowitz and carried them right across the world and into a variety of languages, redefining the notion of belonging in the process. I stood at the Neue Galerie, the Museum of German and Austrian Art in New York in autumn 2010, enveloped in a shimmering dream of Schiele and Klimt. I was moved, thinking, in a muddled, sorrowful way: "This is Vienna as Vienna could have been, had it not been what it was." Perhaps a grandchild of mine will stand one day in a Yugoslav art museum in Manhattan, built with the wealth of a refugee from Sarajevo, Knin, or Peć, thinking similar thoughts. This idea both elated and depressed me with its sense of irrecoverable loss.

A metaphoric "New Gallery" of Yugoslav art is already being built. Members of the Yugoslav diaspora, both those embracing and those rejecting the "old country," continue to re-create it in virtual reality. Visit any "Yugoslav" website and you will find it endlessly revenant, haunted by the former Yugoslavs engaged in an ongoing argument with each other across the continents. It is also there in the works of literature, flourishing in a multitude of languages, in both fictional and nonfictional forms. In 2010 alone, I have read *La vie fantasmagoriquement brève et étrange d'Amadeo Modiglani*, by Velibor Čolić, a writer now much lauded in France; Vesna Marić's *Bluebird*, a poignant English memoir of Mostar; Saša Stanišić's *How the Soldier Repairs the Gramophone*, written originally in German; and the outstanding works of Yugoslav-born American novelists Aleksandar Hemon and Téa Obreht. I am not sure how any of them now describe their national identity, and certainly hope that I would not offend anyone by allowing myself the freedom of listing them together under the shared umbrella of a vanished country. My aim is not to appropriate them for any dubious claim of Yugoslav continuity but to remind others that post-Yugoslav culture now thrives well beyond—perhaps even mainly beyond—those places where we once expected to find it, and often in languages which are not studied in South Slavonic departments.

Just because Yugoslavia is no longer there, it doesn't mean that it has gone away.

Part II

Histories and Common Culture

3

The Past as Future
Post-Yugoslav Space in the Early Twenty-First Century

Dejan Djokić

In 1911, Serbian historian and politician Stojan Novaković published an essay entitled "After One Hundred Years."[1] This futuristic work, published in a pro-Yugoslav almanac in *both* Belgrade and Zagreb, tells the story of an unnamed Croat who travels to Belgrade in May 2011 to attend a lecture by a Professor Vidović (a fictional character and probably a historian).[2] The lecture is delivered in a cultural centre named after Dositej Obradović, an eighteenth-century Serbian man of letters and the first Serbian education minister (the almanac, which celebrated Obradović as an early Yugoslav prophet, was published to mark the hundredth anniversary of his death). Vidović's talk is attended by an audience from across a large, unified South Slav state. The geographical extent of this imagined, future Yugoslavia is described at the beginning of the essay. As he approaches Belgrade, the Croat traveller is impressed by the sight of numerous airplanes flying from the city "like butterflies, carrying mail to Ljubljana, Zagreb, Skadar, Ohrid, Prizren, Skoplje, and Niš"; the reader is told in the same paragraph that the rivers Sava and Danube flow through the state, the territory of which also includes the Dalmatian and Montenegrin coasts. In other words, the territorial extent of Novaković's "Yugoslavia" was remarkably close to that of the Yugoslav state established in 1918, three years after Novaković's death, with the notable exception of Skadar (Shkodra or Shkodër in Albanian, Scutari in Italian), a northwestern Albanian port on Lake Skadar.[3]

Novaković, a former minister of education in several Serbian cabinets, and also a former prime minister, imagined that the culture of the South Slavs would foster a common Yugoslav identity and a unified Yugoslav state. Novaković's argument is not surprising: he shared with many of his contemporaries (not only other South Slavs) the idea that a nation is based primarily on a common linguistic and cultural heritage.[4] His argument was also appropriate for the occasion: the essay was written to mark the centenary of the death of Obradović, the first minister of education in Serbia, while the imagined 2011 lecture by Vidović— Novaković's alter ego—was presumably delivered to mark the bicentenary of Obradović's death.

Stojan Novaković died in February 1915 in Niš, where the Serbian government and the royal court retreated following the Austro-Hungarian bombardment of Belgrade. He died before Serbia was invaded, and the government, the court, and the army withdrew to the Greek island of Corfu in the winter of 1915–16. He did not live long enough to see the creation of Yugoslavia at the end of the war. Despite the Serbian government's public declaration in December 1914 that its main war aim was the liberation and unification of all Serbs, Croats, and Slovenes into one state,[5] could Novaković have foreseen that events would proceed with such speed? Most probably not; in any case, he did not envisage a speedy formation of a Yugoslav identity, but a gradual one, achieved through the fostering of a common Yugoslav culture. It is even less likely he could have imagined that by the time his futuristic alter-ego gave his lecture, Yugoslavia would be dead for twenty years, having twice disintegrated in the twentieth century, both times in violent and tragic wars in which the Yugoslavs fought each other.

Novaković was not alone in believing that the Yugoslavs would unite one day; nor did only Yugoslavs believe in the inevitability, if still a distant one, of their unity. In the same year that Novaković published his essay, the foremost British expert on South Slav history and politics, R. W. Seton-Watson, wrote that Serbs and Croats belonged to one, Yugoslav "race," which would eventually unite, just like the Italian and German "races" had done in the nineteenth century. In the 1910 population census carried out in Austria-Hungary, Serbs and Croats were listed as a single group: the "Serbo-Croats."[6]

In the end, however, it was perhaps more due to the revolutionary zeal of Yugoslavism's fanatical supporters, such as those around the Young Bosnia group, a member of which assassinated the Habsburg archduke in Sarajevo, on June 28, 1914, and due to the Great War sparked by the assassination, that Yugoslavia came into being. The Habsburg monarchy collapsed at the end of the war, which also saw the emergence of several successor states, Yugoslavia among them. Italy's claim on the eastern Adriatic accelerated the unification. As Italian troops entered from the north, Dalmatian Croats threatened to unite Dalmatia with Serbia if Zagreb hesitated. Similarly, predominantly Serb-populated municipalities in Bosnia and Vojvodina pushed for unification with Serbia. The Yugoslav state was proclaimed by the Yugoslavs themselves in Belgrade, on December 1, 1918, and was not recognized by the Allies for another six months. The United States was the first great power to recognise the Kingdom of the Serbs, Croats, and Slovenes, as the country was officially known until 1929—it did so in February 1919, while Britain and France waited until early June. Yet, the Yugoslav delegation at the Paris Peace Conference, which commenced in January 1919, was not recognized until May that year, not even by the United States.[7] Therefore, Yugoslavia was not imposed by the victorious Allies, as it is sometimes inaccurately claimed. Without Allied consent Yugoslavia could not have been created, but it should be remembered that it was proclaimed by Serb, Croat, and Slovene leaders.[8]

.   .   .

Let us imagine that Professor Vidović did indeed give a lecture in 2011. Instead of Belgrade, the lecture was given in London, where Vidović emigrated at the beginning of the Yugoslav wars, and where he studied and then taught history at the "University of Bloomsbury." Instead of celebrating a common Yugoslav identity unified through culture and literature, as Novaković's Vidović did, our Vidović was asked to give an overview of the history of the Yugoslav idea and of Yugoslavia on the occasion of the twentieth anniversary of the country's breakup. Vidović's lecture might have read as follows:

Yugoslavia as an idea had preceded Yugoslavia as a state by almost a hundred years. The idea of Yugoslav unity, or Yugoslavism, originated in the 1830s, when a group of Croat intellectuals began promoting cultural unity between Croats and Serbs. It was a reaction to the growing threat of Magyarization and its most immediate result was cultural integration of the Croats, who had been divided not only territorially within the complex Habsburg structure but also linguistically. The proto-Yugoslavs, better known as the "Illyrians," promoted the *štokavski*, one of the three dialects spoken by Croats, because it was also spoken by Serbs, even though most "Illyrian" intellectuals spoke the *kajkavski*, which was closer to Slovene. (The third Croatian dialect was *čakavski*; the dialects are named after different regional words for "what": *što, kaj,* and *ča*.)

The early development of the Yugoslav idea was inseparable from the development of modern Croatian national integration. Parallel to the Yugoslav idea, the Croats developed a separate Croatian national ideology, based on the "historic right" to statehood. The emerging Serbian state had little understanding of Yugoslavism, a somewhat narrower idea of pan-Serbian liberation and unification dominating the political discourse of nineteenth-century Serbia. The Croatian and Serbian national ideas did not differ much from other Romantic nationalist ideologies of the time, including the Yugoslav idea. They posed a threat to Yugoslav unity, but were not in as sharp a contradiction with it as it might seem from today's perspective. Conflicting claims of Croatian and Serbian nationalists and sometimes even denial of each other's existence were based on linguistic and cultural similarities between the Croats and Serbs, not fundamental differences.[9]

The Yugoslav idea survived the nineteenth century and its "updated" version formed the basis of the program of the Croat-Serb Coalition, which dominated Croatian politics in the years preceding the First World War. At the same time, Yugoslavism, hitherto largely rejected, became accepted by Serbia's intellectuals and, increasingly, politicians—Stojan Novaković was a good example of both. Proponents of Yugoslavism at the beginning of the twentieth century believed that Serbs, Croats, and Slovenes were "tribes" of one *ethnic* nation with three names. Many Slovenes, whose language differed from Serbo-Croat, also became enthusiastic supporters of Yugoslavism, and some even argued that they should give up their separate language for the sake of the nation's unity (a sacrifice that would have overshadowed even that made by the "Illyrians" in the nineteenth century).[10]

The history, idea, and program of this "national oneness" version of Yugoslavism are well summarized in a series of pamphlets published in London during the First World War by the Yugoslav Committee, a group of exiled Habsburg South Slav politicians of the Croat-Serb Coalition and pro-Yugoslav intellectuals. Members of the Yugoslav Committee argued that Yugoslavs—namely Serbs, Croats, and Slovenes—were and had always been one nation, kept apart only by divisions imposed by their foreign rulers. However, they also believed that, like other national ideas, "the idea of Southern Slav unity was modern in its essence," and that its development may be divided into several phases. Employing a remarkably modern language, the author(s) of an essay published in 1916 by the committee stressed that national ideas demand "clear self-consciousness, a wide mental outlook, and an enlightened intelligentsia." According to them, the birth of the Yugoslav idea began in the sixteenth century, but its "final phase" started in 1903 (the year of important political changes in the independent Serbian Kingdom as well as inside the Habsburg South Slav provinces), and that it would be only completed with the unification of the three "tribes" into a single political entity.[11]

Although there were disagreements between the Yugoslav Committee and the Serbian wartime government, especially over the question of whether the future common state should be a centralized or a decentralized one, the notion of "national oneness" was accepted by both sides. Thus, for instance, the Corfu Declaration, issued in July 1917 by the Serbian government and the Yugoslav Committee, stated that "our three-named nation" shared "the same blood" and "spoken and written language," and despite external pressures, "the idea of its [the Yugoslav nation's] unity could never be extinguished."[12]

When it was created in 1918, Yugoslavia was viewed both from inside and outside as a Serbo-Croat-Slovene *nation-state*, in which the South Slavs formed more than 80 percent of the country's population (the largest minorities being ethnic Albanians, Germans, and Hungarians).[13] In fact, the formation of the Kingdom of Serbs, Croats, and Slovenes was facilitated by the principle of self-determination of the peoples, the key to President Wilson's Fourteen Points. Inside the new country, even the Communists, despite the Comintern's anti-Versailles and anti-Yugoslav stance, did not at first oppose the concept of Yugoslav ethnic unity. Nor did the Croatian (Republican) Peasant Party reject Yugoslavism, although it opposed the way the unification was carried out and boycotted the new state's institutions well into the 1920s. Its leader, Stjepan Radić, while calling for a Croatian state *within* Yugoslavia, proclaimed not long after the unification that "we Croats, Slovenes, and Serbs really are one nation, both according to our language and our customs."[14]

As Andrew Wachtel has shown in his study on cultural politics in Yugoslavia, even those most optimistic adherents of Yugoslavism, the intellectuals, recognized that no Yugoslav nation existed in 1918 and that a common Yugoslav culture had to be created.[15] While intellectuals preferred a genuine Yugoslav "synthesis," the country's political leaders argued over the constitution. The Serbs generally preferred centralism, modelled on Serbia's 1903 constitution (which itself was inspired by the French and Belgian constitutions), while Croats, fearing Serb domination, called for a decentralized state. The argument turned into essentially a Serb-Croat debate soon after the unification, although there were prominent Serbs opposed to centralism, and Croats and other non-Serbs who supported Belgrade's vision of the new state. Ivo Banac, one of the foremost experts on Yugoslav history, has argued that this conflict was historically predetermined, due to the incompatible Croat and Serb national ideologies formed prior to the unification in 1918. Broadly speaking, according to Banac, Croats favoured a genuine cooperation among South Slavs, while Serbs preferred a state-sponsored domination over other Yugoslavs and even assimilation of some non-Serbs. While initially there existed a slim chance for a genuine union, by 1921 it had gone. On June 28 that year a Serb-style centralist constitution was promulgated, marking the beginning of Serbian domination and a de facto end to the Yugoslav project.[16] Although powerfully argued, this school of thought fails to explain the full complexity of interwar Yugoslavia. Croat, Serb, and other national ideologies, including the Yugoslav one, may have developed prior to 1918, but they continued to evolve following the unification, and were in any case never as homogeneous as is often assumed. It would also be somewhat simplistic to reduce the politics of the 1920s to a Serb-Croat conflict—during that decade, and even more so during the 1930s, political conflict as well as cooperation often crossed the deep "ethnic divisions" that allegedly undermined Yugoslavia from the very beginning.[17] Finally, during the interwar period and indeed throughout the existence of Yugoslavia, there also existed plausible, pro-Yugoslav alternatives to official Yugoslavisms.

Despite the official discourse, which argued that Yugoslavia was the Serb-Croat-Slovene nation-state, it was only after King Alexander introduced his personal dictatorship in January 1929 that the state embarked upon creating the Yugoslav nation. (In fact, only during the Alexandrine dictatorship of 1929–34 did the state attempt to create a Yugoslav nation—only for five years out of more than seventy years of Yugoslavia's existence did the state engage in Yugoslav nation building. Although Yugoslavia is often viewed as a failure when it comes to nation building, during its existence Serb, Croat, and Slovene national identities continued to be formed, while "new" nations—Bosnian Muslims, Macedonians, and Montenegrins—were promoted.) The dictatorship was ostensibly introduced as a last attempt to save the country from sliding into chaos, after the assassination of Radić and a group of Croatian Peasant Party deputies in June 1928 by a (Serbian) Radical Party deputy. But the dictatorship was too closely linked with the king, despite initially receiving support from many "ordinary" Yugoslavs and even from Vladko Maček, Radić's successor as the Croatian Peasants' leader.[18] The end of the dictatorship would indeed begin with the assassination of King Alexander in October 1934, by a combined action of Croat and Macedonian revolutionaries—the *ustašas* and the Internal Macedonian Revolutionary Organization (IMRO), respectively—although it would never be fully abandoned by the king's successors. Prince Paul, the regent of Yugoslavia between 1934 and 1941, argued that he could not abandon the dictatorship, since he was merely ruling in the name of his minor nephew, King Peter II, and could not risk weakening the position of the king. However, in 1936, Paul was advised by the country's leading experts in constitutional law that a return to democracy would not lessen the crown in any way, but he allegedly ignored their expert opinion.[19]

In 1929 the country's name was officially changed to Yugoslavia. The new name and new administrative divisions were meant to conceal and eventually put to an end divisions created by history, while legal and education systems were to be made uniform throughout the country. Between 1918 and 1929, the "national oneness" version of Yugoslavism was official, but after 1929 the "integral" version of Yugoslavism became compulsory. Despite—or because of—this, it failed. To non-Serbs, especially Croats, it was too Serbian, not only in practice but also in terms of national mythology. Many Serbs came to reject the dictatorship, too, and not only because it put an end to parliamentary democracy, which they claimed to have achieved in their pre-Yugoslav kingdom. From the mid-1930s onward, the Serbs increasingly began to complain that their history and identity were being sacrificed for a wider Yugoslav ideal, and yet they were being accused by Croats of manipulating Yugoslavism in order to Serbianize the country.[20]

The two general, quasi-democratic elections of the second half of the 1930s—in May 1935 and December 1938—were significant not only because they clearly indicated that Alexander's successors, led by his first cousin, Prince Paul, were ready to relax (if not completely abandon) the dictatorship. The 1938 elections in particular demonstrated a growing Serb-Croat cooperation in opposition to the government, which, although Serb-dominated, included the largest Slovene and Bosnian

Muslim parties. The opposition gave the government a very close run, which clearly indicated that many "ordinary" Yugoslavs supported the solution to the "Croat question" and a return to democracy—the two main aims of the united opposition. Because of the government's pressure on the electorate to vote for its list—and the ballot was not secret then—the opposition's success was even more remarkable.

Alexander's desire—to unite the country, but above all to put an end to the Serb-Croat quarrel—was thus being fulfilled, although not in the way he would have imagined it. The Serb-Croat agreement in opposition led Prince Paul to seek an alternative "Serb-Croat" agreement, which would incite the Croatian Peasant Party into the government, and also break up the opposition coalition. This was achieved by the Cvetković-Maček *sporazum* (agreement) of August 1939, which granted Croatia wide autonomy but left unfinished what was clearly a first step toward federalization. The growing external crisis only accelerated events inside Yugoslavia.

The "national oneness" and "integral" versions of Yugoslavism failed for several reasons. Perhaps key among them was that they were too easily associated with Serbian predominance in state and military institutions. Another reason was that there was simply not enough time for the interwar statesmen to reach a viable compromise. Between the world wars Croats and Serbs worked together both in opposition and government towards achieving an agreement. That the "integral" version of Yugoslavism never fully transformed into an "agreement" (federal?) version of Yugoslavism was probably chiefly due to the outbreak of the Second World War. In April 1941, just over a year and a half after the Cvetković-Maček agreement, Yugoslavia was invaded and partitioned by the Axis powers. An enlarged Croatia, which included all of Bosnia-Herzegovina and stretched into northern Serbia, was proclaimed independent, while other parts of the country were either occupied by the Axis and their satellites or annexed by them.

Like in the 1990s, the fiercest fighting took place in Bosnia and Croatia, in ethnically mixed areas, between various regular and irregular forces.[21] In the 1940s, just like in the 1990s, the conflict was in many respects a Serb-Croat war, with Bosnian Muslims caught in between; and yet, in both cases, Serbia and Croatia were officially not at war with each other. Not unlike the political conflict of the interwar period, the armed conflicts that broke out across what was the first former Yugoslavia in the early 1940s were not simply ethnic wars between different Yugoslav groups; the *ustaša* rulers of independent Croatia waging a murderous campaign against the Serbs which apparently shocked even their German mentors, notwithstanding. Wars of resistance went hand in hand with civil and ideological wars; the war between the ustašas and the resurgent Serbs represented just one dimension of a multilayered conflict in occupied Yugoslavia.

Two movements emerged soon after the occupation. A group of army officers led by Colonel (later General) Dragoljub (Draža) Mihailović began the organized resistance, but would be eventually joined, overtaken, and defeated by their main rivals, the Communist-led Partisans. Mihailović's movement, better known as the *četniks*, was in fact a group of loosely connected, dispersed, predominantly Serb, forces. Sometimes they only nominally recognized Mihailović's leadership, especially after he was appointed the war minister by the London-based government-in-exile in January 1942, but often acted independently of him. This was especially true of the Dalmatian and Montenegrin četniks, who at times openly collaborated with Italian troops there. The Partisans, on the other hand, had an able leader in Josip Broz Tito, the general secretary of the Communist Party, who came from a mixed Croat-Slovene background. They were well organized, disciplined, and more willing to fight than the largely passive četniks. The main difference between the two groups, apart from their ideology and tactics, was that the Partisans were able to attract followers among all Yugoslav groups, despite initially being mostly a Serb force. Unlike them, the četniks remained almost exclusively Serb.[22]

Both movements fought for a Yugoslavia, as reflected in their official names: the Yugoslav Army in the Homeland (the četniks) and the People's Liberation Army of Yugoslavia (the Partisans). The četniks were predominantly royalist and fought for the restoration of the monarchy and, at least in early stages of the war, of the old order. While some of Mihailović's advisers openly advocated a Greater Serbia and reprisals against Croats, Muslims, and other "traitors," the četnik leader saw postwar Yugoslavia as a restored kingdom, but with an enlarged Serbia as its dominant core, in addition to Slovene and Croat "units"—the latter without its Serb-populated territories. The Partisans, on the other hand, were a revolutionary, Communist-led movement which promised to restore Yugoslavia as an equal federation of South Slav republics, united around the principle of "brotherhood and unity." The četniks' fear and hatred of communism equalled and sometimes surpassed their hatred of occupying forces—so much that they were prepared to join Germans and Italians in order to fight the Partisans.

The Partisans, on the other hand, considered Mihailović their most dangerous "internal" enemy and in March 1943 even proposed a ceasefire to the Germans, so that they could engage četnik forces (the proposal was promptly rejected).[23] Although the Yugoslav, and particularly Partisan, resistance has been arguably the most effective in occupied Europe, its effectiveness would have been undoubtedly much greater if the two movements had fought together instead of against each other. It may be argued that the Yugoslavs also collaborated more than most other Europeans: in addition to the Croatian ustašas and *domobran*s (the regular army of the Independent State of Croatia) there were collaborationist forces among Serbs, Slovenes, Montenegrins, Bosnians, and Macedonians, as well as Yugoslav Albanians, Hungarians, Germans, and Italians.

Just like in 1918, the Yugoslavia of 1945 was the Yugoslavs' own creation—in other words, it was not imposed by Soviet tanks or Anglo-American diplomatic pressure. The victorious Allies, however, supported a united Yugoslav state in 1945, just as they did in 1918. The post–World War Two restoration was even more remarkable and perhaps unexpected than the country's unification at the end of World War One. Four years of bitter fighting claimed over one million victims (in a country of sixteen million).[24] A majority of Yugoslavs were probably killed by other Yugoslavs, rather than by resisting the occupiers. Yet, the war did not kill the Yugoslav idea. If anything, the Partisans' victory—which was possible largely because they were supported by more Yugoslavs of all ethnic and religious backgrounds than the četniks, let alone the ustašas—showed that the Yugoslav idea had survived the dissolution of the state in April 1941 and had even transformed into a more powerful ideology.

New, socialist Yugoslavia was organized as a federation of six republics: Slovenia, Croatia, Bosnia-Herzegovina, Serbia, Montenegro, and Macedonia. In addition, Vojvodina and Kosovo were granted autonomy within Serbia, the largest republic (Vojvodina initially enjoyed a greater degree of autonomy, but Kosovo's status was later upgraded from that of a "region" to a "province," too). If the territorial federalization was, at least initially, little more than theoretical, because the country was run by the party from its centre in Belgrade, it was altogether different from the "federalization" of the "nation." The "national oneness" of the interwar period was replaced by the "brotherhood and unity" version of Yugoslavism. The former was blamed for the interwar state's internal crises, while the latter was praised for solving Yugoslavia's "national question." The concept of "brotherhood and unity" was one of the key founding myths of Tito's Yugoslavia, together with Yugoslavia's own road to socialism, following the split with Moscow in 1948, the country's leading role in the nonaligned movement and the cult of Tito. And as with other myths, there was some truth in the Communists' claim that the notion of "brotherhood and unity" had offered the best answer to the Yugoslav national question.[25]

The "brotherhood and unity" myth was based on the notion of a struggle for liberation and socialist revolution during the Second World War, to which all Yugoslavs contributed equally. The liberation from foreign occupiers and domestic collaborators also resulted in a "national liberation": the Communists "upgraded" Serbs, Croats, and Slovenes from "tribes" of a single Yugoslav nation into separate, but closely related Yugoslav "nations." Macedonians, who had previously been considered, regardless of what they felt, as "southern Serbs," and Montenegrins, most of whom probably felt Serb but at the same time had a strong sense of a Montenegrin identity, were also recognized as separate nations and granted their own republics. In the late 1960s, Muslim Slavs of Bosnia-Herzegovina and the Sandžak region (on the Serb-Montenegrin border) were officially proclaimed the sixth Yugoslav nation (but not until 1974 at the federal level, when the last Yugoslav constitution acknowledged the change). Instead of apparently being forced to declare themselves as (ethnic) "Yugoslavs," as during the royal dictatorship, the Yugoslavs in Tito's Yugoslavia were free and indeed encouraged to declare their particular national identities: Serb, Croat, Slovene, Macedonian, Montenegrin, Muslim (although not "Bosnian"). Those who chose to be "Yugoslav" were considered "nationally undeclared."

After 1945, "unity" replaced "oneness," but the idea of South Slavic ethnic and cultural proximity had not been fully abandoned. Yugoslavia still meant "South Slavia." It was above all the state of the South Slavs, the others being considered national minorities, regardless of their size. For instance, ethnic Albanians, who vastly outnumbered the Montenegrins, were never recognized as a nation, but were consigned to the status of a "nationality" (i.e., minority) and unlike Montenegro, Kosovo, where most Yugoslav Albanians lived, never became a republic. Therefore, Tito's Yugoslavia, certainly up until the mid-1960s, was somewhere between a nation-state and a multinational state.[26]

The decade between the mid-1960s and mid-1970s was crucial in many respects. It witnessed political and economic reforms and resulted in a new constitution of 1974, which made Yugoslavia a very loose federation at best, a de facto confederation at worst. While Tito was alive it did not matter much, but not long after his death in 1980, arguments over the revision of the constitution would emerge. In 1981, Kosovo Albanians demanded republican status for the predominantly Albanian province of Kosovo, while Serbs would increasingly call for a return to the pre-1974 order. The Serb-Albanian conflict would be overshadowed, for the time being, by a constitutional conflict between Serbia and Slovenia that dominated most of the 1980s. The Slovenes not only resisted Serbian calls for tightening up the federation, but sought to loosen it up further. Not unlike the Croats in the interwar period, who had opposed the centralist constitutions of 1921 and 1931, it was now the Serbs who challenged Yugoslavia's unity by demanding the revision of the 1974 constitution.

Without Tito's prestige at home and abroad and with the end of the Cold War looming, Yugoslavia's international significance, as the only European Communist country outside the Warsaw Pact, slowly diminished. The state had become synonymous with the party, and, as it turned out, it could not survive the party's collapse at its last congress of January 1990. Moreover, the domestic economic crisis reflected the failure of the "self-managing" economy and was only worsened by a rapid decrease in Western aid, which once flowed in regularly. Initially successful attempts to introduce a genuine economic reform by Ante Marković's government in 1989–90 failed, not so much because the reform came too late, but because it was undermined by the three key republics: Serbia, Croatia, and Slovenia.

It was in this atmosphere of economic and political crisis, when increasingly nationalist calls for the reassessment of the "Yugoslav contract" were heard, that Slobodan Milošević emerged from within the party. Although the recent wars in the former Yugoslavia have largely been portrayed as ethnic wars, an "intra-ethnic" conflict within the Serbian Party had a crucial impact on the origins of the wars of the 1990s. In the second half of the 1980s Milošević defeated the moderate faction led by his former political mentor and friend, the late Ivan Stambolić (murdered in August 2000, as one of the last high-profile victims of the Milošević era), before reorganizing Serbia's Communists into the Socialist Party of Serbia, which comfortably won the republic's first multiparty elections in 1990. Milošević's rise and the victory of Franjo Tuđman's nationalist Croatian Democratic Union over the Croatian Communists the same year would have a direct impact on Yugoslavia's fate, as would the emergence of Alija Izetbegović in Bosnia.[27]

The "brotherhood and unity" version of Yugoslavism lost legitimacy by the end of the 1980s, like the other founding myths of Tito's Yugoslavia. Hardly anyone remembered the interwar "integral" version of Yugoslavism, let alone prominent intellectuals who had once advocated South Slav unity. New, often Communist-turned-nationalist, intellectuals in all six republics sought to rewrite official history, apparently seeking to discover the "real truth." Instead, they produced even more problematic, mutually exclusive, and anti-Yugoslav accounts of the past. "Parahistory" (to use the phrase coined by the Serbian historian Andrej Mitrović, an intellectual who maintained a high scholarly standard),[28] nationalist myths, and the language of hatred were readily accepted by the public, not used to critical thinking and open scholarly debate. This was understandable, because socialist Yugoslavia, despite its relative "liberalism," had for years curbed free speech and any form of opposition to Tito and the party. Those who spoke against the party monopoly, such as Milovan Đilas, once one of Tito's three closest allies, were purged and often imprisoned.[29] The irony is that when it became possible to challenge openly the government, nobody took notice of moderate and pan-Yugoslav options offered by some members of the party, such as Ante Marković, or by Đilas or the Zagreb-based Association for Yugoslav Democratic Initiative (UJDI), whose members included distinguished intellectuals from all parts of Yugoslavia. Most Yugoslavs—the "leaders" and the "ordinary" ones—appeared uninterested in moderation and compromise. The disinterested, misinformed, and sometimes ill-intentioned "international community," preoccupied with the end of the Cold War, did not and probably could not help much.[30]

The dissolution of Yugoslavia was a complex process and it can only be explained if understood as a gradual, multifaceted phenomenon. A combination of internal factors—the ideological development of socialist Yugoslavia, the economic crisis, the rise of exclusivist nationalisms and of populist leaders—and external changes—the end of the Cold War and the collapse of Soviet and East European Communist regimes—contributed to the end of Yugoslavia.[31] Yet, even if Yugoslavia's breakup became likely, perhaps inevitable, by 1991, why was it so violent? How was it possible that after living together peacefully for over forty years many "ordinary" Yugoslavs turned on each other? During the existence of Yugoslavia it became clear that many Serbs, Croats, Slovenes, and others may not have become Yugoslavs, but why did so many of them turn into violent anti-Yugoslavs?

The Wars of Yugoslav Succession were extremely violent and had several phases.[32] Croatia and Slovenia both declared independence from Yugoslavia on June 25, 1991. An armed conflict between the Yugoslav People's Army (JNA) and Slovenian territorials over the control of border posts broke out immediately. Croatia remained relatively peaceful during the summer, although sporadic fighting between the Croatian authorities and the republic's Serb minority had begun as early as August 1990. The Slovenian war was short; during two weeks of fighting thirteen Slovenes lost their lives while thirty-nine Yugoslav soldiers and officers were killed. In early July the two sides agreed, under international mediation, that Slovenia would postpone independence for three months, while the army withdrew into barracks. Surprisingly, on July 13, the Yugoslav federal presidency decided to withdraw the army from Slovenia. In December 1991 Germany pressed for international recognition of Croatia and Slovenia, which were finally recognized by the European Community on January 15, 1992. The united Yugoslav state thus formally came to an end. Slovenia, a virtually homogenous nation-state, left Yugoslavia relatively painlessly. Croatia, with its nearly 12 percent Serbian minority, provided the scene for a savage Croat-Serb war.

The Croatian war had two main phases. During the first, which lasted between autumn 1991 and January 1992, roughly one-third of the republic came under the control of Croatian Serbs, who, backed by Serbia, established the Republic of Serbian Krajina. Thousands were killed on both sides, tens of thousands "ethnically cleansed," while the Yugoslav Army and Serbian and Montenegrin volunteers destroyed the Danubian town of Vukovar and shelled Dubrovnik, on the Adriatic coast. The second phase came in August 1995, when during a Croatian blitz (unofficially aided by the United States) the Croatian Serb statelet was crushed. During the first half of the 1990s, between 150,000 and 200,000 Croatian Serbs fled their centuries-old settlements, most of them following the brief August 1995 war.

The war in Bosnia-Herzegovina broke out in April 1992, following the international recognition of an independent Bosnia. The independence was resisted by Bosnian Serbs. By this stage, both Bosnian Muslims (from this time increasingly referred to as Bosniaks) and Bosnian Croats overwhelmingly favoured independence from Belgrade. However, while the Bosniaks wanted an independent Bosnian state, many Croats, especially those living in western Herzegovina, sought unification with Croatia.

These Croats established a breakaway Herceg-Bosna, while the Bosnian Serbs' own statelet, Republika Srpska, stretched over some two-thirds of Bosnia's territory by 1993. The Yugoslav People's Army withdrew from Bosnia at the beginning of the war into the newly formed Federal Republic of Yugoslavia, made up only of Serbia and Montenegro. However, the army's Bosnian-born Serb officer corps and soldiers remained to form the Bosnian Serb Army. Crucially, they also kept much of the JNA weapons and heavy artillery.

Even more than the war in Croatia, the Bosnian War was marked by ethnic cleansing—whose principal victims were Bosniaks—and the siege of towns. Bosniak-held parts of the capital, Sarajevo, were regularly shelled by Bosnian Serb troops, while snipers targeted the city's civilians. In 1993 the Bosniak-Croat war intensified, in central Bosnia and in the Herzegovinian city of Mostar. Although caught between Serbs and Croats, the Bosniak-dominated government survived, partly thanks to international humanitarian aid and political support, sporadic UN military interventions against Bosnian Serbs, and UN sanctions on Serbia, which had been providing aid to Republika Srpska. Croatia came under some international pressure for its involvement in the Bosnian War but escaped without sanctions.

The turning point came in 1994. In March, under U.S. pressure, the Bosnian Croats and Bosniaks ceased hostilities and formed a federation, while in August the government of Slobodan Milošević, feeling the consequences of international isolation, largely abandoned the Bosnian Serbs and their leader Radovan Karadžić. Nevertheless, links between the Yugoslav Army and the Bosnian Serb Army remained. In July 1995 the Bosnian Serb military commander, General Ratko Mladić, led a successful offensive against Bosniak positions in eastern Bosnia. The town of Srebrenica, a UN-protected "safe area," was overrun, and most of its male population—between seven and eight thousand men—were shot dead. This provoked a UN military intervention, which in turn encouraged a joint Bosniak-Croat offensive and coincided with the Croatian attack on Krajina and eventually western Bosnia. Facing a total military defeat in Bosnia as well as Croatia, with tens of thousands of Serb civilians ethnically cleansed, the Bosnian Serbs, represented by Milošević, agreed to a U.S.-backed peace plan in November 1995. Several weeks of difficult negotiations between Milošević, Tudman, and Izetbegović, with Warren Christopher, the U.S. secretary of state, and his aide Richard Holbrooke, in Dayton, Ohio, resulted in a

peace agreement. Bosnia survived as a united country but was de facto partitioned. Republika Srpska, reduced from over 70 to 49 percent of Bosnian
territory, was recognized as one of the two highly autonomous entities. The
other was the Croat-Muslim Federation of Bosnia and Herzegovina, informally also divided along the ethnic lines. The total figure for all Bosnian casualties—once widely, and wrongly, estimated at 250,000—was very high,
probably nearly 100,000 people.[33] Some two million people—around half
of Bosnia's prewar population—were displaced during the war. As of 2012,
hundreds of thousands are still to return to their homes.

Despite acknowledging Milošević's crucial role in bringing peace to
Bosnia, the West kept pressure on Belgrade, only partially lifting the sanctions. The Serbian government survived growing opposition at home, most
notably during the three-month-long demonstrations during the winter of
1996–97 over rigged local elections. However, the greatest challenge would
come from Kosovo, a predominantly Albanian-populated Serbian province. A conflict over a year long between the Serbian government forces
and the ethnic Albanian guerrillas, the self-titled Kosovo Liberation Army
(KLA), could not be resolved by U.S.-sponsored negotiations at Rambouillet and Paris in early 1999. NATO then decided to intervene militar-
ily against Yugoslavia. The official explanation for the intervention was the
suffering of Kosovo Albanians, tens of thousands of whom had been forced
to leave their homes in 1998 and 1999. However, Western fear of having
to deal with another "Bosnia," the feeling of guilt in Western capitals for
failing to prevent Serb atrocities in Bosnia, and the wish to see a regime
change in Belgrade may have been other factors behind the intervention.
Air strikes were launched on March 24, 1999, with the KLA in fact used
by NATO as its ground troops. Nevertheless, Yugoslav armed forces and
various Serbian paramilitaries were able to carry out their war against the
KLA, burning and looting Albanian villages in the process. Over 800,000
ethnic Albanians were forced to flee into Albania and Macedonia, while
many were internally displaced within the province or killed. Thousands of
Serb civilians also left their homes, moving into Serbia "proper" and Montenegro, while many were killed by Albanian guerillas and NATO bombs.

NATO strikes did not seriously degrade the Yugoslav military, but they
damaged the country's infrastructure and eventually the population's mo-
rale. Belgrade was becoming increasingly isolated internationally; even Russia, while condemning NATO strikes, put pressure on Belgrade to accept a
peace deal. On June 3, Milošević backed down, to the relief of the leaders of

NATO countries, some of whom faced increasing opposition to the war at home. Both sides had to compromise: Kosovo remained part of Yugoslavia, if only nominally; a NATO-led UN force (KFOR) entered the province, but not a NATO force with a mandate to move freely across Yugoslavia, as proposed at Rambouillet; and Yugoslav forces withdrew. Albanian refugees returned home, celebrating the end of Belgrade's rule as a national liberation. More than half of the prewar Serbian population of Kosovo—estimated at between 200,000 and 250,000—fled the province, and not many have returned to their homes, more than ten years after the war ended. During the war several thousand Albanians were killed and many are still officially missing (the final figure could rise up to ten thousand) and possibly around a thousand Serbs died. NATO suffered two accidental casualties. Again, like in Bosnia and Croatia, the principal victims were civilians. The Wars of Yugoslav Succession were characterized by a conflict between the nation-state and a multinational state, not unlike the wars of the early twentieth century that saw the demise of the Ottoman empire and the Habsburg monarchy, on whose ruins, ironically, Yugoslavia had once emerged.

Milošević survived the war more isolated than ever but still firmly in power. During the war, the International Criminal Tribunal for the Former Yugoslavia at the Hague indicted him for genocide in Bosnia and war crimes in Croatia and Kosovo. Already weak because of internal divisions, the pro-Western Serbian opposition was further weakened by the NATO intervention. However, the growing social discontent and significant financial and moral support by the West provided the opposition with a badly needed lifeline. Some observers believed Milošević would introduce a dictatorship, but contrary to most predictions he lost power in elections in September 2000. After initially refusing to concede defeat, the Yugoslav president backed down when hundreds of thousands of demonstrators stormed the federal parliament in Belgrade in early October and the police and army refused to intervene.

The new president was Vojislav Koštunica, the candidate of the Democratic Opposition of Serbia, at last united, if only temporarily as it turned out. Koštunica defeated Milošević because he appealed to both conservative and liberal voters. He also won because the election campaign was run by Zoran Ðinđić, a dynamic, able organizer and highly pragmatic politician. Ðinđić, the new prime minister of Serbia and leader of the Democratic Party (DS), and Koštunica, who had broken away from the DS to form the Democratic Party of Serbia (DSS), would soon clash over the speed of reforms and the cooperation with Western institutions, including the Hague tribunal. The Đinđić government extradited Milošević to the tribunal on June 28, 2001 (ironically, the anniversary of the 1389 Kosovo battle and several other key events in modern history) without major opposition, but a continued push for reforms and cooperation with the Hague would cost the prime minister his life in March 2003. Behind Đinđić's assassination was a former paramilitary leader who had once been a member of the French Foreign Legion and who kept close links to the regional mafia. Đinđić had been perceived as a threat both to the mafia and to suspected war criminals. Post-Đinđić Serbia faced an uncertain future. Boris Tadić, Đinđić's successor as the Democrats' leader, also succeeded him as president. Koštunica became the prime minister of Serbia, but as of 2004 his government was in conflict with the Democratic Party and survived only with support from Milošević's Socialists. In 2008 Koštunica lost power and is seemingly a largely irrelevant political factor. The far-right Serbian Radical Party remained strong and in opposition. Its leader, Vojislav Šešelj, was also at the Hague, facing charges for war crimes. The mainstream of the party has since broken away to form a more moderate Serbian Progressive Party.

The Federal Republic of Yugoslavia was renamed Serbia and Montenegro in February 2003, but this increasingly loose union did not survive for long. Montenegro declared independence in May 2006, despite a strong unionist vote,[34] while in February 2008 an overwhelming majority of Kosovo's population voted for independence from Serbia. An independent Kosovo was immediately recognized by the United States, the United Kingdom, Germany, France, and Italy, but not by Russia, Spain, China, and India; it still awaits membership in the UN and most other international organizations. As of 2012, Serbia continues to reject Kosovo's unilateral declaration of independence. While neither side appears ready to compromise, Serbs and Albanians will have to talk eventually and it remains to be seen whether a rapprochement and compromise will be reached.

The end of the last century also saw the end of the political careers of two other key former Yugoslav leaders. Franjo Tuđman of Croatia died in December 1999, while Alija Izetbegović of Bosnia retired from politics in 2000, three years before his death. Post-Tuđman Croatia became a European Union entry candidate in June 2004, despite a difficult relationship with the Hague tribunal and even though most Serb refugees have not returned. Bosnia remains fragile, despite a strong international presence, and nationalist parties continue to enjoy the majority of support among

all three ethnic groups. The former Bosnian Serb leader Karadžić was ar-
rested and extradited to the Hague tribunal in July 2008, after more than
a decade of hiding, while General Mladić was at last apprehended in May
2011, and he too has been extradited to the Hague. Macedonia was nearly
drawn into a war with its large ethnic Albanian minority in 2001, but
partly because of international pressure the country has been peaceful ever
since. Of all the former Yugoslav republics only Slovenia is politically stable and fully integrated into Western institutions. In April 2004 it joined
NATO, and the following month it became an EU member-state. Croatia
is set to become the twenty-eighth member of the union in 2013, while the
other Yugoslav successor states appear unlikely to follow in near future. Although the very survival of the EU is uncertain in 2012, and membership
in the European Union consequently appears less attractive, the former
Yugoslavs should continue to seek further regional integration. Regardless
of the EU prospects, it is in their best interests to forge closer economic,
political and other ties, and many of them have apparently understood
this, despite some still fearing the "ghost" of a restored Yugoslavia.[35] A
loose and informal mini-EU in Southeastern Europe would also make EU
prospects for those remaining in line for Brussels more realistic, should the
European Union survive and the enlargement process continues.

Despite a number of unresolved issues that remain, the increased
economic, cultural, athletic, and political communication among the former Yugoslavs gives hope that stability will take hold in the region. The
rest of Europe should closely watch developments in the Balkans, not least
because the Yugoslavs' attempts to build a viable multinational state in the
twentieth century, and their ultimate failure, could provide valuable lessons for the EU project.

· · ·

If Novaković had been somehow transported to London in 2011—
perhaps in a time machine "invented" by his contemporary H. G.
Wells[36]—and attended Vidović's lecture, he would have been probably
surprised by how soon after his death the South Slavs would succeed in
creating a unified, independent state. He would have seen that the makers of both Yugoslavias, while aware of common cultural and linguistic
ties, sought to unify the state through ideology—integral Yugoslavism
and communism—but ultimately failed in their quest. Novaković would
have been undoubtedly shocked and deeply disappointed with how the

Yugoslav ideal turned out, and how Yugoslavism, instead of replacing the particularistic South Slav identities, would be defeated as a state project by the early 1990s. Although genuine believers in Yugoslav unity existed at the time of the country's disintegration—perhaps most notably Ante Marković, the last Yugoslav prime minister—they were in a minority, or were living abroad, collectively discredited as anti-Yugoslav emigration.[37] Only ten years after Tito's death, Yugoslavism seemed dead, too. Its death preceded the death of the country and yet, at the same time, paradoxically perhaps, it outlives it. It survives as a memory, or more correctly, as numerous, intertwined, individual, and collective memories, that usually "meet" at frequent academic, cultural, business, athletic, or personal encounters between the former Yugoslavs or indeed in cyberspace.[38]

Increasing and multi-level contacts among former Yugoslavs cannot be explained simply by "Yugonostalgia."[39] Common interests, combined with an ability to (in most cases) communicate without an interpreter, increasing mobility facilitated by a liberalized visa regime, similar taste in music, food, and fashion, mean that twenty years after the collapse of Yugoslavia there has survived—and at the same time emerged—a form of post-Yugoslavism. This "Yugosphere," to borrow from Tim Judah,[40] is based on common interests as much as on shared memories and language and culture. Proponents of Yugoslavism in the early twentieth century believed that the Yugoslavs needed their own state in order to achieve freedom and future survival. A century later, when the meaning of state sovereignty has changed rather significantly, could a form of Yugoslavism actually thrive without a common state, which, it may be argued, prevented the Yugoslav idea from fully developing?[41]

Novaković was wrong about the timing of Yugoslav unification and he could not have imagined that well before 2011, the year in which his futuristic essay is set, Yugoslavia would emerge twice and disintegrate twice, the second time surely indefinitely. Yet, perhaps his vision of a common cultural, economic, and even political space in the early twenty-first century between the Alps and the Aegean, the Adriatic and the Danube, was not so utopian after all. If the Yugoslav integration was never complete, it is increasingly clear that a complete disintegration cannot be easily achieved either.[42]

4

What Common Yugoslav Culture Was, and How Everybody Benefited from It

Zoran Milutinović

Most of what has been written during the last two decades about the seventy-year period of Yugoslavia's existence has been decisively coloured by the final act of its dissolution. What is more, many recent studies on Yugoslavia, with some notable exceptions, have been written from either nationalist or anticommunist perspectives, providing ample evidence for the views of those who were its enemies, both inside and outside the country, in whatever shape and form the country was constituted. From either of these two perspectives it is very difficult, if not impossible, to say anything positive about Yugoslavia. Yet, quite beyond nostalgia and sentimentality, which should not be allowed to guide academic inquiry, the historical account of this country must be supplemented by views which explain how Yugoslavs managed to remain together for as long as they did, and how the existence of this state was not entirely detrimental to their national and individual interests. Surely they didn't spend every minute of their days suffering under communist oppression and engaged in nationalist quarrels, kept together only by Marshal Tito's iron fist: wasn't there more to life in Yugoslavia?

My main thesis is that Yugoslavia was not merely an agglomeration of constituent national cultures, but that during its seventy-year existence it managed to create a supranational, common cultural layer in which all Yugoslavs took part. I shall try to explain what I think constituted that common culture, how all Yugoslavs benefited from it, and what appeared in its stead after the dissolution of Yugoslavia.

Calling ex-Yugoslav cultures "small" should neither offend nor surprise anyone. The smallness of small cultures is not merely a matter of small numbers—although strength in numbers certainly influences cultural production to a significant extent—but also refers to what Pascale Casanova aptly expressed with the phrase "cultures poor in resources."[1] Despite all efforts to extend equal recognition to all cultures, the international cultural space is not a sphere of respectful mutual recognition, harmony, and justice, but, as Casanova pointed out, one of inequality between the centre and periphery, of struggle for supremacy, of domination, hierarchy, competition, and resistance. Under such circumstances all cultures poor in resources are driven by two contradictory aims: they try to resist domination by the richer and stronger, which pushes them toward isolationism, and they struggle for recognition in the wider cultural arena, which encourages them to open up. Pursuing these aims, all resource-poor cultures attempt

1. to root themselves in other cultural traditions, in order to appropriate their cultural resources and transform them into their own patrimony, into their own cultural capital, which eases the accumulation of resources;

2. to find a place for themselves within a broader paradigm in which they can encounter other cultures, whether in dialogue or competition, since without that sort of interaction, cultures are sentenced to provincialism, stagnation, and eventual disappearance, and those poor in resources even more so;

3. to find a wider audience for their resources, which again, as is the case with the two previous imperatives, leads them outside of themselves.

While striving to accomplish these three imperatives—acquisition of patrimony, entering a broader paradigm, and widening one's audience—cultures poor in resources also need to choose carefully which foreign patrimony they appropriate and transform into their own resources. While appropriating a foreign patrimony as one's own always entails some form of cultural dependency, an overlap of political and cultural dependency is ultimately fatal for resource-poor cultures. That is part of the reason why Polish and Romanian culture opted for rooting themselves in French, as opposed to German or Russian patrimony. In addition, resource-poor cultures may be in danger of entering a broader paradigm which surpasses their strength to such an extent that neither dialogue nor competition seems possible. If they make such a fatal choice, they are bound to lose their confidence, at the very least, if not to suffocate and disappear altogether. For Yugoslav peoples and the most numerous ethnic minority—the Albanians—common Yugoslav culture was a broader paradigm in which all three imperatives were realized, and both liabilities avoided.

By "common Yugoslav culture" I am not referring to any of the three grand projects of Yugoslav cultural policy—the romantic, the synthetic, or the multicultural—because, as Andrew Wachtel has demonstrated, the romantic was never seriously contemplated and the latter two were not entirely successful.[2] However, both common Yugoslav culture and the three grand projects were rooted in the same series of events that inaugurated cultural cooperation among the South Slavs. This cooperation began to take shape at the beginning of the nineteenth century, and was contemporary with and to a great extent intertwined with the birth of the individual modern South Slav cultures. The story is all too familiar: Bartholomius Jernej Kopitar, a Slovene, convinced Vuk Karadžić, a Serb, to begin a battle for a standard language reform and to collect examples of oral literature which would serve as the patrimony of the new literary culture in the making, which in turn inspired Ljudevit Gaj, a Croat, to initiate a broad movement in Croatia, Dalmatia, Slavonia, and Bosnia and Herzegovina, with the aim of creating a common "Illyrian" or South Slav culture. This cooperation had its ups and downs, and was not the only route to the modernity of Serbian, Croatian, and Slovene cultures; nor was it the only current within them. However, the stimuli it provided, and the results it brought about, must not be underestimated: from Serbian actors from Novi Sad travelling to Zagreb to show the public that theatre in one's own language is possible, to the Croat Josif Pančić becoming the first president of the Serbian Royal Academy, to the many examples from the first decade of the twentieth century which show that many "Illyrians" felt at home everywhere between Austria and Bulgaria, and treated it as a single cultural space.

However, neither spontaneous cultural cooperation nor the post-1918 attempts to synthesize South Slav cultures bore any lasting results, because the synthesis was always conceived as an almost mechanical fusion between whole cultures. It is not difficult to reproach the early Yugoslav cultural enthusiasts for their naïveté and to criticize their unfounded, utopian projections of a coming Yugoslav culture. Nevertheless, a century later we are at a loss when pressed to answer the same simple question: how do cultures grow together, and what does this "togetherness" mean exactly? Historical evidence teaches us only about cultures growing apart: we can accurately trace the disintegration of medieval Latin culture into vernacular protonational ones, but historians still cannot put forward an example that can be analysed, described, and offered as a model for the process of cultures merging. Here, we can only wonder, hope, and attempt wild utopian projections—as we actually do whenever we want to talk about the synthesized European culture yet to come. Yugoslav culture enthusiasts in the 1920s were faced with the same problem. They proposed a number of utopian paths to be taken, and in their proclamations they forged metaphors and competed in lyrical creativity, but ultimately they were no wiser than anyone wondering today how to integrate different national cultures into a European one.

Whenever individual Yugoslav cultures attempted to cooperate as distinct units through their individual representatives, it ended in failure, be it the Novi Sad Agreement, the common core curriculum which never materialized in the intended form, or, quite symbolically, the writing of the history of Yugoslav literatures, planned to be the eighth volume of *The History of World Literature* published by Liber and Mladost in Zagreb in the 1970s.[3] However, throughout the nineteenth and especially in the twentieth century, there were two distinct cultural layers in the territory formerly known as Yugoslavia: a national and a supranational one. Neither the Ottoman nor the Habsburg state—despite their long rules—succeeded in creating a vibrant supranational cultural layer among the South Slavs. By contrast, Yugoslavia managed to create such a supranational layer over the course of its seventy-year existence, despite the relative failure of its cultural policies. The analogy with Goethe's notion of world literature—a literature which transgresses national borders and becomes the patrimony of other nations—only imperfectly explains what I here term as common culture.[4] It does not merely designate a book by a Macedonian author read in Bosnia, but a whole cultural production that ignored the existence of national, republican, and linguistic borders and constituted an international cultural space. It was created independently of any party or state cultural policies, and sometimes in spite of them, thanks to the fact that its creators did not appear as representatives of their respective nations or republics, but as individuals. Its golden era began in the 1960s, at exactly the moment when the state ceased worrying about creating a unified Yugoslav culture.

The first significant take-off of Yugoslav cinema is associated with the genre of the "partisan film." The lists of credits in Veljko Bulajić's war epics show that these films cannot be assigned to any of the Yugoslav component cultures, and must remain the patrimony of all of them. Among the non-linguistic art forms, the best example is the Mediala group: the individual artists who belonged to it represented no one but themselves.[5] Their ethnic background was quite diverse; although individual artists could be assigned to their respective national cultures, the aesthetic ideology of the group remained in shared ownership. The most striking example in the theatre was Ljubiša Ristić's KPGT troupe (an acronym composed of the first letters of the four words for theatre in Serbo-Croatian, Slovene, and Macedonian: *kazalište, pozorište, gledališče, teatar*), which brought together a number of actors, writers, directors, and set designers in a self-consciously supranational artistic ideology, and remained emblematic of the common culture of the Yugoslavs.[6] Other significant examples also come to mind, such as the performance of Slobodan Šnajder's *Croatian Faust* in Belgrade's Yugoslav Dramatic Theatre in the early 1980s, which joined together a Croatian playwright, a Macedonian director, a Slovene set designer, and Serbian actors. Theatre directors worked nationwide. Theatre festivals, such as the Dubrovnik Summer Festival, the Sarajevo Festival of Small Experimental Theatres, and the Sterija's theatre festival in Novi Sad, were also supranational venues; together with other festivals, such as the Pula Film Festival and Struga Poetry Evenings, they constituted the main institutional frameworks in which the common culture blossomed.

The theatre seemed to be the sphere which most easily lent itself to commonality, second only to popular culture, which was truly Yugoslav everywhere: the whole country listened to Bijelo dugme (White Button), Leb i sol (Bread and Salt), Yu grupa (YU Group), and Buldožer (Bulldozer); Fahreta Jahić, or Lepa Brena, was universally popular; Zana Nimani, Đorđe Balašević, Josipa Lisac, and Zdravko Čolić also.[7] The whole country laughed with Miodrag Petrović Čkalja, and with the stand-up comedian Nela Eržišnik, from Banja Luka in Bosnia, who impersonated a woman from Zagorje in Croatia. The weeklies *Start* from Zagreb and *NIN* from Belgrade—the latter being printed in both Cyrillic and Latin script—were read everywhere, and published the works of authors from all parts of the country. The most significant intellectual project in postwar Yugoslavia, the *Praxis* journal and the Korčula Summer School, which was related to it, was also part of that common culture.[8] The scholars who took part in it were united by the pursuit of the same intellectual goal, and did not represent their respective national cultures. Even literature, the most linguistic of arts, allowed and supported this common culture—and not only writers who simultaneously belonged to more than one national culture (such as Ivo Andrić and Vladan Desnica) but also many others who bore witness to the fact that the whole Serbo-Croatian language area functioned as one common literary culture. Krleža's "Ljubljana speech" was an event in each and every national literature, and had a similar effect everywhere.[9] In Jovan Deretić's *History of Serbian Literature*, Krleža is mentioned as often as Isidora Sekulić, and more often than some canonical Serbian authors, such as Momčilo Nastasijević or Branislav Nušić.[10] Even those who in the 1980s and 1990s became ardent nationalists took part in this common literary culture: the first edition of Ranko Marinković's novel *Kiklop* (Cyclops) appeared in Belgrade, in Ijekavian and printed in Cyrillic; popular Bosnian Serb author Momo Kapor published all his pre-1991 books in Zagreb, in Ekavian and in Latin letters; Dobrica Ćosić published his book *Stvarno i moguće* (Real and Possible) in Rijeka, Croatia in 1982. One-fifth of the Yugoslav population did not share the same native language of the Serbo-Croat–speaking majority, yet was included in this common literary culture through strong and extensive programs of translation, which were only a part of wider institutional arrangements for representation and recognition. The state supported these programs, without enforcing them, and there is not a single example of a Slovene, Macedonian, or Albanian writer being dissatisfied with the opportunity to address a wider audience via translation backed by state funding. For most of them, these were the first translations into any other language, and served as a springboard for translations into other, more widely taught and read languages.

Do all these examples indicate that socialist Yugoslavia managed to synthesize or unite all national cultures into a single one? Certainly not. The national cultures remained where they were, sheltered by complex legislation and protected by funding from the constituent republics. However, a number of individuals stepped out of them and created this supranational cultural layer, which can be rightfully called Yugoslav. That patrimony cannot be easily nationalized: most of it will have to remain a common patrimony. This common cultural layer satisfied all three of the previously mentioned imperatives of resource-poor cultures. In addition to helping artists avoid the political pressure of their respective republican administrations by publishing, exhibiting, or directing "abroad" in other Yugoslav republics, which has already been commented on in the literature, it supplied what resource-poor cultures need more than talent: strength in numbers. It formed the broader cultural context in which individuals could find an opportunity for dialogue and competition, without ever running the risk of being dominated and suffocated. The latter was due not only to their relative equality (in numbers, resources, etc.), and the institutional arrangements for representation and recognition, based on the assumption that one should know about the other cultures of one's own country, but also to the fact that the national cultural layer was heavily protected from any outside interference. This common culture was strictly voluntary; one could contribute to it or take something from it at will, but no one was forced to participate in it. It also satisfied the first imperative of all cultures poor in resources—to root themselves in other cultural traditions, in order to appropriate their cultural resources and transform them into their own patrimony, their own cultural capital—although in a manner not envisaged by the creators of Yugoslav cultural policies. The institutional arrangements of representation and recognition failed to ensure, for example, that Macedonian writer Kočo Racin (1908–43), whose poetry was included in school textbooks all over Yugoslavia, and learned by heart in the original Macedonian by pupils, would become the cultural patrimony of, say, Serbs and Croats; although those former pupils may still remember the lines of Racin's poem "Tutunoberachite" (The Tobacco Gatherers), Racin remained of significance only for Macedonian culture, pretty much as the works of Prešern or Njegoš became *known* in other Yugoslav cultures, but remained truly *productive*—as elements of cultural patrimony must be—only within Slovene and Serbian or Montenegrin culture. Racin, Prešern, and Njegoš failed to strike a chord in the souls outside their respective national spaces and they preserved some significance only within their original cultural canons. This failure reveals a systemic shortcoming of not only Yugoslav, but also all other multicultural institutional arrangements of equal representation and recognition. They make promises which cannot be fulfilled: they can provide knowledge of the elements of other cultural traditions, but they cannot guarantee that these elements will be recognized as values, and productively accepted and assimilated within other national patrimonies. Here, the question of value is crucial: Kočo Racin may have failed to become a value in other national spaces, but Macedonian theatre director Slobodan Unkovski has not. Without ever having been a "representative" of Macedonian culture—who would have been taken into account for reasons elaborated by Yugoslav cultural policy—he in fact used to direct all over the former country, and he has enriched other Yugoslav national spaces by offering them his creativity, by raising the standards of theatre directing and thus contributing to their accumulation of cultural capital. The work of Danilo Kiš, recognized as a value and productively included in the patrimonies of all Yugoslav peoples, offers a similar example.

The common cultural space strengthened Yugoslav cultures by providing a wider audience, an enrichment of the various groups' cultural resources, and a shared space for dialogue and competition—free from the danger of suffocation or domination. And they all only benefited from it. If the period between 1960 and 1991—including at least fifteen years of economic austerity not conducive to cultural production—was nevertheless the richest era of cultural history for all Yugoslav national cultures, it is at least partially due to the existence of this supranational cultural layer. Take any fifteen years from that period and compare it with the achievements of all ex-Yugoslav cultures from 1995 to 2010, and you will see what was lost with its disappearance.

It could be argued that the obvious provincialism and intellectual and creative poverty of all post-Yugoslav cultures must be explained by the wars, the transition from socialism to capitalism, and the predominant nationalistic disposition in all of them, in addition to international sanctions and isolation in the case of Serbia. This is certainly true. However, the wars and isolation were the direct outcomes of the dissolution of Yugoslavia, which also destroyed its supranational cultural layer: without the dissolution there would have been no wars and isolation, and the transitional impoverishment would have been easier to bear. As for nationalism, it is at the same time a cause and an effect of the dissolution: it is not only perpetually maintained and stirred up by the successor states, but it is guaranteed to remain in place by the incoherent and ad hoc solutions that the "international community" has devised for identical problems in Croatia, Macedonia, Serbia, Kosovo, and Bosnia and Herzegovina. On the other hand, admitting that there must be a period of postwar recovery, and presuming that the successor nation-states would take better care of all national affairs, including culture, than the supranational Yugoslavia was able to—as was the promise of the nationalist leaders who worked on destroying it—we can proceed to compare the present state of affairs with the previous period of postwar recovery. As I am writing this chapter (2012), it should be 1961 in Croatia and Bosnia and Herzegovina, or 1956 in Serbia and Macedonia. In spite of the incomparably greater level of death and destruction of the Second World War, in addition to the period of Stalinist repression which lasted until at least 1950, there was not only a whole new brilliant generation of artists, writers, and thinkers entering the Yugoslav cultural scene in the late 1950s, which would bring about the most fruitful period in all ex-Yugoslav cultures between 1960 and 1990, but this fifteen-year period had already produced a long list of exceptional achievements, resulting both from individual creativity and from the state's concern for cultural development. Focusing only on Serbian culture, one could list Stevan Hristić's ballet *Ohridska legenda* (Ohrid's Legend) and Ljubica Marić's cantata *Pesme prostora* (Songs of Space); for novels, Ivo Andrić's *Na Drini ćuprija* (The Bridge on the Drina), *Travnička hronika* (Bosnian Chronicle), and *Prokleta avlija* (Damned Yard); Dobrica Ćosić's *Daleko je sunce* (Far Away Is the Sun) and *Koreni* (Roots); Oskar Davičo's *Pesma* (Poem); Radomir Konstantinović's *Daj nam danas* (Give Us Today); and Miodrag Bulatović's *Đavoli dolaze* (Devils Are Coming); for poetry collections, Vasko Popa's collections *Kora* (Crust) and *Nepočin polje*; Miodrag Pavlović's *87 pesama* (87 Poems); Jovan Hristić's *Dnevnik o Ulisu* (A Diary on Ulysses); and Stevan Raičković's *Pesme tišine* (Silence's Poems) and *Balada o predvečerju* (A Ballad on Dusk); the exhibitions of Milan Konjović, Petar Lubarda, and Ivan Tabaković, or of the Zadar Group (Petar Omčikus, Bata Mihajlović, Mića Popović, and Vera Božičković) and of the December Group (Ćelić, Srbinović, and Protić). Despite wartime destruction, the National Library (1946) and the National Museum (1952) opened their doors to visitors fairly quickly—while both institutions have been closed for a number of years in this second postwar period. The state established a number of new theatres: in Sombor, Subotica, Užice, Priština (1945), Kruševac, Vranje, Zaječar (1946), Kikinda (1950), the Beogradsko dramsko pozorište (1947), the Jugoslovensko dramsko pozorište (1948) and the Pozorište na Terazijama (1949), the "Boško Buha" Theatre (1950) and Atelje 212 (1956) in Belgrade, and the Srpsko narodno pozorište in Novi Sad opened for opera (1947) and ballet (1950). A number of new museums were opened: the Muzej Saveza jevrejskih opština (1945), the Muzej grada Beograda (1945), the Galerija Matice srpske (1947), the Jugoslovenska kinoteka (1949), the Vukov i Dositejev muzej (1949), the Muzej pozorišne umetnosti (1950), the Muzej primenjene umetnosti (1950), the Muzej Nikole Tesle (1952), the Galerija Sava Šumanović in Šid (1952), the Galerija fresaka (1953), the Muzej prvog spskog ustanka (1954), and the Muzej srpske pravoslavne crkve (1954). The state organized the highly successful exhibition of Serbian medieval painting in Paris, and residents of Belgrade had an opportunity to see exhibitions dedicated to the works of Henry Moore, Pablo Picasso, Georges

Braque, and Henri Matisse. *NIN*, the weekly which had a huge influence on Yugoslav culture, was founded in 1952, as well as the literary journals *Književnost* (Literature), *Delo* (Work), and *Savremenik* (Contemporary). The film company "Avala film" was founded in 1946, the Academy for Theatre in 1949, and the Sterijino pozorje festival in 1956.

Despite poverty and wartime destruction, culture was taken seriously in this period, and it showed serious results. Anyone familiar with the cultural scenes in the successor states has to admit that the new nation-states do not take culture seriously, nor, thus far, has a creative generation of the same calibre made an entrance. Despite all its shortcomings, despite periods of repression, ideological rigidness, and censorship, Yugoslavia was much more successful in managing its cultural affairs and creating conditions for cultural production than all of its successor states.[11] And it created these conditions not only for the supranational cultural layer which I am focusing on in this chapter, but for all individual cultures as well. It is curious that those who in the late 1980s and early 1990s waxed lyrical about their respective nations' "thousand-year-long dream of statehood," failed to notice that Yugoslavia was an obstacle to the realization of this dream for only seventy years—and not a very significant obstacle at that—and that Yugoslavia had prepared all the necessary cultural preconditions for the fulfilment of this dream. During the Yugoslav period, Slovenia established its first university in Slovene, in addition to the hermetically sealed linguistic space in which the media, publishing, and all levels of education were well protected from the penetration of Serbo-Croatian—in striking contrast to the relationship between Slovene and German throughout the nineteenth century. Macedonians also achieved the standardization of their language and all levels of education only in Yugoslavia; almost all of Macedonian culture falls within that period. Similarly, Albanians achieved the standardization of their northern dialect, accompanied by all levels of education in Albanian, along with a complete infrastructure for cultural development, such as publishing houses, theatres, media, the university, and the Institute for Albanology in Prishtina.[12] Just the list of cultural and educational institutions founded in the second Yugoslavia demonstrates that nationalists, especially those from the smaller nations, should celebrate this period instead of cursing it. As some really have: for Aleš Debeljak, an early promoter of Slovene nationalism, Yugoslavism in 1986 was a "formula which suppresses all specific national characteristics under the same glass bell," the "triumph of unitarism over the autonomy and equal rights of Yugoslav peoples," and the "melting of all peoples into one supra-national organism."[13] Yugoslavism was founded on typification and standardization, in which all "individual national impulses, concepts, traditions, and cultures" disappear, claimed Debeljak; it was part of the conservative project of globalization, based on militant *Aufklärung* ideas, and as such, obsolete in postmodern times, which celebrate the "pulsation of national emotions and identifications."[14] In 1994, however, the same author no longer saw Yugoslavia as an oppressive glass bell but as a multi-cultural country in which "our linguistic, artistic, national, and religious differences converged in productive synthesis."[15] It may simply be a difference between one publication aimed at a Slovene readership, which in the mid-1980s liked to read about the "pulsation of national emotions," and another aimed at an international audience, which in the mid-1990s was horrified by the effect of these pulsations. In any event, Debeljak aptly if belatedly expressed the advantages the common Yugoslav culture had offered him: "The longing for a bigger market, a broader audience, a more numerous readership: all of these are legitimate feelings on the part of former Yugoslavs."[16]

These institutions have survived the dissolution of Yugoslavia, but the layer of common culture to which that state gave birth has been irreparably destroyed, without any substitute being offered. What Tim Judah recently termed the "Yugosphere" can hardly represent such a substitute; rather, it can only be understood as a pale shadow of the vibrant and productive layer of common culture in Yugoslavia.[17] Within the "Yugosphere" the visit of a Slovene actor to Belgrade is an event noted in newspaper articles and television interviews. In the Yugoslav common cultural layer, however, in the late 1980s the Slovene actor Radko Polič flew from Ljubljana to Belgrade several times a month to act in Ljubiša Ristić's production of *Cement* in Atelje 212; neither Polič nor his audience found it unusual, let alone worth mentioning in newspapers.

On the other hand, the notion that the successor cultures, when and if they become members of the European Union, will find there a similar broader paradigm which will offer them a wider audience—an opportunity to appropriate others' patrimony without risking political and cultural dependency, to encounter other cultures in a spirit of dialogue and competition but on more or less equal terms—is an idea that can be examined in the case of Slovenia, which is already an EU member. As for the wider audience, it is absolutely clear that the visibility of Slovene culture in the

European Union is nowhere near that guaranteed to it under the Yugoslav arrangements. There is not a single program of systematic and continuous translation of Slovene literature, financed by a host country, such as those run by Narodna knjiga (People's Book) from Belgrade in the 1970s and 1980s. No other European Union country included France Prešern's or Ivan Cankar's works in school curricula, as had other Yugoslav republics. If you study German literature in Berlin or Spanish literature in Madrid, you do not need to take a compulsory course in Slovene literature, as was required of those who studied Croatian literature in Zagreb or Serbian literature in Belgrade. As for the Slovene language, nowadays it is protected within Slovenia as much as it was before the independence—a higher level of protection is difficult to conceive of—but outside of it, it is less visible than it was in Yugoslavia. The Yugoslav institutional arrangements for representation and recognition may have been imperfect, but the European Union still does not have anything even remotely similar. In the wider European context, such institutional arrangements seem impracticable, given the large numbers of member states and their relative inequality in strength, resources, and numbers. Nor has the demise of multiculturalist policies, which have been quietly abandoned in the United Kingdom, and loudly rejected in Germany, created an atmosphere conducive to thinking about institutionalizing any similar arrangements, which would at least provide knowledge of smaller European cultures, even if these cultures must rely on themselves for the value, productivity, and significance of their elements.

The European common cultural layer in the making is formed solely according to a value criteria, as the Yugoslav one was, but it will necessarily put cultures poor in resources and numbers at a greater disadvantage, because the competition for an opportunity to speak and be heard by others will be much fiercer than it was in the dissolved country of twenty million strong. This means that opportunities for encountering others in a spirit of dialogue and competition, for entering the European common cultural layer in the making, are reserved only for rare individuals who are able to earn it by their own merit: Slavoj Žižek is the only Slovene name that comes to mind in this context. Disregarding this precious exception, the position of Slovene culture within broader European culture is similar to that enjoyed by Croatian, Serbian, and Slovene cultures in the broader Austria-Hungarian one: they were "of it," they "belonged to it," and quietly sitting in the backbenches, they were allowed to appropriate its cultural patrimony and to complain about their cultural dependency but without the benefit of a wider audience and the opportunity to encounter other cultures in a spirit of dialogue and competition on more or less equal terms.

With the disappearance of the Yugoslav common cultural layer and the institutional arrangements which provided for the representation and recognition of national cultures in the dissolved country, former Yugoslavs have lost a lot, and gained nothing. Once this cultural layer was destroyed, what was left was only the national cultures—small, poor in resources, provincial, and unable to step out into the wider arena—but surprisingly satisfied with this state of affairs.

5

Discordia Concors
Central Europe in Post-Yugoslav Discourses
Vladimir Zorić

An Orientalist Prelude:
Central European Debates During the Yugoslav Crisis

In the 1980s, Central Europe offered a seemingly equitable, pluralist alternative to hegemonic impasses of the Communist ideology and a utopian compensation for the increasingly obvious failure of the South Slavic statehood project. Yet, despite the frank attempt to disengage from the doctrinal restrictions of the Communist Party, the late Yugoslav construal of Central Europe remained rather reductive. Disregarding the great variety of historical and literary issues associated with Central Europe, it was guided by divided readings of Kundera's essay "The Tragedy of Central Europe." Kundera considered Russian and Soviet policies of the last two centuries as an anti-European totalitarian force which captured the geographical center of the continent, causing a tragic split in its sense of identity. "Culturally in the West and politically in the East," Central European countries were betrayed by the West and left to languish in the oppressive grip of a radically different civilization.[1] Having identified the threatening Other, Kundera went on to isolate Central Europe's essence: a unique blend of multiculturality and artistry, enabled by the mediatory agency of the Jewish intellectual elite. The destruction of Central European Jewry during the Nazi period was a prefiguration of the destiny meted out on Central European cultural space by the hegemonic powers, primarily the Soviet regime after the Second World War.[2] In Kundera's essay, the Holocaust is not an event in its own right but a *mise en abyme* of an overarching narrative about the downfall of Central Europe.

Kundera's master narrative reinforced the sense of a regional tragedy: Central Europe was undone by an overwhelming foreign force and the Jews were its harbinger victims. In its pathetic essentialism, the argument was too tempting to remain bound by Kundera's anti-Soviet ethos. It migrated and incited a chain reaction of Balkanist and Occidentalist cross-labelling within Yugoslavia.[3] The claim of many Slovenian authors that the northern parts of the country are Central European implied a value judgment of its southern parts. By the same token, Serbian authors' claim that they are not (and do not wish to be) Central European implied a value judgment, not necessarily of Central Europe but of Slovenians who, they believed, denied their share in it. The polemic was based on a gross misapprehension: it is not clear why Central Europe, an open cultural space, should need borders and thresholds of qualification and even less clear why these should apply to national cultures in toto rather than to specific values and practices. The polemic was also damaging to the Yugoslav cultural space itself in that it exacerbated national tensions and prevented the country from becoming a successful example of the multicultural tolerance associated with Central Europe.

Among those trying to avoid this vicious circle was Danilo Kiš, who in his essay "Variations on Central European Themes" held that Central Europe has neither borders nor a center and, moreover, that it should not have any.[4] Kiš's poetic discovery of Central Europe had two polemical thrusts: the first was his skepticism toward the construction of Central Europe as a retrospective utopia devised against present adversaries; the second was his hostility to any rhetorical manipulation of the historical experience of Jews. Consequently, he shunned Kundera's argument that Central Europe had a harbinger victim who anticipated its tragic unity and, in particular, the notion that this victim should be found in Jews. To be sure, Kiš's renunciation of this trope was rather cautious because of his delicate relationship with different participants of the debate. Yet, his essay reveals a discreet critical platform: first, the Central European Jews were not as universalist as Kundera held them to be, and to claim so would itself be a form of essentialism; second, their role in the Russian Revolution and Soviet regime suggests that they were not only victims but also agents of the totalitarian order that allegedly plagued Central Europe.[5]

Kiš's short stories from that period indicate an alternative approach to Central Europe, one that avoids the pitfalls of retrospective utopia and harbinger victimhood. The region's traumatic experience is to be grasped in its absence and precisely *as* an absence. One cannot get a direct experience of obliteration because it is locked in that very event, and any such speculation will end up projecting the mirror image of a present standpoint onto the past. Instead, in his stories "The Apatride" and "The Mirror of the Unknown," Kiš devised a transparent mirror, a complex image that brings together his ethical and poetic concerns.[6] The transparent mirror works as a narrative motif, linking the clairvoyant heroes to the scene of obliteration, and as a poetic allegory, revealing Kiš's own painstaking attempt to reach out to that scene in imagination. Unlike Cartesian true-reflection mirrors, the transparent mirror is a token of endemic occultism that found vent in various nationalist cults of the region; yet it also stands as a token of critical judgment that problematizes access to the past and makes us skeptical of true reflection itself.

Central European History: Between the Yugoslav Federation and the European Union

A deft narrative device in itself, Kiš's occult mirror provided the additional advantage of enabling the keen poetic insight which an author of his aesthetic standing needed to keep his fiction safe from the ideological pitfalls of multifarious discourses on Central Europe. The developments that occurred soon after Kiš's death changed the political map of Europe and, to a present-day observer, may seem to have outdated his meditations on Central Europe.

Yet Kiš's essay on Central Europe and his late prose represented a vocal pronouncement of an author almost unanimously perceived as impervious to the tide of nationalist revival in the Yugoslav republics. In a lyrical necrology, László Végel anticipated the paradoxical galvanizing status of his work in the years to come: "A great spiritual guide has died, a monk, a great mystic of reason, a Central-East-European vagabond; both his friends and his foes have gathered at his grave."[7] In the post-Yugoslav period, Kiš's views on Central Europe gained in significance, becoming as important as Kundera's essay in the past. The immediate reason for his essay's great influence is straightforward: unlike Kundera's narrative, Kiš's essayistic fragments were neither contentious nor divisive, and served as a point of resort and dialogue after the breakup of the country and particularly after the end of the war. Dragan Velikić, László Végel, and Drago Jančar, whose views will be considered here, draw on Kiš as a poetic model, a "spiritual guide," and, at the same time, diverge in important ways from his construction of Central Europe, becoming his undeclared "foes." Whereas for Kiš Central Europe was primarily a matter of imaginative retrieval of the obliterated experience from the past, the post-Yugoslav writers, facing obliteration at their present moment and in uncanny proximity, saw Central Europe as a pressing issue of self-orientation and identity construal.

The one shared feature of post-Yugoslav perceptions of Central Europe is the region's new, mediatory function, replacing its earlier disjunctive role within binary oppositions. This change arises from two simultaneous yet reverse processes occurring in different parts of the region. On the one hand, with the fall of the Berlin Wall in 1989, the countries of Central Europe were regrouped as a cluster of nation-states bound by a limited political partnership under the aegis of the European Economic Community (the European Union after the Maastricht Treaty in 1993). The disappearance of the antagonistic agency brought a profound change to the Central European project: it has shifted from the field of dissident discourses to become an institutional affair, promoted by university curricula, research institutes, and the publishing market. On the other hand, the Yugoslav federation, regarded as the shining example of nonalignment and national diversity, collapsed in a series of civil wars which produced seven nation-states. In a shift of paradigm, Central Europe ceased to be an ideologeme highlighting the national discord within Yugoslavia. Rather, it became a transitional cultural space negotiating between past experience in the fragmenting Yugoslav federation and ongoing political and cultural integration in the European Union.

The second remarkable trait of the post-Yugoslav construal of Central Europe is closely linked to the first one but more thoroughly speculative: disregarding the exigencies of the political field, it excludes any prospect of a practical management of the diversity. It is one thing to talk in an uncommitted way about manifest or concealed similarities between the diverse nations of Central Europe; yet it is quite another thing to manage these similarities in the context of sovereign decision making in a multi-national polity. In the latter case, a whole set of difficult questions arises pertaining to the possibility of a community of political action. Which constitutional mechanisms should be in place to enable the discussion about—and articulation of—a common interest amid the plurality of culture-specific standpoints? Who should be entitled, and with what kind of legitimacy, to make the decisions about specific goals and means on behalf of the constituent units? What kind of legislative and executive balance should there be between the central government and the constituent entities? Clearly, these problems were as pressing to the Yugoslav nomenclature in the past as they are to the Brussels legislature at the present time. However, the post-Yugoslav authors considered them as merely political clutter that should not obstruct the access to Central Europe's main asset—the potential for intercultural dialogue and hybrid identity formation. Unlike the dissident debates of the 1980s, their considerations have Central Europe locked in a free-floating communication without any need for a consensus or action.

The Danubian Route (Upstream): Dragan Velikić

In early 1997, more than ten years after Kiš's *Encyclopedia of the Dead*, the occult mirror reemerges in Dragan Velikić's feuilleton in the Belgrade weekly *Vreme*. Both the title of Velikić's text, "Serbia: A Country on the Other Side of the Mirror," and his elaboration of this arcane image testify to the profound change that supervened in the preceding decade. Velikić's first port of call in the reinvention of the mirror is not Kiš's but Lewis Carroll's fiction, namely Alice's adventures in the looking-glass. Furthermore, the mirror itself turns to another object, capturing Serbia in its cotemporaneous authoritarian confinement rather than Central Europe in its obliterated past:

Serbia is not a country of miracles, it is a country on the other side of the mirror and everything in it corresponds to what Alice experienced. First of all, this country is a big chessboard which has seen, for a number of years, the same gigantic chess game, controlled by the Black King. This king moves all the figures, being the only strategist of the game. For their part, the figures occasionally attempt to deceive the king by changing the rhythm of their movement; they start moving at an incredible speed but, since they live in a country behind the mirror, their speed fails to change anything and all things remain at the same distance, motionless. Everything remains as it is, petrified in eternity.[8]

To be sure, Kiš's and Velikić's specular images are not entirely dissimilar, fraught as they are with nightmarish occultist connotations. Yet, upon closer view, differences emerge. Whereas Kiš attempted to gain the precious insight through the transparent mirror, in Velikić's vision one can enter the mirror with ease, but, once on the other side, cannot get out of it. In this intertextual allegory, the Black King is not an evil genius of an elusive geo-political space. Rather, he stands for Slobodan Milošević as the undisputed ruler of a well-defined polity and the sole deviser of its laws, who prefers a lengthy, ignominious enslavement of his subjects to their instantaneous, ir-revocable obliteration. The author speaks from the other side of the mirror: his thrust is to break free from the lose-lose game and get out of it.

Meanwhile, for all his fatalistic focus on Serbia's self-imposed cus-tody and separation from a win-win situation "out there," Velikić could not dispense with geopolitical analogies. More precisely, the ensuing events prevented him from doing so. The changes in Serbia in October 2000, to which he must have looked forward as the final rupture of the sinister mir-ror, prompted another essay, "Border, Identity, Literature" (2002): "Fifteen years ago, in a country which now reposes but in my private archive, in a reality of mine that is inaccessible to others, in a country which despite all its flaws stood as a marvellous fusion of different nations, religions, cultures, mediocrities emerged from invisible sediments, from errors in the Scripture, from a psychopathology of everyday life, and they could not stand flexions and changes and could not create their own worlds."[9]

Multinationality, multiconfessionality, multiculturality: this nostal-gic look at the Yugoslav past betrays the shining qualities of the dissident utopia of interstitial dialogic space, extolled in the Central European de-bates during the 1980s. Velikić's metaphors are as dense as his syntax and they resonate with dualist tones. The Yugoslav federation, the nearest pos-sible reflection of the scriptural *civitas dei*, was hijacked by the dark mob-sters coming from the sludge of the society and disturbing its everyday civility with pathological visions of homogeneity and changelessness. Inter-estingly enough, this implicit analogy between Central Europe and Yugo-slavia is propped by an explicit parallelism. The Holocaust, argues Velikić, was aimed against the Other, and the undoers of Yugoslavia were equally given to the same task.[10] Like all historical parallels, this analogy conceals contradictions. On the one hand, it suggests that Jewish culture is not a constituent part of Central Europe but its destroyed Other; on the other hand, those who destroy Yugoslavia are viewed as the country's Other.

Whatever the consistency of Velikić's argument, it addresses itself to policy makers no less than to his immediate readership. With the end of the wars and fall of the authoritarian regimes, the malady has subsided but has not resolved, and it still requires an antidote. In Velikić's view, this antidote can take two forms: integration or oblivion.

First, the new nation-states, beleaguered though they are by the legacy of nationalism, should reconvene around their shared geographic conduits: "The only clear legend on the map of Central Europe is the Danube, a powerful artery of its organism. From the observation post of the Kalemegdan fortress in Belgrade, we look at the Danube with a special attention and apprehension . . . knowing full well that in moving through Central Europe we need to take the Danube route, but only upstream."[11] The vexing nature of Velikić's pun—which would not have escaped the Bulgarian and Romanian audience—indicates his part in directing this upstream movement into institutional channels. His diplomatic post as the Serbian ambassador in Vienna, which he held from 2005 to 2009, was a likely place for the voicing of such views. Likewise, his success in the publishing market of Germany and Austria earned him the Central European Prize for 2008 and a place among the writers, academics, and politicians who made a special contribution to Central European thought. Yet, Velikić's extolment of Central Europe is fraught with ambiguity: the Danubian route is only an opportune pathway for Serbia, and for a few other qualifying countries, to reach their real destination: the West, the ultimate repository of the phantasms of Progress.[12] Appropriating Said, Velikić argues that the Western cultural market, driven by the Orientalist fallacy, would not admit a writer from the Balkans who in one way or another did not support the phantasm of Western supremacy. Central Europe has a pragmatic advantage: less likely to appear on the radar of the Orientalist discourse, it is a convenient point of entry for those parts of the embattled Southeastern Europe which are still recuperable for the West.

Velikić's second antidote for the narcissism of minor differences is equally controversial: it is a straight denial of history. Expanding his geopolitical speculation, Velikić argues that the antagonized nations of Yugoslavia failed to follow the example of the Flemish and Walloons who favored the economic welfare of the Pax Belgica over their past divisions: "With some freedom of interpretation, we could argue that the bloody collapse of Yugoslavia at the beginning of the 1990s happened because of the failed oblivion of the antagonisms of the nations of that state during seven decades of their life together."[13] This assumption calls for a Benjaminian gloss: Velikić would have the Angel of History turn his back on the past rather than flee into the future with the terrified gaze directed at the heap of wrecks. The idealistic tinge of Velikić's hypothesis is clear from the contradiction involved in the very notion of a deliberate oblivion. Indeed, how could one ever deliberately forget something? Psychologically, there are ways of suppressing undesirable contents of memory; politically, there are eclectic commemorative practices promoting certain memories at the expense of others. A spontaneous oblivion, however, looks dubious and rings a metaphysical bell. Yet, Velikić's idea is an important semiotic sequel of the mirror-wall complex. The only conceivable way of promoting a policy of oblivion is to remove the walls—and occult mirrors, too—separating nations in geopolitical space and to build them on a temporal axis so as to fend off malicious interferences from the past. The mirrors should thus reflect the ethos of the present rather than give access to the obliteration committed in the past.

Elegy for Minorities: László Végel

Velikić's views on Central Europe represent a semiotic bridge between Kiš's metaphors and our next author, László Végel. Kiš reconstructed the region as the experience of obliteration during the Holocaust, eschewing analogies between Yugoslavia and Central Europe and a possible accession of the earlier to the latter. Velikić, writing in an age in which civil wars and ethnic cleansing produced a closer instance of obliteration, eschewed the trauma and focused on the intercultural link between Yugoslavia and Central Europe, which, to his mind, revealed important similarities. Végel, a Hungarian playwright and prose writer from Serbia's northern province of Vojvodina, also sets forth a comparative case between Yugoslavia and Central Europe; yet, differently from Velikić, he sees them as near perfect antipodes, with the earlier traumatizing and ultimately obliterating the latter.

The theoretical premises of Végel's vision of Central Europe are complex, entangled as they are in his bold metaphors and in his wistful, self-pitying tone. Although he never discriminates between the different respects in which he uses this concept, his reflections on Central Europe give rise to two different lines of development. The first line approximates Mikhail Bakhtin's metahistorical hypothesis of hybrid cultural spaces, which, under auspices of stable empires, stimulate progression from polyglossia (multilinguality) to heteroglossia (multiplicity of ideological standpoints in dialogic interaction).[14] For Végel, too, Central Europe is more of a concept than a geopolitical entity: a patchwork of different individualities and discursive practices brought together by the variety, rather than similarity, of their worldviews. Furthermore—and again in accordance with Bakhtin—the culminating zone of this multilateral enrichment is not the vigorous urban culture of the imperial centers such as Vienna and Budapest but the borderline areas, especially those in the south, like Vojvodina. The medley of languages and cultures rises proportionately to the distance from the centers. The rims of the region negotiate the centripetal and centrifugal forces and set the scene for the dialogue of cultures: the concepts of border and heterocosm, and their semantic derivatives, are catchwords of Végel's writ.

The second aspect of Végel's construction of Central Europe diverges from the idea of a borderline heterocosm and harks back to Kiš's metaphor of occult cognition. In 1988, Végel defined Central Europe as a mystical, apocalyptic space of intersection and evaporation of historical energies, a birthplace of utopian hope: "The great paradigm of Central-Eastern Europe is precisely this feeling of periphery, a traumatic meeting of cultures, the valley where violent historical forces disappear—and, despite all that, an extremely volatile space of hope."[15] In other words, Végel sees Central Europe as a polyphonic region in between East and West but also as a vortex of European history. And vortices, as is well known, do not bother to differentiate subjects: they simply suck them down. This shared lot calls for a shared deliverance. A typical Central European is caught in an eschatological limbo: always in the state of waiting for a herald, he is often ready to lend a docile ear to the call of political ideologies, the resident viruses of the region. His dominant mood is a "dark complex desire," which feeds on the future, and his method of self-definition is an "alchemy," which produces an unknown substance rather than gold. Végel's eulogy of borderline ethos is not of much avail here for alchemy is not linked to borders. Rather, it calls on a different ontological level: "This unconscious and painful spiritual condition is a mysterious workshop of the new alchemy into which they were forced by the caprices of history. The hands are still shivering, instruments remain unknown, there are no decrees and rules, a wrong movement can blow it all up into the air."[16] The intrinsic danger of this state is that ultimately too much power will be vested in the alchemist's shaky hands effectively canceling his minority status. Even worse, he may be transformed into a puppet of a process impenetrable to him.

Whatever the intrinsic challenges of the Central European project, Végel argues that Yugoslavia, a patent counterproject, inflicted a mortal wound to it before collapsing itself in the wars of the 1990s. The pluralist dialogic potential of the country's constitutional diversity was effectively smothered by the heavy-handed dogmatism of the party nomenclature, which Végel rightly identified as a characteristic trait of the Yugoslav public sphere.[17] Furthermore, Yugoslavia's prevalent model of modernization was adverse to the concept of polyphonic space he thought to have been treasured in Vojvodina. Rather than fostering awareness about the everyday interaction of the region's multiple linguistic and confessional communities, the socialist urbanization resulted in a systematic erasure of all historical traces of that coexistence. A despondent flaneur in the changing cityscape of Novi Sad, Végel pays commemorative visits to what he sees as sites of mutilation of Central Europe: the Banovina edifice, a symbol of centralist policy built by the forced labor of the local residents; the ground plan of the demolished Armenian church, an instance of the senseless disposal of endemic communities' remnants; the silhouettes of the Dornstädter cake-shop, a "touching memory" of Central European urban politesse.[18] At the Danube embankment, his view of the river is, unsurprisingly, less buoyant than Velikić's sanguine embrace: "The Boulevard of Marshal Tito terminates as if the city were about to embrace the Danube with both hands. Sometimes, however, we can't escape the impression that these hands are stiff, as if the city drew back, for a moment or two, before embracing the Danube, that mysterious river. In the same way, we were Europeans, and we continue being so, albeit with half-raised hands, without hope, petrified—which is not surprising because in this city Europe was regularly crucified on the cross of Socialist realism."[19]

The second—and, for Végel, more worrying—way in which the Yugoslav experiment affected the delicate Central European rim was tampering with demography. Tito's regime broke with Stalin's hegemonic policy but continued to adhere, albeit surreptitiously, to his legacy of stabilization of geographic and ethnic borders which favored the constituent nations at the expense of ethnic minorities. The suppression of minorities in Vojvodina proceeded, according to Végel, in two stages. The initial and crude form of exclusion was the expulsion of the German population after the Second World War: "The polyphonic Vojvodina sank when the Germans were forced to leave. Everything that ensued afterward was a mere consequence."[20] In Végel's interpretation of Yugoslav history, the enforced displacement of the Germans from Vojvodina has the same portentous role which the dissidents have already ascribed to the destruction of Central European Jewry in their 1980s debates. Their disappearance is not important in itself but as an act of harbinger victimhood announcing the drama of the "small nations" in the present day. The second stage of this drama saw the long-term "velvet repression" by the Yugoslav state.[21] While recognizing that this repression affected all critically disposed citizens, Végel stresses that it had a disproportionately negative impact on the ethnic minorities: "a gradual and cheerful assimilation came to pass under the wing of paternalist rhetoric."[22]

All around the space formerly circumscribed as Central Europe, Végel sees nauseating signs of the maladie du siècle, etatism and nationalism; but is there an antidote? In order to avoid the debilitating implications of historical fatalism, Végel has to make up his mind between the two poles of his thought on Central Europe. He relinquishes the open-ended, polyphonic dialogue and opts for secular eschatology. The minority man ceases to be a regulating principle and becomes a member of an ethnic minority in a present-day nation-state. One can go along with Végel and imagine this member as a Hungarian in Serbia, but the same seems to apply to all other minorities. The ethnic minorities in their respective states will, for once, have a major role in reshaping the cultural profile of the region and reawaken the majoritarian groups to their mission of being Central Europeans:

Milan Kundera noted that in the past the Jews represented a connective tissue of Central Europe. The absence of this noble-spirited cosmopolitan culture is dearly felt in these postcommunist areas overheated by nationalist euphories. When their number was painfully reduced, this European region lost its determinant system of communication. We have all got poorer. Following the cue of Kundera's thought, today one could advance the assumption that perhaps it is Central-Eastern European minorities who could take up the Jewish role, at least partially so.[23]

Despite the lack of clarity as to how exactly the ethnic minorities would dismantle the logic of the nation-states, the dialectic nature of this process is fairly clear. It appears that for Végel, and for Kundera, too, a significant degree of cultural and linguistic diversity within some geopolitical space will not necessarily generate a polyphonic connective environment. Whatever its intrinsic values, a multicultural heterocosm will not be in equilibrium unless one actively gears it to that state. For Végel, this balancing would exclude the involvement of a majoritarian nation-state and circumvent—although not necessarily exclude—a super-state's institutional frameworks of regulated multiculturality. More beneficial than such top-bottom regulations is a grassroots connective action by a group acting as a mediator between diverse worldviews and practices. This agency, with its own set of universal values and informal assignment, would step onto the stage of Central Europe with a Hegelian synthetic role of reconciling all its opposites and providing them with a framework of communication. Indeed, much like Hegel's heroes of historical movement who act on the calling of the World Spirit, Végel's minority men—be they Jews, Germans, or Hungarians—are marginal and yet endowed with an insight into inchoate possibilities of reality.[24] They always rise above the particularism of their position and negotiate the wider acceptance of universal values, even at their own cost.

The irony of Végel's vision of Central Europe is not only that he has to give up his Bakhtinian model of an open-ended dialogue and have recourse to Hegel's dialectics. The irony is also in the fact that, in having recourse to Hegel, Végel uses his dialectical notion of history to dismantle the very same nation-state which Hegel had held as the converging point of all historical processes.

Consolations of the Nation-State: Drago Jančar

The point where Végel parts with Hegelianism is the idea of a stable, self-subsistent nation-state. He doubts its credentials for a simultaneous promotion of the interests of a majority nation and of the rights of a minority group. Yet, the very same idea of nation-state serves as the point of departure for Slovenian writer Drago Jančar. In 1986, in his essay "Terra incognita," Jančar responded to the dissident debates by formulating an ethnocentric, specifically Slovenian, platform for a cultural revival of Central Europe. Jančar's sense of indebtedness to the dissidents, and particularly to Kundera, goes beyond his explicit recognition that the seminal essay "The Tragedy of Central Europe" was read in Ljubljana with as keen an interest "as if it had been written by a Slovenian author."[25] For one thing, Jančar, similarly to Kundera, sees Central Europe as a scene of a struggle for survival: "The Slovenian writer, just as the Slovenian people, did not get any grants: everything had to be obtained in a struggle, even at the price of isolation, derision, and the loss of freedom."[26] The survival in question is one of small nations. The great ones, in Jančar's and Kundera's view, have it secured by the virtue of their numbers as well as by the cumulative effect of their political and cultural influence. Unlike Kundera, however, Jančar has no recourse to the Jews as connectors and harbinger victims of Central Europe; his interest lies elsewhere and commands different explanatory tropes.

Jančar's argument is almost mythopoeic in its simplicity: he never hesitates to use the collective pronoun *us* when describing a shared lot of the Slovenian people from Trieste to Carinthia. Over the last century, according to him, Central Europe saw a succession of multinational states which set themselves the task of negotiating the cultural and ethnic diversity on its territory, the Habsburg monarchy, Yugoslavia, and the European Union. The repeated failure of these statehood projects to resolve that central problem is epitomized by the status of the Slovenians. In each case, they ended up divided between different centers of influence (Vienna, Rome, Belgrade), but also split internally, along the ideological lines imposed by these centers (Catholicism vs. Protestantism, clericalism vs. liberalism, *domobrans* vs. partisans).[27] The recurrence of such rifts in different periods prompts Jančar to posit a transhistorical law: "It is about constants which are deeply rooted, about the return of deep historical and cultural segments, which have remained here as a deep trace, working in us and upon us."[28] Thus, the trope of the harbinger victim announcing a tragedy to come is replaced by a "wheel of history" indicating a cyclical vision of time. The evil occurs at regular intervals rather than through a progressive decline. Likewise, whereas in the harbinger victimhood the tragedy befalls another, contiguous group before striking one's own, in the wheel metaphor the calamity is visited upon different generations of the same group, in this case the Slovenians.

Jančar prefers not to encumber his cyclical hypothesis with historical parallels, opting for a straightforward ethnocentric perspective. In their dual status as the victims and outsiders of history, his fellow Slovenians appear to him as quintessential Central Europeans and, vice versa, all predicaments of Central Europe are reflected in one or another period of modern Slovenian history. This trait of Jančar's argument distinguishes him from his peers, both the ex-Yugoslav writers and the dissidents. Contrary to Velikić, Jančar does not see Central Europe as a viable version of Yugoslavia and a transit region on Slovenia's road to the West. Nor for that matter does he perceive it, like Végel, as a target destination, a precarious zone of multiculturality where Slovenia should firstly reclaim its historical continuity and then redeem the whole region by its minoritarian agency. Finally, Jančar also renounces the sentimental idealism of Kundera and his Slovenian adherent Rožanc, for whom Central Europe is an emancipatory space of "unity in difference" serving to severe ties with an oppressing Other, located in Moscow and Belgrade respectively. Rather, Central Europe appears to Jančar as a specular entity: in a continuous effort to manage ethnic, cultural, and ideological diversity by tolerance and dialogue, it mirrors its resident nations' attempts to overcome their internal rifts and form democratic nation-states. The failure of statehood endeavors is linked with the collapse of multiculturality and tolerance in the region. It is precisely because the small nations fail to establish democratic and sustainable frameworks of sovereignty that the Central European project derails, ending in an endemic clash of ideologies controlled from external centers.

Since in Jančar's view Central Europe and Slovenia are driven by the same "wheel of history" and tempted by similar extremes, mirroring unsurprisingly becomes an important metaphor in his essays. Unlike Kiš's occult looking glass, Jančar's mirror relies on the Cartesian reflection which merely gives back what has already been committed to it: "Can we still show Central Europe in its ideal form? The time has come, I believe, to look at Central Europe in a mirror which would not idealize it but reflect its true face . . . a different face, contorted and scarred by enmities, passion, and envy."[29] The face that Central Europe needs to see in the mirror is not different from the one that appears in the mirror that Jančar holds up to Slovenia. Thus, mirror reflection works in space, in that Slovenia and Central Europe are imagined in a *mise en abyme* link, but it also informs the temporal scale, since the cyclical vision of time produces repetitive patterns of ideological cleavage.

Jančar's views on Central Europe in "Terra incognita" are by no means out of line with the "Contributions for the Slovenian National Programme," collated earlier that year in the famous issue 57 of *Nova revija*.[30] Yet, in the post-Yugoslav period, his statements would acquire a peculiar euro-skeptic spin. In the late 1990s, with EU accession well under way in Slovenia, Jančar discerns monistic and centripetal aspects of this process. He feels that what Slovenia has just gained—a nation-state with sovereign mechanisms of addressing its own issues—is being taken away from it by a distant centralist power in Brussels. The surrender of political sovereignty is aggravated by the impending economic subjection, whereby Slovenian enterprises would soon be owned by multinational corporations serving the interests of global financial markets instead of Slovenian culture and national interests. The ultimate nightmare of Jančar and other Slovenian conservatives revolved around devaluation of the nation's cultural capital rather than the outflow of its financial assets. Slovenia would end up locked in another federal state with supranational European ideology; in this federation, the nations with symbolic capital would be Europeans by virtue of being French, German, or Italian, whereas all others, including Slovenians, would also be Europeans by virtue of being just that, Europeans.

The EU accession gives Jančar a clear signal that history is about to perform another cycle; the map of Europe was being redrawn and, for the first time, Slovenia was being consigned to the East. No sooner had the country espoused liberal democracy and the market economy than it had succumbed to the common ailments of other countries in transition: the abuse of power and corruption, compounded by the political inertia of its citizenry. By qualifying these practices as pathological ("bolni") and Eastern European ("Vzhodna Evropa"), Jančar succumbs to a self-accusatory form of Orientalism: "A paradox has occurred: it is precisely in the European Union that we have finally become Eastern Europeans and we will have to accept this bitter truth."[31] Jančar leaves no space for doubt about the point of his complaint: Slovenians are seen as Eastern European by the West but they also *are* Eastern Europeans because they chose to let themselves go in the first place. Yet, in all fairness, it should be observed that such overtly Orientalist statements are rare in Jančar's essays. By and large, his views aim to replace the anti-Russian platform of Kundera by a less divisive form of essentialism which constructs a monolithic and insulated Slovenian self, "a culturally and historically formed community of individuals who know who they are, where they come from, and where they are going."[32]

Remapping Central Europe:
From the Danubian Capitals to the Triestine Borders

With the collapse of Yugoslavia and initiation of the Euro-Atlantic integrations, the semiotic unity of the Yugoslav debates about Central Europe falls apart. The notion of Central Europe presents Velikić, Végel, and Jančar with different concerns, aligned with their respective political horizons, and enables them to articulate different visions of history. For Velikić, history is a progressive movement with capsular spaces and transitory stations for those who lag behind. For Végel, it involves decline in the form of a vortex engulfing harbinger victims and which can only be stopped by a borderline minoritarian agency. For Jančar, history is a sinister cyclical movement which, like a wheel rotating around a static center, brings the same plots with different agents. What the three authors have in common, however, is their attempt to articulate spatial metaphors for Central Europe clearly different from the received ideas of centrality and in-betweenness. To this geographical remapping we must now turn.

One inspirational attempt to find a spatial form that would capture Central Europe in the intricate plurality of its traditions *and* provide an absorbing narrative template is found in Claudio Magris's travelogue *Danube* (1986). In this foray into Central European history, Magris follows the course of the region's longest river from its humble sources in the Black Forest down its basin through the capital cities of Vienna, Bratislava, Budapest, and Belgrade, to the Iron Gates and the river's delta at the Black Sea. Just as the Danube's watershed brings together the tributaries of many Central European countries, so Magris's work becomes a collection point for different pieces of legend, history, and geography that mark the river's flow through space and time. A potent narrative symbol of Central European harmonious discord, the Danube is also vehemently contested in each of its bends. Magris traces disputes about where the Danube actually begins and ends, how it should be divided into sections and subdued by power plants, and how the longitudinal state borderlines should be drawn. Thus, not only are the concept and function of Central Europe relational and dependent on individual perspectives, the very geographical metaphors, supposed to stabilize and determine it, are also unstable, and bear witness to the conflicting views and ideologies of the region.

None of the three post-Yugoslav authors follows Magris in constructing the Danube as the formative geographic metaphor of Central Europe. Velikić implicitly cuts the river into two sections: the upper, Central European one, ending with Serbia, and the lower one, beginning with Romania, which belongs to the unnamed Other. For Végel, the Danube is a mysterious river which brings to Novi Sad "the white crests of the Babylonish waves" but also testifies to the city's perennial, martyr-like encounter with the "bloody drama and volcanic craters of Central-Eastern Europe."[33] Even though Velikić and Végel envisage different directions—upstream and downstream—they agree in seeing the Danube as merely a link to Central Europe rather than a comprehensive metaphor of that region. Jančar, finally, does not assign the Danube any major symbolic role; his rhetoric, imbued with national conservatism, draws on local geographical features, and Slovenia is not a Danubian country. Thus, the contrast with

Magris seems complete: whereas Velikić and Végel perceive the Danube in a metonymic way, as a relational image, Jančar does not even include it in his rhetoric horizon.

Implicitly renouncing the Danube as a geographic metaphor of Central Europe, the three authors turn to another corner of the map and claim to discover a more promising literary space: Trieste. Although never a part of Yugoslavia, the former Austro-Hungarian seaport acquires, in their optic, an aura of the quintessential Central European city, which exemplifies the region's diversity more faithfully than its capitals Vienna, Budapest, and Prague do. To be sure, the argument is not without a precedent: himself a native of Trieste, Magris produced a cultural history of the city (coauthored with Angelo Ara) in which he made a case for its status as a literary capital of Central Europe.[34] Yet, in the volatile context of the Yugoslav debates on Central Europe during the 1980s, this early extolment of Trieste remained in the shadow of the Manichaean divide between Central Europe and its threatening Other, advanced in Kundera's essay "The Tragedy of Central Europe." There are two aspects explicating the revival of interest in Trieste in the post-Yugoslav period: a historical and a literary one.

Trieste as a Multicultural City

The prosperous commercial role of Trieste in the Habsburg empire provided a favorable setting for the formation of diasporic communities from both Central Europe and the Mediterranean. Among other minorities, Trieste has been home to strong Slovenian, Serbian, and Hungarian communes which left their imprint in the material culture of the city, through architectural endowments and private edifices, as well as in its artistic life. Moreover, Trieste's borderline position in the Habsburg empire, and its later neutral status as a free territory between Italy and Yugoslavia (1947–54) enhanced its centrifugal attributes. As the Central European debates of the 1980s brought the critical examination of all sovereign projects in the region, the boundary location of Trieste came as a welcome vehicle for its reinvention from the geographic margins. Trieste represented that part of Central Europe which, unlike Vienna or for that matter Belgrade, enabled and invited cultural access of each former Yugoslav nation on non-hegemonic terms.

Having spent a part of his youth in Istria, Velikić seems predisposed to put this point in the most explicit way: if Vienna had been the capital of the Habsburg empire before it sank in the First World War, nowadays it is Trieste that must be seen as "the capital of the underwater Empire."[35] To Velikić, that empire, glowing below the surface of cultural memory, is nothing else but Central Europe itself, free of the sovereign designs and colonial ambitions of its organizing center. Velikić does not define Trieste as a multicultural space, a stable home of many cultures; indeed, when specifying the intrinsic balance of the city, he falls back on vague attributes such as "full of contrasts" and "schizophrenic locale."[36] More importantly to Velikić, Trieste nourishes the tradition of an open space and a transit zone. Much like Bakhtin's chronotope of the road, Velikić's Trieste is a hub where people coming from the East can meet people from the West and vice versa. Furthermore, it is also a clearing field for the same people to move into the opposite zone in both directions. It is the paths of these fleeting visitors, rather than residents, that interest Velikić. A home with many doors, Trieste variously evens out or emphasizes differences between its visitors. On the one hand, it unites the cacophonous Yugoslav nations in shopping tours: "To generations of Yugoslavs, Trieste represented a shopping window to the promised land, an anteroom of Europe, a border-line territory on which over a weekend they could sense the scent of the West, even if only in laboratory conditions."[37] On the other hand, Trieste also has the capacity to bring hidden differences between its visitors to surface. People as different as Dositej Obradović and Njegoš visit Trieste and leave ample evidence of their resentments. Thus, in Velikić's view, not only is Trieste a symbolic, nonhegemonic successor to Vienna; it is also a paradigm of what he thinks Central Europe is all about: a transit zone between East and West.[38]

For Végel, Trieste is a poignant reminder of what Novi Sad could have become had it remained faithful to its multicultural roots as the free city that Maria Theresia aptly named Neoplanta, permitting appellations in local vernaculars (Novi Sad, Neusatz, Újvidék).[39] The two cities take pride in such institutional forms of multiculturality, but they also superimpose cultural boundaries upon the state borders: "Here the Balkan culture meets the Central European one just as in Trieste the Central European culture meets the Mediterranean one."[40] In Végel's view, this elicits a comparison: both cities stand as potent symbols of the transformative power of Habsburg colonial policy in the borderline regions (the Adriatic Sea and Pannonia), yet, in the twentieth century, they developed in very different directions. Whereas Trieste benefited from its boundary position and created a thriving mixture of the local and the universal, Novi Sad appears to Végel as a declining metropolis that has succumbed to the pressure of the nation-state and its hegemonic center. For the latter city, the consequences have been dire: the ethnic homogenization of Novi Sad was initiated during the Yugoslav period by the expulsion and assimilation of minorities, carried on in the post-Yugoslav period with the resettlement of Serb refugees and, overall, brought an unprecedented parochial drift to the city's urban culture. Végel's perception of Triestine multiculturality thus may not differ from Velikić's in evaluation, which is positive in both cases, but it certainly differs in gist. While Velikić praises the porous borders of the city, its openness to ever new discourses, and the responsiveness of its visitors, Végel insists on a preestablished, precarious balance of diverse cultural discourses which can easily be compromised by an undue openness.

Jančar's view of Trieste is starker: ironically, it fills the lacunae left by Velikić's and Végel's idealistic portrayal of the city as a cosmopolitan enclave. For all its modernist credentials, the recent history of Trieste appears to Jančar as a blatant example of the mismanagement of cultural diversity in a maladjusted, and often malevolent, sovereign framework. It is from Trieste, Jančar warns, that the ill-fated military expedition of Archduke Maximilian sailed to Mexico to have him enthroned as the emperor. Yet, for the Slovenian community, the critical moment arrived after the fall of the Habsburg empire: the city was handed over to Italian governance, and the subsequent rise of fascism led to repressive measures against non-Italian communities. The most traumatic of these events—and one which Jančar repeatedly revisits—is the burning of the Slovenian National House by the blackshirts in 1920, which resulted in an exodus of most of the Slovenian population from the city.[41] The endemic particularism, to which Trieste has been all too susceptible, lives to the present day in the guise of the Habsburg revival espoused by some local irredentist parties.[42] It is unsurprising, thus, that Jančar sees the north Adriatic boundary zone in terms of a knife: "This rim of the Mediterranean, its hand-sleeve that makes the deepest incision into the European mainland, has been a scene of bloody dramas, of national and ideological conflicts."[43]

Velikić's, Végel's, and Jančar's shared focus on Trieste as a microcosm of Central European multiculturality conceals three very different understandings of what multiculturality itself should be: an open space for cultural transitions, a preestablished equilibrium of cultures, or a cultural conflict as a natural state. Furthermore, it must equally be admitted that the three authors use Trieste as projection for their divergent perceptions of Yugoslavia, ranging from bittersweet illusion to totalitarian reality.

Trieste as Joyce's City

The second aspect of the post-Yugoslav rediscovery of Trieste is specifically poetic. Seemingly, it is as straightforward as the aforesaid notion of multiculturality but, at a closer view, turns out to be equally contentious. It abandons the abstract field of cultural formations to focus on a single man, James Joyce, and the literary implications of his "voluntary exile" in Trieste, which spanned, with only a few breaks, from 1904 to 1915. This tumultuous period of Joyce's life became a target of narrative quest in Velikić's novel *The North Wall* (*Severni zid,* 1995), and in Jančar's short story, "Joyce's Pupil" ("Joyceov učenec," 1998).[44] Such thematic convergence is not a mere coincidence. The fact that Velikić and Jančar saw Joyce's experience in Trieste as critical to his literary experiment seems all but natural given the evidence of his effervescent creativity during this period. The fact that they ultimately produced works of narrative fiction centering on Joyce's experience in Trieste is an indicator of an important poetic spin of their essayistic pronouncements on Central Europe. While their essays on Trieste aim to present a pluralist, borderline alternative to all centralizing and essentialist aspects of Central European debates, their narrative focus on Joyce in Trieste represents a poetic step away from Central Europe itself. What comes into view here is the principal paradox of the post-Yugoslav authors' framing of Central Europe as a *literary* rather than only cultural space. While they may talk, often enthusiastically, about a literary tradition of Central Europe, listing such names as Kafka, Musil, Roth, and Hašek, when it comes to shaping their own poetic reference to Central Europe they have recourse to the maverick visitor Joyce rather than to these supposed insiders to the tradition.

Velikić's and Jančar's imaginative grasp of Joyce's life in Trieste is neither firsthand nor symmetrical in terms of width and depth. First, in both authors, it is mediated by another narrative instance: Richard Ellmann's authoritative biography of Joyce.[45] The narrative summa of Joycean studies at the time, Ellmann's monograph still leaves something to be desired in terms of Joyce's transactions with the Slavs in Trieste and Pola. Secondly, while Jančar selects only a fraction of Joyce's life, captured by a brief paragraph in Ellmann's book,[46] Velikić opts for a comprehensive reconstruction of the entire eleven-year period, and extracts from Ellmann the network of Joyce's acquaintances (from a young Berlitz employee, Amalija Globočnik, to Ettore Schmitz, better known as Italo Svevo), the complete load of his memories from Dublin, and the inchoate plans for *A Portrait of the Artist as a Young Man*, *Ulysses*, and *Finnegan's Wake*. Another point of difference is the extent to which they involve Yugoslavia. *The North Wall* unravels two parallel plots: Joyce's life in Trieste, which precedes the constitution of Yugoslavia, and the life of Yugoslav émigrés in Vienna during the 1990s, following the breakup of the country. Jančar's take on Joyce stretches from his last years in Trieste to the establishment of the Communist regime in Yugoslavia after the Second World War, when he is qualified as suspect and gets the protagonist of the story into trouble.

All these differences in emphasis cannot overshadow the main line of convergence between *The North Wall* and "Joyce's Pupil": through their protagonists, both works present a distinct national perspective on Joyce. In *The North Wall*, the heroine, Olga, a stymied Joyce scholar from Belgrade, joins her husband, Andrej, who emigrated from Yugoslavia to Vienna to avoid army conscription for the war. Ironically, it is in Vienna, as she tries to piece together her life as an émigré, and during her brief trip to Trieste that she gets a deeper insight into the subject of her scholarly inquiry. The sections of the novel which trace Joyce's life in Pola and Trieste can thus be seen as focalized narration but also as the expanding content of Olga's imaginative reconstruction. If Velikić's *The North Wall* introduces Serbs to Joyce, "Joyce's Pupil" relies on Boris Furlan, a Slovenian law student from Trieste, who took private English classes from Joyce but apparently benefitted from the tuition in other ways, including philosophical debates and exercises in style. After the beginning of the First World War they part ways for good: Joyce moves to Zurich to escape "the whirlwind of history," and Furlan, given to political activism, is "drawn . . . into the whirlwind."[47] The writer's lessons disappear from Furlan's memory as he rises to prominence, firstly as an antifascist activist in Trieste during 1920s, then as the presenter of the Slovenian program of Radio London during the Second World War, and finally as the dean of the law school in Ljubljana in the first years of the Communist rule. Yet the insidious impact of Joyce's lessons follows him at the key moments of his life: in 1941, as a political refugee in Zurich, he visits Joyce's grave, and in 1953, just about to be lynched as an enemy of the people, he hears Joyce's voice telling him how to describe an oil lamp.[48]

Even such a brief summary of *The North Wall* and "Joyce's Pupil" raises a sensible question. Is this selection of Serb and Slovenian characters as narrative focalizers and reverent disciples of Joyce a form of national particularism that befits the conflictive space of Yugoslavia rather than the multicultural reputation of Trieste? In other words, in the present-day postconflict status of the former Yugoslav cultural spaces, is it conceivable that a Serbian author address Joyce's life in Trieste through the eyes of a Slovenian character and vice versa? Speculative though this question is, it still touches upon a key aspect of Joyce's own work: just as he accessed Dublin through Trieste, so he approached the many layers of classical mythology through the eyes of an Irishman *and* a Hungarian Jew. There is no easy answer to the question as to whether an analogous narrative is probable in the post-Yugoslav context.

What can be established with more certitude is that both narratives contain imagery and symbolic scenes encapsulating their authors' respective visions of history. In *The North Wall*, Olga intuits the presence of the Great Chess Player who tries to take control of her life, and she feels that the only way to escape him is to settle in Austria.[49] Linking the Danubian capitals on a train journey from her benighted country, she thus takes the very same route from Belgrade to Budapest to Vienna that Velikić would outline in his Mitteleuropa Prize speech fifteen years later. The destination of her exilic journey is hardly a place for literary invention. What Velikić sees as the Viennese—and, in another sense, Central European—monotonous focus on the past is epitomized by the tram rides which Olga takes around the Ring district, and by her visit to a graveyard where she discovers memento mori—a grave of a Serbian merchant. Yet, Vienna has the strategic advantage of being a median point allowing Olga to contemplate the peripheries of Central Europe. She pays occasional visits to her family in Belgrade and confronts the niche of history created by the advent of primordialist forces of national revival: "In that blockade and isolation from the world, there is only imitation of life."[50] Likewise, it is from the senescent Vienna that Olga accesses Trieste and its more dignified imitation of life: Joyce's literary world in the making which takes her beyond Central Europe. The focus of Velikić's interest is not the importance for Central Europe of Joyce's sojourn in Trieste, but the importance of Central Europe for Joyce's art. In a critical segment of his novel, he embarks on a narrative divination of Joyce's Istrian and Triestine epiphanies, which he subsequently links to his masterful prose works published later in the West. Thus, Velikić's Serbian characters may take the Danubian route to get to Central Europe only to find that they need to go further. Central Europe itself only finds its self-fulfillment in something that transcends it both spatially and ontologically: the fictional world of a modernist work addressed to the audience in the West.

"Joyce's Pupil" establishes a rather different link between the narrative orders of Slovenian (and Central European) history and Joyce's story. Just as Joyce's literary work synthesizes many discursive traditions from different periods, so Boris Furlan's career in the political field brings together all key moments of Slovenian national history in the first half of the twentieth century. Yet, differently from Velikić, who looks into what the Triestine experience means to Joyce as a creative writer, Jančar's interest lies with what Joyce's sojourn in Trieste may mean to Slovenian culture. Once parted to take their opposed paths, Joyce and Furlan remain unconcerned with each other and their fateful link is cunningly woven into the plot through the repetitive motif of the lamp. The first (and determinant) appearance of the lamp, during their private lesson, is based on a cue from Ellmann's biography of Joyce.[51] After the language class, the pupil is given the painstaking task of describing an oil lamp which is quickly taken over by "Professor Zois," who "goes on for a full half hour, indulging a habit that many years later the student will call descriptive passion."[52] The lamp appears in unexpected yet decisive moments of Furlan's life: in the university library in Ljubljana, as he discovers Joyce's obituary; in the bomb shelter of a London hotel, during a Luftwaffe air raid; in the interrogator's office and on the ceiling of his prison cell, as he is prosecuted by the Communist regime. Finally, the lamp is Furlan's very last thought as he is about to be dumped into a freezing river.[53] The recurrence of the lamp at different points of Jančar's narrative highlights his cyclical vision of historical time in respect to the upheavals of modern Slovenian history. Crucially, this approach echoes Joyce's own narrative strategy in *Ulysses*, in which the seemingly chaotic appearance of everyday life is permeated by mythical patterns and cues. Joyce thus provides both a historical stimulus and narrative template for Slovenian self-understanding. From Jančar's point of view, narrative insight into repetitive patterns of experience is needed in both literary and historical imagination. The lesson is learned by Furlan (albeit at the price of his life) but repeatedly ignored by the Slovenian intellectual elite, who has yet to come to grips with the foundational polarities of the Slovenian nation-state.

Since Central European debates have been about discovering unity in variety and vice versa, one could agree to a conclusion that would recall a time-honored rhetoric distinction. The post-Yugoslav perceptions of Central Europe illustrate a transition from *concordia discors*, or dissonant harmony, to *discordia concors*, or harmonic discord. The last decade of the Yugoslav federation saw a relatively stable and coherent—even if somewhat simplified—concept of Central Europe which was employed to polemical and divisive purposes in the context of the escalating political crisis. For all their polarizing force, these disagreements were based on a prior agreement over the common core of the concept: it was a retro-utopia raised against a threatening Other. After the breakup of the country and the fall of the Berlin Wall, this semiotic unity of the Central European idea gives rise to pervasive pragmatic differences. At one level, Velikić's, Végel's, and Jančar's views on Central Europe are functions of the specificity of their nation-states' political contexts; at another level, however, they arise from their radically differing visions of the nature of historical process and cultural space. True, the three authors occasionally agree in isolating one or another aspect of Central European space, such as the denunciation of nationalism and Trieste as a literary capital of the region. Yet, their harmony is precarious and should be considered against the backdrop of a deeply ingrained disagreement over the concepts and premises related to the politics of multiculturality.

Part III

Legacies of Yugoslavia: Cultural Returns

6

"Something Has Survived . . ."
Ambivalence in the Discourse About Socialist Yugoslavia in Present-Day Slovenia
Mitja Velikonja

The Lost World

I borrow the title of this text from *The Lost World* (1997), a sequel to *Jurassic Park*, a film about dinosaurs that reappear on an isolated island after having been exterminated, ultimately taking control of it. However, the inspiration also comes from a billboard for a Slovenian commercial radio station in the autumn of 2009, boasting a silhouette of Yugoslavia and the promise to play more "Yugo" music than any other radio station. That same autumn was also the time of countless conferences, books, documentaries, interviews, celebrations, and manifestations about "the fall of the Berlin Wall," "the end of dictatorship," "the start of a democratic transition," "the reunification of Europe," and "long-awaited freedom." And yet here we found, twenty years after the collapse of Yugoslavia, a ten-meter-high image of our former state, and not of the present one, for which we, as is repeated over and over, "fought so long." This little example, which is not an isolated one, places the "Slovenian story of success" (as one of the most popular political slogans in Slovenia in the 1990s used to put it) in a different light.

Today, speaking about "socialist Yugoslavia" in Slovenia is controversial precisely because of these two words—*socialist* and *Yugoslavia*. From a distance, and judging by dominant nationalism discourses, one could get an impression that the attitude is very simple, binary, "evolutionary": Slovenia realizes its "thousand-year dream of being independent"; it escapes from—to use one of the frequent Balkanophobic terms of the late 1980s—the "Balkan cloak," and rejoins its "natural environment," that is

"Europe." However, if we look closer, we see that the situation is much more complicated.

My aim in this chapter is to briefly show and analyze this ambivalent attitude in different narratives and social practices in contemporary Slovenia. In other words, I am interested in the "othering" of socialist Yugoslavia in different Slovenian discourses. In the face of critical approaches to discursive constructions of different "Easts"—Orientalist and Balkanist—I believe it is time to approach the former Yugoslavia in the same way;[1] not how it really was, a political, social, cultural, and multiethnic entity that collapsed in 1991, but how it is constructed and perceived today. I consider the "Yugoslavist" discourse to be a complex, multilayered ideology, often inherently contradictory, and coming from outside ex-Yugoslavia. However, I believe "Yugoslavist" discourse also comes from the inside, from "ex-Yugoslavs," "post-Yugoslavs," and "never-truly-Yugoslavs" as well. I am interested in how this discourse constructs, discusses, and affects the "lost Yugoslav world." In this discourse, the category "Balkans" is often a synonym for "Yugoslavia"— so when there is a reference to something being "Balkan," it is meant to modify only "Yugoslavia" and not other Balkan countries.[2]

I approach my topic from two different research perspectives. First, I will concentrate on the Yugoslavist discourse in Slovenia, a state that found itself in a specific situation. As a constituent republic, Slovenia was part of Yugoslavia, but at present (2012) it is the only successor state to have joined the European Union. Is it more appropriate to consider Slovenia an ex-Yugoslav republic or a new European country? To illustrate this unease for some Slovenians, let me quote a Slovenian speaker at a NATO conference in 2000: "Slovenia is a country of Southeast Europe, but not a Balkan state."[3] Second, my analytical approaches are drawn from cultural studies: from the theoretical perspective of Roland Barthes, the Birmingham school of cultural studies, the Frankfurt school of critical theory, and French "la nouvelle histoire." I will begin by presenting voices and opinions that demonize Slovenian socialist and Yugoslav pasts and then I will present those which favor it. Finally, I will explain and interpret these Yugoslavist discourses.

No to YU

On the surface of dominant national discourses, everything seems clear: Slovenia was trapped and suppressed in Yugoslavia for decades, and it finally gained independence in 1991, followed by acceptance into its "natural environment." This is a typical political mythology of transition: from dark ages to splendid times, from winter to spring, from backwardness to progress. Its constituent elements are self-victimization, "the last bastion" myth (or the Antemurale myth), the founding fathers, the conspiracy theories, and the new EUrocentrism, as I call it—the myth of the united Europe (which is in fact limited only to EU states).[4] All this is accompanied by usual Balkanist stereotypes that are, in the end, logically incorrect: Yugoslavia is a synonym for the whole of the Balkans, Byzantinism is joined with Ottomanism, "Serbian hegemony" with Bolshevism, and so on. But at the base of this mythology lies an unsaid practice, very typical for Slovenian political life in general: being opportunistic and loyal toward neighboring or distant centers of power—to put it sarcastically, "in search of the good master."

Anti-Yugoslav views prevail in dominant national discourses and in the state apparatus: from media to politics, from new public holidays to school curricula. They are shared by all leading political parties, with some nuances, of course, among nationalists, liberals, and so-called social democrats. For example, national celebrations are peppered with practically identical speeches about socialism and Yugoslavia from representatives of the right, center, or the so-called left. Similarly, national television offers another apt example: repetition of news programming from the months after the establishment of independence (from the collapse of Yugoslavia, the so-called "ten-days war" and the international recognition of the new state) are broadcast at the end of the daily programming (from about eleven-thirty in the evening until one in the morning). This same interpretation is present in the right-wing, neonazi subpolitical groups that consider themselves "patriotic." Their views differ from the dominant one only in their brutal tone, expressed in graffiti, posters, and online postings. They say nothing new relative to mainstream politics.

Let me mention two examples from the spring of 2010. A leader of the extreme nationalist party, Zmago Jelinčič, declared in parliament that "Croats will infiltrate the Slovenian government!" and that "only an idiot would allow a Croat to be in the government," at a moment when the new minister of environment—one of Croat origin—was to be appointed. Meanwhile, a former foreign minister, Dimitrij Rupel, wrote that there is "an evil under the Slovenian sun." In other words, he considers old communist attitudes and personalities to be returning to Slovenian political life, and that "Slovenia is not able to cut the links to its communist past." In autumn 2010, right-wing politicians warned that special programming on national television aimed at ex-Yugoslav communities living in Slovenia (Serbs, Croats, Bosniaks, and Albanians) would "bring Yugoslavia back, with all its quarrels" and that this was nothing less than "unconstitutional Yugo-nostalgia." The fervent Catholic conservative theologian Ivan Štuhec was sure that "Slovenia . . . was moving away from the precious spirit of Europe and was wading through the Balkan marsh of corrupted *bratstvo i jedinstvo*, which always needed mafia godfathers."[5]

The notion that Slovenians and "the Southerners" (often termed "Jugosi," "Jugoviči," or "Čefurji," to mention the most frequent xeno-phobic terms) have nothing in common—even further, the latter are an inferior group in Slovenian society—appears in popular movies, television series, and comedy skits. From the early 1990s, there were stereotyped characteristics of "them" as noneducated, with a poor grasp of Slovenian, identifiable by their bad teeth and low-paying jobs, and often involved in criminal activities. The cleaning lady Fata in the popular series *Dober Dan* is one such example. Fata is uneducated, ugly, underpaid, terribly dressed, has bad teeth and speaks poor Slovenian. These stereotypes are often created by Slovenian directors, but—what I find particularly disturb-ing—Bosnian directors who found refuge in Slovenia during the Bosnian War are surprisingly complicit as well—Branko Đurić Đuro, for example, the creator of the Yugoslav cult series *Top lista nadrealista*. The concluding scene from Đuro blockbuster *Kajmak i marmelada* (2003) shows a pretty, blonde, hard-working Slovenian girl leaving her Bosnian exboyfriend, a dark, macho character involved in petty crime. The message is clear: they tried, but they failed because they are too different.

Yes to YU

On the other hand, in popular culture, consumerism, design, alterna-tive culture, and leftist subpolitical groups, Slovenia's "Yugoslav"-"Balkan"-"socialist" past also plays a very different role. Bands like Zaklonišče Prepeva (Shelter Singing) or Rock Partyzani (Rock Partisans) play rock songs in which socialist ideas, Partisan struggles, and Yugoslav experiences are glorified. In consumer culture, the term *Balkan* becomes a brand for wild partying, drinking to excess, and exotic beauty. Designers often refer to socialist aesthetics in their work. In alternative culture, progressive ideas, practices, and symbols of "those times" are reappropriated in activities and images. The same is seen in anti-establishment leftist groups like alterglobalists, pacifists, punks, anarchists, left-oriented students, and others who are fighting for a more just world. Here, experiences from the decades of socialist Yugoslavia serve as one of the most precious inspirations, together with other examples—new or old—of radical-left movements (from Zapatistas and squatters, to anarchists in the Spanish Civil War).[6] In times of recession, massive unemployment, growing social injustice, and dissolution of the welfare state, people are starting to look at the "old times" with sympathy. At workers' demonstrations, old revolutionary songs are sung and flags of the old regime are seen on Slovenian streets once again (in spring 2010, during an interview on national television, one unemployed worker started to sing the "Internationale," a song that had not been broadcast on prime time for more than twenty years).

So it is no surprise that public opinion surveys show that Slovenians, in fact, appreciated the past socialist decades. The data must be understood alongside widespread dissatisfaction with political, social, and economic conditions of transition. In my opinion, this is not because Slovenia did not make any progress, but because the promises of politicians and the expectations of the people in the late 1980s and the early 1990s were highly exaggerated. For example, more than 90 percent of the respondents in 1995, 1998, and 2003 described their life in Yugoslavia as "good" and "very good."[7] Two-thirds to three-quarters of the same respondents "agreed" or "completely agreed" that "despite communism we lived relatively freely in the decades before our independence."[8] Other data shows quite balanced even slightly positive attitudes of Slovenian respondents toward the socialist-Yugoslav decades. In 2009, a survey showed that Slovenians identify terms like *freedom, welfare,* and *justice* more with socialism than the capitalism.[9] A survey of the student population, again in 2009, showed that 27 percent of Slovenian students would like to live in socialist Yugoslavia.[10]

Explanations of the Yugoslavist Discourse

How can all these contradicting features and data be interpreted? It is not an easy job. I think that there are many answers to this question, and that they might show a complexity of the Yugoslavist discourse in Slovenia. I do not think that there is a simple mechanical divide between opposing discourses of "bad socialism/Yugoslavia" and "good socialism/Yugoslavia." Nor do I think that we can understand these attitudes separately, as ideological currents of the two antagonistic groups within Slovenian society. I am convinced that one must be understood in relation to the other, and read in relation to the other, in all of the internal contradictions that follow in the explanations below.

First, the Slovenian transitional political elite and dominant national political parties have symptomatic strategies of dealing with the socialist-Yugoslav past: they either fiercely attack it or simply ignore it. We must keep in mind that most leading Slovenian politicians from the period of independence, ranging from right, liberal, and so-called social democrat parties—were members of the League of Communists, and that some of them even held very high positions or jobs in state institutions such as universities, institutes, and publishing houses. In this regard, it can be said that the socialist-Yugoslav past "haunts" them like an unpleasant memory. In a typical Freudian situation, instead of confronting what they consider to be trauma—their communist past—they ignore it or attack it (and especially attack all those who did not convert as swiftly as they did).

Second, the institutionalized "left" politics (Social Democratic Party) that directly originate from the former communist party likewise do not refer to the former state. Even more: during one heated political discussion in Slovenia, it was explicitly pointed out by representatives of the Social Democratic Party that "they do not have any wish, any ambition and any right to restore that political system that lost its legitimacy and legality." Even the Union of Antifascist Partisans emphasized its nation-liberation campaign with more fervor ("We liberated our country, Slovenia!") than the socialist revolution that was an inseparable part of independence. This position toward socialist-Yugoslav times can be understood with regard to their political conformism and an efficient, silent, and only seemingly illogical pact of the neoliberal economy and nationalism.

Third, when they realized that socialist-Yugoslav heritage did not interest anyone in the main political parties, populists began to employ it. For example, Ljubljana's Zoran Janković, a popular local politician, in the summer of 2010 insisted on naming a new street in Ljubljana after Josip Broz Tito, despite strong opposition from right-wing parties. After almost twenty years, Ljubljana again has a street named after Tito. But even more illogical is Jelinčič's aforementioned veneration of Tito: Jelinčič consistently refers to Tito as a positive personality from our history and a "cool dude" (*frajer* in Slovenian). He even erected a monument to Tito in his own backyard.

Fourth, it is important to consider that the ex-Yugoslav region is now identified as "Western Balkans," a new category that offers many possibilities for discussion. Here, old ties are to be redefined. The Balkans are considered an economic opportunity for Slovenian enterprises, one not very present in public discourse. In other words, the economy works silently. More attention is given to the new or better role of Slovenia in the region: Slovenia as an EU member should lead the process of European integration of the so-called "Western Balkans." This paternalistic and outright colonial discourse started as early as 2004, just after Slovenia joined the European Union, first from high EU representatives and then from Slovenian politicians themselves. The situation has changed, but the words are the same—the same lessons that had been directed at Slovenia until 2004 are now given by Slovenia to other non-EU Balkan states. The dominant political discourse in Slovenia about the Balkans is schizophrenic: on the one hand, the Balkans are avoided as backward, violent, and dangerous while, on the other hand, the region seems to be a new priority in foreign policy and economy. For example, an editorial in the daily *Delo*, on March 6, 2010, was titled "Direction: The Balkans," while a story in headline news, "The 'Personal Trilaterale SHS' Is Born,"[11] reported on the meeting of Slovenian and Croatian prime ministers with the Serbian president. However, this new Slovenian interest in the Balkans is not always successful. Another, later example is the March 2010 conference organized by Slovenian and Croatian prime ministers on the topic of the Western Balkans, which had conspicuously missing elements: the Serbian president, the president of the European Council, Herman Van Rompuy, and the Spanish foreign minister, Miguel Angel Moratinos, were absent, while the European commissioner for the enlargement and European neighborhood policy, Štefan Füle, attended for only an hour.

References to the "old days," nostalgic or just retro, can serve as subversive social, political, and aesthetic statements and activities—against everything that was so unconditionally advocated and implemented in the last twenty years. In this way, small but active groups or individuals, primarily composed of younger practitioners, can deliberately irritate dominant discourses and institutions. But it can also become a base for emancipative strategies, identity politics, or simply business that creatively unites Slovenian with other Balkan identities (again, some may find it paradoxical, for it is a reflection of reality: a good example is the "pizza-*burek*" that originated in Slovenia in the early 1990s and symbolically unites the "West"—pizza—with the "East"—*burek*).[12]

And finally, my sixth proposed answer: I believe that the manifestation of Yugo-nostalgia in Slovenia must be understood differently than in other post-Yugoslav countries. Yugo-nostalgia does have the subversive and emancipatory dimensions mentioned above, but it lies in the impossibility of the curious emotion itself: nostalgia. Nostalgia is a wish that cannot be realized, an impossible, broken wish, a wish-for-the-wish's-sake. When Slovenians who hold quite positive opinions of their previous lives in Yugoslavia were asked in 2001 if they should "return to the rule of communists," more than two-thirds "strongly disagreed" and "quite disagreed," while only one-fifth "quite agreed" and "strongly agreed."[13] On one hand, they had a good opinion of it, even desired it, but they would not want to go back to it. Or, perhaps, they appreciated it then precisely because it was clear that those days could not return. This is the very definition of nostalgia.

To conclude, I will add that the Slovenian-Yugoslavist discourse creates and reproduces this "impossible," divided, and ambivalent attitude of Slovenians toward their socialist-Yugoslav-Balkan past and their "new European" present. As in other similar discourses, refusal goes hand in hand with fascination, demonization with adoration, arrogance with envy, attraction with fear. To borrow the term from popular psychology: it is a love-hate relationship. The closeness—temporal and territorial—of socialist Yugoslavia and the Balkans is what generates distance. Slovenian dominant discourses are firmly oriented toward the West, "Europe"; however, when it is party time, during New Year celebrations, for example, thousands of Slovenians flock to Belgrade or Sarajevo, cities that have only recently become major tourist destinations. Many of them go to the Guča folk festival in Serbia, while Slovenians are the most important group of visitors in the recently reopened museums in Bosnia that celebrate the Partisan past.[14] One-third of Slovenians spend their summer holidays on the Croatian coast. Interestingly, I have never heard of Slovenians going to party en masse to Brussels, Maastricht, or Strasbourg.[15]

Slovenian Yugoslavist discourse is not fixed in terms of content or ambition. It is clearly contextual, adaptive in its ambitions and objectives. As such, it speaks more about Slovenians and their changing attitudes toward their socialist-Yugoslav past than how the Yugoslav socialism really was. By creating this curious place—exotic yet dangerous—it insists that we, contemporary citizens of Slovenia, and they, people living in Yugoslavia until its end, are not equal. But differences in social reality are usually indicative of a hierarchy. And here another question arises: what political, social, and cultural differences and inequalities does this ideology produce? But this will be the topic for another study.

7

Vibrant Commonalities and the Yugoslav Legacy
A Few Remarks
Gordana P. Crnković

1.

While political elites and new governments continue to assert the distinctiveness of the Yugoslav successor states and the nonconnection with a shared Yugoslav past, the art created in the region in the last two decades frequently seems to make, assume, and even emphasize these connections. In doing so, this art works against the dominant political establishments, but is often congruent with the region's grassroots activities, as well as the tendencies apparent in other social realms such as sports, tourism, the economy, and so on. The works of art shape the fluidity of space and time, as well as ties with the past. These artworks also make and map connections with artistic and intellectual living legacies of a particular space, which was once multicentered yet also common, and which is now divided yet also not entirely uncommon, as the following examples may briefly demonstrate.

The Macedonian film *Before the Rain* (*Pred doždot*, 1994), for instance, written and directed by Milcho Manchevski, starts with a prologue coming from the Yugoslav and Bosnian classic novel, Meša Selimović's *Dervish and Death* (*Derviš i smrt*, 1966), and the whole film could be interpreted as having a dialogue with that quote and that novel: "With a shriek birds flee across the black sky, people are silent, my blood aches from waiting."[1] The first-person narrator of Selimović's novel, dervish Ahmed Nurrudin, writes this line after he has sowed the seeds of violence that he believes will bring justice, and is waiting to see if the desired result will indeed come about.

Violence does happen—the dervish was not waiting in vain—but it brings both justice and injustice, the death of those who were guilty and the death of innocents, as well as an irrepressible chain of further events which the dervish seems to be unable to stop or redirect. Emphasized by its placement at the very opening of the film, this implied dialogue with *Dervish and Death* points at the realms of *Before the Rain* associated with that novel, and at the intimate connection between this Macedonian (and British-French-Macedonian coproduced) film of the post-Yugoslav period with a Yugoslav-era Yugoslav and Bosnian classic literary text. A viewer aware of how these lines, used in the film's prologue, are positioned in Selimović's novel, aware of the moment in which they are written by the dervish, of what they stem from (a criminal murder of the dervish Nurrudin's brother that made him plot revenge) and what they precede, will appreciate this film in a different way. Such a viewer will remember the murder of an innocent in the novel, that causes hatred in those left behind, and their will for revenge, and what comes next—an unstoppable torrent of violence. The question that the film's main character, war photographer Aleksandar Kirkov, poses to the inflamed leader of an armed group searching for an alleged murderer of their kin, "And what after?" contains a whole world of complexity and experience, if one thinks of Selimović's novel and its own articulation of "what comes after" an act of violent revenge.

The actor who reads this significant prologue and also plays the lead role of Macedonian-born and London-based war photographer Aleksandar Kirkov is Rade Šerbedžija, whose very appearance strongly recalls and brings back to the present many aspects of the Yugoslav past. A Croatian actor of Serb ethnicity and a decades-long resident of Zagreb, Rade Šerbedžija was one of the most popular and prominent actors in the former Yugoslavia. His life story seems symbolic of those artists who were committed to working on both national and supranational levels (Croatian and Yugoslav in his case); recalling it may show how this orientation has fared in recent times.

During the Yugoslav period, Šerbedžija worked on a number of projects including the filming of Croatian national classics, as in a television series' adaptation of the nineteenth-century novel *In the Registrar's Office* (*U registraturi*), by Ante Kovačić. But he was also one of the founders and main promoters of the Yugoslav theater troupe KPGT (each letter beginning the word for "theater" in four languages of Yugoslavia: Croatian, *kazalište*; Serbian, *pozorište*; Slovenian, *gledališče*; and Macedonian, *teatar*), which was initiated by Belgrade theater director Ljubiša Ristić and which created one of the most fascinating theater productions of the 1980s, Dušan Jovanović's *The Liberation of Skopje* (*Oslobođenje Skoplja*). The actor also played leading roles in numerous Yugoslav-era films, was for years the most beloved Hamlet of the Dubrovnik Summer Games, and created and performed a monologue based on Miroslav Krleža's book *My Settling of Accounts with Them* (*Moj obračun s njima*). He actively participated in Sarajevo's peace protests of April 1992, which ended with demonstrators being shot at, an event that would mark the beginning of the war in Bosnia and Herzegovina. Šerbedžija stayed in the besieged Sarajevo for some time and then left for Belgrade to be with his wife, theater director Lenka Udovički, as she was giving birth to their baby. He appeared on Croatian state television in December 1993, in a show where he was treated like an enemy of the Croatian state on account of his (mis)represented actions. He smoked one cigarette after another and tried to talk sense and communicate it to the audience, while selected callers phoned into the program, mostly to abuse him. Later he moved to Slovenia; friends and colleagues there helped him obtain Slovenian citizenship, which allowed him to travel. After this he went to London, where he was a long-time guest of Vanessa Redgrave. (In honor of Redgrave, he and his wife named their second daughter Vanessa-Vanja.) In London he met Macedonian-American director Milcho Manchevski, who cast him in *Before the Rain*, a film that opened up for him, as the phrase goes, the doors of Hollywood. He moved to Los Angeles with his family and has been a sought-after actor in Hollywood and international productions for years, working with a number of directors including Stanley Kubrick in his last film, *Eyes Wide Shut*. In the year 2000, Šerbedžija founded the summer theater *Ulysses* in Croatia, on the island of Brijuni off the coast of Istria, and with his family has most recently relocated to the Croatian city of Rijeka, to establish a graduate program "Acting, Media, Culture" at the University of Rijeka. In the last two decades, he has appeared in Bosnian, Serbian, Macedonian, and Croatian films, linking them all with his presence and invoking with his very appearance some aspects of the Yugoslav cultural realm. When a post-Yugoslav viewer sees Šerbedžija in Manchevski's *Before the Rain*, or in any of the other films in which he has recently appeared, she will likely be aware of at least some of his previous roles in films and outside of them, and this awareness will bring a specific "Yugoslav legacy" into the present reception of these post-Yugoslav films.[2]

2.

A number of literary and cinematic works from the Yugoslav successor states create direct or indirect ties with the common Yugoslav history and with the realms of other Yugoslav successor states. The Slovenian film *The Border Guard* (*Varuh meje*, directed by Maja Weiss, 2002), for example, has a Slovenian character looking across the River Kolpa/Kupa (a natural border between Slovenia and Croatia) into Croatia, and saying: "This really makes no sense. Before we fished together . . . and now . . . ," leaving unsaid what this now is, and how it actually relates to that "before." Warned against the "wild Croats," three Slovenian girls cross the border anyway, and then form the one positive relationship of the film with a retired Croatian actor. Another Slovenian film, the very popular *Cheese and Jam* (*Kajmak in marmelada*, 2003), written, directed, and starring Branko Đurić Đuro, not only has a multi-ethnic (reminiscent of old Yugoslav) relationship at its center, between a Bosnian emigrant and a Slovenian local, but also inscribes, with the appearance of Branko Đurić Đuro, the memory of the *Top Chart of Surrealists* (*Top lista nadrealista*), Sarajevo's 1980s hit radio and TV series, whose special brand of surrealism and Monty Python–like political commentary was endorsed and loved throughout the former Yugoslavia, and one of whose main founders and faces was Branko Đurić Đuro himself. An established Croatian writer of the younger generation, Zagreb's Zoran Ferić, dedicates his story "The Island on Kupa" ("Otok na Kupi") to Serbian author Milorad Pavić, "with trepidation," and Croatian writer Ante Tomić mentions that he modeled the main character of his novel *Nothing Should Surprise Us* (*Ništa nas ne smije iznenaditi*, 2003), Ljuba Vrapče, after the main character from the Yugoslav-era Serbian writer Dragoslav Mihailović's novel *When Pumpkins Blossomed* (*Kad su cvetale tikve*, 1968). Set in the late Yugoslav era (the 1980s), Tomić's novel features characters from Montenegro, Slovenia, Bosnia and Herzegovina, and other formerly Yugoslav states and autonomous provinces, and revolves around the unlikely friendship between a doctor from Split, Siniša, and a young Belgrade hoodlum, Ljuba Vrapče. Another well-liked Croatian novel revolves around multi-ethnic relations among people from now separate countries: Renato Baretić's *The Eighth Representative* (*Osmi povjerenik*, 2003) spins the story of a young Croatian politician sent to a small, distant island off the Croatian Adriatic coast, where he forges an unlikely friendship with an odd Bosnian couple. Mirjana Karanović, a popular and excellent actress, formerly Belgrade-based and now residing in Sarajevo, plays a Croatian mother in Vinko Brešan's *Witnesses* (*Svjedoci*, 2003; a Croatian film), a Bosnian Serb mother in Ahmed Imamović's *Go West* (original title, 2005), and a Bosniak mother in Jasmila Žbanić's *Grbavica: The Land of My Dreams* (Grbavica, 2006; both Bosnian films).

The young Bosnian writer Muharem Bazdulj includes not only a number of literal "Yugoslav" references in his stories but also the cosmopolitan attitude embraced both by educated young people in the post-Yugoslav region and by much of Yugoslav-era artistic production (as opposed to the more recently promoted nationalistic stance): his stories, for instance, open with a poem by Ezra Pound, or include a poem by Emily Dickinson, or are simply entitled in English.[3] The Serbian film *The Tour* (*Turneja*, directed by Goran Marković, 2008), features some of the most prominent Serbian (Dragan Nikolić), Croatian (Mira Furlan), and Bosnian (Emir Hadžihafizbegović) actors. In particular, Furlan brings into the film associations with the cinema of the former Yugoslavia, given that she was one of the most prominent Yugoslav and Croatian actors of the 1980s; she emigrated to the United States in 1991 and has not appeared in much of the regional film production since that time. The film also includes theatrical performances of parts of literary classics from Croatian, Serbian, and Bosnian national literatures. In general much of the cinematic production in the Yugoslav successor states is characterized by its crossing of national borders, a condition due to both artistic and economic factors. Funds are drawn from more than one country in (and outside of) the region, as are the stories, locales, actors, and crew. This cooperation has resulted in a number of films, such as *No Man's Land* (*Ničija zemlja*, 2001), a Bosnian Academy Award winner but also a French-Belgian-British-Italian-Slovenian coproduction; *All for Free* (*Sve džaba*, 2006), a film written and directed by a Zagreb-stationed Antonio Nuić, but set in Bosnia and featuring a mixture of famous Bosnian, Croatian, and Serbian actors; *Armin* (2007), written and directed by Croatian Ognjen Sviličić and mostly set in Zagreb, but revolving around a Bosnian story and starring a preeminent Bosnian actor and the face of much of the Bosnian new cinema, Emir Hadžihafizbegović; or *It Is Not the End* (*Nije kraj*, directed by Vinko Brešan, 2008), a film shot in both Zagreb and Belgrade (among other locales), and drawing from both Croatian and Serbian financial and artistic resources.

3.

But then, other than simply recognizing in the present moment these post-Yugoslav, yet in a sense rather Yugoslav-looking cultural connections, what could one identify as a feature related specifically to the region's history within Yugoslavia? In other words, how does a connection with the Yugoslav past appear as a distinctive aspect of post-Yugoslav cultural space?

To briefly mention only one item, it seems as if it is a specific Yugoslav socialist attitude, or more precisely, a certain "Krleža-like" attitude toward recent changes and the world of progress and success, the attitude articulated in select works of art, that characterizes some of the new cultural production. One remembers Krleža as being among the principal writers of socialist Yugoslavia, and one forgets that he lived most of his life in a pre-socialist society. He was fifty-one years old when World War II ended and the FNRJ (later SFRJ; Socialist Federative Republic of Yugoslavia) started to build itself as a society distinct from its prewar identity; in his novels he writes not about a socialist society but about a capitalist one out of control. His 1938 novel *On the Edge of Reason* (*Na rubu pameti*), for instance, focuses on the world in which success of all kinds, and primarily financial success, is all that matters, and provides a supreme justification for injustice, immorality, and violence. "Success is an end in itself, and success is for the sake of success, and everything is for the sake of success: big and trifling lies, dinners and tea parties, circles of people, friendships, deceptions, hatreds, wars, and careers. . . . Ideas are confused, and success is the only criterion."[4]

There seems to be a clear connection (though it does not have to be conscious or intended) between Krleža's take on the absolute elevation of success in a certain form of capitalism, on the one hand, and a perception of transition from Yugoslav socialism to largely laissez-faire capitalism, a perception articulated in a number of works appearing in post-Yugoslav cultural production, on the other. As newcomers on the world stage of "everything is allowed if it is for success or profit, and all is justified for the needs of work or career," the characters in post-Yugoslav texts or films often do not fare well in their contact with "the West" or with the global space in general—which is surely not globalized legally, even less ethically, but is very palpably being globalized in its economic sphere. In the film *What Iva Recorded on October 21, 2003* (*Što je Iva snimila 21. listopada 2003*, directed by Tomislav Radić, 2005), a Croatian entrepreneur ends up being played for a fool by a Western one: after offering his family's intimate realm (his daughter's home birthday party) to a Western partner in hopes of securing a business contract, the Croatian man discovers that it was the Western man who actually got the better of him and also tried to seduce his wife. The Westerner was much better at the same game that the Croatian man tried to play, the game of playacting a human relationship while actually aiming for gain and profit. He also had a vision of all he wanted to take (the unsuspecting host's wife), which surpassed the native man's imagination of all that, or how much, one may actually want to get and try to take from others, including from one's host, a still privileged figure in post-Yugoslav space.

In the film *Armin* (2007), revolving around teenage Armin and his father, who come from a small Bosnian town to Zagreb in order to audition for a German film on the Bosnian War, the attitudes of local and foreign professionals handling the father and son, professionals who are "all business" as the saying goes, and the space in which they function, are shown in an almost surreal light, which makes visible the machinery of work, career, success, and efficiency. It is a system that may include humans but is not driven by them anymore.

By using . . . cinematic device[s] which turn average hotel spaces into claustrophobic traps, and people doing their jobs into disturbing automatons, *Armin* creates a penetrating view of this world, which corresponds with the mute experience of this world acquired by the hastily appraised and belittled father and son. . . . And it is these cold objective lights, these quietly moving elevators, these huge buildings and walls and machines, that make these people, rather than the other way around. The people obey and "succeed" by their obedience, gradually becoming parts of the system with a bit of the system's power—a receptionist, a film director, a producer—doing their job while losing all the other aspects of life and of possible joy, which become vague and distant.[5]

A number of Bosnian films feature symbolic scenes in which the West is seen as exploiting, deserting, avoiding, or simply not bothering with Bosnia, despite the huge amounts of Western money and energy that were extended to post-Dayton Bosnia, and despite numerous individual Westerners who have been helping and who are also often featured in these films. There is nothing personal in the way that the West or the world—or rather their economic or institutional systems—deal with Bosnia. In other words, it is not that the systems in place have anything against Bosnia or the post-Yugoslav region per se, but rather that any place that is so weakened and vulnerable after a war, and with such a largely unproductive or even damaging institutional framework as Bosnia and Herzegovina has at the present time, becomes a fertile ground for standard actions that bring in various kinds of profit and success. The poverty that pushes women into the sex trade is thus exploited by some UN soldiers who become patrons of underage Bosnian prostitutes in *Summer in the Golden Valley* (*Ljeto u zlatnoj dolini*, directed by Srđan Vuletić, 2003); in *No Man's Land* some UN commanders cynically stage a show of care for the media, while actually deserting the victims, in order to maintain the appearance of help and their comfortable positions—and that in opposition to the genuine attempts to help by the common UN (here French) soldiers and the Western (here British) journalists. In Aida Begić's *Snow* (*Snijeg*, 2008), a Western real estate corporation attempts to buy a whole village in eastern Bosnia—fertile land alongside the private homes, the whole lot—from the impoverished women left in a village after the men were killed, or "ethnically cleansed." The sale would probably not better the lives of these women, who would be forced to leave their land with probably not too much money and without the skills needed to live well in another place, but there is clear profit to be made by this transaction. This real estate transaction is, again, not aimed at harming these women or Bosnia, but is just a rational way of doing business in a globalized world in which financial success is the sole principle of operation. And aside from the exploitation for profit there is also a desertion of the unfortunate in order to pursue a life of success: *Summer in the Golden Valley*, a film set in Sarajevo, is punctuated by a recurring image of a beautiful silver plane carrying foreigners and flying as fast as it can away from the valley afflicted by the "sickness of misery" (*bolest bijede*); and *Fuse* (*Gori vatra*, directed by Pjer Žalica, 2004) includes in its fantastic story a scene of President Clinton's limo that never stops or even lowers its tinted windows as it furiously passes through the Bosnian town of Tešanj. These and a number of other works from the post-Yugoslav era seem to draw some part of their critical vision (which is often also ironical, satirical, or grotesque), from the intellectual and cultural environment of the socialist Yugoslavia, profoundly marked by the work of people like Miroslav Krleža.

4.

And then there are also very literal examples of bringing back, retrieving, and reactivating the Yugoslav intellectual and artistic past in the present. These take the form of reprinting or publishing for the very first time not only the artistic works but also the most "literal-level" words of those who were elements and energies of that Yugoslav reality—the words of their interviews or even previously unpublished notes. These include the 2001 reprinting of Predrag Matvejević's *Conversations with Krleža* (*Razgovori s Krležom*, the first edition was published in 1969), and the first printing of Krleža's conversations with Belgrade's Miloš Jevtić, recorded or assembled from Krleža's writings for Radio Belgrade and printed in Zagreb in 2009 under the title *To the Much Respected Gentlemen Ants* (*Mnogopoštovanoj gospodi mravima*).

Given that there is presently, in 2010, so much talk in the Yugoslav successor states (with the exception of Slovenia) about "joining Europe" and "becoming part of Europe," let us quickly remember the stance regarding Europe by some of the most prominent Yugoslav-era writers like Miroslav Krleža, Ivo Andrić, or Danilo Kiš. Cosmopolitan and polyglot, these writers have lived in and experienced "Europe" firsthand, from Krleža's many travels and residencies abroad—including the one in the USSR in the 1920s, recorded in his *A Trip to Russia* (*Izlet u Rusiju*, 1926); to Andrić's diplomatic service, sometimes compromised, in European capitals; to Kiš's later life and work in France, with his first stay there recorded in his youthful *A Trip to Paris* (*Izlet u Pariz*, 1960). More importantly, they studied this "Europe" and knew the works of European culture—its literature and art—deeply and thoroughly. This intimate knowledge allowed a discerning, nongeneralizing, and critical attitude, the one of an intellectual equal, instead of the inferior attitude of a pupil who is always behind and always having to learn from "Europe," or desiring a mimetic approximation of the "European" ideal, which is often felt in the post-Yugoslav cultural space.

Consider, for instance, Danilo Kiš's reflection on French literature, from the March 3, 1965, interview with Milan Vlajčić in *Mladost*:

You spent a lot of time in France and had a chance to see how the translations of our distinguished writers fare with French literary critics. Which of our [i.e., Yugoslav] values get a real response?

We have a better writer than all of the contemporary French writers, including Sartre: that is Krleža. His book *A Banquet in Blitva* [*Banket u Blitvi*, 1961] was unnoticed in Paris. His other books will fare the same in France and in the West. And Krleža is a greater writer and greater philosopher than Sartre. A French bourgeois is not interested in our artistic values but in our tourist attractions. I am convinced that our literature today, and especially poetry, is above the French, and particularly this unread, unrecognized *Karleja*, who cannot be found in the [missing word] dictionary because he is transcribed as *Kerleja*. But what do we care? We still learn at his side.[6]

So what are some of the things that one could learn today from Miroslav Krleža or, as Kiš puts it, "at his side"? ("Learn" does not mean here to uncritically accept, but rather to engage in a dialogue with or be aware of Krleža's positions and of his reasoning.) Let us look at a few fragments from these new editions of conversations with Krleža. Here, for example, is Krleža answering questions on various topics.

On socialism:

Socialism means a peaceful life under warm roofs and not feeding fires across the whole world. Socialism means hospitals, and not the creation of mass hunger and sickness. Socialism means a cult of good books and beautiful arts, and not a betrayal of ethics and manslaughter. Socialism means human morality among peoples and countries, and not the cult of lies, death, and political murder. . . . Socialism is nothing else but a preventive, prophylactic action that decreases all kinds of Suffering, thus Pain, thus Evil. Accordingly, socialism is exactly "only that," the fight against earthly evils by earthly means, and not any "idea from above."[7]

On technology:

In that regard the results are usually merciless caricatures of hopes and expectations. Here is one contemporary example: landing on the Moon. . . . I will add, without intention to undermine the technical success of the endeavor, that during this first flight one of them [the astronauts] celebrates mass like a Protestant priest, which means he believes in and prays to God, and the other, when he saw the Moon up close with his own eyes, could think only of naming a crater after his wife. A touchingly sentimental gesture! They thus carried to the Moon their own earthly views of the world . . .

In connection to that I would remind you of one excerpt from [Krleža's text] *Ten Bloody Years (1914–1924)* (*Deset krvavih godina*): "In accordance with Divine Command, the ranks and orders of the Triple United Kingdom undertook with their deepest servility the expedition to the Moon, landed on the coast of Plato's Sea, waiting in unison and obedience the further Divine orders and always ready to sacrifice their lives out of loyalty, not only for the invasion of Luna, but also of the other planets, within the realm, and if necessary outside of the frame of our solar system."

With this I wanted to say that if one goes on with such low logic, we should not be surprised if one day comes the news that the astronaut forces of Block A or Block B landed on the coast of the Sea of Silence and exchanged rocket fire from posts at the craters Copernicus and Aristotle.[8]

On science and art:

A scientific consciousness rose up above the problems of various human worries and sicknesses . . . but it is utterly helpless in the face of politics. . . . [A human being] has command over a whole range of destructive forces, but cannot yet figure out how to protect himself and future generations from the cobalt bomb. Curing measles and diarrhea and pneumonia with the injection of viruses, a human being, on the other hand, menaces his survival with much more refined "antibiotic" inventions, losing his way so much that one could assert without exaggeration, that the mind has become the greatest danger for human life. . . .

Science actually dreams, and that, if one sees it right, is not such a stupid thought. Science often sleeps with a dead dream devoid of ideas. It snores at the university departments and that thunder resounds through all the halls of the world.

Art makes its way through the centuries under the unclear, unintelligible, and often nervously aggressive dictates of so-called scientific truths. Scientific hypothesis changes on a whim through the ages. . . . Scientific formulae follow rhythmically the game of blind and destructive forces, the forces regarding which poetry had its own melancholic picture a long time ago.[9]

On history or, as Predrag Matvejević puts it, on Krleža's take on history, which is much closer to Nietzsche than to Marx, where the "class struggle" is only a "superficial episode whereas the negation of that which is human is a veritable tragedy," Krleža said:

It is true: history detached itself from everything that is human. But what here is a human being? In what measure is he a constant? A human being, of the Old Testament type? The Hellenist of the fourth century, who fears for his life day and night because he secretly reads Sophocles and Euripides?

Around him scream hermits, ascetics, future metaphysical career-makers. Saints. Before illiterate masses they burn books, temples, libraries, kill women and children, make history. These are the "superhumans" who will in the name of their moral-intellectual consciousness control history for the next two millennia. And the Hellenistic decadents will dissolve into the air like laments from Boethius to the present day. The lyrical resignation of the lonely mind in a long night. That too is history. And those saints were the engines of progress.[10]

Reappropriating Krleža today with these reprinted or first-time-published interviews may show a way of reactivating and reutilizing other vibrant commonalities of post-Yugoslav cultural space, other Yugoslav legacies. As a realm of ideas, thoughts, philosophy, and art, the intellectual

Yugoslav legacy is not a matter of the past but a matter of the present, which starts living the moment one looks at it, reads it, thinks about it, or enters into a dialogue with it. And one of the more useful aspects of this legacy today is the informed knowledge of the "world" and Europe, instead of manipulated and manipulating myths about them, along with the critical understanding of these realms in all of their complexities, potentials, and histories, instead of the simply mimetic attitude of the desire to approximate them without much understanding of what they are about. This Yugoslav legacy also includes post-Yugoslav intellectuals and artists finding and building connections among themselves, not unlike the ones that were built between Kiš and Krleža, or Matvejević and Krleža, or Jevtić and Krleža. These connections strengthen each individual entity and do not homogenize, but instead help to create a vital field of intellectual energy and experience, of vibrant commonalities, which everyone in post-Yugoslav spaces can benefit from, as these realms become integrated into the European Union and increasingly drawn into global processes.

8

Zenit Rising
Return to a Balkan Avant-Garde
Marijeta Božović

A Critical Revival

The last five years have seen an explosion of interest in what, by all respects, should be a small and forgotten avant-garde publication. The experimental magazine *Zenit* (1921–26) was the output of a tiny core group of Serbs working initially in Zagreb in the early 1920s, and in the country then known as the Kingdom—not yet of Yugoslavia—but of Serbs, Croats, and Slovenes. Such circumstances hardly predicted a revival nearly a century later.

Yet one glance at a recent bibliography reveals a veritable flood of articles, books, monographs, exhibits, and conference presentations on the subject.[1] In the past several years, Belgrade and Zagreb have released rival catalogs of the complete issues of *Zenit*, alongside an impressive and expensive complete facsimile reprint of the magazines for collectors. Recently, the National Library of Serbia has made the complete set available online.[2] The Ubu Gallery in New York City faithfully collects the original issues, as well as an archive of related ephemera: advertisements, flyers, requests for payment from subscribers, and invitations to *Zenit*-related events. Whence the resurgent interest?

The titles alone of these recent articles speak volumes: "Croatia Has an Avant-Garde!"[3] claims one headline. Another proclaims "The Vitality of Avant-Garde Art,"[4] and yet another more enigmatically celebrates "8 ½ Decades Since the Foundation of *Zenit* and Zenitism."[5] Meanwhile, a Belgrade publication sums up the work produced in and around *Zenit* as the "Zagreb intermezzo of the Serbian avant-garde." Given the context of post-Yugoslav spaces and regional rivalries, there is nothing unusual in this interweaving of national claims. However, the very interest in a marginal, nationally slippery avant-garde publication such as *Zenit* signals something of a sea change. The internationally known writer Dubravka Ugrešić, a scholar of *Zenit* before disintegration, some years ago thought there would be little chance of reviving interest in the journal in Zagreb.[6] It is also fair to say that fifteen years ago, there would have been little chance of a *Zenit*-related gallery show, with no mention of any wars except, perhaps, World War I, in a New York gallery. The landscape has shifted, and even the leading center of cultural capital is invested in emerging, rediscovered, plural modernisms.

I propose to examine this marked and sudden return of interest in a slim journal originally conceived of as a monthly provocation. Who needs a marginal avant-garde? Who needs a *tradition* of the avant-garde, even more curiously; and why might these post-Yugoslav spaces, in the current critical parlance, be so interested in reviving this one?

The First Balkan Avant-Garde

The *Zenit* journals were collections of essays, poems, and manifestos in two alphabets and a handful of languages, including Esperanto; avant-garde art objects; revolutionary events; and a collective experiment headed by Ljubomir Micić, the group's André Breton. The collective grew still smaller with each quarrel: by the end, one suspects that only Micić's brother, Branko Ve (or Virgil) Poljanski, and wife, Anuška (pseudonym Nina-Naj), could stand him. But for almost six years, the *Zenitisti* glued together word and image on cheap press, declared themselves the local avant-garde, and sought to make their double marginality an integral part of the manifesto.

In 1921, the new kingdom was stretching fledgling wings toward the West, but these Zagreb troublemakers looked elsewhere for inspiration. "I am the brother of Raskolnikov!" claims the title of one manifesto. The motto provokes: "Balkanize the world!" "We aren't Gnostics to ponder how the sky is composed of spirit. We are heretics who hate your God. . . . We Zenitists are the first who in art listen to the commandment of our wild blood. (You call us barbarians!) We are the first to discover that there is a land of the Barbaro-genius—the Balkans!"[7]

Yugoslavia was born out of Ottoman and Austro-Hungarian wreckage, and from the nightmare of World War I. As Miško Šuvaković reminds us, "All the transcendent political models of the late nineteenth and twentieth centuries were part of the Yugoslav rise and fall," including, as he puts it, "bourgeois national capitalism and liberal capitalist fascism, nationalism and revolutionary communism, Stalinism, real socialism, self-governing socialism, post-socialist patriotism, and transitional post-socialism."[8] That alone should make the region worthy of study and critical attention: the rise and fall of Yugoslavia encapsulates much of the twentieth century's bloodshed, ideological struggle, and idealism.

However, the interwar avant-garde, and especially the Zagreb circle centered on Micić in the early 1920s, met the recent wreckage with perhaps the region's most ambitious artistic response. I limit my attention here to Micić and *Zenit*, and to 1921–25, the first five years of the journal's life. These early Zagreb years catch *Zenit* at its most ambitiously internationalist and deliberately radical. One of *Zenit*'s first manifestos opens as follows:

> Man—that is our first word. From the solitude of stiff walls and cursed streets, from the dark depths of the subconscious and unearthly nights, we emerge before you like apostles, like prophets, to prophesize: Man-Art . . . We are entering today into a New Decade and we have to get past the borders of Yugoslavia. In the last decade we were soldiers of war and murder for "the freedom of the people" outside of those borders, and from today on we want to be soldiers of humanity. Of Culture, Love, and Brotherhood. We are entering as the suffering and the converted. We are entering crippled and wounded as a people, but in us lies the strength of those who suffered, who were humiliated, who were stoned on the pillory-stocks of Europe. Let our entrance into the third decade of the twentieth century be a fight for humanity, through Art.[9]

Arguably, this avant-garde was doomed before it began. In interwar capitalism, such provocations represented the excluded far left; after World War II and Yugoslavia's metamorphosis into a socialist state, they would be treated as "extreme expressions of Western bourgeois or civilian decadence, cosmopolitanism, and political subversion."[10]

Yet in 1921, Micić tried almost single-handedly to launch a movement and to introduce *Balkan avant-garde* as a serious term. It was a moment in European culture defined by such projects, but one that Micić and his colleagues, in their newly pieced-together country, took as entirely theirs. The *Zenit* group worked from their position on the margin of other avant-gardes, and took advantage of their relative cultural "youth": from scraps of Nietzsche, Russian modernism in all its forms, expressionism, futurism, dadaism, and constructivism, the Zenitists built the Balkan barbarogenius.

The Collective Event

As an art object and as a collective project, *Zenit* challenged multiple preconceptions about artistic production. Conflicts between avant-gardists and Yugoslav modernists centered on the question of collectivity: while the avant-gardists aspired to and proclaimed the triumph of collective art in manifestos, modernist poetry remained "rooted in individual, highly aestheticized artistic (poetic) practice."[11]

Šuvaković points out that, unlike the paradigmatic Russian and German avant-gardes, to which the marginal European movements looked for inspiration, "the utopian ideas of the entire work (*Gesamtkunstwerk*) in Yugoslav avant-gardes were embodied only in manifesto platforms and utopian or projected trends." He contrasts an art that consisted mostly of manifestos to grand collective accomplishments in "architecture (the Bauhaus building), theater (Oskar Schlemmer's mathematical dance), monumental sculpture (Tatlin's *Monument to the Third International*), and public mass performance and theatrical experiment (the art of *LEF*)."[12] However, the utopian exclamations of *Zenit* were their own legitimate events.

Journals were *the* medium for the Yugoslav avant-garde: "The history of the Yugoslav avant-garde from 1921 to 1932 [is] defined by the magazines. . . . These magazines were not only literary works or literary mediators (communicators) with a specific art typography, but intertextual and interpictorial experimental creations forming an avant-garde model of textual visual expression."[13]

Sonja Briski Uzelac adds that magazines did more than "transmit" literary works or even add a decorative or illustrative visual component: they "assumed the function of an elementary medium, a fundamental space, and material avant-garde invasion of the institution of art."[14] An added and not to be underestimated benefit was social: these publications provided a "communication system of art, primarily among artists but more broadly among the cultural centers. . . . These ties created the basis for an entire artistic archipelago."[15] For readers and participants alike, serial publications served as a kind of social network.

Today and for similar reasons, experimental art magazines, often wildly reinvented and in electronic form, have never seemed more relevant. The imperfection and vitality of serial publication, the compromise of art pieced together by group effort, suggest an aesthetic increasingly our own.[16]

The Politics of Word and Image

One wants to read and frame a *Zenit* simultaneously, and ends up using the journal to wrap fish. The breakdown of borders between word and image has been so successful in the twentieth century that by now it is ubiquitous and unavoidable in commercial design; but to better grasp the political significance of the visual-textual experimentation in the early avant-garde, we need only turn to Walter Benjamin's seminal writings on media and technological reproducibility.

In "The Author as Producer," originally given as an address at the Paris Institute for the Study of Fascism in 1934, Benjamin writes with fascination about the novel potential of the Soviet printing press. Innovative use of technology seemed to abolish "the conventional distinction between genres, between writer and poet, between scholar and popularizer . . . even the distinction between author and reader."[17]

Benjamin called for technical progress to lead to the way to political progress, to

overcom[e] another of the barriers, transcend another of the antitheses, that fetter the production of intellectuals—in this case, the barrier between writing and image. What we require of the photographer is the ability to give his picture a caption that wrenches it from modish commerce and gives it a revolutionary use value. But we will make this demand most emphatically when we—the writers—take up photography. Here, too, therefore, technical progress is for the author as producer the foundation of his political progress. In other words, only by transcending the specialization in the process of intellectual production—a specialization that, in the bourgeois view, constitutes its order—can one make this production politically useful; and the barriers imposed by specialization must be breached jointly by the productive forces that they were set up to divide.[18]

What is striking about *Zenit* as a particular example of the avant-garde assault on barriers is that it presents such a conscious reach for a new art form. The paradoxically local and international issues, with their increasing breakdown between visual and semantic uses of text, as well as between the roles of poet, organizer, and revolutionary, show the formal manifestations of a progressive art in the very process of *becoming*. Thirteen years before Benjamin's essay, Micić and his colleagues were struggling toward artistic and theoretical formulations of just such a stand, simultaneously evolving theory and praxes. One of the privileges of the double outsider, located on the margins of cultural production as an avant-garde artist and geopolitically on the margins of other avant-gardes, is an acute and prescient self-consciousness.

The pages and images of *Zenit* offer word-image conflations, differing from mere collage in that they include the dimension of time. The experience of leafing through pages, or potentially through issues of the serial publication, adds a phenomenological and experiential element for the reader-viewer. To push a bit further, the experiment begins to resemble montage done on the cheap, a textual version of early avant-garde cinema.

The Zenitists worshiped American films. Micić once gave the following as a formula: "U.S.A. = Poe + Whitman + Chaplin"; the last was to him the most important ingredient. *Zenit* looked to popular forms and used the smallest-scale means of production to twist and radicalize aesthetic principles stolen from Hollywood, and from signs and advertisements. They learned to flatten the surface from soup advertisements as well as from Kandinsky, and cribbed geometry from road signs and Malevich. The productive tension shows in the journals, which devoured the popular culture of mass capitalism and regurgitated leftist avant-gardes—as in the later phenomena of French New Wave cinema. (With a beautiful circularity, late 1970s and early 1980s "Yugoslav New Wave" films nod to this early local print avant-garde.)

Throughout, the *Zenit* experiment followed a single dominant, a "'zenith' in the projection of a new civilization of image and sign."[19] The aspiration upward and as a progressive struggle signals an attempted Lamarckian evolution in art. We can compare this struggle with Benjamin's words in "The Work of Art in the Age of Mechanical Reproduction":

The history of every art form has critical periods in which the particular form strains after effects which can be easily achieved only with a changed technical standard—that is to say, in a new art form. The excesses and crudities of art which thus result, particularly in periods of so-called decadence, actually emerge from the core of its richest historical energies. In recent years, Dadaism has amused itself with such barbarisms. Only now is its impulse recognizable: *Dadaism attempted to produce with the means of painting (or literature) the effects which the public today seeks in film.*[20]

Film infected the entirety of the international avant-garde, as the Zenitists were openly aware. Micić writes that one must "learn from film the speed of changing place and space, but this film miracle should stand on the firm basis of a single unique idea."[21] Actual film projects were rare and remained unfinished even in later years, as Nevena Daković has discussed in her work on Yugoslav film theory: "The first avant-garde generated a number of film forms never intended to be made into actual films, but devoted to developing *the technique of the imagined work*. . . . [Instead it generated] written film designed to induce highly subjective imagined film, like that destined to be projected onto the personal screen in the viewer's head."[22] Looked at in such a context, the highly visual *Zenit* journals begin to resemble illustrated film scripts, with included stage directions and implicit sound effects: each "viewer" might come away with a slightly different version of the shared and implied "film."

Boško Tokin, one of the core founders of *Zenit*, was in reality a frustrated filmmaker who went on to become a pioneer of Yugoslav film theory and criticism. Such leanings were unsurprising: in the 1920s cinematography was a "fetish apparatus," and film was considered by many to be "the only art linked to a modern technique able to reflect the essence of an urban environment and the rhythm of a technological age."[23] Tying his interests together, Tokin argued for the "linguistic nature" of film in his articles, and concluded that "film is a type of 'new Esperanto' . . . since any idea written in light and movement is universally understood."[24] The Zenitists as a group were aiming at nothing less than a new and universal language. They lacked the resources to make movies, and so they made magazines.

Balkanizing Europe

Micić's people gorged on Cézanne and expressionism; drank in the same toxins as Siegfried Kracauer and the early Frankfurt school; dissected dada; would soon out-séance surrealism; and conducted epistolary romances with both Muscovite *and* Parisian Russians—alternately cursing and currying favor with such white émigrés as Zinaida Gippius and Dmitry Merezhkovsky. Šuvaković calls these "contradictory, eclectic, and shocking ideological characteristics," roughly definable as "an anarchist approach using a variety of strategies for provocation within the greater ideologies of pan-Slavism, nationalism, Nietzsche's *Übermensch*, Bolshevik revolutionary rhetoric, Trotskyism,"[25] and so forth.

To overemphasize the anarchy, however, is to downplay the experiment's potential. Rather than view *Zenit* as a grab bag of radical strategies merging into pan-Slavism, we can read it as an ideology and artistic form struggling to emerge out of the available materials. If the "Balkanness" of the barbarogenius was so prominently stressed (see for example the Evgenije Dudek poem in *Zenit* issue 13: "Ja sam zenitista da strašan Balkanac [I am a Zenitist, a frightening Balkanite]"), it was primarily to provide a counterstance, a dialectical opposition to everything for which "mainstream" Europe stood. From the start, this wild man was emphatically *Balkan*, not Serbian, Croatian, or Yugoslav—despite the utter lack of other Balkan participants in the project.

The movement, or rather its troubled leader, did eventually and notoriously slide into nationalism. Micić moved his headquarters to Belgrade in the mid-1920s, and then fled to Paris, only to return in 1936 to publish a single issue of "an obscure, rightist, nationalist magazine," *Serbianism*. "He spent the rest of his life in complete anonymity," as Darko Šimičić grimly summarizes.[26] Arguably, this tendency toward nationalism was present from the beginning—every radical impulse contains the germs of its opposite bent. But at the start, the mission of the Balkan barbarogenius was, as *Zenit* claimed, not to "retain" cultural supremacy behind one's own borders, but to Balkanize Europe. Aleš Erjavec writes: "*Zenit* promoted the idea of an 'eastern-metacosmic type of superman,' who would have 'a superior relation to Mme Europe' and its worn-out values. . . . Micić's ideas are reminiscent not only of Nietzsche but of the 'national' wing of Russian futurism [Khlebnikov, etc.] which promulgated (counter to the cosmopolitan futurism of Mayakovsky's circle) a negation of culture, an animality, troglodytism, and the Slavic tradition at the expense of the Italo-German one." But Erjavec too notices that any clear antinomy is in fact undermined by the conflation just sketched out: by blending the ideas of German expressionism with those of Russian futurism, Micić was developing a "link between the two parts of the continent: *Zenit* was to be the voice of Europe's East speaking to Europe's West."[27] For hardly the first or last time, the very language of its critique comes from the Western tradition.

Šimičić in turn points out that, despite being "strongly under the influence of the European avant-garde, Micić insisted on the autochthonous Balkan 'barbarogenius' opposing Europe."[28] The seeming contradiction does not quite undermine the *Zenit* stance: Micić aimed to appropriate the best other cultures had to offer, from a position on the margins that, in his hands, suddenly seemed privileged. How? Why? "Micić believed that the time had come for the Balkan region to be more than just Europe's cultural colony, 'in which the importation of cultural trash is unlimited and unhindered by law.' He criticized the aesthetic and unconscious adoption of Western styles and their pale and empty imitation."[29]

The language of colonization is entirely appropriate to the *Zenit* project. Pascale Casanova, in *The World Republic of Letters*, posits a geographical model for the distribution of cultural capital. Casanova argues that cultural blocks struggle for power and fight over borders that are related but not identical to their political counterparts. Culturally colonized spaces (i.e., the minor languages) are left in the conundrum that the Algerian writer Mohammed Dib has described powerfully in "Thief of Fire." In what language is the "thief of culture" to write?

The poverty of the means granted to [the thief of fire] is so impossible to imagine that it appears to defy all credibility. Language, culture, intellectual values, scales of moral values, none of these gifts that one receives in the cradle are of any possible use to him. . . . What to do? The thief gets hold at once of other instruments, ones that have been forged neither for him nor for the ends that he means to pursue. What matters is that they are within his reach and that he can bend them to suit his purposes. The language is not his language, the culture is not the heritage of his ancestors, these turns of thought, these intellectual, ethical categories are not current in his natural environment. How ambiguous are the weapons at his disposal![30]

Tellingly, an acute interest in the revolts of Europe-apportioned Africa registers in the "Makroskop" sections of the *Zenit* journals.

The peculiar solution towards which *Zenit* aspired was not at this point a "greater Serbian," but a cobbled-together Esperanto. The issues contain a veritable Babel of languages, with most poetry published in the original, and nearly always include pieces in both Latin and Cyrillic alphabets. In recent years, post-Yugoslav nations have used translation as a divisive tool, for example insisting on the presence of simultaneous translators from Croatian into Serbian at political events, or on subtitles for regional films.[31] By contrast, the lack of translation in these early *Zenit* journals suggests a radical unity through implied mutual comprehensibility. *Zenit* issued a cry of support for actual Esperanto—and for the figurative Esperanto of an increasingly visual language, whether experienced as modern hieroglyphics or as a magazine mimicry of film.

The Zenitists stole fire where they could. They mixed original Nietzsche with the Nietzscheanism of Russian modernists: the Balkan barbarogenius is the acknowledged country cousin of Aleksandr Blok's Scythian. *Zenit's* issue 3 opens with Blok's famous poem "We Are Scythians!" which itself went on to influence a century of Russian thought. Here, Blok's verses are printed in the old imperial Russian orthography and paired with an etching by Egon Schiele. The barbarogenius has Germanic DNA and Eastern European foster parents, or vice versa; to keep mixing family metaphors, a marriage was meant to follow the great divide: the East, through a transfusion of healthy barbarian blood, was to save old Europe from Spenglerian decline.

The cry of the barbarogenius is thus a plea for the mixed breed, and a bold claim that the margins might be the coming centers of a new world. If the Balkans could spark World War I, could they not spark salvation and the art of the future? Here is the rebellion of a small culture, a peculiar cultural postcolonialism, as well as the small-scale realization of *Gesamtkunstwerk*. *Zenit* appeals because it combines modesty with arrogance, and provides a kind of utopia that remains possible to get behind. Magazine utopias, at least, do not cause ecological catastrophes.

Avant-Garde Tradition

To return to an earlier question: who needs a tradition of the avant-garde? Many recent publications in the post-Yugoslav countries and abroad almost instinctively compare historical avant-garde experiments with contemporary art practices. Audiences and critics alike sense continuity between early dada shock art and the more recent work of someone like Marina Abramović, perhaps the most famous performance artist in the world today.

The most impressive English-language anthology on the subject of Yugoslav "historical, neo, and post-avant-gardes," Đurić and Šuvaković's *Impossible Histories*, suggests that historical avant-gardes are seen as "the precursor to modernism, while the neo-avant-garde is considered a critical practice on the fringes of mainstream modernist culture."[32] The post-avant-garde in turn takes a "posthistorical" stance, commenting on earlier narratives at will, among them the previous avant-gardes. But this overview posits continuity, or rather contiguity, without much examination. Surely the post-avant-garde, should we accept such a term, is not actually posthistorical?

The real question is why should iconoclastic new praxes, defined precisely by their radical break with tradition, repeat earlier artistic movements? Is it unavoidable? Do these "returns to an avant-garde" merely repeat formulas that consistently *épater la bourgeoisie*: for example, by subverting an accepted cultural institution, whether by drawing a mustache on the *Mona Lisa* or by bringing naked bodies into the New York Museum of Modern Art? Or is the link between the two performances more profound?

The debate on the continuity of radical praxes has of course a life outside the Balkans. In the context of the Anglo-American poetic tradition, Marjorie Perloff has argued in *21st-Century Modernism: The "New" Poetics* that we are currently experiencing a "carrying-on, in somewhat diluted form," of the avant-garde project "at the very heart of early modernism." She writes:

> Indeed, what strikes us when we re-read the poetries of the early twentieth century is that the real fate of first-stage modernism was one of deferral, its radical and utopian aspirations being cut off by the catastrophe[s of the 20th century]. . . . Indeed between the two world wars (and well beyond the second one) it almost seems as if poems and art works made a conscious effort to repress the technological and formal inventions of modernism at its origins. Now that the long twentieth century is finally behind us, perhaps we can begin to see this embryonic phase with new eyes. Far from being irrelevant and obsolete, the aesthetic of early modernism has provided the seeds of the materialist poetic which is increasingly our own.[33]

Perloff intuits something deeply compelling, and her insights can be turned to suggest telling similarities as well as stark differences between the experiences of the pre- and post-Yugoslav avant-gardes. Any post-Yugoslav art must in some way acknowledge and grapple with the legacies of very recent violence, and cannot simply resume the deferred potential of an interrupted avant-garde project.

There is perhaps a counterintuitive conservatism to Perloff's project, which seems to project authenticity and origin onto the early English avant-garde; but a similar note tends to creep into any discussion of a return to the avant-garde. However, Perloff's primary concern is with *the* internationally dominant language, and with the solitary intellectual practices of the so-called language poets—a sharp contrast to the minor, marginal, and collective Balkan avant-garde. Does the very marginality of Balkan avant-garde art create continuity for artists from the region, as a recurring theme and leitmotif of their work? Does that marginality encourage or necessitate an interest in local precursors, despite the expected antitraditional bent of any avant-garde?

A recent Belgrade publication, Gojko Tešić's *Otkrovenje srpske avangarde* (*The Revelation of the Serbian Avant-Garde*) argues that in the local context it is entirely necessary to consider the avant-garde a tradition. After gathering the Serbian avant-gardes of the twentieth-century under one cover, he concludes that the "stroll through the forest of the avant-garde naturally imposes talk of an avant-garde tradition."[34]

Tešić argues that this Serbian avant-garde tradition shakes the paradigm of the avant-garde as discontinuous with modernism. As he puts it, "Even Ezra Pound at some point said that tradition should be understood as something beautiful to nurture, not as chains that bind. . . . The modern or rather avant-garde creator, in the act of negation, of overturning [a certain] tradition is in fact tracking after these earlier types of poetic experiment, which can be productive."[35] The "terminological chaos" that suggests otherwise, according to Tešić, confuses the issue and results from adopting terminology from the West, with its entirely different cultural context. "The strong influence of Anglo-American theoretical thought, covering a space in which the avant-garde radicalisms of the beginning of the previous century were not a massive phenomenon . . . imposed modernism as an established concept . . . on all tendencies of the modern type which came into conflict with every sign of poetic radicalism."[36] Yet Tešić turns repeatedly to Anglo-American thought to conceptualize his countertheory. His paradigmatic thinkers, no less than Perloff's, are Pound and Eliot. Furthermore, it is evident that his model is fundamentally internally oriented, positing continuity through national—that is to say Serbian—culture. Such criticism goes the way of Micić's own fate, moving away from the "Balkanization of Europe" to a retreat into the far less provocative "Serbianism."

The contemporary art praxes that are attracting the most attention, meanwhile, be it in the medium of film, in video or performance art, in new journals, or in various online incarnations, are doing just the opposite: opening the region up to international discourses and finding global relevance. It is precisely the work of artists such as Abramović, with her unapologetic post-Yugoslav identity, unflinching gaze at a history of violence, and resulting international significance, that to me continues most in the spirit of the early *Zenit* radicalism. And that spirit has never felt more modern.

Part IV

The Story of a Language

9

Post-Yugoslav Emergence and the Creation of Difference

Tomislav Z. Longinović

Language Falls Apart

The language I still can't help but call Serbo-Croatian, despite political changes and violent national-identity shifts within my destroyed homeland, acquired its latest avatar in 2007. After Montenegro's separation from Serbia, the newly independent parliament voted to introduce Montenegrin as the official language of the new sovereign state, adding a fourth version of the formerly common language to the collection of new-yet-old idioms. The first three, Bosnian, Croatian, and Serbian, have been given their present name by the pragmatic translators of the International War Crimes Tribunal in the Hague, creating the virally echoing BCS acronym to name the former lingua franca of the region. Interestingly, the judicial origin of the name immediately invokes the prosecution of war crimes on the territory of the former Yugoslavia, positioning the new-yet-old idiom as part of the palliative political and military apparatus that was to decide on the readiness of the former warring parties to enter the European Union. This article merges my own experience of a person trying to come to terms with the linguistic divisions imposed as a result of Yugoslavia's violent dismemberment and my scholarly interest in understanding translation as a cultural practice promoting communication and understanding. In fact, the conclusions drawn from the post-Yugoslav case will prove that translation can be effectively used as a political tool for the production of differences and for tearing down cultural bridges that promote understanding.

The recognition of linguistic particularities was especially necessary to support the painful birth of Bosnia-Herzegovina as a separate political entity after 1992, inspired by the notion that an independent state needs a language that bears its name as well. For those of us teaching this language to foreign students at the university level, the dilemma of the language's name will become even more complex with the introduction of M into the BCS formula, especially if we take into account the fact that these four incarnations of the former Serbo-Croatian are mutually intelligible on the level of everyday communication for a vast majority of its speakers.

In fact, the case of Serbo-Croatian is a painful reminder of the cultural reality whose language is the marker of collective identity and the extension of national territory. Structured by extralinguistic forces tied to the power of social elites and their projected political aims, language performs the most basic interpellation of those subjected to the national imagination. Discussing quite a different relationship between Québécois and French, Annie Brisset comes to a conclusion that rings very true in the case of Serbo-Croatian: "Translation becomes an act of reclaiming, of re-centering of the identity, a re-territorializing operation. It does not create a new language, but it elevates a dialect to the status of a national and cultural language."[1] The literal reclaiming of national territories through the violent breakup of the common South Slavic state during the Wars of Yugoslav Succession (1991–95) and their aftermath (Montenegro, 2006; Kosovo, 2008) has witnessed at least seven recentering operations of the kind outlined by Brisset, performed through different operations of linguistic cleansing accompanying the ethnic one. Each of the seven post-Yugoslav political entities (Bosnia-Herzegovina, Croatia, Macedonia, Montenegro, Kosovo, Serbia, Slovenia) has retaliated against the former lingua franca of the common state in a cultural mode, reflecting its new identity by creating different visions of the national territory by linguistic means. I will limit myself to the discussion of Serbia and Croatia, although it is possible to imagine a book-length study mapping this type of opposition to a common code of communication. The production and exaggeration of linguistic difference required by the new creation of each of these political entities raises the issue of translation between them. The issue is particularly problematic since many of the emergent cultures do not require translation to come to terms with meanings articulated in the other one.

The very beginning of the translation conundrum was engendered during the war between the two largest of the post-Yugoslav nations, Serbia and Croatia. This brings to the foreground the issue of cultural relations between these "nonidentical twins," joined in their linguistic identity through the name of the dominant language of the former common state: Serbo-Croatian. By symbolically removing the hyphen between them, the ethnic conflict created the need for translation as a cultural practice that would confirm and amplify differences between the two warring parties. In fact, some of the differences were already there, but they were more on the level of dialect, word choice, and orthography within a single linguistic continuum, than on the level of insurmountable semantic difference necessary for a language to declare its independence on scientific grounds and to require translation.

It is commonly held that that there is about 20 percent difference in vocabulary items between Eastern and Western versions of Serbo-Croatian; Western ones largely use the Latin script, while the Eastern versions use both the Cyrillic and the Latin one. The complexity of Bosnian identity is in fact the main problem in simply naming the Western variant of Serbo-Croatian "Croatian" and the Eastern one "Serbian," especially after the breakup of the common Yugoslav cultural continuum. For example, the Serbs of Bosnia speak a dialect of Serbo-Croatian closer to Croatian, but would never agree to call their language "Croatian"; they will insist that they speak "Serbian." They are also reluctant to call their language "Bosnian" since that would conflate their national identity with that of Bosniaks, that is, the Bosnian Moslems, the only group that wholeheartedly accepts the new name of the language. The Croats of Bosnia have the same issue with "Bosnian," since they call their language "Croatian," despite the fact that they live within the political confines of the territory of Bosnia-Herzegovina. The case of Montenegro reproduces the same type of linguistic issue, since approximately half of the population opposing national independence calls the language "Serbian," while the other half favoring the new state entity insists on "Montenegrin" as the name of the language they speak. In the case of this new independent state, both of these names refer to the absolutely identical linguistic code shared by its speakers.

Translating the Nation

The effect of translation as a cultural instrument of sovereignty and a vehicle for national reinvention manifests both the obvious absurdity of the attempt to discard similarity and the legacy of identity based on the common *štokavian* dialect chosen by the South Slavic enlighteners Vuk Karadžić and Ljudevit Gaj. The 1850 Vienna agreement to champion a common tongue serving as a platform for the political unification of Serbs-under-Turks and Croats-under-Hungarians envisioned a unified philological territory that was to serve as a cultural weapon in their struggle against the imperial rule of the Ottomans and the Habsburgs. This anti-imperial move of the nonidentical linguistic twins was based on the idea of the common Slavic *ethnos* that would use the kinship based on the shared language to develop a nation. Besides this historical decision by Vuk and Gaj, the other dialects within the Croat national domain (*čakavski* and *kajkavski*) were quite dissimilar from the *štokavski*, so the linguistic standardization based on the idiom shared with the Serbs also made sense from the point of view of even the narrowly conceived Croat nationalist politics. It was the majority dialect, and the alliance with the Serbs could be used tactically, especially since the latter had led the anti-imperial struggle in the Balkans since the first 1804 uprisings. Siding with the stronger Slavic brother, who was supposed to embody rebellion against foreign rule, could only be a tactical move, at least until the right to full independence could be realized under the banner of Croatia as a sovereign state entity.

After the 1991 declarations of independence from the common South Slavic state, Croatia was the first to invent and emphasize the existing minor linguistic differences in order to justify the discourse of ethnic particularism, despite the fact that the *štokavski* speakers from Serbia and Croatia could understand each other much better than the speakers of *kajkavski* and *štokavski* dialects within Croatia itself. The latest political platform of ethnic particularism required the emphasis on insurmountable distinctiveness of the constituent peoples based on pseudo-clerical interpretations of differences between the cultures of Christian Orthodoxy and Catholicism. In the case of Bosnia, Islam would be used with a similar purpose in mind, attempting to define culture as a prosthesis of religion and not of language. In fact, the failure of the Yugoslav state confirmed that the Romantic notion of the nation-state, imagined as a territory based on common linguistic heritage and a shared folklore, had been radically shaken, as the historically residual cultural formation based on religious affiliation and identification with the former imperial master suddenly became dominant during the 1990s in the public discourse of the emergent nations in the Western Balkans. There was a palpable shift in the definition of the imaginary foundations of culture, as an uncanny return of old imperial alliances began its repeated haunting.

Therefore, the birth of post-Yugoslav nations was accompanied by the reinforcement of the fantasy resting on the twin pillars of monolingualism and freedom. "To acquire a native language is to be reborn in a free country, to have a country entirely to oneself."[2] The monolingual fantasy of the pure native realm not shared with any other nation or language intentionally mistakes any mode of cultural sharing as domination, intent on placing full faith in the operative force of what Freud has labeled "narcissism of minor differences" to account for the discourse of Eurocentric nationalism of his day.[3] By creating a gap between those who are in possession of the national prerogative (derived from religious affiliation this time) and those sudden aliens not sharing the strictly policed symbolic order deriving from Roman Catholicism, the Croat elites intentionally fostered the separation of the languages spoken by the nonidentical Yugoslav twins to destroy the notion of the nation based on a common Slavic origin. The rebirth of Croatian as a separate language required translation as a distancing practice that would preclude sharing the language with the Serbs, both as the conquering external other and the insidious alien within the country, which could not be imagined as free and pure unless this residual element of exaggerated difference was expelled from the realm of shared signification and renounced as incomprehensible.

This type of separatist political practice sets itself against what is assumed about translation as the par excellence activity devoted to the bridging of cultural gaps and palliating misunderstandings after the Babelic punishment, to provide humanity with the potential of overcoming legacies of conflict, war, and trauma. A community engaged in this kind of translational nationalism struggles to discover and invent differences that would anchor it in the territory belonging to a single country, an imaginary monoculture that would not compromise its sovereign and independent status even at the price of a superfluous translation, whose unstated political aim is the separation from a cultural location shared with its previous linguistic twin-turned-adversary.

Hyphenated Difference

"The miracle of translation does not take place every day; there is, at times, a desert without a desert crossing," writes Jacques Derrida, while addressing the growing issue of "unreadability" haunting the extended public space created by globalization.[4] The issue of the former Serbo-Croatian is therefore even more puzzling, since the desert crossings were available on many different levels between the two warring states, yet the choice of the nationalist elites was to lose oneself in the desert sands of one's own particularity and make sure that the paths disappeared in the violent hurricanes of nationalist becoming.

One of the most bizarre episodes in the history of unnecessary translation took place in Zagreb, Croatia, on the occasion of the first Serbian film premiere after the end of the Serbo-Croatian war. The film was *Wounds* (*Rane*, 1998) by Srđan Dragojević, a surreal story reflecting on the violent life of Belgrade youth during the worst years of the Slobodan Milošević regime. Although the idioms used by the youth in both cultures are almost equivalent and mutually highly intelligible, the movie distributers in Croatia decided the film ought to be subtitled. This is how the journalist of the *Feral Tribune*, the voice of the antinationalist Croatian intellectuals, described the atmosphere in the cinema: "First the original title shows up on the screen in Latin script, *Beograd, jesen 1991*, and then right below it the subtitle in Latin script explains, *Beograd, jesen 1991*. . . . Pandemonium erupts in the movie theater. Laughter, tears, and enthusiastic knee slapping, although we've only been two minutes into the film. There's no doubt; this is perhaps the most insane film event in the history of cinema, comparable maybe only to the premieres of American silent comedies."[5]

Reminiscent of the poetic device employed in Jorge Luis Borges's story "Pierre Menard, autor del Quijote," where the translation of Cervantes's masterpiece is really a nontranslation by Pierre Menard a few centuries later, the reality of this event points to the cultural mechanism involved in the production of difference at any price. The reaction of the Croatian audience is symptomatic of the division between the official cultural dictates of the new nation-state in the making and the general public that sees through the transparent attempts to exaggerate differences and separate one cultural space from another, however absurd that may appear in the virtually identical language of the Croats, Serbs, Bosnians, Montenegrins, and so on. Since the film itself uses highly localized speech patterns of Belgrade urban youth, redolent with obscenities familiar in both Serbian and Croatian versions of the language, the task of the translator becomes even more complicated and bizarre as s/he is interpellated by the national demand to create difference where there is none to be found.

One of the most difficult problems arose in the translation of the vulgar signifier for the female sexual organ, often used to denote a person bearing the moral qualities of spinelessness, cowardice, and a lack of masculine power: *pička*. One of the characters, a young thug from the urban wasteland of New Belgrade, shows his masculine pride by declaring he will not run away from any sort of confrontation as if he were a coward: "Neću da bežim k'o pička!" The subtitler uses a synonymous word for the female sexual organ, *pizda*, claiming it for Croatian as a *differentia specifica* of the new national identity: "Neću bježati kao pizda!" In American English, it would be roughly translated as: "I won't run off like a pussy." Besides pointing to the most frequent syntactic difference (*da bežim/bježati*, or *da* + verb present tense as Serbian preference, and infinitive as a Croatian one), the use of the *pička/pizda* for the female sexual organ is absolutely exchangeable across the BCSM territories. Miljenko Jergović, one of the most popular post-Yugoslav writers to emerge on the Croatian literary scene, questions exactly this inability of the subtitler to produce difference when translating a dialogue saturated with obscenities. "Namely, our language makers have invented no less than three words for helicopter (*uvrtnjak*, *vrtolet*, and *zrakomlat*), but have not until the present day reported what's the score in the sexual acts and organs game, which are, perhaps by pure accident, most common in the creation of curses both among Serbs and Croats."[6] His irony is poignant, recalling the relationship between the two nations and their widely shared arsenal of obscenities; this demonstrates how similar the two nonidentical twins of Yugoslavia are when it comes to the most profane level of speech culture, which remains out of touch with the high literary standards that the nationalist language creators try to impose on the general population. It is at this most colloquial level of language that the translation between the two former warring sides proves to be unnecessary if not ridiculous, giving rise to the direct opposition of viewing audiences to artificially imposed official standards of linguistic (non)difference.

There were no polemical articles in the Croatian press attempting to argue for the new cultural policy of translating from Serbian, since the linguistic facts for such a practice were obviously very difficult to come by. Returning to Derrida's desert metaphor for untranslatability, one could say that the crossings were created to get to an already familiar place, the one that the translator had set out from even before the winds had began to obliterate the paths between the two nonidentical cultural twins. And while German is used as the name of the language spoken in Switzerland, Austria, and Germany, and English as a name of the language spoken in the United States or Australia, the former Serbo-Croatian has been convicted to the removal of the hyphen and subjected to the nationalist cultural cloning, which strives to produce linguistic difference as a metaphor of its political and national sovereignty.

Fiction After Yugoslavia

Croatian author Borivoj Radaković uses the term *politolect* to account for the creation of what can be seen as a "field-specific sociolect,"[7] used by a closed circle of political functionaries and bureaucrats intent on promoting the monocultural vision of a country in its struggle to gain the status of absolute semantic and linguistic difference.[8] The collective identity based on this principle is similar to that of other closed in-groups (prisoners, criminals, soldiers, sports fans, etc.) who create their particular idioms out of the need to prevent understanding by other social groups sharing the same "national" language. One of the features of the *politolect* invoked by Radaković is its distinction from other types of jargon: its obvious intent is to come up with terms and usages that would require translation even from the perfectly comprehensible "brotherly" idiom. This creation of the new *politolect*, based on the intentional invention of a language that would serve the dual purpose of instituting the necessity of translation on the one hand and excluding the ethnically opposing forces from the public sphere of the nation on the other, was the most conspicuous cultural effect of the Yugoslav breakup.

The 1997 statement of the leading Croatian literary critic, Stanko Lasić, that as far as he is concerned, "Serbian literature now occupies the same status as the Bulgarian one," has galvanized the discussion regarding the issue of translation and contact between the two formerly related literary traditions, providing the new impetus for translation between the two nonidentical cultural twins.[9] Bulgarian is a Slavic language, distinct from both Serbian and Croatian, whose similarity is much greater than its difference. Lasić's statement is performative within the context of a dissolving country since it employs the notion of differentiation between the Orthodox-based (Bulgarian and Serbian) and Catholic-based (Croatian) cultures to reinforce the political sense of separation. The choices made in the translation of literary works since the secession of Croatia from

Yugoslavia in 1991 are themselves quite symptomatic of this cultural trend. Kostić writes about the first translation of a novel from Serbian into Croatian: the novel *Gifts of Time* (*Darovi vremena*, 1997), by Zoran Živković. The examples provided parallel those offered in the translation of captions for the film *Wounds* discussed above; some sentences are never translated, while those that are translated are so minimally different from the original that the act of translation just draws out its absurdity as a cultural practice in the context of the former Serbo-Croatian. An apt example of this practice can be seen in an excerpt quoted by Kostić.[10] The "original" Serbian by Zoran Živković reads as follows:

Prešao je pogledom po zidu naspram prozora. Nije mogao dobro da vidi u polumraku, ali to nije ni bilo potrebno. Znao je šta se tamo nalazi.

The translator of the novel, Stanislav Vidmar, rendered this very same sentence as follows:

Prošao je pogledom po zidu nasuprot prozora. Nije mogao dobro vidjeti u polumraku, ali to nije ni bilo potrebno. Znao je što se tamo nalazi.

[His gaze moved along the wall across from the window. He was not able to see well in the semidarkness, but that proved unnecessary. He knew what was there.]

The differences between the two versions are mostly dialectal and often present the former Serbo-Croatian synonyms as terms embodying the national *differentia specifica* between the formerly related Serb and Croat cultures (e.g., *naspram/nasuprot*—in English, "across"—are synonyms). This trait of translation as the agent of literary difference offers a glimpse into the processes of nation building that have been regulating the standardization of modern European languages ever since the end of the eighteenth century. As the evolution of Italian or German after the 1870s testifies, the process of national self-identification relied on the literary canon to imagine the new national territory and establish laws that would regulate the proper linguistic usage at the expense of the former heteroglossia of the territories inhabited by a variety of ethnic subjects. The dominance of one dialect over the other (e.g., the suppression of southern dialects as well as Milanese, Venetian, and some other northern ones) during the formation of standard Italian would have been similar, except for the fact that a certain standardization of usage already occurred in Serbo-Croatian during half a century of the common Yugoslav state. The usage of the *šta/što* pronoun from the last sentence of the quote is indeed so fluid and undecidable between different speakers of Serbian, Croatian, Bosnian, and Montenegrin that its minimal vocalic *a/o* alternation is probably the most vivid linguistic manifestation of the absurd nature of the conflict between the separate political entities whose languages are commonly intelligible to each of their respective subjects.

Some of the responses to this kind of absurdity were themselves quite ingenious—the Croatian antiwar magazine *Arkzin* established a literary prize evocatively named *Bvulgarica* (Latin for "Bulgarian"). This act of framing a public narrative of division by "labeling" was done in order to respond to the already-mentioned statement by Stanko Lasić about Serbian literature slipping further Eastward into the Bulgarian cultural zone for the Croat reader.[11] This "Orientalization" of the Serbian is in tune with the overall political struggle for asserting sovereignty by claiming incompatibility between the two formerly fraternal cultures. After all the barbarity exhibited by the "other side," by the Serb twin one loves to hate, the translation is now imagined as a necessity despite the mutual sense of understanding. The two South Slavic twins cannot speak the same language, since the Serbs are labeled/framed as genocidal *guslars* whose culture could only serve as an instrument of oppression if the tiniest sign of understanding were shown to them. Therefore, the translation has to be instituted, even when it brings with it the *a/o* divide in *šta/što* to emphasize the difference—which has a hard time being a difference. The common idiom of Serbo-Croatian is simultaneously recognized as a trace of that abject and scorned Other and the glorious illusion of a proper national identity born in the struggle with that demonic other. The similarity of myself to that demonic Other has to be denied in every aspect of culture, especially in language shared for more than a century and a half. Some of the scholarly responses from translators working in the former Yugoslavia have tried to come to terms with this issue from the perspective of the cultural outsider, who is forced to take sides in the conflict and fit himself or herself into the liberal paradigm used to explain the conflict to the Western observer. A notable example is the writing of Francis Jones, who embraces the Bosniak narrative in order to distance himself from the Serbs and to some extent Croats as well.[12] Although he translates into English and his work is therefore only tangentially relevant to this article devoted to mutual Serbo-Croat translation, it is symptomatic of a trend created by Western intellectuals to assuage their conscience and divide their loyalties between the warring parties.

Can the opposition to translation, which paradoxically promotes cultural understanding between Serbs and Croats and resists the monolingualist fantasy of pure difference in the guise of an official national tongue, be understood as the force of an old nostalgia for Yugoslavia? If nostalgia rests on the rational demand to preserve what is common in the service of understanding, then the resistance to translation between the nonidentical twins could be construed as a preservation of common Slavic roots as a linguistic legacy apart from the nationalist call for misunderstanding and hatred. The imaginary economy of borderline tendencies dominant in the psychic life of small nations, whose identity is reinforced by the fallacy of monolingualist hallucinations, yields separatist political outcomes, the cultivation of state *politolects* as tools of ethnic separation from the evil twin, and the enforcement of the vision of a pure beauty of the native landscape belonging to a single national configuration. It is more likely that the impulse to choose nontranslation in the case of nonidentical twins comes from the everyday life of subjects engaged with otherness as part of a new global call for understanding despite hostility. While the common South Slavic standard will not be required under those circumstances, the translation between the formerly fraternal nations will not be required as well.

The translation practices outlined in this article have been instituted during a particularly volatile postconflict period in the former Yugoslavia and reflect a desire of the new nationalist elites to establish political sovereignty by cultural means. It is also true that this practice has been largely abandoned in Croatian cultural activities after the defeat of the right-wing Tudman government. The translation between the cultures of nonidentical Serbian and Croatian twins still persists within the legal system that now certifies official translators for administrative documents originating in Serbia. This soft return of the hyphen in Serbo-Croatian has been a proof that the cultural bonds between the two Slavic cultures are definitely stronger than the overpolitical agendas of nationalist leaders, who are poised to strengthen their power through the production of difference at the expense of bridging the gaps between the sides involved in the conflict. The case of post-Yugoslav translation during the 1990s will serve as an example for scholars who tend to take translation as an exemplary vehicle for intercultural understanding, by demonstrating that misunderstanding can be manufactured within the contexts in which understanding already exists as a cultural given.

10

What Happened to Serbo-Croatian?
Ranko Bugarski

An Unusual Situation

This chapter presents a brief overview of the unusual life story of a language bearing many names but internationally best known as Serbo-Croatian. Its course is traced from its construction at the turn of the twentieth century, through its deconstruction some ninety years later, to its eventual reconstruction as several national official languages (Serbian, Croatian, Bosnian, Montenegrin) following the breakup of Yugoslavia.

The answer to the question posed in the title is by no means obvious and has hence generated a great deal of controversy; in fact, in the analysis to be offered it admits of several possibilities depending on the perspective taken, as follows:

1. Nothing much has happened; Serbo-Croatian is alive and well.

2. Very much has happened; Serbo-Croatian is no more.

3. Something has happened; Serbo-Croatian is partly alive.

Answer (1) arises from focusing on the language, thus taking a *linguistic* perspective which here subsumes that of communication. Answer (2) arises from focusing on the state(s) where the language is officially used, thus taking a *political* perspective, which here also covers legal and symbolic aspects. Answer (3) arises from focusing on the speakers, thus taking a *psychological* perspective which here refers to variable native reactions to the identity and name of one's mother tongue.

Such a state of affairs is remarkable in that Serbo-Croatian turns out to exist, not to exist, or to only partly exist, depending on the perspective one takes. One is reminded of de Saussure's famous dictum that the point of view creates the object of study. In what follows the three answers will be briefly discussed in turn; before that, however, it is necessary to cast a historical glance at the relationship between the term *Serbo-Croatian* and the content behind it, in order to be clear about what exactly we are talking about at any given stage. As just implied, there is a problem here since the name is by no means consistently coextensive with any idiom(s) so named. The fact that this term (with its alternatives Croato-Serbian, Croatian or Serbian, Serbian or Croatian) has several different concepts associated with it has caused much confusion among commentators, and has opened the way to various ideologically motivated interpretations, frequently including not a little political manipulation.

The Meanings of "Serbo-Croatian"

First of all, it must be borne in mind that "Serbo-Croatian" originally was and essentially remains a linguistic term and not a popular name, the speakers mostly calling the language either Serbian or Croatian, depending on their nationality (with some additions and complications setting in later, to be noted below). The compound term was actually first used in several versions by foreign scholars—Jacob Grimm as early as 1824, Jernej Kopitar from 1836, to be followed somewhat later by native Croatian and finally Serbian grammarians as well.[1] It referred to the vernacular, or folk language, of Serbs and Croats—what would later be described as a diasystem comprising three macrodialects: štokavian, kajkavian, and čakavian. This acceptance of the term, long recognized by dialectology and historical linguistics, has retained its validity to this day despite the more recent developments and changes on the superimposed level of the standard language.

At the time, however, there existed no actual linguistic entity on this level to match the dual name, with Serbs and Croats living in different empires and sharing some of the vernaculars but having several literary idioms each. This was rather the gestation period of the Romantic idea that the two kin peoples should share a common literary language, in a declarative manner culminating in a joint meeting of Croat and Serb philologists in Vienna in 1850, which issued such a call (known as the Vienna Agreement). It combined the ideals of the pan-Slavic Illyrian movement led by Ljudevit Gaj in Croatia with Vuk Karadžić's insistence on a literary idiom based on

Serbian vernacular speech. But it was not before the turn of the century that Vuk's followers in Zagreb actually produced the basic normative handbooks codifying the neo-štokavian "Croatian or Serbian," which marked the beginning of what would come to be known as the Serbo-Croatian standard language. Finally, this language made its way into the constitutions of the successive states emerging on its territory in the aftermath of World War I, starting with that of the Kingdom of Serbs, Croats, and Slovenes, thus becoming an official language. It was removed from such use during and after the recent Wars of Yugoslav Succession, in a process which began in 1991, to be replaced with the newly recognized distinct national languages: Serbian, Croatian, Bosnian, and finally, in 2008, Montenegrin. Yet this administrative move in itself does not imply that Serbo-Croatian as a linguistic entity (either as diasystem or as standard language) likewise automatically disappeared as a result, since languages as systems of communication are not simply created or abolished by political decree. Indeed, as will be argued below, it definitely survives, with no apparent intention of slipping into history.

In sum, then, we must distinguish between as many as four references of the term *Serbo-Croatian*: (1) diasystem, (2) imagined literary language, (3) standard language, (4) official language. The situation described is summarized, in a simplified fashion, in Table 1.

Table 1   Chronology of the Meanings of "Serbo-Croatian"

Serbo-Croatian:	1824	1850	1900	1921	1991	2010
diasystem		x- >				
literary language			x - >			
standard language				x - - - - - - - - - - - - - - - - >		
official language				x - - - - - - x		

The above table disregards several complicating details which we shall only mention in passing.

1. The literary and standard language levels are separated because of the considerable chronological gap involved, although they have traditionally been treated as one and the same despite the sociolinguistic difference between the two concepts.

2. In the constitutions of the Kingdoms of Serbs, Croats, and Slovenes (1921) and of Yugoslavia (1931) the language was officially named "Serbo-Croato-Slovenian," for purely political symmetry and with no basis at all in linguistic fact, Slovenian being linguistically distinct.

3. During World War II the language was labeled Serbian in Serbia and Croatian in Croatia, the compound term gradually reemerging in different arrangements in the constitutions of the postwar Yugoslav republics—especially after the Novi Sad Agreement of 1954, which called for a renewed administrative unification of the language (though recognizing shortly thereafter that it contained ethno-territorial varieties, called *varijante*, the two major ones being the Eastern or Serbian and the Western or Croatian).

From the dates given it follows that, as of 2010, the term Serbo-Croatian in its various meanings has been known for some 186 years. The idea of a common literary language arose 160 years ago but took half a century to materialize, with a standard language of that name being codified about 110 years ago. Its life span in the status of an official language extended over seventy years, the former thus both predating and postdating the latter by some 20 years now. (This also shows that "standard language" and "official language" are categorically different notions, which must not be confused even though they often coincide in reality; and as regards linking the language to a common state, Serbo-Croatian had existed in some form long before the creation of Yugoslavia in 1918, so there is no inherent necessity for it to be simply written off with that state's ultimate destruction in 1991.) All told, the picture reveals a marked lack of systematic correspondence between the name and the named, a state of affairs much given to various interpretations—and misinterpretations.

The Resulting Confusion and Rival Claims

Under the circumstances outlined, in combination with conflicting ideologies and political agendas usually inspired by the opposed ethnic nationalisms, and with the help of a selective and creative handling of historical events, it has been easy to advance with extraordinary zeal some strange notions about the existence, identity, and status of Serbo-Croatian. A favorite method has been to ignore the polysemy of the term, along with the time frame sketched out in the table and to conflate under the same label the different levels of analysis. Among the extreme claims put forward are the following:

- Serbo-Croatian was and remains a mere fiction, since such a language never actually existed except as a unitarist political construction, the real languages being Serbian and Croatian (and later also Bosnian and Montenegrin).

- Serbo-Croatian is the only truly existing language, these four having been invented and artificially differentiated by the respective national elites in their quest for power.

- Serbo-Croatian exists merely as a manipulative misnomer; in reality it is just renamed Serbian, as are also Croatian, Bosnian, and Montenegrin.

- Croatian and Serbian are wholly different languages in all respects.

- The Croats stole their language from the Serbs and called it Croatian.

- Croatian is several centuries older than Serbian.

- Since every self-respecting nation must possess its own distinct language and state, both Serbo-Croatian and Yugoslavia were unnatural creations and as such rightly doomed to death.

- Even if Serbo-Croatian ever actually existed, it definitely ceased to do so after 1991, as this label was dropped from all the constitutions and laws of the post-Yugoslav states.

Rather than discussing such extravagant pronouncements, a superfluous exercise in a serious publication such as this book, let us now return, against the background provided, to the three answers initially offered.

Taking Stock

First, a linguistic perspective clearly shows that Serbo-Croatian can still legitimately be regarded as a living language, despite its present lack of political or legal status. Its former ethno-territorial variants have officially become distinct national languages, and due to linguistic engineering the differences among them have increased in the postwar period. However, these differences are still far outweighed by deep-seated similarities, in terms of structure and everyday lexicon frequently reaching the point of identity. As a consequence, communication among the speakers of Serbian, Croatian, Bosnian, and Montenegrin for all practical purposes goes on as smoothly as before. If these four were in fact different languages linguistically, we would find within this group widespread bilingualism and multilingualism, contrastive grammars and bilingual dictionaries, translation and interpretation services, and so on. Yet none of this exists, with such negligible exceptions as (1) the so-called "differential dictionaries" of Serbian and Croatian, whose sole actual purpose is to warn Croatian speakers against perceived or invented Serbisms, and (2) translating official documents bearing the state imprint. Therefore, treating Serbo-Croatian as a single polycentric standard language with several national variants remains fully justified, regardless of the altered extralinguistic circumstances.[2]

Second, from a political point of view Serbo-Croatian has ceased to exist, as the compound label no longer appears in any of the constitutions or laws of the post-Yugoslav states. It is hence a legal nonentity, its place having been taken by the national official languages—Serbian, Croatian, Bosnian, and Montenegrin—as important symbols of the identity and sovereignty of these states. Mother-tongue statistics may serve as an illustration here. While in the 1981 census, the last to be taken in Yugoslavia, some 16.4 million, or 73 per cent of the total population of 22.4 million, declared Serbo-Croatian or Croato-Serbian as their mother tongue,[3] that language name is all but absent from official classifications in postwar censuses, not even being a recognized option. In the Serbian census of 2002, for example, the 39,000 who still declared Serbo-Croatian were in the final figures added to the nearly 6.6 million speakers of Serbian, and the 3,000 who claimed Croato-Serbian automatically joined the 24,000 Croatian speakers; 135,000 speakers of Bosnian were also recorded.[4] So, just as the Yugoslav federation was torn to pieces, its by-far largest language, which had served as a major cohesive factor and symbol of its precarious unity, was administratively and statistically dismembered as well.

Combining the findings in the previous two paragraphs, then, what we have here may be described as one language linguistically but four languages politically. This is not to say that these four lack linguistic status— only that they are variants of an overarching polycentric standard language. As such they should be identified and described first and foremost in terms of their defining linguistic properties of pronunciation and script, grammar and lexicon, and only secondarily and to a limited degree correlated with the geopolitical spread and ethnic distribution of their speakers. This needs to be stressed because defining, say, Serbian or Croatian as, respectively, the languages of Serbia and Croatia, or of Serbs and Croats, while often convenient for scoring political points or enlisting emotional support, badly misrepresents the far more complicated reality. Impartial readers will hardly need reminding that these languages are spoken in several other post-Yugoslav states too—to say nothing of the "outer diaspora"—and by members of other nations than the titular ones. So simple equations such as these, mainly serving to engender futile battles over ownership, historical priority, or contemporary territorial claims, say very little about the nature of these idioms themselves or of the relations among them, and much of what they do say or imply with their vague approximations is misleading if not plainly wrong.

Finally, the psychological aspect of the issue is not nearly as clear-cut, being by its very nature less amenable to objective analysis and especially to quantification, so the verdict on this point must be one of partial existence. Namely, it is a safe guess that a large majority of Serbs have always intimately thought of their language as Serbian, and of Croats as Croatian, and informally named it accordingly, even while it was formally labeled Serbo-Croatian or Croato-Serbian. The main exceptions were to be found in multiethnic areas with a high percentage of mixed marriages (such as Bosnia-Herzegovina, Vojvodina, or parts of Croatia), where the compound name would have been felt to be more appropriate. This majority has certainly increased as a result of the war and of the official reinstatement of the traditional language names, to which the sudden emergence of a large number of people formerly declaring Serbo-Croatian and now opting for Bosnian should be added. Nonetheless, there must still be a significant though probably dwindling minority, dispersed throughout the former Serbo-Croatian area and particularly in diaspora situations, who continue to identify with this common language rather than with any of its offspring (and frequently call it simply "our language" so as to avoid taking sides and possibly offending others in their immediate environments). I suspect there is often an added element of "Yugonostalgia," or emotional protest at the loss of one's home country, in this practice as well.

As an aside, I might illustrate from personal experience the frequent mismatches between official and habitual language names and their relationship to the entities named. For most of my life I have lived in only two cities (which, incidentally, have been in no fewer than six states during that time!) and have spoken what to me—and to most people belonging or close to my generation—has been one and the same language, though its official designation changed several times. I was born and bred in the ethnically mixed city of Sarajevo, where during my schooling the language was constitutionally called first Serbo-Croato-Slovenian but later on (1941–45, when Sarajevo was part of the so-called Independent State of Croatia) it became Croatian, and subsequently Serbo-Croatian. When I moved to Belgrade in 1961 it was Serbo-Croatian there as well, but three decades later it became Serbian (while back in my hometown the everyday language— still much the same—now officially counts as three national languages: Serbian, Croatian, and Bosnian). Having lived here for half a century now, I have no problem with calling the language Serbian, although I regard it, as both linguist and speaker, as a form of Serbo-Croatian. So whatever official or popular names have been used, I have actually identified with Serbo-Croatian as my native tongue all my life and continue to do so, even if this now makes me in the eyes of some people—somewhat paradoxically perhaps—a native speaker of a dead language!

Conclusion

To return to the main argument and conclude our investigation, the three possibilities listed constitute, at least in the view advanced here, a hierarchy ranging from most to least important. They all reflect reality, only different aspects of it, and as such must be taken into account—but without implying that they therefore carry equal weight. Since what is under consideration is a language, a linguistic foundation naturally must be given priority. As this is a standard language, and such languages are normally associated with the formation and functioning of states, the second place goes to the political angle. And because all languages are spoken by people, their feelings, attitudes, and habits also deserve to be considered, even if only marginally due to their inevitable and not infrequently haphazard subjectivity. This, then, rounds off an approach rather more comprehensive, and probably more insightful, than many other treatments, typically one-sided in stressing only a chosen perspective at the expense of the others, and as such offering much special pleading instead of an objective analysis.

To end with a direct reference to this volume's general topic, it should be clear from the preceding discussion that the system of Serbo-Croatian has essentially survived the partitions that have been imposed on it over the recent period of intense destruction and reconstruction of its entire speech area. If this book aims to explore from different directions the possibilities of enriching post-Yugoslav cultural encounters, our analysis confirms that the communicative network of the language whose situation we have examined undoubtedly remains adequate to the task. There is a growing awareness that this is so throughout the "region" (Serbian *region*,

Croatian *regija*: an increasingly popular concept more or less coinciding with the former Yugoslavia, especially the Serbo-Croatian speaking parts of it), of which evidence is provided elsewhere in the volume. We may just mention here the frequent "international" meetings of writers and artists, exchanges of theatrical, film, radio and television productions and broadcasts, live pop music shows drawing large audiences, the joint publication and dissemination of books in their original versions, the free circulation of newspapers and magazines, the same authors and journalists contributing columns to media in several states, shared running commentaries of sports events, and so on. Underlying all these activities is a widespread feeling common to the participants—though, needless to say, not necessarily shared by the nationalist political and intellectual circles, whose interests are better served by further alienation than by improved communication—that, while Yugoslavia as a political project is definitely a thing of the past, its heritage as a cultural space is well worth preserving and developing, to the benefit of all concerned. Indeed, a closer look at the larger scene may even leave the observer with the impression that in purely cultural terms Yugoslavia never really disintegrated. Along with this goes the realization that the full mutual understanding among the idioms officially replacing Serbo-Croatian, which eliminates the need for translation, offers welcome assistance in pursuing such goals; how much of this potential will actually be made use of in the years to come, and in what ways, is then no longer a linguistic question.

11

Language Imprisoned by Identities; or, Why Language Should Be Defended

Milorad Pupovac

Prolegomena

Language can both open up the world and close it: so thought Hans Georg Gadamer from the perspective of hermeneutical philosophy,[1] and so thought Noam Chomsky from the perspective of linguistic philosophy.[2] Not infrequently we ourselves think so when we encounter a language that speaks of the world more than the world itself does, or when we encounter inarticulate language compared with the abundance of ways in which the world itself "speaks up."

Speaking from the perspective of critical-satirical journalism and literature, Karl Kraus claimed that language can both liberate and enslave,[3] and Dubravko Škiljan made a similar claim from the perspective of critical linguistics.[4] Some of us have made this claim when we encounter the power of our own or of someone else's speech that provides liberation from fear or injustice, or when we encounter our own, or someone else's, imprisonment in an uncomfortable, constricted, and enslaving language.

Language needs to be continually defended, sometimes from itself at other times from us. It needs to be defended from itself because it enables itself and us to become routinized and ideologized. It needs to be defended from us because we are prone to use language and to "identitization" of language.

This study is intended to defend language from the phenomenon of its identitization, with reference to the historical and current phenomena of identitization among speakers of South Slavic languages, and especially in cases when *language has obtained the status of dialect, while its standard idioms obtained the status of languages.*[5] By *identitization* we mean a hypostatization of an identity, whether in its entirety or in its fragments. We speak of identitization when the communicative function and the linguistic structure of language come under the dominance of identity. The result of identitization is *identitized language*, that is, language whose communicative and linguistic functions are captured by identity.

Identitized language is in fact language as identity. While it often appears that identitization of language and standardization of language are, if not identical, then at least complementary processes, it needs to be emphasized that in our understanding of things that is not the case. The primary effect of identitization of language is not a language. Language in that process appears only as a vehicle of *standardization of identity*. What is more, this identity is one of great names—such as Nation, State, Language, and, sometimes and in some places, Church and Party. The point of identitization of language is not for the language to be asserted but for the identity to assert itself. For this reason, the identitized language most often comes into being as a vernacular that is ascribed one of the great names.[6]

In order to understand more fully what we mean by identitized language, we shall compare it with secret language and metalanguage. A secret language, practiced by individuals, groups, and institutions, comes into being and is used for the purpose of excluding everyone who is not supposed to know the content of the communication. A secret language excludes others. The metalanguage, practiced by researchers, scientists, and their popularizers, is created for the purpose of providing cognition or the procedure of arriving at knowledge with a language of its own, so that in effect it is not directed toward other people but toward the object of cognition. It simply ignores the other. In contrast, identitized language does not exclude or ignore the other; it seeks to exist in place of the other. Even before it enters into any kind of interaction with the other, it seeks to take the other's place. This comes at a high price; one can lose one's own identity. However, all these three types of language also have a common trait: *they are not dialogical.* Other languages, regardless of the degree of difference there might exist among their identities, are not guided by the *nondialogical principle,*[7] but by some species of dialogical imperative. As von Humboldt states, languages survive because they meet and combine with each other.[8] The same is true of identities.

From Grammar of Nation
to the Vernacular of the State

Many, from ancient writers to more recent ones, have spoken about the significance of language for the constitution of human societies.[9] *Gentem lingua facit*, "language makes the people"—this had been said even before Dante's *De vulgari eloquentia* (On Eloquence in the Vernacular; written circa 1305, printed in 1577), and before Herder's *Abhandlung über den Ursprung der Sprache* (Essay on the Origin of Language; published in 1772). During that period of time, from the first printed book (1461, in German) to the French Revolution, or as Peter Burke states, from 1450 to 1750, the first discovery of language took place. Burke calls this "the period of rediscovery of language; others call it "the vernacular revolution." The beginning of this period was marked, on the one hand, by the formation of a philosophico-political ideology of language and, on the other hand, by the founding of the modern science of language. The foundation for the former had been laid by Herder when he spoke of the "genius of the language of the people" (*Genius der Volkssprache*), "language as the soul of the people" (*die Seele des Volkes*), and the "storehouse of the people" (*das Vorratshaus eines Volkes*). After Herder, Wilhelm von Humboldt developed the theory of universal linguistic competence, the diversity of the makeup of human language, and its influence on the development of humankind. The contributions of the two thinkers had a crucial impact on that which constituted the grammar of nation—that is, on language, history, culture, literature, science, education, and institutions of the state.

During that period many European vernaculars obtained either their translations of the Bible, once that was allowed, or their grammars. These vernacular languages emancipated themselves from Latin and paved the way to the time in which many of them would become grammars of nation,[10] while others would fail in this effort. The period in which languages formed something like grammars of nation took two entire centuries, from 1750 to 1950.

Herder and von Humboldt, as well as those who followed them over the course of the nineteenth century and the beginning of the twentieth century, had a decisive influence on the formation of the ideologies of language and the science of language among peoples speaking the South Slavic languages. The professions of the individuals who took part in the formation of South Slavic grammars of nation of their peoples included collectors of folk traditions, philologists and linguistic enthusiasts, literati, poets, politicians, public officials, teachers, priests, and printers. The making of the grammar of nation was to be achieved through orthographies, grammars, dictionaries, short stories and novels, poetry, and music. Among those who formed the ideology of language as well as its literature was the Croatian poet Petar Preradović, an ethnic Serb and an Austrian general. His poems "Rodu o jeziku" (To My People About Our Language) and "Jezik roda moga" (Language of My People) (printed in *Danica* [Morning Star], 1860, and *Naše gore list* [One of Our Kind], 1862) provide examples of both ideologism and creativity. The first two stanzas are from "Rodu o jeziku"; the other two are from "Jezik roda moga":

Tuđ tuđinu, tebi tvoj doliči,
Tuđi poštuj, a svojim se diči!
Dičiti se možeš njime:
Njim carevi carevahu,
Njim kraljevi kraljevahu,
Slavne mu je loze ime,
Slavan puk ga svojim zove . . .

On ti svakoj tuzi i radosti
On ti duše cijeloj nutrnosti
Jedin pravi tumač biva.
. . .

Zuji, zveči, zvoni, zvuči,
Šumi, grmi, tutnji, huči—
To je jezik roda moga!

Njime milim, krasnim zato
I odievam svoje pjesme,
Oj! Spievi su njemu česme,
S kojih teče obilato
I put neba silno štrca,
A odozgo rosom blagom
Po rodu se siplje dragom,
I uvela kriepi srca.[11]

[Alien to foreigner, it becomes you,
Respect the foreign, but be proud of yours!
You can be proud of it (your language):
With it the tsars ruled,
With it the kings reigned,

Its name stems from glorious stock,
Glorious people call it their own.

In every sadness and joy
It becomes the only real interpreter
Of the soul of entire inner life.
. . .

It hums, rattles, rings, sounds,
Rustles, thunders, roars, booms—
That is the language of my people!
With this dear and beautiful language
I therefore adorn my poems,
O! Its songs are fountains,
From which they flow profusely
And spurt forth strongly toward heaven,
And from above like mild dew
Pour down onto my dear folks,
And strengthen the faded hearts.][12]

In these four groups of verses we can clearly recognize what socio-linguists would recognize, more than a century later, as key concepts of linguistic identity. In the first group Preradović endorses two things: the *autonomy* and *historicity* of the language of his people. In the second he underscores the *authenticity* of the language in communicating the uniqueness of the people. In the third group he stages its *creativity* and *wealth*, or in a word, its *vitality*.[13] In the fourth group he again underscores its vitality, but also its *formative* power with regard to the people (*rod*).

From the time of Preradović to the present much has happened with regard to language ideology and the linguistics of the "language of his people": the language of his poems is still the language of his people, no matter what else it is called and no matter what people are feeling at the moment. This is not surprising since that notion follows from the formative idea of the grammar of nation. I make this point in order to preclude the thought that Preradović's period does not communicate with the period that follows him. In the area of the former Yugoslavia Preradović's period begins around the middle of the twentieth century. The period of the grammar of nation in this region ends with the selection and codification of the Macedonian language, an act that is a temporal as well as an ideological and scholarly border, even a border that marks the end of one period and the beginning of another—the period of "state vernaculars."[14] This period continues to the present day, and can be considered a ramification, a byway, and in some respects even a cul de sac of the previous period. In this new period the language has lost its autonomy and the mechanisms of its vitality are being restrained; aside from research into the standardization of language, significant contributions have been lacking.

With the two following examples, both from the realm of vocabulary, I want to demonstrate the relationship between language and the state vernacular. That is, I want to demonstrate what happens when language is placed in the mold of the state vernacular. The first example is from the beginning of the 1990s, when terms and words were being changed in Croatia with a lot of enthusiasm and with little thought. Differences were produced in both time and space, in attitudes both toward others and toward ourselves. For instance, the word *radnik* (worker; cf. *rad, raditi, radni*) was replaced by the word *djelatnik*. Consequences of the change were twofold. A very common and productive word was put out of use, taken over by a word lacking current usage in the Croatian language, a word belonging to a different lexical generic order (*djelo, djelovati, djelovanje*), which in its new role either could not produce what its predecessor did or did produce unusual syntagms. On the other hand, a word was put out of use that had a specific and complex semantics (comprising several centuries of human societies, while here it was excluded for its being marked by communist society), and its place was taken by a word without either that history or that semantics in the Croatian language. Confronted with such intervention into language, the linguistic intuition of the loyal speaker of the Croatian language started—in accordance with the grammar of the language—to act autonomously, so that, as one can read in the earliest newspaper reference, and as one still can see on web pages of numerous companies and institutions, that *radno vrijeme* ("working hours"; usually posted on shop and office entrances) was renamed as *djelatno vrijeme*.[15] We do not know what happens to *nedjelatnici* (that is, *neradnici*, those who do not work) when they are not at their *djelatno mjesto* (that is, *radno mjesto*). One should probably read up on that in *Zakon o djelovanju* (that is, *Zakon o radu*; Labor Law). Be that as it may, this type of intervention into language produces two serious consequences. First, it erodes and limits linguistic productivity and creativity, thereby creating a sense of insecurity in speakers. Second, it produces fruitless words which are made into the idioms of a language (that is, its vocabulary)—labels with no history or meaning. It is fortunate that this intervention did not succeed completely, so that *Sv. Josip Radnik* was preserved (St. Josip the Worker is a holiday celebrated on May 1, since the 1990s, as a substitute for May Day, the holiday of working people celebrated on May 1 during socialism). Perhaps that will be enough for the restoration of the excluded paradigm.

The second example is from the present day, and does not concern intervention into language that restrains or blocks the productive linguistic syntagmatic axis, as was the case in the previous example. The second example illustrates the limitation of selection in language, and the lack of differentiation or permissiveness of different spoken registers. On February 12, 2010, *Večernji list*, a Zagreb daily, published a report from Županja about one Branko Berać being detained by the police and taken to the police station, where he was kept in custody all day and reported to Misdemeanor Court for issuing the following words of advice to his nephew and his friend going to a football match in Split: "Pazite se tamo, budite dobri da vas milicija ne mora batinati! [Take care there and behave so that militia (*milicija*) won't have to give you a clubbing!]."[16] For that he was issued a misdemeanor fine of two thousand kuna. Instead of being commended as a loyal citizen and a good guardian, he experienced something quite different: "Just as my nephew and his friend drove away in the car, a man approached me and asked why I referred to *policija* as *milicija*. I answered that that was the same thing—what was once done by the *milicija* is now done by the *policija*. The stranger took a step back, opened his jacket and placed his right hand on the handle of the handgun he had in his belt, and with his left hand took a police badge on a chain out from under his sweater, and, introducing himself as chief officer of crime police, ordered me sharply not to move."[17]

After that, other policemen who arrived took him to the police station, took away his personal belongings, including the key to his car, which he found after the whole day in detention in the same place where he had left it, but with an empty tank. To a journalist's question of how something like that might have happened, the head of the Department of Public Order in the police precinct with a jurisdiction in the case said: "The law on misdemeanors against public order and peace forbids disparagement and insult of officials, and the penalty is determined by the Misdemeanor Court." He added that there had been no *milicija* since 1991. On the surface everything is fine. Moreover, this was an excellent example of the efficiency of the *rule of law*! If the citizen X is an example of civic loyalty, and the policeman Y an example of police professionalism, where then is the problem? Obviously not in the disappearance of a tank of gas, but in *milicija*! The policeman Y held that the use of the word *milicija* by the citizen X was against the law. On the one hand, the citizen, however, did not know, and could not know, that using words from a language that does not exist any more is against the law. Let us set aside the fact that he could not know that in a private conversation he must refer to police using the name that it uses for itself, and not perhaps *murija, panduri, drotovi* (slang words for a policeman, like *cop* in English), and the like. On the other hand, the policeman is not really required to know about the functioning of the human mental lexicon, especially the one that did not undergo *onomaktomia* (removing those words that do not belong to a proper language), nor does the official need to know what to do when encountering words from former or future languages. To ask of native linguists to help them and explain to them that they are both victims of the state vernacular would be naïve, considering that it evolved from the maker of the grammar of nation to the custodian of the state vernacular.

From Standardization of the Vernacular to Vernacularization of the Standard

The history of language standardization as a linguistic and sociolinguistic phenomenon has been poorly researched. There are numerous and highly developed theories of the standard language and language standardization, but there is no theoretically elaborated overview of the historical evolution of the phenomenon of language standardization, not only concerning the question of what was standardized and how, but also concerning the question of what kind of language and linguistic communication should result from the total effort of standardization. The course and duration of the first stage of standardization, which relied on the written text and which largely or at least occasionally understood the speech community as a *community of texts*, vary from language to language, but this stage does undoubtedly possess principles of its own. The same can be said of the second stage, in which emphasis shifts from a community of texts to *outstanding or good authors*.[18] In the third stage, in which the term standard language is introduced, standardization becomes a much more complex and demanding task, taken on by *institutions of linguistic scholarship*.[19] The task at hand here is more complex and demanding because of the increase in the number of so-called functional styles, but also because of demands for revision of the standard in accordance with new political or communicative motivations. The fourth stage is marked by an increase in the awareness that standardization ultimately has to do with the *public language*,[20] that is, the standardized language is a public language in all its functional diversity and communicative forms (written or oral, textual or interactive, monological or dialogical).

These four stages (should this periodization prove well-founded) have been mutually intertwining and overlapping, but I am convinced that they can be recognized in the majority of languages of what Burke calls the period of "rediscovery of language," or the period of the "vernacular revolution." I am also convinced that in some of the general periodizations of standardization stages of European vernaculars each of them could be associated with one or more corresponding names in circulation, such as written language, literary language, general language, standard language, and public language (*pisani jezik, književni jezik, opći jezik, standardni jezik, javni jezik*).[21] Each of these stages contributed in its own way to the strengthening of both horizontal and vertical axes of communication within language communities: at one time by programs of general literacy and mandatory education, and at another time by means of general military conscription and the tax system, and at yet other times by means of the print media and the media that evolved later. This development contributed not only to the lessening of the communicative distance between the standard and the nonstandards, but also to a polyfunctionality of the standard. Therefore, the standard increasingly developed into the language of public communication, with all the internal dynamism that this earned or spontaneous autonomy can bring with it—especially the *ability of autoregulation*. The evolution of a vernacular into the public language should be the final and finishing activity of standardization, after which a good portion of the roles played by institutions of standardization is transferred to the language itself, with its capacity for autoregulation. For various sociolinguistic and politico-historical reasons, some European languages have not reached that stage—among them the majority of South Slavic languages, and I especially have in mind the languages declared in the linguistic space of Croats, Serbs, Bosniaks, and Montenegrins. Because of a lack of continuity in language policy, these languages move between the first and the third stages in the practice of standardization, not infrequently ignoring the second stage and entirely disregarding the potentials of the fourth stage.[22]

The example of the Montenegrin language, until recently a standard variant of the Croato-Serbian language, is a good illustration of this situation. It could be said that just as the Macedonian language is a borderline case of the grammar of nation, so is the Montenegrin language a borderline case of the vernacularization of the standard. However, one should immediately add that what is at stake here is not vernacularization with respect to a growing role of society vis-à-vis the state, but the other way round—because of the strengthening of the symbolic role of the state vis-à-vis the communicative role of society.

"The state must have its own language," has been repeated by the Montenegrin intellectuals gathered around poet Jevrem Brković.[23] That is, after declaring state independence, it is necessary to declare language independence as well. The authors of *Pravopis crnogorskoga jezika* (Orthography of the Montenegrin Language) write similarly in their foreword: "The achievement of state independence and the passing of the constitution that defines the Montenegrin language as the official language of Montenegro have conditioned the need to create a new orthography of the Montenegrin language, mandatory at the level of state."[24]

As is obvious, the foreword to this *Pravopis* prescribes a "language . . . mandatory at the level of state," that is in all forms and at all levels of official communication. If one is to infer from this that this is the definition of orthography, that would mean that it is related primarily to written forms of communication. The foreword defines not only the official *status* of the Montenegrin language, but also its *corpus*, so that it is much more than an orthography—*it sets the principles of language planning*.[25] The next passage states that clearly:

In the Montenegrin language one can differentiate between three layers: (1) the general *štokavian* language layer (which is common to Bosnian, Montenegrin, Croatian, and Serbian languages; (2) general Montenegrin [*koine*] language layer (common to all Montenegrin speech representatives); (3) dialectal language traits (that concern Montenegrin local speeches). We have codified all the characteristics of the contemporary Montenegrin language that belong to the first and the second layers. Herein lies the crucial difference between this orthography and the previous official orthographies in Montenegro, which treated characteristics of the second layer as dialectological.[26]

If we add to this the following passage, placed among orthographic principles, then the above statement appears even more clearly justified:[27] "The model for the Montenegrin standard language norm is the common, general [*koine*] language layer that belongs to all *autochthonous* Montenegrin citizens" (emphasis in the original).[28]

Each of these three quotes could be given manifold, multilayered, and extensive interpretations. And each of these interpretations could amount to a small treatise. However, within the framework of this chapter, we shall leave these quotes to interpret themselves. In order to facilitate such autointerpretation, we shall add only one more quote: "Finally, in order to follow the logic of language standardization, it was necessary to deduce the orthography from the grammar. However, the urgent need to standardize the Montengrin language imposed an opposite logic: to present to the public an orthography and a dictionary first."[29]

Considering what is to be read in chapter 8 of *Orthography of the Montenegrin Language*, "Grafemi *ć*, *đ*, *ś*, *ź*," it is not clear what was the "urgent need" that "imposed the opposite logic." Or is it in fact the logic of the thing itself, namely that *the orthography here is the true grammar*, so that it could not have been any different? How else can one read the next fragment: "The phonemes *ś* and *ź* are the characteristics differentiating the Montenegrin standard language from the other three *štokavian* standard languages (Bosnian, Croatian, and Serbian). In view of the fact that they form a noteworthy feature of the contemporary Montenegrin language, that they have persisted as generally present sounds in spite of many decades of orthographic and orthoepic scholarship that treated them as dialectal, they are part of the standard language norm."[30]

A person whose tongue is quicker than his mind or whose tongue does not limit his mind might evoke here the popular saying: "Spala knjiga na dva slova! [The book came down to two letters!]." If we keep in mind the history of the standardization of vernaculars from its beginnings, and if we remember that over the course of this long history the book represented its reality both symbolically and functionally, then it truly can be said that from the first printed grammar of a vernacular, Nebrija's *Gramatica castellana* (1492), to *Pravopis crnogorskog jezika*, the book has again become the Book.

Therefore, what is at stake here is obviously not a text containing the rules of writing supposed to be in effect in a language, but a Book that symbolizes, or as the authors say, "marks," a vernacularization of a standard. What has happened with this *Pravopis* book is in fact a rule of sorts. In this regard, the authors of *Pravopis* and those who authorized them, have not done anything that others before them have not done with orthography. A good portion of controversies of Croato-Serbian standardization began and ended with orthography. The fact that this situation in the case of the Montenegrin standard is more exposed should not be reason to blame the Montenegrins. They have, at the price of following a process to absurdity, done what others have tried to do. And for that reason their Book is not so much just theirs but it is also common to Croats, Serbs, and Bosnians. It is also common to all those who deal with language from a sociolinguistic perspective, especially from the point of view of standardization and the relationship between language and identity, because such efforts at vernacularization of the standard open up the question of the end of one type of standardization or one type of theory of standardization and debates on standardization, which in the area of the former Yugoslavia are hopelessly closed and becoming even more closed. Standardization has in these theories and debates become hypostatized, just as has the logic of identity on which it rests. Its hypostatization is especially prominent in circumstances of a changed communicative paradigm. In the communicative paradigm that is being constructed the public language is based increasingly less on the linguistic text alone and on the text that is finished in advance. The interactive and dialogic character of new media and the intertextual and polyphonic structure of messages themselves obviously change the traditional relations between the sender, the message, and the receiver. Under the influence of all these transformations of media the manner in which the public language is formed changes too. For that reason it is impossible that the methods of standardization would not also be affected by these processes. Therefore it can no longer be justified to base standardization exclusively on the *polymorphic* nature of language, that is,[31] on phonological, morphological, or lexical fragments of its identity, if for no other reason than because it no longer corresponds to the circumstances of a changed communication paradigm. Because of that, attempts like the one in Montenegro, but also in other places, create more misunderstanding than can be set before language by claims for it to perform an identity role—one could say: without faith in the language or measure in identity!

Polyglossia Instead of Polymorphy

So, in the area of the former Yugoslavia, but also in other parts of Southeast Europe, we encounter several identitized languages that have come into being as a result of the polymorphic logic of language standardization. A paradoxical consequence of this polymorphic logic is that two crucial protagonists of this logic have become its prisoners. Both the identity function of language and its standardization have become this, thus losing the autonomy that gives meaning to the relationship between identity (ethnic, national, state, or other) and language, on the one hand, and between standardization and language, on the other hand. If language is imprisoned by the identity function, and if standardization is reduced to polymorphy, then both these things undermine the ground they stand on. Regardless of the specific and reduced communicability of identity,[32] and regardless of the containment and stabilization of the standard, neither one nor the other proves itself only in relation to the other, but solely in a communicative interaction with other identities and other standards. And that means in interaction with those with whom you are in some sort of identity and standardization dispute, and not with those who can relate to that dispute at the level of argument, but not at the level of reality. In order to achieve that, I maintain it is necessary to restore the logic of polyglossia or heteroglossia, both in the politics of identity and in politics of standardization.[33] In contrast to the logic of polymorphy, this logic affords both the politics with the necessary conditions for vitality and autonomy.

The working of the logic of polyglossia can be observed in the following example taken from Alija Lakišić's cookbook *Bosanski kuhar: Tradicionalno kulinarstvo Bosne i Hercegovine*. In this cookbook (*kuhar*, while we in Zagreb would more commonly say *kuharica*), abundant in recipes for various dishes, sweets, pastry, and drinks, we glean knowledge of dietary customs and the culture of food, but we can also find excellent linguistic examples, among them the following:

Adolmljeni Tukac[34]

Kod nas se za tukca upotrebljava pet naziva: tukac (tuka), morac (moruja), bibac (bibica), puran (pura) i ćuran (ćurka).

Ovo jelo imalo je a i danas ima različite nazive: tukac na pirjanu, tukac na tiritu, punjeni tukac tiritom, nadjeveni tukac.

Cijeli tukac, mlada džigerica (može i bijela džigerica i srce), majdonos (list i korijen peršuna), đereviz (list celera), mrkva. Džigerica i zelen treba da su u količini koja može popuniti ½ šupljine tukca, riže ¼ od ove količine (znači, količina za oko ⅛ šupljine tukca) so, biber, mesna voda (juha), nešto masla.

Tukac se očisti. Bijela džigerica i srce se obari, voda baci, te meso isjeca. Crna džigerica se isjeca. Riža se donekle prodinsta na maslu. Zelen se isjecka. Sve ovo se posoli, pobiberi i sve izmiješa. Zatim se tukac nadolmi ovim pirjanom (dolmom, punjevinom), zalije juhom i eventualno sa malo masnoće od pečenja, ako tukac nije dovoljno debeo. Peče se u dubokoj tavi—tepsiji.

Kad je tukac pečen, rastvori se (rasiječe) napola, istrese pirjan na pervazliju ili na lenger (oval), a odozgo postavi rastvoreni tukac i tako servira.

Kao dodatak servira se kiselo mlijeko i drugi odgovarajući prilog.[35]

The language of this text is polyphonic through and through. It is polyphonic in terms of the origin of some words (there are Turkisms like *tirit*; some are recognizable as standard words such as *puran* [Croatian] and *ćuran* [Serbian], some are trans-standard like *tukac*, some are substandard like *prodinsta*, some are regionalisms like *morac* [Herzegovinian] or *bibac* [Bosnian], and some are probably neologisms like *punjevina*); in terms of communicative intent (it seeks to communicate with the largest possible number of people, regardless of their degree of polyglotic ability); and in terms of communicating different identity characteristics (regardless of their religious, ethnic, or regional identity). On the basis of the language of this text we can understand just how polyglot our language is; on the same basis we can also understand just how nonpolyglot someone else's language is; thus, we can understand the entirety of our linguistic identity. On the basis of this entirety we have a possibility of choice, and with that, freedom in language; on this basis we have the possibility of verifying our identities, and with that, of affirming them. To have the possibility of choice and the freedom in language should be as important as it is to have a language. Be that as it may, of one thing I am certain: polyglossia defends language both from itself and from ourselves, whoever we are and whatever we are called.

A recent decision, by the government of the Republic of Croatia,[36] to donate Croatian translations of *acquis communautaire* of the European Union to the "countries of the region" (Bosnia and Herzegovina, Montenegro, Serbia, plus Macedonia), inspired by the logic of Europeanization of the region, could also be seen as a step toward a transformation of "these spaces" into an area of polyglossia.[37]

Part V

Post-Film

12

The Vibrant Cinemas in the Post-Yugoslav Space

Andrew Horton

"None of this should have happened," says a contemporary Belgrade middle-class protagonist in the opening line of Srđan Golubović's 2007 post-Milošević era Serbian drama, *The Trap* (*Klopka*), which was Serbia's submission for the Foreign Film Oscar in 2007. Our narrator then unfolds his tale of what happened when he found out his ten-year-old son had a deadly illness that could only be treated in Germany for the price of twenty-six thousand euros; he and his wife have nowhere near that kind of money. When his wife puts an ad in the newspaper, a "stranger" who is a criminal agrees to provide the funding if the father will murder another criminal for him. Suddenly film noir meets the Balkans in this finely etched drama that represents a surprisingly wide variety of engagingly powerful films—dramas, comedies, and dramatic comedies—that are emerging from the countries that now make up the former Yugoslavia. These include, as we will survey, films made both by award-winning popular filmmakers from the "prewar" days of the 1970s and 1980s, and by a younger generation of emerging filmmakers such as Golubović and others who are finding their own voices and cinematic visions with influences from Hollywood, changing technologies, the internet, and beyond.

Meanwhile our troubled father, Mladen (Nebojša Glogovac), and his concerned wife, Marija (Nataša Ninković), are struggling to deal with their son in a contemporary Belgrade with signs of poverty everywhere, including street urchins, gypsies, and teen punk criminals; yet we see expensive SUVs and fancy villas as well. Of course everyone in the film seems to have a cell phone too, except the young son who begs for one and finally receives one from his father. Mladen meets up with his criminal benefactor, Miloš (played with dark power by the popular actor Miki Manojlović), and after a number of well set-up scenes showing his doubts about what he is doing, Mladen commits the murder only to discover that Miloš doesn't have the cash after all.

Based on a novel by Nenad Teofilović, *The Trap* pulls us in through Golubović's true-to-life handling of "family affairs," fine acting, and a subplot that soon becomes part of the main plot: it turns out that the gangster whom Mladen murders is the father of a girl who is a school and playground friend of Mladen's son, and whose mother, Jelena (Anica Dobra), has become their acquaintance through playground conversations.

This Serbian film, now distributed in the United States by Film Movement, is representative of the emerging world of coproduced "post-Yugoslav" films, since the credits list Hungarian and German funding as well Serbian producers. I would add that part of what makes this film representative of many of the emerging "post-Yugoslav" films is that it reflects realistically the complexity of life in post-Milošević Belgrade without ever directly bringing in the troubled politics and religious conflicts that have made up so much of the history of the collapse of Yugoslavia and the related wars.

In fact, these "post-Yugoslav" films actually reflect a spirit present in Yugoslav cinema before the breakup of the nation. The film industry that evolved in the former Yugoslavia was an unusual one in that it embraced both popular entertainment and artistic filmmaking. Yugoslav filmmakers won awards at international film festivals including Cannes, Venice, Montreal, Berlin, Karlovy Vary, Istanbul, Mannheim, Hollywood, and elsewhere, while also pleasing a home audience with surprisingly high box office receipts. Hollywood traditionally supplies eight or nine of the top ten films in most countries every year, including in nations such as Britain, France, and Germany. But, until the very end of its existence, Yugoslavia often had four or five local films in the top ten, a phenomenon that continues today in Serbia and some of the other former Yugoslav republics. In 1991, for instance, Srđan Karanović's *Virgina* (*Virdžina*, 1991) outsold *Terminator 2* in Yugoslavia. Then came the wars of the 1990s, multiple changes, and the current period of recovery and development.

Consider the transition since the turn of the new century in what was Yugoslavia. While many former communist nations of Central and Eastern Europe have taken on the complexities of democracy and capitalism relatively peacefully, and many have already been accepted into the

European Union, the former Yugoslavia entered a deeply troubling era of war and social-political upheaval, beginning in 1991. The result, after two wars and many other military and political skirmishes, was the breakup of the Yugoslavia into six independent countries—Slovenia, Croatia, Bosnia, Macedonia, Serbia and Montenegro, plus the NATO- and United Nations–monitored territory of Kosovo, which became independent in 2008. Once a showcase independent socialist nation led by Marshal Tito until his death in 1980, Yugoslavia had distinguished itself since 1948 by saying "no" to Moscow's Stalinist approach to communism and had, in many ways, successfully charted an independent course between East and West, as well as between socialism and market capitalism. In recent years, the trials at the Hague for Milošević and others associated with war crimes during the 1990s have continued, and each republic has worked to establish its own identity and to move beyond the difficulties and pain of the 1990s.

What I wish to trace by briefly examining a few specific films is the surprisingly vibrant body of cinema production throughout the former Yugoslavia despite economic and other limitations. These difficulties in the new republics include high unemployment, often over 50 percent; the continuous departure of young people to other countries; lack of political security; and a huge illegal trade of goods, drugs, and women, often controlled by local "mafia." And we should add that despite the Yugoslav Communist Party's call for equality for all, women have had and continue to have a difficult position in post-Yugoslav culture. Yet, if in the 1980s Yugoslavia counted on twenty-five to thirty feature films being made each year, today the total that the various republics are producing is roughly the same (and we might add even more than this if we count the many low-budget homemade digital films that do not make it into cinemas).

These "former" nations are, of course, also affected by the same changing media conditions that exist around the world. Consider, for instance, the drastic decline of cinemas everywhere. Croatia, for instance, has gone from about four hundred screens in 1980 to roughly fifty in 2004, and a drastic decline can be seen in the other republics as well. The rise in video and DVD viewing, partly on illegal bootleg copies, is yet another factor to consider in assessing "contemporary cinema" in the former Yugoslavia. To this reality can be added the endless screening of feature films on the many television channels available throughout the republics of the former Yugoslavia. Thus if it is the case that the average American sees only four films a year in an actual cinema, many people I have met throughout the former

Yugoslavia have said it might be more like two films per person in the five successor republics. Add to this the fact that while a few multiplex cinemas are beginning to appear in Belgrade, Zagreb, Banja Luka, and Ljubljana, they are out of reach for many people. Similarly, filmmakers all over the world are competing with a youth more interested in reality television shows and games (video and internet) than in film. Thus while many filmmakers used to write and direct for television as well as in feature films, current trends in the five republics have made such dual careers more problematic.

Film financing has also changed over this latest period. Yugoslav film production always maintained an interesting and creative balance between state cultural funding (often in large part derived from ticket sales) and private funds raised by particular companies such as Jadran Film (Zagreb), Avala Film and Centar Film (Belgrade), Viba Film (Ljubljana), and Studio Film (Sarajevo). Today the picture is even more complex as filmmakers draw on state film funds, individual producers, and increasingly often, international co-producers. Milcho Manchevski's Oscar-nominated film *Before the Rain* (*Pred doždot*, 1994) was a Macedonian-British-French coproduction and Danis Tanović's Oscar-winning *No Man's Land* (*Ničija zemlja*, 2001), though shot in Bosnia with a basically Bosnian cast and production crew, received Slovenian, French, British, Italian, and Belgian funding.

Add to all of the above the fact that the digital filmmaking revolution is also an important factor in films being made today in the former Yugoslavia. Thus the cost of filmmaking has gone down and many young filmmakers are able to shoot, edit, and then transfer to 35mm. But they can also simply project these digital films as video in festivals and local theaters or simply go "straight to video or DVD" as a guerilla form of filmmaking.

Let us now turn to how many filmmakers—both young and already established—are managing, despite the difficulties we've mentioned, to make quality films that reach their targeted audiences, often winning international awards as well. Any country would be jealous of the numbers of awards and honors that the countries of the former Yugoslavia have won and continue to win.

The "Prague Group" Revisited

I first wish to note that many of the most significant films in the former Yugoslavia were made by a group of filmmakers commonly known as "the Prague Group," which I wrote about in *Cineaste* in 1981.[1] Educated at the FAMU (Film and TV Academy) film school in Prague at the end of the 1960s, this group of talented filmmakers returned home to make television series and films that drew in large numbers of the public and won numerous international awards. In brief, each of these filmmakers—including Rajko Grlić, Srđan Karanović, Goran Marković, Goran Paskaljević, Lordan Zafranović, with Emir Kusturica joining FAMU a few years later—has been quite active during the past dozen years as well. I personally, for instance, was impressed that even throughout the Milošević years, most of this group continued to be in touch with each other no matter whether they are Croatian, Serbian, or from other republics, and worked to actually help each other keep film projects going. This was the same spirit I observed before the wars when I was working on several screenplays in Belgrade, including cowriting *Something in Between* (*Nešto između*, 1983).

Consider one of this distinguished group, Rajko Grlić of Croatia, who has for many years now been a professor of filmmaking at the University of Ohio as well. Grlić not only has continued to make films in the former Yugoslavia, but he has managed to organize and run one of the most admired film festivals in Europe, the July Motovun Festival held in a beautiful mountain top village in Croatia attended by more than forty thousand each summer.

His first feature after the wars of the 1990s was a popular kind of Balkan *Butch Cassidy and the Sundance Kid* entitled *Charuga* (*Čaruga*, 1996), which tells the tale of an actual Robin Hood–like figure in 1918 and years following who, influenced by Lenin (at one point he even dresses like him) and Marx, was robbing from the rich to give to the poor to start a true "revolution." The fact that he ends up simply robbing from everyone and forgets the "revolution," with the film ending in his own execution, provides a wry take on what was happening to communism across the former Soviet Union and Eastern Europe.

Several years later in his documentary *Croatia 2000: A Winter to Remember* (*Novo novo vrijeme*, 2001), Grlić (codirecting with Igor Mirković) captured social and political change by making a fascinating film about the Croatian national elections in 2000 after Tuđman's death. Allowed to shoot "inside" each campaign as it was taking place, Grlić made a film that played to large audiences in the Croatian cinemas. It is a fascinating look at grassroots democracy in action. The fact that the election led to the defeat of Tuđman's HDZ (Hrvatska demokratska zajednica, Croatian Democratic

Union) party by a coalition SDP-HSLS group, insured there would be a more liberal government open to true social and political change in Croatia.

The film to highlight here, however, is Grlić's award winning action-comic-drama *Border Post* (*Karaula*, 2007), based on a novel by Ante Tomić, set in prewar Macedonia on the Albanian border with a Yugoslav army unit. Grlić, who is Croatian, represents the strong positive values of post-Yugoslavia cooperation between the former republics, since this film was the first film after the Yugoslav wars to be coproduced by companies in Serbia, Slovenia, Croatia, Bosnia, Great Britain, Macedonia, France, and Austria. That the film was a large box office and critical success in each of the former Yugoslav countries says a lot about the growing possibilities of future cooperation in co-productions.

Quite simply, the plot of *Border Post* depicts a trend in post-Yugoslavia films by not directly focusing on politics, nationality, or religion. The blame for a breakdown in peace on the Albanian border in Grlić's wryly dark tale is based on a true story of a Bosnian officer who kept his unit together on the border once he discovered he had syphilis and didn't want his wife to find out. Such an awkward and absurd situation leads to the beginning of armed conflict on the border, as each character is shown to be trying to live out several lives with different values. Grlić's statement for this set-up says much about so many of the films made during and since the war. According to Grlić: "The film enquires about those people, who were to transform in a matter of months into soldiers, refugees, victims and criminals. How did they live? What did they really want? What was the everyday life that engendered war and who were the ones who had war implanted into their minds so quickly and so easily?"[2] Certainly during the late 1940s through to the early 1960s many of the "war" films being produced and made in Yugoslavia were "Partisan films" that celebrated the World War II victories of Tito's army and the Yugoslav people over the Nazis. But in this post-Milošević era and even during the war years of the 1990s many filmmakers have echoed Grlić's statement that they were or are exploring how such disasters came about and how ordinary people managed or manage to continue their lives.

Croatian New Wave Cinema

If we move from Grlić as an established Croatian director to the younger Croatian directors who have started up since the end of the wars, we find a number of talented filmmakers emerging. Representative of this group would be Kristijan Milić and Goran Kulenović, who had a hit with their first feature, *24 Hours* (*24 sata*), in 2003. The film is actually made up of two films, one by each director, and both depicting the frustrations of today's Croatian youth. Kulenović's piece is entitled "Straight to the Bottom" and deals with four friends who meet in a bar in Zagreb in 1994. In a tale of sudden twists and dark humor, we discover that they each have very different lives. One of them is killed in an attempt to rob a café, leading to the problem of how to dispose of the body. Milić's Tarantino-style "Safe House" tells of three policemen guarding a witness, who are aware of the connection between police and the local criminals and of how it will all play out in their lives and jobs.

More recently, Arsen Anton Ostojić, who has worked on more than twenty feature films and has an MFA in filmmaking from New York University, made his first feature, *A Wonderful Night in Split* (*Ta divna splitska noć*), which became not only a hit but also the 2005 Croatian submission for a Foreign Film Oscar in Hollywood. Once again, like Gobulović's *Trap*, Ostojić's film echoes film noir not only in its focus on aspects of crime involving criminals crossing with average citizens, but also in its impressive style and black-and-white cinematography by Mirko Pivčević. Split is a historic Croatian seaside town with medieval narrow alleys not accessible to cars and motorcycles. During a New Year's Eve celebration, Ostojić weaves multiple intersecting tales between ten in the evening and midnight as thousands are gathered to celebrate in the portside plaza to see and listen to a pop rapper, Dino Dvornik, who, like Ostojić, was from Split (he died in September 2008), sings, raps, shouts, and continually exclaims to much applause that "Split is the greatest city in the world."

The title "Wonderful Night" turns ironic and dark very swiftly as we track a drug dealer and former soldier from the Yugoslav wars who is having a passionate affair with the widow of his best friend, also a soldier, who died in the wars. But then everything begins to go from bad to worse as the woman's seven-year-old son sees his mother making love. Next we have a nineteen-year-old girl, who is a drug addict desperately in search of drugs to celebrate the New Year. She agrees to make love to a black American sailor in order to get drugs, but he has a pistol and this story too goes from worse to total disaster. That leaves another intertwined tale of a lead drug contact man who winds up in trouble with the bigger drug lord, which leads him to the teenage girl and the former soldier drug dealer before his tale becomes far less than wonderful. Finally, a young couple wishes to lose their virginity before midnight as the rapper raps and as all stories intertwine only to, of course, meet their "noir" by midnight. The film becomes overly long and many viewers may lose interest because, with too many characters wrapped up in drugs, there is little real human interest in character or story development past the stereotyped noir set-up; yet the music, cinematography, and atmosphere speak well, not only for Ostojić's talent, but also for a developing Croatian "new wave" cinema that is finding its audiences and its own voice after the tragedies of the Yugoslav wars.

Bosnian Cinema:
From Sarajevo to Hollywood with Oscar Winners

Cinema is very much alive and flourishing in Sarajevo and the rest of Bosnia-Herzegovina since the wars. Witness the importance of the Sarajevo Film Festival, each August since 1993. Started by a dedicated group of lovers of moving images, these Sarajevo cineastes led by Mirsad Purivatra have built on the spirit of those in the city who love to see movies despite all odds. Along with Thessaloniki in Greece, it has become a "regional cinema center," where filmmakers can gather from around the Balkans. Support for the festival has come from Vanessa Redgrave, Francis Ford Coppola, Martin Scorsese, Miloš Forman, and even Ingmar Bergman. In the past few years, the festival has helped to set up a Balkan Film Development fund (CINE-LINK) that works to identify and aid good scripts and projects not only in Bosnia but the whole Balkan region. *Los Angeles Times* film critic Kenneth Turan captured much of this "Sarajevo spirit" in his book *Sundance to Sarajevo: Film Festivals and the World They Made* (2002).

Together with the flourishing of the Sarajevo festival, Bosnian films have also been thriving. In 2001, the Oscar for Best Foreign Film went to Danis Tanović's *No Man's Land*, the stirring, darkly comic drama of several Bosnian soldiers and one Serb trapped in a trench during the Bosnian War. "This one is for Bosnia," said Tanović when accepting the Oscar, despite the fact that the film was financed through Slovenian and European production houses (although it is a Bosnian story with a predominantly Bosnian cast). The success of Tanović's film, which drew in over two hundred thousand viewers to the less than thirty-five cinemas in Bosnia, outselling Hollywood's *Pearl Harbor* ten to one,[3] has been a blessing for the recovering film community of Bosnia.

We should remember that *No Man's Land*, made by someone who had experienced a real war, appeared at a time when Hollywood was flooding the market with war movies such as *Behind Enemy Lines* (1998), *Spy Game* (2001), and *Black Hawk Down* (2001). These films capture wars ranging from Bosnia to the Middle East and Africa but always with an attempt to establish American "heroes" fighting the "enemy." It is a strong character-istic of Tanović's film, and of those not only from Bosnia but also from the former Yugoslav republics, that the films tend to celebrate common folk who are not heroes and who often seem unable even to point a gun in the right direction.

A very positive corner was turned in the Bosnian film community in 2002–3 as three feature films emerged, each with its own merits, thus shat-tering what had become a rhythm of "one feature film every three years." Dino Mustafić's debut feature, *Remake*, cuts back and forth between World War II and the recent Bosnian war as two stories—one about a father and one about his son—unfold. A second very popular debut film for 2003 was *Summer in the Golden Valley* (*Ljeto u zlatnoj dolini*), by Srđan Vuletić. This is a wry and emotional coming-of-age tale about a Bosnian Muslim teen-ager who learns at his father's funeral that his father owed a lot of money to a Sarajevo crime lord, Hamid. Postwar Sarajevo and the crime, drug, and youth scenes open up in this well-paced film.

Finally Pjer Žalica's debut feature, *Fuse* (*Gori vatra*, 2003), is a darkly comic update in many ways of Gogol's *Inspector General*. This award-winning and popular film (which even made the top ten in Belgrade for 2003–4) focuses on a small Bosnian town, Tešanj, just after the Dayton Agreement, when the word is out that President Clinton will drop by as a symbolic act for a day. We track a variety of characters through moments sad or hilarious or both as they try to come to terms with each other after the recent war and their stated and unstated grudges, hatreds, and misun-derstandings. The ending is perfect for, as anyone can guess, Clinton does not appear and they will have to live their own lives their own Bosnian way.

Before leaving our coverage of Bosnian film, we should mention the "former Bosnian" filmmaker Emir Kusturica. Before the wars he was the most internationally known filmmaker of the former Yugoslavia of the previous twenty years. With *Time of the Gypsies* (*Dom za vešanje*, 1989), for instance, Kusturica built on documented accounts of the Yugoslav gypsy mafia selling children into crime and prostitution in Italy. In collaboration with screen-writer Gordan Mihić, he added strong "magic realism" elements together with a memorable gypsy music sound track by the popular composer Goran Bregović.

Once the Bosnian War began, however, Kusturica became a controversial figure when he removed himself from any support for his native city, denied his Muslim culture, and tied himself quite strongly to "Yugoslav" and thus Belgrade-centered concepts of Serbian nationalism, leaving his native Bosnia behind. His film made during the war—*Underground* (*Podzemlje*, 1995)—had the appropriate subtitle of "Once upon a Time There Was a Country" and won the Palme d'Or at Cannes in 1995. Based on theatrical works and a script by Dušan Kovačević, the narrative centers on a Serbian black-market profiteer named "Blacky" (Miki Manojlović) who, during the German occupation of Belgrade, takes a group of people—men, women, and children—underground to protect them from the Nazis while they in turn create goods for sale to the Nazis. Blacky and his crew play the middle men and fail to tell his underground society that the war ends in 1945. The result is that this underground culture continues until the 1990s when the angry citizens break out of their subterranean world to discover that the Bosnian War is in progress. Many scenes such as an underground surrealistic wedding are memorable in and for themselves. But as Dina Iordanova has explained, Kusturica is caught between historical allegory and Serbian propaganda. "The overall critical reception of the film classified it as an esoteric piece of elitist cinema."[4]

Slovenian Popular Cinema

The situation in Slovenia since the late 1990s shows a cinema and media alive and well and growing by leaps and bounds. With a population of two million, Slovenia has more per capita cinema screens than any other location in the former Yugoslavia. One hundred screens exist in sixty-two cinemas with two multiplexes and almost three million ticket sales a year. In 2003–4, for instance, an all time box office record for a Slovenian film was set by Branko Đurić's *Cheese and Jam* (*Kajmak in marmelada*) with almost 140,000 tickets sold.

Written, directed, and starring Đurić, who came straight from his starring role in the Oscar-winning *No Man's Land*, *Cheese and Jam* is an at times joyful and at other times tragic contemporary story, as Đurić writes, "about those of us who are mixed."[5] Đurić, who was born in Sarajevo of a Muslim mother and Serbian father, came to Slovenia as a refugee during the Bosnian War and is himself in a mixed marriage. The film is drawn from his experiences and touches among other topics on the issue of smuggling refugees across borders. Yet, despite the hardships, Đurić and wife (in the story) Tanja Ribić, demonstrate that it is, finally, a love story. Clearly, what attracted audiences was a film that spoke about the times rather than about Hollywood special effects and alien invasions. Seeing such an amazing variety of films of such high quality coming out of Slovenia in recent years, it is easy to speak of a "new Slovenian wave." But Nika Bohinc, in a publication about recent Slovenian film, notes that we should recognize the solid past provided by such Slovenian filmmakers as Boštjan Hladnik, Karpo Godina, Franci Slak, and Žarko Lužnik.[6] Such recognition of past accomplishments is important. Yet the astounding fact is that most of the new films by young filmmakers have pulled audiences back into cinemas across the country and walked off with numerous awards internationally as well.

A lot of credit goes to the Slovenian Film Fund (established in 1994), which has certainly made a real contribution to helping young filmmakers and has also enabled established names to get films made. Yet there is also a special close relationship between all of the following organizations: the Slovenian Film Fund, Slovenian Cinematheque (Slovenska kinoteka), Slovenian Film Archive (Slovenski filmski arhiv), Academy of Theater, Radio, Film, and Television (Akademija za gledališče, radio, film in televizijo), Association of Slovenian Filmmakers, Association of Slovenian Film Producers, Festival of Slovenian Film, and Ljubljiana International Film Festival.

An equally impressive hard-nosed drama is Damjan Kozole's *Spare Parts* (*Rezervni deli*, 2003). Rudi is a young fellow who gets a job as a driver with Ludvik, an old motorcycle champion who has fallen on hard times and makes his money driving illegal aliens from one border to another. "Spare parts" is what Ludvik calls these people from Africa and the former Soviet Union and the Middle East, who are tortured, forced into prostitution, and more, in this relentless story of a young man trying to become an adult in an ugly world. Taking place in Krško, a small industrial Slovenian town with a failed nuclear plant that has killed many with cancer including Ludvik's wife, the story acknowledges the 135,000 illegal aliens who pass through Slovenia each year. The film was a large commercial success in Slovenia and was, according to producer Danijel Hočevar, sold to ten countries in 2003.[7]

Offbeat comedy and youth culture seen from the inside are traits of a number of recent Slovenian films. *Idle Running* (*V leru*, 1999) is Janez

Burger's seductive comedy whose main character, Dizzy (played by Jan Cvitkovič, who also wrote the script) is a sometime university student with the philosophy that "life sucks." Passive, pessimistic, alienated, and afraid of commitment to anything or anyone, he does not quite become an adult by film's end, but certainly begins to share some relationships. Jan Cvitkovič has since written and directed the extremely popular dark comedy *Gravehopping* (*Od groba do groba*, 2005) about one young fellow who specializes in being paid for village funeral orations and his mechanic best friend. Very much in the Eastern European and especially Czech tradition of offbeat humor coming from common characters and simple situations, the film speaks well for Cvitkovič's talents and for the future of Slovenian popular film.

A Revitalized Post-Yugoslav Serbian Cinema

We began this brief survey with the contemporary Serbian film *Trap*, and we now conclude by returning to Serbia and the young filmmaking generation that has come forward after the wars of the early 1990s. Cut to one scene in a recent film: A crippled young Belgrade man sits in a wheelchair talking to a video camera, crying out, "I look like an ordinary guy, but that's not true!" As soon as the camera stops shooting, the young man stands up, clearly showing he is not crippled as he talks to his friend, the cameraman. The scene comes from the main character in the first of seven stories within Miroslav Momčilović's *Seven and a Half* (*Sedam i po*, 2006), each of which takes on one of the seven deadly sins, in this case, "Greed." The film looks at contemporary Belgrade life in which everyone is caught trying to live in a world of conflicting and overlapping values that often contradict each other. In short, in this film (which was Momčilović's directorial debut; he had previously scripted the popular ironic comedy *When I Grow Up I'll Be Like This Guy Kengur* [*Kad porastem biću Kengur*, 2004]), we the audience are set up for a world in which we cannot trust anyone or anything we see or hear.

Momčilović's *Seven and a Half* offers seven "takes" on the confusion in contemporary Belgrade as seen through sections, each reflecting one of the seven deadly sins; the "half" is playfully winking at us, of course, by referring to Federico Fellini's *8½* and Ingmar Bergman's *The Seventh Seal*. In the final episode, "Envy," two unemployed Serbs are sitting at a simple café-restaurant owned by a Bosnian refugee who is taking his pregnant wife to the hospital to deliver their child. But when he and the Serbs get in an argument about who makes the best kebabs, Serbia or Bosnia, they later pour sugar in the gas tank of his Mercedes when he is not looking. They make it clear that they are jealous that this "refugee" has done well in postwar life whereas they have no jobs, wives, families, or cars. When the Bosnian gets a call that the baby is a boy but he is not breathing well, there is panic when the car won't start. Finally the Serbs get a taxi and help the desperate Bosnian to the hospital.

Instead of going for a violent ending as in earlier postwar Serbian films such as in Srđan Dragojević's *Wounds* (*Rane*, 1998), Momčilović goes for a "carnivalesque" coming-together of the whole seven tales in a healing conclusion (yes, the "half" for the other seven tales!). At the hospital we meet each character from the previous tales, each at the hospital for a different reason, and all join in singing the same lullaby for the Bosnian baby as we see the child in close-up; it is in a special see-through machine to help it breathe, and it begins to move and cry. As if we were ending a Hollywood musical or a Fellini comedy, all are singing together as a child has been saved and will begin his life in the complicated new Serbia! As one Belgrade viewer of the film comments on Internet Movie Database (IMDb): "The film doesn't tend to moralize—it discovers that there is and should be a moment of catharsis and redemption although the characters make mistakes. Their lives, in Christian terms, aren't sinful, and their weaknesses are caused by the context we live in. Therefore, this story repeatedly calls out for laughter. To conquer the fear and problems, to be self-ironic to laugh at themselves—it's the way of transcending one's pain." It is possible to say, then, that Momčilović's approach, like that of several other Serbian filmmakers, echoes Nelson Mandela's vision and values, as Mandela said even after twenty-seven years in prison, "We cannot forget, but we must forgive."

Despite all that Serbia has been through in recent years, films such as *Seven and a Half*, which draw in large audiences and win many awards, offer signs of a revitalized cinema. There are other encouraging signs as well. Serbia now has, for instance, at least fourteen annual film festivals including the well-respected FEST (Belgrade International Film Festival) held each winter, and festivals of animation in Čačak, screenwriting in Vrnjačka Banja, acting in Niš, and even underwater films in Belgrade. Furthermore, as recently as 2006, four Serbian films were in the top ten box office films of the year (*Ivko's Fete* [*Ivkova Slava*], *We Are No Angels* [*Mi nismo anđeli*], *Border Post*, and *Seven and a Half*), a fact rarely duplicated by any country outside the United States, and thus Serbian filmmakers can be proud they are continuing to connect with their own people. Furthermore, the reorganized Film Center Serbia (Filmski centar Srbije), under acting director Miroljub Vučković, has taken on at least four overall missions: (1) the promotion of Serbian film throughout the world as seen by the screening of films in over twenty-eight festivals; (2) the support and financing of documentary films that concern Serbia in many ways; (3) encouraging young and new filmmakers, particularly through script development programs; and (4) developing books and publications related to Serbian filmmakers and subjects on Serbian cinema.

Among the postwar Serbian generation, let us mention one more of the growing number of successful filmmakers finding their own voices but also clearly influenced by Hollywood and new approaches to cinematic story telling: Radivoje Andrić. His debut film, *Three Palms for Two Punks and a Babe* (*Tri palme za dve bitange i ribicu*, 1998), is refreshingly offbeat and became very popular at home and at festivals; it was followed by an even more popular second feature, *Thunderbirds* (*Munje*, 2001), written by Srba Anđelić. This was a playfully exaggerated mix of romance, musical, and crime film like many contemporary American mixed-genre films, clearly aiming at the teen and young-twenties market. It also managed to capture first place at the box office that year. It follows the story of three young male friends—Mare, Pop, and Gojko—who are trying to break into the hip music scene of Belgrade and score with some chicks at the same time. Shot on digital video and referencing many Hollywood and British teen films in visual and story style, the film could easily be enjoyed by teens everywhere, although ironic references to postwar Serbia come through as well. This is most obvious in the final shot as our buddies accidentally drive a car through a guardrail on top of an elevated parking lot and they hang precariously—shouting "Serbia" as if their dangerous condition represents the whole of their life. Something of a Balkan *Snatch* (2000), Andrić's film steered away from the depressing nihilism of some Serbian films made during and after the wars toward a playful hopefulness despite the ineptitude of the main characters.

Andrić's *When I Grow Up, I'll Be Like This Guy Kengur* (*Kad porastem biću Kengur*) became an upbeat 2004 celebration of Belgrade's current postwar, twenty-first-century reality and diverse population of natives and refugees. We focus on an evening in which a host of characters are watching Euro soccer on TV in a café and admiring a real Yugoslav player named

"Kengur" (Kangaroo). Meanwhile we follow the story of Braca, a young man, intent on romance with the girl of his dreams. A lot of humor derives from a zany date in an almost deserted movie theater as Belgrade goes through an earthquake and, at the end of the film, Belgrade experiences, yes, the appearance of flying saucers over the city (welcome a nod to Hollywood sci-fi!). A third "layer" to the story involves several male friends who have reduced their lives to drinking beer on the rooftop of their apartment building and urinating over the side whenever moved to do so. Somewhere between *Dumb and Dumber* and *Pulp Fiction*, Andrić's film echoes familiar Hollywood youth characters.

I think we can take such comic Serbian films as a positive sign for a country and a culture with a troubled past that is now resolved to move forward. As the ending of *Seven and a Half* celebrates, it may well be possible in the emerging Serbia to transcend the "seven deadly sins" and sing a lullaby together no matter what values we follow, to celebrate the newborn child who must grow up in a changing Serbia.

13

Marking the Trail
Balkan Women Filmmakers and the Transnational Imaginary
Meta Mazaj

The emerging transnational configurations of women making films since the late 1990s have been making a significant mark at international film festivals, reshaping the parameters of specific national cinemas as well as the discourse of world cinema. In her article "To Each Her Own Cinema," Patricia White argues that while the festival discourse is still largely dominated by "individualist" and "auteurist" notions, "we are standing at a moment of change and promise at the intersection of world cinema and women's cinema."[1] As the increasing group of respected women directors who symbolize the traditionally masculine *cinema d'auteur* urges us to rethink the intersection of world cinema and women's cinema, it also redraws the coordinates of many national cinemas and their shifting position on the international stage.

The case of Balkan cinema serves as a particularly instructive example, since the recent emergence of women filmmakers from the former Yugoslav republics is contrasted with the complete absence of women's films in the 1990s, a defining decade for the region as well as for the development and international recognition of Balkan cinema. There were women artists, writers, journalists, and scholars whose voices were internationally heard and who offered a vocal critical alternative: feminist writer Jasmina Tešanović, young playwright Biljana Srbijanović, internationally renowned performance artist Marina Abramović, and academics Svetlana Slapšak and Renata Salecl, to name only a few. But not so in filmmaking. A large group of films that emerged in the 1990s and made Balkan cinema visible, were not only all made by male directors but presented, without a slight hint of ambiguity, a hypermasculine and patriarchal image of a nation, constructed in a thematic and stylistic framework that appealed to international audiences, in no small amount because it affirmed the stereotypical image of the Balkans.

After more than a decade of silence, in a period often defined as transitional, women filmmakers are bursting onto the scene, achieving recognition at A-category international film festivals and considerable success at home. This turnover was announced by young women filmmakers from the former Yugoslav nations with basically no history of women's filmmaking (such as Bosnia), and their debut feature coproductions. In 2002, Maja Weiss became the first internationally visible woman filmmaker from Slovenia with her feature *Varuh meje* (*Guardian of the Frontier*), which was selected and received awards at many festivals.[2] In 2006, Jasmila Žbanić and her debut feature *Grbavica*, a coproduction with Austria, Germany, and Croatia (and only the third feature film in Bosnian and Herzegovinian filmmaking directed by a woman), won a Golden Bear at the Berlin Film Festival, which was followed by twenty more festival awards and an official submission to the Oscars.[3] In 2008, Aida Begić's *Snijeg* (*Snow*), a coproduction with Germany, France, and Iran,[4] won Grand Prix for best film in the Cannes Critics' Week program, opened the fourteenth Sarajevo film festival with a smash, won numerous awards, and continues to tour festivals. In 2009, Marina Andree's debut documentary, *Sevdah*, received the prestigious audience award at the Sarajevo film festival, got overwhelming audience and critical responses, and also toured the festival circuit. In fact, premature as this claim may be, in recent years women have not only emerged but have dominated the regional film festivals in the Balkans, both bigger ones such as Sarajevo and smaller ones such as Portorož, where a considerable percentage of competition films for the years 2008–11 have been made by women directors.

In examining the phenomenon of this recent emergence, and a previous gap, of women's films, I want to argue its significance on a dual level. On the most superficial level, the presence of the new generation of women filmmakers from the former Yugoslav region, and their success on the international stage, fulfills a very significant lack and provides a crucial reflection on the postwar, transitional reality of the nations in the region. More importantly, their films, not only transnational in their production background but firmly embedded in the discourse of transnational imaginary, bracket the realist aesthetic that translates too smoothly into a familiar signifier for "genuine" descriptions of transitional societies (and that so strongly characterized Balkan cinema of the 1990s), and pose significant questions about the positioning of a film's enunciation vis-à-vis the international gaze. Specifically, the examples of *Grbavica* (Žbanić, 2006), *Snow* (Begić, 2008), and *Guardian of the Frontier* (Weiss, 2002) will demonstrate the importance of the transnational not so much as a spatial but as a visual territory that displaces the viewer and the processes by which we accommodate and appropriate the threat of the foreign. They thus show ways in which their cinema, as women's cinema, is uniquely predisposed to rethink not only the nation-building project in the newly transformed European space, but the status and the visibility of such "national" enunciation in the larger transnational sphere.

The Intervention of Women's Cinema

The breakup of Yugoslavia in the early 1990s placed the Balkans at the center of Western consciousness, and the ensuing crisis overshadowed many other conflicts around the world, defining the 1990s as "the Balkan decade."[5] While the role of journalism in constructing a perception of the Balkans in this period was certainly significant, it was cinema that constructed the strongest perspective on the Balkan crisis. Suddenly, the West "discovered" Balkan cinema, and filmmakers from the region grasped this moment to articulate their own vision of themselves. Films like *Pred doždot* (*Before the Rain*, 1994), *Podzemlje* (*Underground*, 1995), *Lepa sela lepo gore* (*Pretty Village, Pretty Flame*, 1996), *Bure baruta* (*Cabaret Balkan*, 1998), *Ničija zemlja* (*No Man's Land*, 2001), achieved wide international attention and praise, but also invited fierce criticism and fury.

While certainly diverse and unique in their own right, this group of films was marked by similar thematic obsessions (the political turmoil of the former Yugoslavia) and a stylistic unity that the scholars of Balkan cinema referred to as "the cinema of voluntary self-exoticism,"[6] or "the cinema of self-Balkanization."[7] If they were on the one hand seen as providing a welcome window into the otherwise complex and almost incomprehensible conflict, they were also critiqued for constructing an ideological lens of Balkanization, an ambivalent discourse whereby the Balkans are perceived as an integral part of superior European cultural space but simultaneously demonized as primitive, barbaric, uncivilized, and chaotic. That is, the films represented the region as a land with strong tribal culture and medieval ethos, marked by senseless violence, a ruthless and consistent celebration of destruction, cold treatment of ethnic strife, and a carnivalesque atmosphere toward their own present, past, and future. Often consciously integrating within their structure the perspective of the outside gaze,[8] or framing the narrative as a self-conscious and carefully constructed performance for this outside gaze (as in *Cabaret Balkan*), the films were nevertheless perceived in a rather straightforward manner, according to the conventions of realism, as authentic representations of the local conflict or, as Iordanova put it, as "instant history."[9] The criticism of the films was thus double-sided, attacking the films both for deviating from Balkan reality as well as catering to a specific market niche and art-house festival circuit norm that lends the films the credible form of "authenticity" and conveniently fits them into a preconceived framework of "local style."

During the first decade of the new century, the changed political and ideological landscape also had a rather profound influence on the cinematic landscape. As Pavičić explains, all post-Yugoslav countries started a process of political and economic reforms "that is usually called by a blurry, seductive term 'normalization.'"[10] Following the elections that removed the previous regimes and began reviving the countries' economies and cultural exchange, this process of normalization included "the reform of the judicial system, the prosecution of war criminals, adopting European Union 'acquis communautaire' (EU legislation), the closure of shipyards, iron mills and old industrial mammoths, reform of universities, introduction of tax numbers and VAT, pension reform,"[11] and so on, with a clear goal of joining the political and cultural sphere of the European Union. These dramatic economic, social, and ideological changes had a profound effect on the cinematic expression which began reflecting, Pavičić argues, this discourse of normalization as well as a clear rejection of the previous stylistic dominant of self-Balkanization. In contrast to the films of the 1990s, these "films of normalization" tend to deploy realistic, everyday, and often urban settings, and characters capable of transformation "who have to surpass traumas and obstacles inherited from the past" and "take an active attitude to problems, engage themselves in problem solving, trying to sort out a better future for themselves."[12] As such, these films implicitly illustrate the dynamics of transitional society and endorse the values of liberal capitalism that define the larger sphere of European Union.

While women's films that emerge in this period are undoubtedly an important part of this "cinema of normalization," they also go beyond it and present a unique intervention in that they not only serve as a corrective to the previous stylistic dominant that conveniently constructs the Balkans as the exotic other, but construct a transnational imaginary that critically negotiates the relationship between a specific "local" enunciation and an international gaze—in this way, they urge us to rethink not only the discourse of the national but the ways in which this discourse is integrated into the larger sphere of world cinema. In his recent article on realism in world cinema, Thomas Elsaesser argues that the new aesthetic of world cinema is less about "national provenance or geopolitical location" and instead revolves around "theoretical issues in what is clearly a global context."[13] That is, traditional markers of realist aesthetic (deep focus, long takes, fixed frames, etc.) are now put to different use in what Elsaesser calls "an ontological turn" or "a post-photographic reality,"[14] which provokes perceptual insecurity and a cognitive switch that not only disturbs the stability of the time-space continuum but our own (traditionally stable) position as spectators. In the films of Balkan woman filmmakers, as we will see, this aesthetic is not only a theoretical issue but has important political implications in that it questions and subverts the ways in which "foreignness" or "otherness" is made visible, familiar, and attainable to the international gaze.

The epistemological shift discussed by Elsaeeser has assumed a crucial role in transnational women cinema and has been explored in several recent studies, such as *Transnational Feminism in Film and Media*, that show how the increasing presence of women filmmakers on the world cinema stage is not merely the presence of "alternative voice." The editors of *Transnational Feminism*, for example, view women's cinema as particularly well placed in taking on the dilemmas of transnational cinema: themes of borders and border identity, displacement, fragmentation, otherness. But they go further and argue, "Transnational feminism, in our understanding, is not a decorative addition or an optional perspective that can be applied to studies of transnational media but an acknowledgement that transnational processes are inherently gendered, sexualized, and racialized."[15] The implication here is not only that given women's position as a silenced, abject subject, women's cinema in fact is particularly well placed in taking on the dilemmas of transnational cinema that revolve around the themes of borders and border identity, displacement, fragmentation, otherness, and so on. Their statement argues for an epistemological shift that establishes the issues of transnational women's cinema as a necessary framework in understanding the dynamics of "transnational imaginary."

Establishing the grounds for this epistemological shift, however, also exposes its fundamental dilemma. If the value of women's films in the transnational framework seems indisputable, the conditions under which women's films do and can become visible raise more problematic questions. That is, to what extent does a woman's film which achieves festival success conform either to the generic conventions of auteur and art cinema, or the more plural category of "woman's cinema," thus falling into the danger of being reduced to a women's cause or agenda? If transnational women's films effectively explore the underside of borders and displacement, to what extent is there a risk that both the filmmakers and the audiences become mere border tourists? Underlining these questions is a contentious relationship in such cinema between transnational modernizing forces that are aligned with "universal" feminism and the "politics of location" which may resist such globalizing forces.

It is precisely this dilemma, the disputed relationship between the universal and local, that is most instructive in examining the work of Balkan women filmmakers whose transnational productions have gained recognition at prestigious international film festivals. On a more immediate level, it reveals the nature of the relationship between their decade-long silence and their current visibility. The Balkan War is a particularly interesting example because it is seen as the first modern war that was an explicitly gendered war. Rape, while always a "bad and inevitable side effect" of any war, was here an officially outlined strategy of ethnic cleansing, systematically used as an essential tool in warfare. Far from being random occurrences, rapes occurred not only on a massive scale but were institutionalized by an efficient apparatus of numerous rape camps that often escaped the myopic vision of human rights watch-groups. It was this explicit use of rape as warfare that finally prompted the UN International Criminal Tribunal in the Hague (1996), for the first time in history, to clearly define rape as a war crime (this was unprecedented, since this was the first time that a gender-related crime is specifically treated, without any other charges, as war crime). On the one hand, women filmmakers' projects in the Balkans were thus buried underground on the local level by the intense gendering of nationalism that provided the ideological impetus for use of rape as a strategy of war. On the other hand, they were buried on a global level, ironically, by the involvement of high-profile feminists like Catherine MacKinnon and Beverly Allen who, while making Balkan women's issues visible on a global stage, diverted attention away from equally important issues of suffering by women (displacement, lost children, homelessness, complete loss of means of survival) and from local voices.[16]

On a broader level, this framework reveals how the women filmmakers not only construct a radically different vision of the Balkan war and address its fundamentally gendered nature, but how they deploy cinema in order to rethink the role of the signifier of the nation in the discourse of world cinema. The work of women filmmakers like Žbanić, Begić, and Weiss seems to circle precisely around the divide between the postulates of universal feminism and problems posed by specific local conditions—a divide that determines their reception as well as their textual politics. The films received positive reception and were embraced by international audiences because they talked about the specific conditions of Balkan women in universal terms that in many ways addressed and catered to the expectations of women's cinema that circulates on a global stage. Clearly targeted to international audience, they seem to address the demands of universal feminism by recuperating the female voice under the huge pile of masculine rubble of war and reveal and critique the strong patriarchal community they are a part of. However, their aesthetic, while commanding the attention of international gaze, also displaces it, making difficult if not impossible the viewer's quasi-documentary or ethnographic engagement with the image, without disavowing its indexical quality.

Jasmila Žbanić and *Grbavica*

Jasmila Žbanić's *Grbavica* directly addresses "the elephant in the room" that seemed to be ignored for so long, the massive rape of Bosniak women as part of ethnic cleansing efforts, the devastating condition of women as a consequence, as well as a whole generation of unwanted children that are material products of the rapes. Žbanić softens this unspeakable event by framing it in a personal story that is more acceptable for international context, a story of mother who is a victim of war rapes and her struggles with a love/hate relationship with a child who is a product of that rape—her story is an exception, not a rule, since an overwhelming majority of women in Esma's situation either had abortions, or killed or abandoned their children after birth. Set in the present-day, famous, Sarajevo neighborhood of Grbavica that was converted into a rape camp during the war, the film uses vivid simplicity and simple realist style to address the identity of the women for whom the war is an immediate reality and who have to reconcile the banal everyday with memories of the past, and on the other hand the identity of the young postwar generation for whom the war is an indirect but necessary source of identification.

Underneath this surface accessibility, however, *Grbavica* is infused with representational and aesthetic tactics that scrape the veneer of this surface and reveal a structure that is at once enticingly complex and evasive, built on gaps, silences, and absences rather than on the materiality of visual depictions. The film's quasi-narrative structure is rough, hesitant, replicating not the structure of events but the difficult process of recovering memory, as well as the difficult process of translating this embodied memory into the logic of narrative and the demands of the international gaze. The memory of the past is buried deep and inaccessible to the viewer, and Žbanić never invokes the past either by means of flashbacks or any other visual representations of war, although it is felt as a constant presence that shapes the experience of the film. If the unattractive and difficult combination of letters that make up the word Grbavica (the etymologically meaning of which is a woman with a hump) is meant to offer an insight into Esma's inner world by giving "a very good sound picture" of it, as the director remarked, it also makes clear that it is this suppressed inner world (suppressed visually and in terms of narrative plot) that will come to mark the film more than what is directly shown. This embodied memory constantly remains at a level beneath the realm of speech and communication, placing the film in a paradox of commanding our gaze and needing to communicate something that is unreachable both to the self and to others.

This paradox of how Žbanić positions her film vis-à-vis the international gaze is already revealed in a distinctly nonnarrative opening sequence. Opening with a static shot of a luxurious hand-woven carpet, a pattern at once asymmetric and coherent, the camera begins a slow and surreal pan, revealing first the disembodied hands and legs, and then the stillness of women's intertwined bodies that recalls the image of mass graves. Much like the complex, intricate pattern of a rug, the women are defined by their singularity but connected into a complex textile of their own. The shot pans slowly to Esma and focuses on her face as she opens her eyes and gazes straight into the camera. Esma's gaze poses a challenge for spectators and lays the foundation for the chief challenge of the film: to elicit empathy with Esma, but from a distance that doesn't flatten her into a one-dimensional victim. Commanding our attention, Esma's gaze is also decidedly confrontational, reinforcing the tension between the need to communicate and the pressure of silence.

In one of the most powerful and disturbing moments in the film that takes place during a group therapy session, one woman's tragic description of her painful experience is accompanied by another woman's hysterical laughter, which only gets louder and more hysterical as the therapist tries to quiet her down and remind the women that "being closed up is the worst thing you can do," and that "talking is the first step toward healing." Soon, all the women, including the therapist, join in a collective laughter. In this scene, strikingly reminiscent of Marleene Gorris's *Question of Silence* (1982), the collective laughter is anything but crazy. It shows rather that for these women who have been traumatized, marginalized, and left without the possibility to reconstruct their lives, "telling a story" is not like opening a shoe box. Reflecting Žbanić's hesitation to let the coded structure of the filmic narrative define her utterance, these women's laughter is laughter of resistance, laughter at the absurdity of imposing a coded, rigid, institutional language on an experience that defies such language. Esma's struggle to reconcile the unspeakable experience of the past with a clearly coded and structured routine of group therapy thus reflects the viewer's struggle to reconcile the realism and simplicity of language that depicts her everyday life with the unattainable and elusive one that ultimately marks the film. Interestingly, while clearly targeting her film to international audiences, Žbanić insisted on an international release title, *Grbavica*, that is inaccessible and difficult even to an insider, and defies the attractive and romantic promise of "the land of dreams." Likewise, her film insists that we contend with the unknown, foreign, terrifying territory of its text without the possibility of assembling it into a familiar structure.

Aida Begić and *Snow*

A similar textual strategy is at work in Aida Begić's *Snow*, an Iranian coproduction that recalls the work of Makmalbaf sisters. Set over the course of seven days in a small village in Eastern Bosnia in 1997, *Snow* shows the lives of six women whose families were killed, their bodies never found, so the village is under the spell of mourning that cannot end. Their lives are very much defined by mourning, but they have also moved beyond this frozen historical moment and are actively involved in transforming their lives by producing and selling jams and chutneys. The film revolves largely around the detailed visual depictions of their daily routines of making jams, weaving, praying, and the communal spirit required by this process, but at the same it depicts irreconcilable differences between women. Begić shows nicely how for these women, remarkable in their solidarity and singularity, the issue is not so much how to survive; they're already making their mark, their "authorial inscription" just needs to be heard, seen, recognized. Hence, the title of the film: for Begić, the significance of snow lies not in the fact that it covers the ground and transforms reality, but in this authorial inscription, in the fact that in snow, all beasts (as she says) can leave a visible trail and put themselves on the map.

Again, however, while the film seems firmly placed within the obligatory mode of realist narrative, and while it frames the historical and cultural specificity of its story within the paradigms of universal feminism, its representational and aesthetic strategies question both of these frameworks. Similarly to *Grbavica*, the film refuses to offer any spatial, national, or contextual aesthetic markers that tend to be so crucial to the process of reading and decoding the "foreignness" in a foreign film. The town or the larger community is never shown, with the exception of a few dilapidated buildings and house interiors, and the relationship between the women and children in a large extended family, while seemingly crucial for the narrative, is never explained.

Most notable perhaps is Begić's use of magic realism, which displaces and undermines, rather than complements, the realist narrative: a recurring sequence in which Alma twists her beautiful veil while walking, washes herself at a fountain, and carries a cup of water and towel to the prayer site; the mystery of the little boy's growing hair; the prayer rug which Nana throws over the water to form a floating bridge as they walk to the site of the mass grave. In these sequences, the boundaries between the world of magic realism and realism, between dreamscapes and landscapes, between physical and metaphysical are never drawn, never explained. Trying to establish the coordinates the film seems to promise becomes as difficult as the game of pantomime that the film opens with, where meaning is to be reconstructed not from the tangible, the visible and audible, but from the often unreadable gestures that can be understood only in the intimate and internal world of the characters. It is the elusive poetry of every day that takes precedence over contextual markers of space, time, and event, and makes the film inviting but ultimately evasive and impossible to accommodate within familiar (either feminist or national) paradigms.

Maja Weiss and *Guardian of the Frontier*

Maja Weiss in her *Guardian of the Frontier* similarly uses the function of a woman's narrative to complicate the assumptions of realism. Hers is an explicitly political project: she not only explores the possibilities of a woman's cinema and its role in (re)discovering and (re)building a nation, but also projects her film outward and beyond the nation, and then deploys the female narrative to expose the very homophobic, nationalist, and racist discourses that this transnational community is supposed to have transcended. In her film, a new transnational imaginary implies not only a different understanding of "frontiers" that define the nation, but a "transformation of perspective," to put it in Elsaeeser's terms, a different way of seeing, a different way of conceiving a relationship between the spectator and an image. While showing the necessarily gendered nature of the nation-building project, she also shows that controlling women's voices is as much about controlling the structure of the nation as it is about controlling and drawing borders that represent it in the broader sphere.

The film, promoted by the festival circuit as the female *Deliverance*, is embedded in the traditionally male genres of a road movie and psychological thriller, where bracketing the foundations of the genre has implications both for our understanding of cinematic conventions as well as our understanding of forces that provide the basis for the project of nation building. On the surface the film is a simple story of three young women friends who, during their semester break, decide to canoe down the Kolpa River, on the border between Slovenia and Croatia. The three women are rather stereotypical representations of different poles of female subjectivity: Simona is very traditional, introverted, kind, romantic, and naïve in her perceptions of relationships; Žana is strong, daring, direct, extroverted, manlike in her posture and attitude; and Alja possesses qualities of both, torn in between the two poles. When they head down the river along the recently ravaged Croatian border, news of a girl murdered by a serial killer heightens the tension brewing beneath the idyllic landscape and peaceful villages. As the relationship and differences between them intensifies—Simona becomes haunted by the visions of "the King of the Forest," and the sexual tensions between Žana and Alja escalate into a full blown affair—they become tormented by a "Guardian of the Frontier," a man in many guises who keeps reappearing to monitor their behavior and to make sure that all the frontiers—spatial, social, gender, and racial—remain safely in place.

The road, the staple iconographic feature of the road movie, is here substituted by the Kolpa, whose flow still indicates some kind of a forward movement, although this slow movement seems rather regressive, not transcending borders and limitations of space but moving us slowly yet surely toward numerous—physical and mental—border zones. If this is a border-crossing film, those borders are internal as much as they are external, and the film can be seen as a journey from image to image, where the final image is stripped naked with all the fears and frontiers out in the open. And if it relies on the psychological-thriller genre to build the suspense in the conventional way, it places the reasons for that suspense in the magical and supernatural, so that it is often unclear what is real event and what is fantasy.

The distinct yet closely interconnected spaces—landscape and mindscape—are established from the very beginning by Weiss's technique of constructing a complex visual space. On the one hand, the borders that the film invokes and the discourses of power that enforce them are depicted in a very literal manner; they are tangible and an essential part of the women's journey. The river Kolpa itself is a border between Slovenia and Croatia, and the women deliberate in one of the early scenes the consequences of swimming across it. Soon after they set off on their canoe trip, they are stopped at a police roadblock. Later, they stand next to a sign announcing the border between Slovenia and Croatia, and take pictures. As they transport their canoe across the river, they notice a group of refugees crossing the river, and we later see the same group being chased by the police. All these frontiers and institutions of power behind them are literally embodied by the "Guardian of the Frontier," sometimes simply called the "Great Man" or the "Great Slovenian," an ominous figure who keeps reappearing in different locations and different roles (a fisherman, a policeman, a hunter, and a nationalist politician preaching about the need to keep Slovenia "pure"), and who is at war with anything that appears to be unconventional or "unnatural." However, while these literal borders are present everywhere the women go, they are not the frontiers really affecting or obstructing their journey. In fact, the women readily and fearlessly dismiss them and ridicule them; they daringly swim across the river, jokingly dismiss Alja's boyfriend and father's warnings about the serial killer, dismiss the presence of the Guardian as "just a hunter" or "just a normal man," and dismiss the threat of police activity as chasing "after the refugees, not us."

However, the deeper they are into their nature-inspired journey—freeing themselves from the confines of their everyday life, relationships and institutions, exploring their desires and their sexuality and revealing their naked bodies to the sun—the more the threats presented by the frontiers assert themselves into the visual field and into their (and our) unconscious, moving back and forth from the real and the imaginary. And as these frontiers start blurring the distinction between reality and fantasy, and the discourse of the nation becomes entangled with the discourse on gender, sexuality, and family, we also witness a breakdown in the ontological status of the image, where it becomes impossible to distinguish real events from fantasy and mythical stories.

The correspondence between landscape and mindscape, physical and mental borders, which reveals how nationalist discourse becomes effective through the connection between physical politics of inclusion and exclusion (border drawing) and discursive, representational practices (which cinema is an important part of), is effectively announced by the opening sequence. Panning across the idyllic, lush green landscape, without being attached to a specific subjective point of view, the opening shot slowly zooms in on a shoe in the water. This zoom-in, combined with the eerie, mystical soundtrack, disturbs the neutrality of the transcendental gaze, and as it assumes the subjective perspective despite its nonattachment, it establishes the place as a haunted, ominous, and uncanny one. This opening scene is immediately followed by a shot of our female protagonist traveling, sitting in a fast-moving train, with camera in her hands, and there is Western music in the background. As Doro Wiese points out in his analysis of the film, this visual and aural construction of the sequence points to a person missing from the frame, someone who must have explored and tried to conquer the depicted "virgin" territory before, but failed, carried away by the river. In *Guardian of the Frontier*, he says, "the nation originates in a loss, as the first sign of human life refers to a missing person."[17] If the three female characters are seen as claiming the traditional male role of traveling, exploring, discovering, conquering the land, these uncanny elements "refer to the threat imposing itself to their claim, to the fact that this ought to be prevented." The missing person is thus turned into a "symbol of punishment for crossing a border," forcing a question: "Which cultural differences are silenced, doomed to remain invisible or sentenced to death for the purpose of nation building?"[18]

It is this uncanny, both real and imaginary, threat, that ultimately determines the narrative trajectory and proves crucial to the nation-building enterprise. The sense of danger cast by the subjective camera-eye and music in the opening scene cast a shadow on the women's adventure that is real yet empty and devoid of any tangible "evidence." As Žana breaks the first "border policy" and swims across the river to the Croatian side, the music brings back the sense of the uncanny despite the fact that nothing happens. With every warning, unfounded as it may be, the visual and acoustic elements build "something" that presents a threat of violence to the women. The more they dismiss every sign of danger and turn it into a joke, the more they are captivated by these signs, and the empty and undetermined threats nevertheless start affecting their journey and their behavior. It ceases to matter whether these threats are merely empty signifiers; real or imaginary, literal or discursive; they set up a firm structure that regulates their behavior, their sexuality, their subjectivity.

As the lines between the physical and discursive borders of the nation begin to blur, and as the difference between real and imaginary threats begins to break down, we also witness a breakdown in the ontological status of the image, where it becomes impossible for the viewer to locate themselves in the diegetic space of the film and maintain even a minimal distinction between real events, fantasy, and mythical stories. In the second part of the film, Simona becomes completely entangled in the magical story of the "King of the Forest," a mythical figure in one of Alja's tales who makes fireflies to put a spell on virgins to keep them under his power. This mythical tale mixed with the murder story, Simona's visions of the Guardian and her fantasies about men on the one hand, and escalating sexual relations between Alja and Žana on the other, end up in a series of disorienting sequences that blend the fantastic and the real, the violent and adventurous. This displacement climaxes in the most unsettling sequence, where the three women wander into a folk festival with the townspeople drinking and dancing, and the Guardian (this time as a politician) preaching about family values, the danger of refugees, and the basic principles of the nation (family is sacred, mothers have to stay home, and homosexuality is a sin). The women eventually flee this collective expression of nationalist longing, and a crosscutting, dreamlike sequence advances several contradictory scenarios: Simona is shown leaving her tent, and as Alja and Žana are having sex, Simona's sexual fantasy turns into a surreal scene with her in a traditional costume, surrounded by water, fire, dancing, and the Guardian's bizarre sexual advances.

If up to this point some semblance of time and space continuum was maintained, this sequence finally forces an ontological switch, and the question of what happened—was Simona raped, as she later claims, or did she construct this fantasy to cope with Žana and Alja's relationship—becomes impossible and redundant. Although the women record all the events on camera and rely on this photographic evidence to determine and restore the "real," it turns out that the film was spoiled and the status of reality that so depends on the indexical quality of the image is forever suspended. The moment of "recognition" that the final song speaks of never arrives, and is never established by the visual apparatus of the film. Not only is there no evidence of what happened during their journey, but once back in their old setting, the women seem to return to their old subjectivities and prejourney relationships.

However, if the three characters, despite their adventures, remain complicit in the project of the nation, unable to alter its discursive structure, it is the working of the camera that frees us from its bounds and offers us freedom to explore new ways of seeing and new possibilities of thinking. As Wiese nicely concludes, the film's "staging of an unpleasant and unacceptable camera perspective entices the viewers to de-identify themselves, so that they can read the very fabric of power: a de-identification that is not a freedom *from*, but a freedom *to* recognize mechanisms of subjectification."[19]

Further, I would argue, the women filmmakers discussed here not only construct female subjectivity as one that refuses to be contained within the tangible concepts of "womanhood," but they use what may be called "feminine aesthetic" to problematize dominant tropes of visibility and to suggest a new transnational imaginary. Contrary to the majority of films that defined the 1990s, their aesthetic serves not so much as a historical statement (though foreign films are most often perceived in this vein)—as just another, updated vision of the former Yugoslav region—but rather as a platform to open up a discussion about world cinema vis-à-vis certain kinds of "foreignness" that cannot be easily translated into familiar paradigms of knowledge, that refuse to make foreignness into what Marziniak has called "palatable foreignness."[20]

That transcending the national is an essential component of debates about the transitional and transnational processes in the region is a proposition that can be taken for granted. But, the films discussed here point to the necessity of moving beyond the usual markers (geopolitical or textual) of "transnationalism" and the obvious context of transnational production and circulation. Transnational in these films is not so much a spatial category, involving either journeying, migration, or question of borders. In fact, these films remain confined within a rather limited geopolitical space. Here, transnational space is marked instead by a viewing space, a visual territory that dislocates the viewer from her familiar viewing position and introduces a new, foreign territory that has to be contended with from within its "foreignness," rather than from the outside looking in. Dudley Andrew has argued that a study of world cinema should put the viewer "inside unfamiliar conditions of viewing rather than bringing the unfamiliar handily to them," that it should "let us know the territory differently"; the viewer's strategy of mapping becomes a strategy not of orientation but disorientation.[21] Such a methodological and spectatorial stance, while certainly imperative, is difficult to envision when the discourse of international film festivals still places world cinema on familiar grounds. By showing how the process of transition is not an internal or regional matter but involves an epistemological switch that is positioned in the in-between of local and global, young women auteurs from the former Yugoslav region seem to be breaking new ground that makes this theoretical stance vis-à-vis world cinema into a tangible and necessary film experience.

Part VI

The New National Literatures

14

Traumatic Experiences
War Literature in Bosnia and Herzegovina Since the 1990s
Davor Beganović

There are two crucial texts by Sigmund Freud that can relocate contemporary Bosnian literature in a completely new light. These two intricate essays deal with states of mind and soul, particularly in extreme situations. They could be relatively easily uncoupled from the individual, and interwoven with society and its secondary manifestation in particular (culture, for example). Those two essays are, of course, "Beyond the Pleasure Principle" (1917) and "Mourning and Melancholy" (1920). How do these concrete scientific treatises influence, penetrate, or describe Bosnian literature and culture as a whole? Is it not far-fetched to think that two nearly century-old texts resonate in modern, contemporary culture, giving it an impetus, a push to move forward, to repeat patterns of loss obsessively, matrices of mourning and paradigms of suffering that would leave lasting traces on the subject—individuals as well as a collective? I cannot come close to analysing all the details of Freud's complex thought elaborated in these two essays that entered European civilisation as a reformulation of ancient medical teaching. The aim of my paper is to trace, only briefly, the way in which Freud transformed concepts of trauma and melancholy and then to try to connect this transformation with its concrete manifestation in Bosnian culture (especially literature) during the war and in its aftermath.

As is well known, trauma is a medical term for a physical wound, used extremely broadly in Greek medical theory. The slow path from this general concept of bodily injury (which is still maintained in the name *trauma clinic*) to the narrower sense of psychical disorder can be seen as paralleling the development of so-called modern societies. Cathy Caruth shows that the domestication of medical concepts in the field of cultural studies happens through a paradoxical turn that was constructed by Freud himself.[1] His example of traumatic behaviour is not a concrete patient, but a literary figure—Tancred from Tasso's *Jerusalem Liberated*. Freud describes the scene as follows: "Its Hero, Tancred, unwittingly kills his beloved Clorinda in a duel while she is disguised in the armour of an enemy knight. After her burial he makes his way into a strange magic forest which strikes the Crusaders' army with terror. He slashes with his sword at a tall tree; blood streams from the cut and the voice of Clorinda, whose soul is imprisoned in the tree, is heard complaining that he has wounded his beloved once again." This initial affinity between art and medicine ultimately advanced to become almost exclusively an object of cultural studies analyses. The medical approach to trauma was "reduced" to a level of secondary realization. But let me move a step forward and ask if there is an intrinsic affinity between the structure of a narrative and the structure of consciousness of so-called *Unfall Neurotiker* (accident neurotic): clearly, there is: consider *Wiederholungszwang*, repetition compulsion. It seems to me that Freud's central reflection pointing in this direction is contained in the following sentence: "But we come now to a new and remarkable fact, namely that the compulsion to repeat also recalls from the past experiences which include no possibility of pleasure, and which can never, even long ago, have brought satisfaction even to instinctual impulses which have since been repressed."[2] Is there a connection between this repetition, from which any sort of pleasure is excluded, and a narrative, which is always centred on pleasure? I would say yes, and add that this repetition forms the very characteristic of modern literature. Now, I would ask you to memorize Freud's sentence before I move to his second text that I think is important with regard to contemporary Bosnian literature.

"Mourning and Melancholy" and "Beyond the Pleasure Principle" are closely connected with World War I, though the wounds are positioned differently. Whereas the former essay analyses psychological disorders of physically wounded persons, the latter differentiates between two affects. One is normal (*Trauer*, mourning) and the second one pathological (*Melancholie*, melancholy). The mourning develops after a loss. Mostly it is the loss "of a loved person, or the loss of some abstraction which has taken the place of one, such as one's country, liberty, an ideal and so on."[3] In connection with this, mourning is dependent on the passage of time: it is assumed that, under normal circumstances, mourning can be overcome and the affected person can find his or her way back into normality. Under certain preconditions, mourning can last longer—this could lead to a disorder that should be denoted as a psychic disorder. It is a disease which Freud, in an analogy with ancient temperament theory, calls "melancholy." His definition, or rather the enumeration of its symptoms, reads as follows: "The distinguishing mental features of melancholia are a profoundly painful dejection, cessation of interest in the outside world, loss of the capacity to love, inhibition of all activity, and a lowering of self-regarding feelings to a degree that finds utterance in self-reproaches and self-revilings, and culminates in a delusional expectation of punishment."[4] All but one of these qualities—the disruption of ego (*Selbstgefühl*)—are, according to Freud, also contained in the feeling of mourning. But what separates melancholy from mourning is, on the one hand, its obstinacy in defying loss and, on the other, its persistence in the unconscious. Freud again: "In yet other cases one feels justified in maintaining the belief that a loss of this kind has occurred, but one cannot see clearly what it is that has been lost, and it all the more reasonable to suppose that the patient cannot consciously perceive what he has lost either."[5] Another distinction is to be sought in the division between "who" and "what." The patient can know who is lost, but not exactly *what* in this *who* is not present anymore. Now this loss in substance leads to a lack of knowledge, which is the ground of melancholy: "This would suggest that melancholia is in some way related to an object-loss which is withdrawn from the consciousness, in contradistinction to mourning in which there is nothing about the loss that is unconscious."[6]

I will stop here and concentrate my attention on one annoying fact. While Freud makes extensive use of culture in the "trauma text," the cultural dimension of melancholy is almost obsolete in the other essay. How can I make this discrepancy useful for my own conceptualization of the double origin of postwar Bosnian-Herzegovinian literature? First of all, let me return to the coincidence of Freud's two texts with the event of World War I. It is impossible to overlook that there is a close connection between Freud's writing and the slaughterhouse of Europe between 1914 and 1918. In a strikingly analogous development, if I may use this word, the literature in Bosnia and Herzegovina shows exactly these two dominating features as a discursive paradigm: on the one side, there are narratives of trauma; on the other, those of melancholy. This is not an accident, nor did it happen by chance. In the tradition of Yugoslav literatures dealing with World War I, there is a clear tendency toward thematizing traumatic or melancholic events as a source of narratives. The first indication of this is an inauguration of the topos of nonrepresentability as the rhetorical nodal point. So-called realistic literature always made the claim of having a direct approach to atrocities. The modernists, after their personal experience with a "modern kind of warfare," tried to find another mode of representation that escaped the traps of drastic images but was still able to communicate the pictures of mutilated, decayed bodies of men.

The first means of this mode of representation is, certainly, the grotesque, the specific mixture of horror and humour of which is almost the ideal device for concealment, hiding, and suppression of the scandalous and terrible precisely by its transposition into a new narrative world that is able to uncover the pseudorationality of warfare and its mendacious character. In a paradoxical turn, these "alternative" narratives mutate—in their capability for distance reduction—into realistic and mimetic representation par excellence. Dignity, which gives bodies individual independence, is withdrawn. They are grotesquely disfigured, declared disabled, and left in a state of dissemination. The most prominent example of such a narrative is *The Croatian God Mars* (*Hrvatski bog Mars*, 1924) by Miroslav Krleža. The novellas in this collection, besides their strong socialist engagement connected with criticism of dying Austro-Hungarian monarchy, use the poetics of expressionism to describe the atrocity of war and its consequences for the people involved in it. All of them deal with small peasants from Croatian hinterland that became the victims of social and economic injustice. In the precarious time they are used as cannon fodder, misused as pawns in the game of foreign empires.

If this strategy is to be bound to trauma, there is another one that I would associate with melancholy, one characterized by a phenomenon that I call "poetization of represented reality." The paradigmatic texts illustrating this approach are two small volumes by Ivo Andrić, *Ex ponto* (1918) and *Restlessness* (*Nemiri*, 1920). As distinct from Krleža's avant-garde literature connected with Russian revolution and German expressionism, Andrić's two lyrical texts deal with his personal experience during World War I. A member of the Mlada Bosna (Young Bosnia) organization, which was directly responsible for the assassination of Archduke Ferdinand in Sarajevo in 1914, he was first imprisoned and then interned in the Bosnian province, where he stayed, under house arrest, until the end of the war. He dealt with this experience in highly elaborated and complex prose poems in which there is a feeling of melancholy. The "angst" in these pieces is generated by the lyrical self's being captured in extremely narrow space, left alone with their own time (which is abundant). The time is transformed into an endless circulation leading to apocalyptic and melancholic reflections and meditations. The narrativization of the plot and events is moved into the psyche of the protagonists, time is suspended and brought to a standstill. In such a constellation, the role of space becomes the central modelling principle of the narrative. Andrić proves himself a master of this perspective, becoming a creator of war literature whose theme is not war as such or even at all.

Before I fast-forward more than seventy years to contemporary Bosnia and Herzegovina, I will provide a short summary of the interim. In the years during World War I and immediately after, Sigmund Freud wrote two papers on a new contextualization of physical loss—trauma and melancholy. Both of them are influential in literature and cultural studies, both crucially touching on the problems emerging in the aftermath of war. Literature itself reacted in a similar way. My two examples bear witness to the appropriation of melancholic and traumatic discourse as two modelling approaches in a representation of menacing reality threatening to dissipate the body and to disintegrate the individual. Seen in retrospect, the "task" of literature dealing with the civil war in Bosnia and Herzegovina (I am using this highly controversial denotation of the war act for the sake of simplicity) was a cyclic attempt at the art of classic modernism created in the aftermath of World War I. At the same time, it was a breach with war literature that only dealt with the myths of nation building, conservation, and fixation of given and prescribed traditions. Or, even more bluntly, one can interpret this literature as openly polemical with regard to the literary experiences of a former generation (namely the one that emerged during World War II and immediately after it), as an experiment in enthronization of its literature during the civil war in Bosnia. These are aesthetically valueless or misshapen texts, on the one hand, which tend to claim to possess the one and only historical truth, on the other.

Two dominant genres in the contemporary literature of Bosnia and Herzegovina should support my somewhat daring thesis. Riccardo Nicolosi's name for the first genre is "the literature of besieged Sarajevo."[7] I would characterize the other genre, with reservations, as that dedicated to the trauma of the warrior. Returning now to my cyclic conceptualization of Yugoslav literary history, I associate the first genre with Andrić's space-oriented, poetological conceptual and the second one with Krleža's poetological concept that postulates time as the highest principle of construction in literary aesthetics.

To further differentiate between the two, a very important distinction can be found in their approach to the problem of space or, more accurately, the set of problems concerning topography. The Sarajevo narratives are topographic, while the trauma text is more temporal. Space assumes a central position by focusing on claustrophobic narrowing. It becomes an attribute of the world that is closed—in itself and by itself at the same time. This is a world that is also in a state of change, transforming from the place of intimacy into the place of foreignness; through this alternation, it becomes what Michel Foucault calls a heterotopy.[8] The change that the familiar landscape experienced is so essential that it is almost impossible to recognize it. Its new configuration or, more precisely, disfigurement, turned it into a certain negative object of art that is aesthetically drained but not refilled with ethical substance. The prose on besieged Sarajevo acts in a moral sense. It is not interested in positing an ethical statement concerning guilt or punishment. If it does, such ethical perspective is on the margins, in occasional reflection on the destruction, fury, and ruthlessness of besiegers and their principles.

The concentration on space has further consequences. The individual's dealing with his or her psychological condition are left almost unconsidered, a fact that brought the charge of alleged insensibility with regard to many of these authors. It is often forgotten, however, that this conversion of psychologisation means a consequent denial of postulates of classical modernism and the Yugoslav prose of the 1960s, dominated by existentialist discourse, above all Sartre's and Camus'. When Semezdin Mehmedinović, Aleksandar Hemon, Miljenko Jergović, or Alma Lazarevska removed the last traces of realism from their characters and left them to act in a world void of significance, they not only aimed to performatively express their powerlessness before the eruption of war's horrors, but they tried to create a new paradigm, one capable of presenting the emotion of hopelessness in a concrete form. In this respect the war exercised a liberating impact on the young Bosnian literature. The canonized and prescribed models were displaced by new ones, oriented toward topographical, postmodernist literary forms, and this in turn led to the exclusion of the old tradition.

What happened with the model inherited from Krleža? What happened to the authors who preferred the representation of war from the warrior's perspective? The second form of narrative dominating Bosnian literature is set in two places: on the front and in the mental institution. Since the war's front line in general is drawn and situated outdoors, claustrophobia is suspended and the feeling of displeasure and resentment is relocated in the protagonist's inner life. It is therefore possible to detect in this literary genre a stronger focus on the psychological factor, which consequently provides space for the discursive representation of trauma. Trauma, as already shown by Freud in "Beyond the Pleasure Principle," has narrative potential, found in the structure of repetition—primarily compulsive repetition. For Freud, as we have seen, the repetition of plot is most important. Yet the narratology is significant too, because the plot that is repeated tends to abolish the linearity. This is precisely the central component of the postwar Bosnian prose dealing with the "trauma of the warrior."

Two exemplary authors I will shortly consider are Josip Mlakić and Faruk Šehić, both of whom participated in and witnessed the war. They have tried to make their experiences present to the public but, at the same time, tried to avoid the autobiographical prose model as much as possible. This way of representation is consistent with a specific commitment to their individual and collective identity. According to Margot Norris: "Readers of twentieth century war writing enter into communion with acts of witnessing that entail both psychological and ethical risks, as well as ontological and ethical responsibilities. The crudest negative risks—of having representations of violence exciting pleasure, or having images of cruelty feed what Michael André Bernstein calls, 'an appetitive fascination with evil'—are most often incurred by war writing that is not testimonial in structure or intention."[9] Josip Mlakić innovatively describes this double inability. His narrator is conscious that he can find the way out of his trauma only by constructing a coherent narrative. Therefore he tries to tell his story. The attempts are unsuccessful because they can only be formulated in a fragmented form. The narrator approaches the moment of nonrepresentability of trauma or a traumatic event. In the hospital he is treated with mixed speech and writing therapy. The psychiatrist tries to approach his trauma with a persistent in-depth search for the initial event that triggered the character running amok. But the narrator continually denies an appropriate answer and involves his analyst in an intricate cat-and-mouse game. What is denied to the doctor in the notebooks appears openly in "dialogue" with the reader. The mixture of emotions and insights gives an opportunity for interpretation of the traumatic effect that war events have on the "heroes":

I can't describe it better; I'll try to make it clear in this way: in your vicinity dies a man, you don't know even his name. At first you feel nothing, except fear that this could have happened to you and a certain feeling of emptiness; we were dull as a stone. And then, for example, you see that this man wears a jumper knitted by his wife, mother or sister, and something changes in you. You think about all the people to whom this man means something and who in this moment think of him as if he were alive. At first you feel that you're losing breath, and then that your throat is slowly tightening, and then you feel some sort of bitterness; just, death gets its usual meaning. . . . Just as if you overcome some kind of paralysis and see everything with different eyes: the eyes you had as a normal man who, even if he knew the difference between an automatic and a semiautomatic rifle, didn't think about such stupidities.[10]

When talking with the psychiatrist, the narrator who should be cured cannot heal because he is not able to tell his story in a linear way. As a result, a construction is developed in which trauma itself is repeated (a repetition of repetition). It mimetically mirrors the structure of trauma itself. Unable to deal with it, the narrator dissipates his energy in new, unarticulated fragments, which, in turn, make the therapy, and thus the narrative, collapse.

Faruk Šehić was, like Mlakić, a soldier who, at least partially, represented his own war experiences in his narratives. Moreover, he was seriously wounded in a fight, an autobiographical fact that should be kept in mind if one reflects upon the disgust occasionally emerging from his prose. In this segment, Šehić approaches most clearly the discourse I associate with literary modernism. His narrative is abundant with grotesque and carnivalesque moments; it comprises elements of black humour used to somewhat overcome the horrors the narrator had witnessed. But the horrors still prevail. The following quotation is a representation of the Bosnian slaughterhouse:

With his nail Zgemba scratches human brain from the pie. He tears the pieces with his right hand, dips them in the salt and puts them in his mouth. With fingers of the other hand, from the white sachet (spotted with a mixture of brain and blood) he takes a snack of cottage cheese. His face is sooty from gunpowder. In his lap he holds an automatic rifle, caliber 7.62mm. A couple of minutes ago in this trench sat the "autonomists." Over the battlement a still-hot corpse is bent. Machine-gun fire bisected his breast. I turn him around. From the inside pocket of his parka I take the wallet.

I look at his photo. He had a high brow and thin hair. Big and melancholic eyes. With a sharp edge of the photograph I pick out the pieces of apple from between my teeth.[11]

Is this not what Cathy Caruth postulates at the end of her essay about Alain Resnais' *Hiroshima, mon amour*? Caruth writes: "It is the event of this incomprehension and in our departure from sense and understanding that our own witnessing may indeed begin to take place."[12] In this element is the kernel of differentiation between trauma texts and the matrix inherited from Krleža: minimalism and compactness dominate on the one hand and rhetorical abundance and densification on the other. While Krleža builds one rhetorically determined and dominated world of the grotesque body with great expenditure, Šehić and Mlakić aim for a construction that persuades with its terseness. The world of warriors could be, if one follows their poetics, best expressed with such narrative devices.

Now my theses can be summarized. In the era of modernism, two discourses developed in Yugoslav literatures concerning the war. One of them deals with those not directly involved with the war actions but who feel its consequences retroactively. This is a topographic literature marked with melancholy. The other discourse concentrates on the warrior figure and tries to capture the traumas they carry inside. This is communicated by means of the grotesque or carnivalesque. The literature of Bosnia and Herzegovina from the war spanning from 1992 to 1995 follows and modifies that paradigm: it is split into traumatic and melancholic "branches" that are not clearly divided but that often show elements of hybridity. The most successful works follow and further develop this model.

15

Culture of Memory or Cultural Amnesia
The Uses of the Past in the Contemporary Croatian Novel
Andrea Zlatar-Violić

Introduction:
Changes in the Literary Market (1990–2010)

If Croatian literature in the 1990s was marked by a series of questions—about continuity and discontinuity, about changes in the genre system and the emergence of a new poetics—contemporary Croatian literature is characterized by a steady output, predominantly of novels and short story collections. Poetic production is considerable in terms of its range, while its quality is perhaps higher than that of prose; however it is marginalized, especially in the media. While this does not detract from its symbolic value, poetic texts, and generally spoken drama as well, have a significantly smaller readership.[1]

The Croatian Ministry of Culture receives nearly two thousand applications for the cofinancing of books every year—a lot for a country of some four million inhabitants. Despite the ministry's support for authors and its policy of buying books, and although significant numbers of titles are published, it is clear that the publishing industry is not autonomous. The main reason for this is that, save for the partial efforts of the larger publishers, there has been a failure to restore the distribution network after it was destroyed in the 1990s.

Cultural columns are gradually disappearing from daily newspapers; either that, or they overlap with "lifestyle" items or scandals connected with the entertainment industry. On public television channels, features about culture are reduced to minimal "cultural news" items, while they never even existed on commercial stations. It would be hard to describe more than a handful of writers as professional "literary critics"; literary criticism has become a secondary and irregular activity limited to literary magazines with print runs numbering just a few hundred. Bestseller lists, and lists of books borrowed from public libraries, are almost invariably topped by translations of international hits, on the whole Anglo-American. *The Secret Life of Hitler? Climate Cataclysm? The Causes of the Global Crisis?* Yes, those are all potential titles of Croatian bestsellers, which can only be outsold by the scandalous memoirs of some celebrity-star. Discussions about the loss of distinction between high- and low-brow literature, about the blossoming of popular genres and "the democratization of writing," and about the relation between literary quality and the large number of nonprofessional publishers, has had one positive effect. It has contributed, namely, to raising the *average* standard of literary production and to forming a relatively stable reading public. People now regularly choose new titles by Croatian authors: Ante Tomić, Miljenko Jergović, Zoran Ferić, Slavenka Drakulić, Julijana Matanović, Ivana Sajko—tried and tested local writers.

Individual Poetics

Although it is reasonable to try to assess new literary titles in terms of their context, and thus to link them with recognizable trends, it seems to me that the key quality of contemporary Croatian literary production is the simultaneous existence of several individual poetics. We could choose to follow the formation of certain groups or identify common denominators (women's writing, war writing); yet the output of many writers, male and female, bears witness to the distinct identity of their literary opus. We can start with the interpretation of novels published in the last few years by Irena Vrkljan, Slavenka Drakulić, and Dubravka Ugrešić, whose writings could be analyzed as "paradigmatic" in the sense of continuity or discontinuity of literary poetics. While Irena Vrkljan (b. 1931) cannot be considered an explicitly feminist writer, her novels may be analyzed within that framework. In her first novel, *Svila, škare* (1984; published in English as *The Silk, the Shears*, 1999), Vrkljan creates a fragmented narrative about her own growth to adulthood, through the prism of specifically female experience, such as emancipation and sexuality, social status and the family, and questions of intellectual and artistic activity. In her second novel, *Marina ili o biografiji* (1986; published in English as *Marina or About Biography*, 1999), she writes the biography of the Russian poet

Marina Tsvetaeva in parallel with the story of her own life. Vrkljan returns to similar themes in her later works, *Pisma mladoj ženi* (*Letters to a Young Woman*, 2003), her intimate essays *Naše ljubavi, naše bolesti* (*Our Loves, Our Ailments*, 2004), and the novels *Zelene čarape* (*Green Stockings*, 2005) and *Sestra, kao iza stakla* (*Sister, as Though Through Glass*, 2006). Through these works, Vrkljan creates an exceptionally coherent opus in which the specifically female narrative voice in her writing is emphasized. The title of her latest work of prose, *Svila nestala, škare ostale* (*The Silk Went, the Scissors Remained*, 2008), clearly refers to the *The Silk, the Shears*, her first novel, published twenty years earlier. This work, too, contains her characteristic narrative procedure, with key moments poetically highlighted, familiar from the novel *The Silk, the Shears*, through *Marina or About Biography*, right up to *Our Loves, Our Ailments*, with its quality of a testimonial.

The opus of writer and journalist Slavenka Drakulić (b. 1948) has from its inception been characterized by the treatment of women's themes, particularly the body and sickness. Following her collection of feminist essays, *Smrtni grijesi feminizma* (*The Deadly Sins of Feminism*, 1984), the cult book of Croatian feminism, Drakulić published the novels *Holorami straha* (1988; published in English as *Holograms of Fear*, 1992), *Mramorna koža* (1989; published in English as *Marble Skin*, 1993), *Božanska glad* (1995; published in English as *The Taste of a Man*, 1996), and *Kao da me nema* (1999; published in English as *As If I Am Not There*, 1999). Drakulić's latest novel, *Frida* (2007; published in English as *Frida's Bed*, 2008), relates in narrative form the artistic and personal biography of the Mexican painter Frida Kahlo.

The central theme of all Drakulić's novels is the female body—from a body exposed to illness to a body devouring out of love and a body subjected to violence. All the basic features of a feminist text are connected in her novels: the female narrative voice speaks from a female perspective about specifically female experience. In addition, in the sense of public engagement, Drakulić takes the emphatically feminist position that every private action is at the same time public. Her narrative interest in Frida Kahlo focuses the theme of the female in the central connections between the body and sickness as trauma, the body and pleasure, the body as the object and subject of artistic expression.

On the other hand, the novel *Baba Jaga je snijela jaje* (2008; published in English as *Baba Yaga Laid an Egg*, 2009), by Dubravka Ugrešić, represents a marked thematic divergence from the novels that preceded it at the end of the 1990s (*Muzej bezuvjetne predaje*, published in English as *The*

Museum of Unconditional Surrender, 2002; *Ministarstvo boli*, published in English as *The Ministry of Pain*, 2007). In it, Ugrešić has abandoned the position of "a first-person narrator in exile." By means of its narrative-essayistic construction, which combines autobiographical narrative, parodic fiction, and ethnological essay, the novel emphasizes Ugrešić's *authorial* impulse to play with narrative stereotypes. Critics on the one hand have characterized it as a compendium of postmodern strategies of writing, and on the other have stressed Ugrešić's interest in transforming both the mythic figure of the Slav Baba Yaga and the stereotype of femininity—and particularly female aging—in contemporary Western culture. Ugrešić's early novel, *Štefica Cvek u raljama života* (1981; published in English in *The Jaws of Life and Other Stories*, 1993), with its fundamental poetic qualities, its parodic tone, and its play with the stereotypes of the love story, could be seen as a precursor of contemporary Croatian urban women's writing. In *Baba Yaga*, too, irony, parody, and witty narration have freed both readers and critics of the burden of thinking about elderly female characters as oppressed subjects, even though the text produces a distinct sense of bitterness.

The Anglo-American popular genre of chick-lit has not inspired an equivalent movement in Croatian literary space, despite initial indications that it would. Postfeminist literary trends are most evident in "marginal" literary genres such as newspaper columns. There are several such columnists in the contemporary Croatian literary scene, all of whom use the first-person narrative: Rujana Jeger, Milana Vuković Runjić, Arijana Čulina, Vedrana Rudan, and Julijana Matanović. All these writers have tried their hand at other genres (novels, short stories), but it is their journalism that has given them a prominent media presence and made them popular with their readership: their collections of journalism are among the most widely read titles on the market. The hatchet that cut chick-lit off from serious literature during the war has not been buried to this day. The conviction that newspaper columns written by female journalists are a lesser form of literature is so strong that even the writers themselves often deny any connection with chick-lit or with postfeminism and feminism as a whole.

The Issue of Continuity in Cultural Space

The basic issue that appears in the cultural space which has since the 1990s been developing on the territory of the countries of ex-Yugoslavia is the issue of continuity or discontinuity. This issue arises on various levels, ranging from the numerous individual poetics that form personal images of the past and generation-formed images, to the issue of "collective memory." This latter is especially significant in the first "post-Yu" period, the 1990s, when media mechanisms and state politics were used to try to create a uniform new image about the cultural memory of a nation, based on a break with the past. This break is visible in several forms: as a selection of the past, as a suppression of the past (a need for amnesia), and as a subsequent creation of a new image of national history.

The cultural symbolic capital in Croatia was created in the 1990s to serve on a formal level as the national representation of the country and the nation. The cultural policy encouraged the production of artistic projects (megaprojects, such as those in film and music or theater performance), which were supposed to create a set of images of a national history, that is, to shape the crucial spaces in Croatian national history.

The basic characteristics of the 1990s are, therefore, the autoreproduction of national cultural space, the suppression of the individual and the collective memory of the Yugoslavian period, and the construction of new memory through a reconstruction of a mythological past.[2]

Literature in Exile: Personal Mechanisms of Memory

A key role in the formation of the right to individual memory of the 1990s was provided by writers in exile or belonging to the political opposition and who in their fiction developed individual texts about the past. In that respect, the writing of Dubravka Ugrešić, Slavenka Drakulić, and Daša Drndić was based on ethical and intellectual issues: how to face recent history in literature? The issue of continuity and discontinuity of literary memory is perhaps most easily demonstrated by analyzing the works of Dubravka Ugrešić. Within her work, the question of inner poetic continuity certainly gets an affirmative answer in the "reading back," but the ironic and the autobiographical have switched places. While in the 1980s the autobiographical was written on the margins of the text, and self-conscious literary devices represented the content itself, now the (auto)irony is an inner point, the starting and the finishing one. The framework of reality within which Dubravka Ugrešić writes during the 1990s is comprised of historic, social, cultural, and political layers. The construction of a "fictional identity," constructed by the ideologies of the newly founded states, is analyzed in *The Culture of Lies* (*Kultura laži*, 1996), a text that is simultaneously shaped by two discourse strategies: reflection and narration. While reflection serves to identify problematic places in the present, the narrative strategy provides Ugrešić with materials from the past for the comparative analysis of analogous regimes. Although ideologically different, the mechanisms of these regimes are the same: Dubravka Ugrešić is predominantly interested in those that reject the past and construct new history to suit the political goals of the new states. "It seems that it was not only fear, the awakened national (and nationalist) sentiment, hatred toward the enemy, jeopardy, the establishment of an autocratic system, media propaganda, and war, that has established a culture of lies. One of the strategies for establishing a culture of lies is the terror of forgetting (they make you forget what you do not remember) and the terror of memory (they make you remember what you do not remember)."[3]

In Dubravka Ugrešić's novel *The Ministry of Pain* the thematic focus is very similar to the motives for the creation of the *Lexicon on YU Mythology* (*Leksikon YU mitologije*, 2005)—everyone brings to the seminar fragments of their past, told in a personal language, in order to renew the space of collective memory, of what could perhaps still be ours, since our language and our country are no longer ours. Only the people are still our people. That familiar plastic bag with blue, red, and white stripes is used as the metaphor for collecting memories, the bag which is a trademark of the refugees.[4] This bag is introduced by the student Meliha:

The plastic bag with red, white, and blue stripes travels around Eastern and Central Europe, perhaps even further, to Russia, and perhaps even further, to India, China, America, around the whole world. This plastic bag is the luggage of the poor: of petty thieves and smugglers; of buyers and middlemen; of people from the flea markets, the drycleaners, the washrooms, and cheap tailor shops; the luggage of the immigrants, refugees, and homeless. In these bags, jackets, T-shirts, and coffee came from Trieste into Croatia, Bosnia, Serbia, Bulgaria, Romania. . . . The plastic bag with red, blue, and white stripes is a nomad, a refugee, a hobo, a master of survival; it crosses borders without a passport and rides the cheapest transportation without a ticket.[5]

Into this imaginary bag, during the first semester, the students put their confessional fragments, bits of their personal lives. The seminar becomes a place of therapeutic practice with the intention to comfort and find one's own identity. What will it be based on? In addition to the common state and the political platform, the foundations of a common language, of joint cultural and historic experience are also missing. How does one build identity based on a literature that no longer exists, on a language that is no longer a single and common one? "I had to find a territory in this madness which would belong equally to all of us and which would be the least painful one. It could only be, I thought, our common past. Because we all had our right to memory taken away from us. With the disappearance of the country, the memory had to be erased as well."[6]

Literary Map, 2000–2010: City and Memory

The voice of the new generation in the second temporal cycle, after 2000, is represented in the novel *Sloboština Barbie* (2008), by Maša Kolanović, whose growing up parallels the development of the new country in transition. Maša Kolanović (b. 1979), by profession a literary scholar, is in this respect a representative figure of *the new age*, the generation that has to reconstruct by itself the cultural memory destroyed in the 1990s. It is a sort of a bildungsroman that takes place during the beginning of the 1990s, which were the war years, the years of political and cultural change. Maša Kolanović writes from the perspective of a young girl, growing up in one of Zagreb's skyscrapers in the neighborhood of Slobuština, whose biggest problem is how to protect her collection of Barbie dolls and their accessories during the war:

The best fun is fucking a bald doll and then, in the middle of it, taking its wig off to put it on your own head!

When Svjetlana's Ken said this to Dea's Barbie, a siren marked the end of the air raid so the game finished, which was just as well because it had started to turn into a farce. A Barbie farce.

Because every time the playing got old, when we had already changed and brushed our Barbies for the thousandth time, when all the intrigues had already been resolved, and our Barbies, sitting at a small tin bar, had finished gossiping with all the other Barbies in the world and its surroundings, Svjetlana's Ken (whom we called Doctor Kajfeš, after the snoring medicine we'd seen in a commercial) would always start doing some pranks, and we would get angry with Svjetlana, laughing our heads off at the same time. There were all kinds of situations. Doctor Kajfeš would love jumping into Barbie's bed uninvited, putting on Barbie's clothes, telling dirty jokes into Barbie's ear (Babe, y'know why they have female workers in candy factories? To make it hard, ha, ha), plant his head onto a Barbie's body or snore loudly to show that the medicines he was selling were not working (hmm, that was really just an excuse to get Barbie to open the door, and then he'd brutally rape her five times before she could say blueberry pie, or sometimes, by mistake, screwberry pie, which would only get him more into it). All of which would not be so terrible if Doctor Kajfeš wasn't the most disgusting Ken that would ever be found in an illustrated history of Kens, if such a book should ever be written. Doctor Kajfeš was not of Mattel race, he was made of some disgusting kind of plastic, and had some disgusting overburned skin color, although he was not a black Ken. But the strawberry to top the cream was that Doctor Kajfeš had one of his eyes slowly falling off and the fingers of his right hand destroyed, bitten off one time when Svjetlana's cousin Marijana was visiting. On that fatal day Svjetlana was bummed because Marijana had destroyed most of her belongings, which were unimpressive to start with. It was a really hard day for Svjetlana. She cried her eyes out because Marijana had not only maimed her Ken, but had also stolen a pair of golden shoes (not made of real gold, of course), passed a glowing hot iron over her small synthetic pair of tights and throughout this horrid episode Svjetlana's mother was yelling at Svjetlana so the poor thing had to continue playing with that stupid little brat who had devastated all the decent things she owned. If on that day Svjetlana didn't wish for a nice little coffin for one to nicely rot in, she never would. I mean, why don't they put an age limit on playing with Barbie dolls? If it says on the Legos that they are not for kids *under three years old*, why *on earth* cannot the same be done for Barbie dolls? They could have it engraved on their bums instead of that stupid *Made in Taiwan*! If someone from Mattel had seen what a three-year-old Marijana had done to Svjetlana's belongings, they would surely have done something to protect that fragile little being from a nervous breakdown.[7]

Maša Kolanović is an ironic narrator but a warm one, voicing a generation that was growing up in a period when the socialist patterns of identity were breaking down, so her ironic narrator observes many changes which she in her young mind puts together in a critical but also humorous way. Literary critics prone to popular culture will find in this novel a lot of material for cultural analysis, from the social and the political context, to the formation of girls' identities. If we put aside other qualities of the novel (a representative of the new type of female writing, playing with forms of popular literature, etc.), the novel, which puts the name of one of Zagreb's neighborhoods (Sloboština) in the very title, gives us the key for the analysis of *space, the physical space*, as a site for transfer of both individual and collective memory. The category of historical time is written into the category of space, especially urban space. The mechanisms of memory in the fiction of Maša Kolanović are linked to metonymic bonds, either dealing with spaces of family and personal intimacy (apartment, room, basement), or culturally marked spaces (city, Novi Zagreb). Literally put, the bodies of the narrator and the characters are those who occupy a space, and the bodies remember spaces which they have occupied; it is the way in which sensorial memory acquires its spatial existence.

Although a newer urban neighborhood, such as Sloboština in Novi Zagreb, in itself has no cultural past, this novel confirms the potential of urbanity as a place of remembering in literature. The city comes into being by its mapping in the text. In the same way, literature comes into being through the subsequent, as well as anticipatory, writing of the city in the text. Precisely through the process of its own fictionalization, the city, in the words of Renata Lachmann, becomes a privileged site of memory; it starts functioning as a system of signs and as a specific text of culture.[8]

Postwar and Posttraumatic Literature

When attempting to sum up recent trends in Croatian literature, one can further identify a common denominator, shaped also in the fiction of Maša Kolanović, through the themes of shift and transition in postwar and posttraumatic literature. A body of texts dealing with war marked the second half of the 1990s, while, in the next decade, it tackled—both in prose and drama—the issues of illegal privatization, corruption, and the social marginalization of war veterans.[9]

The social chronicle comes in 2008 in Tarsiiformes (*Rod avetnjaka*), a novel by Slađana Bukovac. The second novel of this young author, born in 1971, reveals the development of her narrative interest in an ironic analysis of Croatian reality, where Slađana Bukovac as the narrator goes to the outpatients' ward of the psychiatric hospital. This space is shaped by the fact that various prototypes of marginal characters can be found there: they are the people at the fringes of the Croatian reality. They are mostly war veterans, whose PTSD diagnosis is closely related to their problems with survival and existence. A few characters (Dugin Ratnik, Mrs. Bonnars, a daughter of a suicidal patient) stand out for their personality and indirectly form the basic relation of the confronted characters, whose different destinies are seen through the eyes of the narrator—the psychiatrist Pavel. His perception of reality combines the personal and the political: he attempts to understand the individual through his psyche, while at the same time viewing psychological problems as reflections of politics. In other words, he sees that the personal is to a great extent shaped by the superpersonal, that the private is subjected to public laws, and that social consciousness precedes intimacy. The narrative dexterity of Slađana Bukovac develops here precisely in an analysis of daily urban life. On the one hand, Bukovac wants to show the possibility of forming a personal consciousness and of building characters with a complex inner being; on the other, as an ironic and socially conscious narrator, she simultaneously develops characters who warn us about the impossibility of constructing personal identity in the sociopolitical context of contemporary reality. The central issue of trauma (a psychiatric term for what in ordinary life stands for misfortune), which connects all the characters and their observer (the psychiatrist), presents itself as an issue impossible to fully represent (trauma eludes representation) and a problem impossible to solve. Therefore, the characters are left to carry on with life without a cathartic resolution. The suicide of the main character is the only possible narrative option in a novel in which the individual memory of a traumatic and war-ridden past becomes a burden too difficult to bear—since the "collective" cannot unburden the individual.

Finally, *Half-Sleep* (*Polusan*), the second novel by Ratko Cvetnić (b. 1957), also occurs along the lines of reexamining the personal and the collective past. In 1997 Cvetnić, a writer of both fiction and nonfiction, published *Brief Excursion* (*Kratki izlet*), in which he demonstrates that he is both an ironic and a socially conscious storyteller and a writer of essayistic criticism. In his fiction, the fates of exceptionally individualized characters who resist the mechanisms of collective identity—so often present in war situations—collide with the manifestations of mass psychology.

Cvetnić's *Half-Sleep* shows Zagreb in the late 1980s, when the socialist system dissolved and new values and new political and ideological models began to form. Linking his story to the characters of one generation and within a relatively short period, Cvetnić gives a representation of a particular time, precisely articulating its paradoxes.[10] On the one hand, the second half of the 1980s is a period during which history seemingly "stops without prospect," while on the other hand, this same period contains the events following the fall of the Berlin Wall: the creation of the first civil political parties and the complete change of political life. Cvetnić is aware of all this, as an author and as the narrator, through the principal character, Vjekoslav Modrić, so the historical and documentary reality forms the background of the novel. Cvetnić's *Half-Sleep* is neither a satirical novel nor a story based on real fact. It is a novel which depicts contemporary characters in the context of a certain historical moment. We could say that, in a paradoxical way, we are dealing with a postwar novel which tells the prehistory of the war. The key value of Cvetnić's writing is definitely his storytelling competence, intertwining narrative and reflexive segments, connecting them to the character of the protagonist. A certain "fictionalization" of history is here employed to create a credible narrative world that is close to the contemporary version of existentialist narratives.

The last example will be the new novel by Croatian drama and prose writer Ivana Sajko (b. 1975), *The History of My Family from 1941 to 1991 and After* (*Povijest moje obitelji od 1941 do 1991, i nakon*, 2009). Sajko writes her novel precisely from the point of someone who couldn't be an actor in or witness to collective history, but wants to reconstruct—in a very personal way—the memories of the past. In her relatively short narrative (she combines first- and third-person narration) she gives us one brief overview of the last sixty years, focusing on important historical and political events, even giving a very clear ideological perspective.

The foundations are her personal history, while at the same time it is the history of people she has lived with and met, the fragments of a common, collective history that has only narrative links with her own: members of her family narrated to her what happened in the past; she was listening, reading books on history, comparing them, and finally she wrote a novel based on her historical investigations. The result of her findings is that the past defines us. Similarly to Dubravka Ugrešić, Sajko also confronts the *"new past."* Are those who remember a different past burdened by a sense of guilt? Yes, they are, answers Ivana Sajko. This newly produced guilt is imposed by the new history of the new establishment in the 1990s. Two new novels published in 2010, *Hotel Zagorje* written by the young author Ivana Simić Bodrožić, and *Father* (*Otac*) by Miljenko Jergović, are opening new traumatic pages of the Croatian past. Ivana Simić Bodrožić writes about the 1990s from the point of view of a young girl; her intimate past is subverted by images of the collective past. Miljenko Jergović, in *Father*, reexamines the problematic Croatian historical heritage from World War II. His first-person narrative is focused on personal and family memoirs and their relation to public representations of the past.

Toward a Conclusion: Neither Amnesia nor Amnesty

The fictional strength exhibited by these authors in the last two years is poetically diverse but all the novels exhibit an intention to deconstruct existing stereotypes and to dismantle the key collective images which have dominated our fiction, nonfiction, and the media scene. In this way, different narrative devices are used to create individual worlds seen from the perspective of individual characters and not by employing ready-made cultural and historic perceptions.

Aware of the tension that exists between personal and collective identity, contemporary Croatian writers choose to represent fictional situations that emphasize the protagonist's difference from standards of common behavior. An inclination toward the marginal and marginalized often leads them to represent urban daily life and the "little narratives" that do not belong to the dominant majority.

These characters function in the present, while the reality of their lives—through memory—is shared with the past. In *La mémoire, l'histoire, l'oubli*, the French philosopher Paul Ricoeur dedicates his last chapter to a hermeneutic meditation on the matter of forgetting and on human existence between memory and forgetting. "Too much memory in one place, too much forgetting in the other"—this is Ricoeur's conclusion, based on his observation of the mechanisms of reality, commemorative meetings (such as the grotesque deformations of the "sites of memory" from Pierre Nora's analysis), and public representations of the past. We are faced with three obstacles which preclude memory: the Freudian interpretation of the mechanisms of suppressed memories, the ideological manipulation of history, and the forced memory of the collective. Ricoeur is primarily interested in a reverse mechanism of memory and forgetting, that is, the relationship between an individual and the community. It is not by accident that Ricoeur begins his discussions by citing examples from recent political history: Algiers, Rwanda, Bosnia, Kosovo. His analysis is sharply clear and directed at the core of the problem, precisely at the point of the subconsciously forced shaping of memory, which determines the position of the witness and the victim. The victim, according to Ricoeur's analysis, shuts himself or herself within the historical community and interprets or accepts personal trauma through the logic of the community. Modern societies revise their own past and suppress problematic areas in history, so that when they are unable to recreate an innocent past, they create the possibility of redeeming guilt and damages. It is clear that societies cannot be in conflict with themselves all the time, so they need to have some "therapeutic" mechanisms. However, the most vulnerable and unstable line is the one, Ricoeur believes, that separates *amnesia* from *amnesty*. Every political body, in order to protect its own identity, will choose amnesty as the mechanism that protects its unity. Amnesia is only the consequence of a collective amnesty: if we are smart enough not to investigate deeper into our own past, everything will be fine; we are all good and we are united. The mechanism of suppressed memory, however, does not stand still: what was hidden from the public eye thus comes to the surface, that from which the society is only seemingly given amnesty—the collaborationism, the executions, the retaliation.[11]

The texts of contemporary Croatian literature analyzed here underline the strength of individual choice, the level of the individual "I choose," "it is my choice," or finally, "I decide for myself." As much in the world of legal and political choices as in the world of literary memory represented by individual gestures: "I remember" and "I recall."

16

Cheesecakes and Bestsellers
Contemporary Serbian Literature and the Scandal of Transition
Tatjana Rosić

Go, go, go, said the bird: human kind
Cannot bear very much reality.
                    T. S. Eliot, *Four Quartets*

The Scandal of Transition

Since the idea of provocation rules the global culture of the media, advertising, broadsheets, show business, the stock market, the screen, and the stage, more and more writers and critics are trying to learn the rules of the game. Provocation is aimed at launching its protagonists and creators into the galaxy of celebrities as soon as possible, absolving them of any political, esthetic, or ethical responsibility for abusing the media space.

Theorist Henry Giroux qualifies this as the culture of fear and depression, the culture of fear from risk.[1] This culture is a form of new totalitarianism, in which reading and writing are no longer of interest to anyone, as critics and all protagonists of the (non)existing literary scene in Serbia are trying to persuade us. In brief, reading and writing are boring in today's world, which is characterized by the ever faster consumption of newer and newer information and digital images. The idea of someone spending his life reading and writing may seem as senseless as it is impudent in the age in which "fun" and "entertainment" are the imperative, in the high-tech era when passionate interest in new gadgets reigns.

The era of consumption is riding strong. Moreover, consumer society has reached its decadent stage: no one is surprised by the fact that reading is seen as just another easy and readily available form of entertainment. The unspoken mantra of modern-day literary criticism in Serbia can thus boil down to the pseudo-emancipatory catchphrase "reading can/must be fun." This gives critics the role of entertainment-prophets, linked to the thriving industry of the pseudobook and its market. What such "entertainment" entails has not, however, been clarified. All those who ever felt the famous pleasure that Barthes derives from a text always experience the miraculous challenge of a transgression, characteristic only of genuine, supreme, unique fun.[2] Everything else is merely consumption, which Adorno and Horkheimer defined as the neutralization or stifling of individual social resistance.[3]

Current Serbian literary texts appear to have forgotten this central experience of reading as a transgression, and seem to fear the market imperative of producing a bestseller at all costs. Has the postmodernist cultural scene of the 1980s failed to prepare Serbian literature for confronting the challenges of contemporary social and political changes? And to what extent? Indeed, the postmodernist writers and critics active in the 1980s did not "face" the consequences of their actions until the 1990s—during the beginning of wars in the former Yugoslavia and the defeat of the idea of Yugoslavism. Having abruptly lost its cosmopolitan Yugoslav cultural context, this generation suddenly found itself internally divided: on the one hand, its prior practice entailed the cosmopolitan dream of "re-Europeanizing" or even "re-globalizing" Serbian literature, while on the other hand, its ideals of globalist society were being achieved only in the form of totalitarian demands for social and economic changes, to which small cultures in transition cannot adequately respond. The neocolonial spirit of the late twentieth and early twenty-first centuries fatally impacted Serbian culture, redefining and redistributing the discourse of Serbian "postmodernists." The initial premises of Serbian literary postmodernist criticism have never been redefined, for many reasons, including careerism and political opportunism. The new "theoretical training"—within which postmodernism accepted the discourse of gender and postcolonial studies, finally recognizing the importance of the long ignored or stifled feminist criticism—was embraced with a lot of resistance, two decades late. The war was over, the disintegration of Yugoslavia complete. The literary and cultural arenas had, however, disintegrated to such an extent that there could be no pluralist, creative decentralization: dialogue and exchange of opinions proved impossible in tabloidized everyday Serbian reality. If we agree there is something resembling a "scene" in the transition-era of Serbian culture by the end of this chapter, we may even conclude that the political and literary "scenes" strangely reflect each other in their struggle to create a "third Serbia," like the mirror room in a fun house.

The futile attempt to revive or create esthetic communities has thus become one of the main tasks of those trying to understand transition-culture in Serbia. The definition and purpose of such communities is not always clear to those searching for it—this endeavor is hindered by con-temporary theories of "community," which indicate that community is always an imaginary and short-term project, the unattainable embodiment of fiction and/or phantasm. The new theories of community, however, are based on the insight that each community, even if only esthetic or fic-tional, has *real* social and critical impact. Lack of faith in that impact has turned the Serbian literary scene into a phantom fleeing its own shadow, all the time hoping it will one day wake up in "reality."

This is why the real question, for those aspiring to address the on-going problems of Serbia's culture and literature, is whether there can be belief in the possibility of genuine social action. Is there somewhere in Ser-bian culture a possibility of reading/writing as transgression, which would turn an ordinary citizen into an unpredictable person, unsuitable for social institutions but still capable of recognizing a kindred, wild spirit and ex-tending it a hand of friendship—the one that the poised Corto Maltese offers hysterical Rasputin in the Siberian steppe?[4] Or do we in Serbia prefer to believe that the time of antiheroes is almost over, that the fictional es-thetic experience of the community, along with the idea of imagination as the last haven for social resistance, is a scandalous and outdated fashion—which may yet break out in the posh transition era?

Cake Parlor as an Apocalypse

Cake Parlor Stories (*Poslastičarske priče*, 2008),[5] an unusual collection of stories edited by David Albahari and Vladan Mijatović Živojinović, writ-ten in response to the editors' call for stories about sweets, appeared in Serbian bookstores in 2008. At first glance, the concept of the collection appears nostalgic: the topos of nearly all the stories is the old-fashioned, al-most forgotten cake parlors, with plastic tables, checkered vinyl tablecloths, dented ashtrays (yes, smoking was allowed in these cake parlors!), and metal chairs, offering a comfortingly predictable variety of pastries (Turkish sweets such as baklava, halva, and tulumba; custard pie, coconut chocolate puffs, chestnut puree, cooked wheat with whipped cream, etc.). They have nearly disappeared from our everyday lives in the transition-era, replaced by chains of comfortable, cozy cafeterias offering all types of coffees, cakes, and sandwiches, their cake stands dominated by a brand new cake unknown to Serbia until recently—the cheesecake and its various fruit toppings. The cake parlors described in this book appear as a cautionary metaphor of human modesty, a prerequisite for happiness: with a plateful of cake, sipping lemonade or *chicha de jora*, this is where your first childhood dreams and puppy loves came true, where the middle aged indulged in innocuous hedonism. Compared to the modern-day variety, those communist cake parlors now appear not only modest but also poor, stirring melancholy for the time when one needed so little for real human contact.

But to the surprise of the unsuspecting reader, this apparently nostalgic collection takes a very odd turn indeed. The ode to the sweet and sumptuous but still affordable poor man's luxury turns into painful self-examination. The modest cake parlor of forgotten communist times transforms into an arena of gory transition conflicts, confirming the belief of everyone who voted for Slobodan Milošević that hedonism cannot ever be innocuous. The best "cake parlor stories" turn the good old communist cake parlor into the site of an absurd and antiheroic hara-kiri (David Albahari, "Hara-kiri in the Cake Parlor" ["Harikiri u poslastičarnici"]); abduction (Srđan V. Tešin, "Tulumbas and Death" ["Tulumbe i smrt"]); mafia extortion (Branko Anđić, "Entrance" ["Ulazna vrata"]); terrorist and anarchist conspiracies (Saša Ilić, "Chinese Quarter" ["Kineska četvrt"]); grotesque vying among gastarbeiters (Svetislav Basara, "Summer Solstice" ["Letnji solsticij"]); and refugee confessions (Đorđe Jakov, "Koshava in No 83" ["Košava u broju 83"]), but never again into the site of the fairy-tale fulfillment of innocuous hedonistic dreams.

How did this view of the cake parlor as an apocalypse, uniting writers of various generations and diverse poetic orientations, come about? It is difficult to believe that David Albahari asked the "invited" writers to depict such a metamorphosis, especially since some stories in the collection deviate from the apocalyptic pattern (Ljubica Arsić's story, for instance). The *Cake Parlor Stories* editors, and some of the authors (to note, five of eighteen have lived abroad for over a decade now), nevertheless present the Serbian cake parlor as a venue possessed by foreign, demonic, and colonial—or potentially colonial—forces.

Culture studies reveal that the history of small, everyday things tells us more about society in a given period than any history textbook. The stories about cakes thus reveal the secret history of communist hedonism and its lethal effects, which were suppressed in collective memory: with a few rare exceptions, the owners of "communist" cake parlors were Albanians and the pastries sold in them reflected a conflict between the two empires that continued their war through their different concepts of "sweet." The followers of the Austro-Hungarian school were fully devoted to refined creams and strudels, and disdained the sugar sherbet with lemon that was poured over the Turkish delights. It was logical that this communist empire would "fall apart" precisely in the Albanian (i.e., cake parlor) territory and that cake lovers would be punished for their political ignorance and inadvertence, which resulted in involuntary political transgressions and subsequent atonement. The reader of *Cake Parlor Stories* sees that these erstwhile, small Sunday treats, which went by the name of "visits to the cake parlor," were actually a special war, in which citizens unknowingly participated—by choosing this or that cake, this or that cake parlor, this or that concept of hedonism and "dolce vita." This war paradoxically inflicts the fatal blow to itself, the antiheroic hara-kiri.

The authors of the "sweet stories" were almost unanimous in their ambivalence toward the postcommunist and postwar transition era. Cake parlors have been selling neither dreams nor cakes for quite a while now. Something entirely different has been sold in them for a long time, something we still lack the real name for, because we have not fully comprehended it yet. Just as Belgrade bookshops, publishers, and printers have not been offering merely books and the delicate world of brutal imagination for a long time. The bookshops that we remember from the idyllic days, when we wandered from one to another in search of rare titles, no longer exist, just like the modest communist cake parlors. To the eternal nostalgists, these new modernly designed book shops aiming to attract buyers in a variety of ways—from organizing promotions to creative workshops—seem like a mere stage set for negotiations and blackmail, for the turnover of money and union strikes, for amassing illustrated encyclopedias and an endless number of similar new titles.

"Female" and "Male" Teams

The time has come for us to get used to buying instant cakes and books at airports, cafes, grocery stores, or at nearly every newsstand in town. It is only the pseudo-elitist spirit that drives us to perceive this as the "death of all values"—although apparently we should be doing the opposite, reveling in the carnivalesque joy and the abolition of demarcations between high and popular cultures, which has come to Serbia as well. We should even go a step further and forget about the dangerous interaction between neoliberal commercialization and totalitarianism. We should also forget about poetry and short stories as literary forms. As Tihomir Brajović, a literary critic and professor of comparative South Slavic literature, has aptly pointed out, the era of bestsellers is also a renaissance of great epics and historical sagas, the novel as the dominant genre, particularly in Serbia, torn by transition and national and political passions.[6]

But now that the alluring bestseller, like cheesecake, is proudly exhibited on bookstore shelves and bestseller lists, instilling euphoria about the alleged return to reading in the confusing transitional system of literary values, the Serbian cultural and literary public still wonders—what about the cakes? More precisely, what happened to good books and literature, which should rise to the demands of the times while also absolving national literature, since the latter cannot even comes to terms with itself. The answers, more precisely the recipes, offered by various stakeholders can be grouped around two main questions: (1) How can Serbian literature, too, attract readership and be translated into foreign languages (as if these two were of equal value?!) so as to achieve enviable circulation both in Serbia and abroad? And (2) which kind of literature, group of writers, or literary titles can be considered as the genuine, worthy representative of transitional and postwar Serbian reality? It is very important to stress that those who attempt to revive national literature mostly disregard that "reality." Furthermore, as Vladimir Nabokov wisely warned, "reality" is one of those dangerous words that make no sense if they are not written in parentheses.[7]

Thus, the (non)existing literary scene in transitional Serbia is being mapped around the idea of "reading as fun" and "writing about reality." These two codes reveal the Serbian literary scene to be tense, dramatic, and, at times, extremely divided. What is surprising is the division of writers into "male" and "female" teams, which is one of the symptoms of transitional re-patriarchalization. The race for market domination was won by women writers—much to everyone's surprise, particularly the feminists. The "boom" of female writers and the commercial success of "female writing" shows that women have, true to form, remained in the domain of the market, not wavering from their historic concern for private life and everyday survival, while male writers (this noun is necessarily in the masculine gender in the Serbian language) are preoccupied (yet again!) by concern for the public good, involved in debates about reestablishing a Serbian literary scene that will not depend on market conditions.

Serbian Bestsellers: "Female Writing," "Female Authorship," and "Nostalgia for the Historical"

The boom of "female writing"—characteristic of the postfeminist era and linked to media promotion of female authors—began in Serbia in the early 1990s and continued, with even greater success, after 2000. Like cheesecake and bestsellers, it is an imported item and follows foreign recipes: love drama, thriller, a war or two, and the obligatory tinge of the exotic or mystical. Serbian female authors realized that a national Serbian bestseller, which would not be advertised as a mere item but as an authentic literary text offering good entertainment, would sell the best. The proliferation of dangerously similar titles on the bestseller lists clearly indicates the components without which an inflammatory, desirable Serbian literary cocktail cannot exist: a love plot, poetics of glamor most often reflected in the idea of the existence of an original Serbian jet set, a family chronicle and genealogy, historical retrospective, revival of the Serbian bourgeois tradition, parody of the everyday lives of women in Serbia providing the illusion that women are actually transcending it, urban female characters living female gender roles from *Cosmopolitan*, adventure in the form of exotic tourist/shopping trips.

But it no longer suffices to ask the question about the legitimate reasons for female literature posed by Julia Kristeva, the famous French theoretician of Bulgarian descent.[8] If one wants to understand the commercialized female experience it is easy to see that the modern-day market is ruled, not so much by innovative hunger for the formal innovations of "female writing" of the 1980s, but by a daunting frenzy in both elitist and mass cultures for the naked depiction of all forms of gender experience. In combination with the dominant sophisticated neoconservatism, this frenzy creates genuine confusion about social and cultural changes, the consequences of which we are not yet able to fathom. What is at issue is the changing discourse of diversity, linked to media representation of new perceptions of female authorship, in which women authors are recognized as new, attractive pop heroines associated with showbiz.

This image is defined by the new technology and esthetics of spectacle which the media employ in shaping the image of female authorship in today's Serbia. The appearance of several female authors, of whom Isidora Bjelica is a heroine, thus substantiates Boris Groys's qualification of media as the crucial institution forging the tastes and values of contemporary consumer society.[9] During the 1990s, in her novels such as *The Defamed* (*Ozloglašena*, 1994), *The Protocols of Polit-Art Wise-Men* (*Protokoli polit-art mudraca*, 1994), or *The Fiancée of the War Criminal* (*Verenica ratnog zločinca*, 1994), Isidora Bjelica alternatively represented the woman-author as the local personification of a Hollywood diva, a retro-avant-garde scandal artist, or a national heroine of Serbian Orthodoxy, coinciding her "new character" with media depiction of armed conflicts in the former Yugoslavia, in the form of a glamorous spectacle. In *Sexepistolary Novel* (*Seksepistolarni roman*, 1996), Bjelica expanded the media palette of female authorship, bringing in, as coauthor, Luna Lu—the cult journalist of the opposition Radio B92—who posed as the Warholette of urban Belgrade. Fascination with one's opponent ultimately resulted in open love between rightist Isidora Bjelica and rocker Suzana Zlatanović also known as Luna Lu, suggesting a glamorous market-esthetic integration. Scandal mongering, of course, played a key role here as well, modeled after both mainstream Hollywood and its parody—both in Serbian style—along with the possibility of mutual understanding. Along the way, the classical scenario of Hollywood thrillers, where the persecutor and victim swap identities, was transformed into a burlesque-swap of fashion-media representations of new conservatism and radical urban leftism. Exaggeration and transgression were the key words allowing their dialogue, which ignored the allegedly insurmountable ideological-poetic differences, particularly when something as rare as *money* was at issue. This explains the claustrophobia that arises when one grasps the commercial nature of their understanding: this is not an experiment for reexamining different poetical discourses, but a political pact in which each party aims to boost her own media effectiveness.

After 2000, the media presented the women authors in this group (Isidora Bjelica, Ljiljana Habjanović Đurović, Vesna Radusinović, Mirjana Bobić Mojsilović, et al.) as professionals, making a living off their own writing, no longer voicing the support of the political coteries that had launched them. Their media affirmation and commercial success, measured in thousands of books published and sold, were further supported in the regional context, which also registered a boom of female writing.

The media image of the woman writer, promoted by the authors of so-called "trivial literature," successfully assimilates all the available patterns of female authorship in Serbian media-discourse: both turbofolk and rave-techno, showbiz and new financial elites. This assimilation is facilitated by the insistence on, first and foremost, the "femininity" of the author! Both in their texts and media appearances, most of these female authors represent and support an idealized, successful, business-patriarchal woman-mother. This type corresponds to the "nostalgia for historical" contents and forms that dominates official Serbian culture, while simultaneously boosting the success of a "female writing" that no feminist would recognize as "female." New titles published by Isidora Bjelica confirm that change: she devotes herself to the fulfillment of traditional female desire, depicting love stories in exotic destinations (Cairo, Tunis, Beirut) or mysterious women coming from distant, noble destinations (Santorini island or—Serbia!). Love, fashion, and national tradition are still intermingled in her quasi-ironic bestsellers (*My Grandfather Louis Vuitton* [*Moj deda Luis Vuton*, 2009]); while sex appears as political provocation (*Serbia Without Orgasm* [*Srbija bez orgazma*, 2003]; *Secrets of Josip Broz Tito's Bed* [*Tajne kreveta Josipa Broza Tita*, 2004])! This product of patriarchal capitalism bases "female writing" on the ancient myth that seductiveness is a woman's strongest weapon—precisely in the epoch characterized by the closing of departments studying female and feminist literature and the failure of numerous utopian gender projects.

Bourdieu's idea of the symbolic violence of the patriarchate helps us discern an interest-based alliance in Serbian culture, an alliance between the repression of universalist literary-critical speech and academic social practice, on the one hand, and the implacable commercial demands of the market, on the other.[10] Official critical-literary discourse in Serbian culture appears to be seriously shaken by both the market and media boom of "female writing" to which it gladly caters. This discourse is apparently prompted by concern for its own status, and invokes new politically correct standards of tolerance and "diversity," although diversity is nonexistent at a time characterized by the defeat of feminism. Another political-esthetic and economic-showbiz pact is on the horizon.

For very few people realize that women in Serbia write with more verve and variety than one might conclude by looking at bestseller lists. The policy of evaluating "female authorship" and exceptional authors such as Judita Šalgo, Mirjana Novaković, Radmila Lazić, Milica Mićić Dimovska,

Danica Vukićević, Ljiljana Đurđić, Nina Živančević, Milena Marković, and the Bogavac sisters, has thus not changed for three decades; notwithstanding the generational differences among these authors, none of them have abandoned their artistic experiments and concepts, believing that they are the only guarantors of the future of books and readers. The devastating status of the above-mentioned female Serbian writers becomes clear when the curious, uninitiated reader chances upon a cheaply illustrated edition of *Fear and Its Servant* (*Strah i njegov sluga*, 2009), by cult female author Mirjana Novaković, with an amateurishly designed pop art vampire grinning on the front cover, in the popular vampire section of the largest Belgrade bookshops. These writers are not only exposed to the humiliation of the market but also ignored by the critics. Official, predominantly male criticism insists on catering to populist female literature in Serbia, ignoring even authors like Mirjana Đorđević or Mirjana Mitrović, who have successfully mastered the world standards of the bestseller; they do not lay claim to laurel wreaths but they do offer their readers intelligent, sophisticated, and tense plots spiced with witty details and dialogue. This recognizable atmosphere of the "Serbian" crime thriller is also found in the latest novel by the very popular writer Mirjana Đurđević, *Kaja, Belgrade, and the Good American* (*Kaja, Beograd i dobri Amerikanac*, 2009); she blends it with love of knowledge, passion for adventure, and attachment to a tomcat, a house, and leisure, above all.

Too Much (")Reality("); or, On the Impossibility of Literary Policy in Serbia

As opposed to the commercial success of "female writing," the (non) existent Serbian literary scene is ruled by teams of male authors and critics, who energetically argue over the appearance of "new literature" in Serbia and the means for reviving a nonmarket value system (or at least striking a balance between it and the market value system). In the context of this polemic, they suggest that the reconstituted literary scene play the role of a "dam" suppressing the deluge of bestsellers, so that the transition market would be structured in terms of values, not just commerce. Structuring the book market in terms of values would enable us to single out the unique, attractive book that we would qualify as a *good, valuable, and important book*. Singling such a book out of an amorphous pile would lead to the formulation of a standard and constitute the process of classification.

The revival of "negative criticism," whose authors fight against the prevailing opportunism and conformism, was presented to the Serbian public as an opportunity for open dialogue between those with different opinions, and as a means to revive the lethargic, passive, cultural community. Such a revival would also allow the desired restructuring of the entropic literary market. Insistence on reviving "negative criticism" has been the focus of a group of writers and critics for years (Saša Ilić, Saša Ćirić, Marjan Čakarević, Adrijana Zaharijević, and others, with support from colleagues in the region, such as Boris Buden, Svetlana Slapšak, Pavle Levi, Serb Horvat) The group has rallied round the cultural supplement *Beton*, which has been published every two weeks since 2006 in the Belgrade daily *Danas* (its activity is available at www.elektrobeton.net).

The members of the group passionately advocate negative criticism as a means to decontaminate Serbian culture and literature from the authoritarianism of national (or nationalist, in their view) institutions, in the context of the debate on Serbia's responsibility for the disintegration of Yugoslavia. *Beton*'s critics apparently aim to relaunch a set of a literary and cultural issues perceived as outdated. The group emphasizes that the current scene is being stirred by vociferous and topical activist theories of cultural practices. These practices cannot be understood without awareness of their interaction with the historical moment, the social environment, and the community in which they are conducted and which they produce. Within this reform, literary activity is merely one aspect of social and cultural engagement, merely another form of assuming responsibility for the historical-epochal moment in which we live. Thus it is logical that the postmodernist pessimism embodied in the question "Why literature?" be succeeded by the question "Why literary criticism?" This is a prerequisite for "cleaning up" the literary scene and promoting new topical, market-oriented Serbian prose. Therefore this group wants to demystify nostalgia for "the golden era of postmodernism," which could be seen as nostalgia for the readership and communities of the last decadent decade of the communist regime (which, however, were not Serbian but Yugoslav).

The representatives of this group want to demystify the hermetic Alexandrian paradigm of postmodernist Serbian prose in the latter half of the twentieth century, whose self-referentiality, in their view, paralyzes the authenticity of the artistic act and precludes critical "writing about reality." The revisionist reviews of the *Beton* group about key Serbian postmodernist figures, such as Radoslav Petković, Svetislav Basara, or Mileta

Prodanović, are based on their conviction that Serbian literature has become boring and unreadable—and thus unacceptable in the market—precisely because of its ostrich-like approach to reality and its refusal to write openly about the historical, political, and social experience of two decades of war in the Balkans. The Alexandrian paradigm, in their view, was particularly lethal to critical thinking, confining it to an academic discipline, from which postmodernist literary criticism derives its idea about its elite status. This group believes that the ineffectiveness of Serbian postmodernist criticism lies in its duality; on the one hand, it aspires to the turgidity of an academic discipline, and, on the other, it toys with its manufacturing-media nature, preventing the articulation of a clear value judgment and critical viewpoint.

The task of creating a new type of literary criticism would not be as utopian if the *Beton* critics were not so ambivalent (to put it mildly) toward the postmodernist paradigm. Postmodernist criticism still seems to be a "gold mine," which becomes starkly obvious in the defense of the myth about Kiš's perfection as writer and esthete (this defense extends to other writers in the "Kiš circle," of whom Mirko Kovač, who has lived in Croatia since the beginning of the 1990s, is definitely the most privileged—although it is not clear what they need to be "defended" from). In this myth, the figure of the author is constructed, as Foucault emphasizes, as an ideological figure whose social role, contrary to the Romantic vision of a genius, is to control the "flourishing of imagination" and the subversive multitude of literary discourses in a society.[11] This is why the attempts by Saša Ilić, the most relevant writer in this group, to deal with his own literary legacy—such as in his afterword to the anthology of new Serbian prose *The Dog's Century* (*Pseći vek*, 2000)—appear unconvincing. (In the spirit of the mainstream postmodernism of Aleksandar Jerkov and Mihajlo Pantić, whom he accuses in his afterword of mannerism and conformism, Ilić fails to include any women writers in his anthology of up-and-coming Serbian prosaists). Ilić's prose works—*Odysseus's Catalog* (*Odisejev catalog*, 1998, coauthored by Dragan Bošković), *Premonition of a Civil War* (*Predosećanje gradjanskog rata*, 2000), and *The Berlin Window* (*Berlinsko okno*, 2005)—demonstrate that Ilić remains loyal to the postmodernist tradition even when he parodies it. He successfully explores its potential with a fragmentary, jigsaw-puzzle narrative and rich references to both popular media and traditional elite cultures. As in his novel *The Berlin Window*, he achieves a minimalist, purified, postmodernist, novelistic form free of unnecessary hermeticism. This form gains narrative speed and ideological assertiveness in the context of topics like the disintegration of the state (first, second, third Yugoslavias), exile, the diaspora, historical guilt, and responsibility. All this renders Saša Ilić one of the most interesting writers in modern-day Serbian literature and *The Berlin Window* one of the most provocative novels on the disintegration of Yugoslavia and the psychosis of postcommunist transition.

The question, therefore, is whether reducing literary criticism to negativity and the articulation of value judgments is a one-way gesture serving political purposes. *Beton*'s critical mission is to finally legitimize the link between the ideological and the esthetical—the link Adorno and Horkheimer focused on in their critical theory—in contemporary Serbian culture.[12] This link, however, reveals that the creation of literary-critical and cultural-political platforms is impossible without the support of the media. Yet the media is always in a co-relationship with the interests of hegemonic social groups, or groups aiming to achieve social hegemony in the future, as Gramsci has demonstrated.[13] The *Beton* protagonists need to be aware of neoliberal totalitarianism, the global situation, and a market-media policy which impacts their own work and actions. Their provocative, alluring, theoretically well-conceived program is valid *only* as long as they also question their own raison d'être, since hegemonic ideologies rarely grant creative freedom to subversive individuals or rebellious groups. (Their attack on national institutions is odd, for instance, given that the key two figures in the group, Saša Ilić and Saša Ćirić, are themselves employed in leading national cultural institutions—in the National Library and Public Radio Service!) Trust in the *Beton* group is thus undermined by its vociferous call to others to help decontaminate Serbian culture. This group will function well as long as it continuously reexamines its own critical-literary reasons for rallying.

The decades-long insistence on "literary and esthetic values" in Serbian culture has delayed any reflection on the link between ideology and esthetics. This link marked the history of the twentieth century and was ignored for a long time in Serbian culture precisely in order to naturalize "universal esthetic values," and to conceal the social and cultural context in which they were created. In that respect, the appearance of the literary group P-70, whose first manifesto was first read aloud at an "evening of surprises" in the Belgrade Student Cultural Center (SCC) on November 5, 2009, constitutes a backward step toward the rehabilitation of the universalist story of genuine, ideologically pure, literary, and esthetic values. The excerpt from P70's first manifesto appears anachronistic when one considers that it was presented in the SCC: the SCC's historical role in Yugoslav and Serbian conceptual art was a reexamination of social community within performance practice. The reading of the manifesto in the birthplace of Yugoslav conceptual art, whose quality does not fall short of world standards, can be perceived as a bad performance aiming to stop time and abolish history:

We have nothing against subsidies, but we have no intention of serving any political concept because we believe that we are superior to all ideological mantras. And we have nothing against market success, but we are not willing to abandon our own creative dignity to achieve it. Our objective is to win over and reaffirm the literary scene by helping each other, through our individual and joint appearances, to adjust the criteria of subsidies and the market to ourselves, rather than adjust ourselves to them.[14]

These commonsensical statements by the manifesto signatories indicate the interest-based nature of their association, a nature no one appreciating common sense can criticize. A group of writers born after 1970 (Vladimir Kecmanović, Slobodan Vladušić, Nikola Malović, Dejan Stoijljković, and Marko Krstić—the only critic in the group) decided to publish its generational manifesto and declare biological war against those who believe that it is impossible to beat the phantoms persecuting Serbian writers (small circulations and the state institutions' humiliating attitude towards and negligence of towards their own culture). Capital *P* stands for the first letter of the word *prose* which in Serbian is also written with a *p*. Thus, P-70 symbolizes the new generation of writers born after 1970 forming a group whose manifesto tries to announce the U-turn in contemporary Serbian literature. The group asks for a return to the roots and "old good values" of Serbian language and literary tradition, as well as to the realistic type of narration and mimetic representation of reality. The visual logo of the group is seventy-kilometer-per-hour speed limit traffic sign with the capital *P* added before. Although contradictorily designed the logo should suggest cultural acceleration for which P-70 is voting to— acceleration which is maybe slow but inevitable. Subsidies, of course, can be foreign, but as the above excerpt shows, they are considered acceptable only if they do not jeopardize the integrity and pride of this commonsensical, interest-based, and success-craving group, which placidly claims that it feels superior to "all ideological mantras" after everything that happened in the former Yugoslavia. Another frequently quoted statement in P-70's second manifesto again demonstrates its anachronistic and methodologically unclear position on literature and ideology: "We have joined forces because we do not want to bury living authors, as those who perceive literature merely as a prostitute of ideology are doing."[15]

All this, of course, would be funny if it were not dangerous: insistence on the superiority of the esthetic over the ideological has proven to be a fatal attraction with tragic historical consequences. However, despite the clear snow job, Group P-70 soon attracted the attention of the public prone to retrograde and contradictory views, with some mutual help from disparate literary fellow travelers. Part of the first manifesto was published in the popular conservative Belgrade daily *Večernje novosti*. P-70's second manifesto soon followed. In it, the group revealed their common wish—that they do not have to feel ashamed "for writing in Serbian."

The poetic incoherence of the group is obvious; in its manifesto it insists on explaining the inexplicable association of those sharing an interest but not poetics. But they seem to feel compelled to neutralize their poetic diversity (driven by common sense, feeling they had to make up a reason for their association) by a collective catharsis of loyalty to the language as homeland—whether of the nation or the writer. But the literary diversity of the group is much too evident to be ignored: especially since it reveals that pragmatism is their fundamental and only common platform.

Vladimir Kecmanović, the most prominent writer in this group, is said to write prose that cannot otherwise be found in Serbian contemporary literature. Surrounded by the high standards of wartime prose in the region (in novels written by Miljenko Jergović, Josip Mlakić, and Boris Dežulović in Croatia; by Andrej Nikolaidis in Montenegro; by Nenad Veličković, Faruh Šehić, and Lajma Begović in Bosnia and Herzegovina), Kecmanović wrote the novels *Felix* (*Felix*, 2007) and *So Hot Was the Cannon* (*Top je bio vreo*, 2008), characterized by minimalist dialogue and a successful, paradoxically lyrical depiction of the wartime atmosphere. These novels, giving readers an impression of the "authentic" Serbian version of the war in Sarajevo under siege, have been extremely successful. The secret of Kecmanović's popularity, however, does not lie in the "authenticity" of the Serbian version of Sarajevo's destruction, but in the refined balance he strikes between political correctness, on the one hand, and the nationalist message, on the other. Kecmanović's novel thus stands out among texts on similar topics. Similarly, Dragojević's movie *Pretty Village, Pretty*

Flame (*Lepa sela lepo gore*, 1996), which Kecmanović calls the masterpiece of Serbian cinematography, stands out among Serbian-made movies on the war in Bosnia. Pavle Levi's lucid study points out the diverse components Dragojević manipulated to confuse the viewer.[16] Kecmanović, too, skillfully combines various narrative strategies, manipulating the reader's trust. Kecmanović's effective narrative skills, the lyrical atmosphere underlying the naturalistic narration and general feeling of human misery, cannot be disputed. The choice of first-person narrator, a Serb boy who loses his parents during the shelling of Sarajevo and temporarily loses his speech due to the shock, renders impossible any rebuke of the nationalist position: a child's perspective is by definition vulnerable, leading to the reader's identification with the horrors of war, in which everyone is victim and everyone is perpetrator. The amount of positive and negative characters in the Serb and Muslim camps are mathematically precise and identical—the transformation of a positive character into a negative one guarantees the transformation of a negative character into a positive one in the same camp (Muslim) and vice versa (Serb camp). All this leads to the pacification of the war theme; the novel becomes a story about the solidarity of those who suffered losses in the war or who perceive war as an extraordinary situation in which everyone sustains losses for higher, inexplicable reasons—as indicated by the fantastic leitmotif of male legs in gray pants (not in uniform!) appearing in the crucial scenes, without indication of which force (demonic or godly) is in play. Add to all this the author's exceptional skills for self-promotion in the media and it comes as no surprise that his novel *So Hot Was the Cannon* was warmly welcomed by readers, reprinted a couple of times, and translated into foreign languages (thus achieving the ideal of local market success and entry into foreign markets!). An invitation to the National Prayer Breakfast in February 2010 as well as Kecmanović's warm acceptance of this invitation confirmed his contradictory public status rooted in several politically opposed positions. It is strange, but not impossible, to imagine the presence of this young, nationalistic Serbian writer at one of the most famous global political events organized by the so-called "enemy" of the Serbian nation who initiated its bombing in 1999. Therefore, the unexpected invitation as well as Kecmanovic's puzzling acceptance of the mysterious call remain the subject of conjecture and speculations in Serbian literary and cultural circles.

While Kecmanović represents the "new reality prose" of Serbia's transition-era literature, characterized by the revival of realistic-naturalistic narration, the other members of the P-70 group nurture a kind of retro post-modernism. Like Nikola Malović in his novel *The Boka Wanderer* (*Lutajući Bokelj*, 2007), Dejan Stojiljković resorts to postmodernist, historical meta-fiction in his novel *Constantin's Crossroads* (2010), reconstructing an epic-nostalgic story about a lost time. Slobodan Vladušić's first novel, *Forward* (*Forward*, 2009), demonstrates another kind of ambition: written in the mold of Kiš's novel *Hourglass* (*Peščanik*, 1972), it is a combination of Ser-bian postmodernist literary tradition and postmodernist theory regarding the relationship between technology and the human body/text. Vladušić toys with technological and physiological narrative in the context of the impoverished community at the Serbian-Romanian border, touching upon "hot" transition topics, such as prostitution, pornography, and human traf-ficking, but with a self-referentiality difficult for readers to follow.

One of the most quoted statements in P-70's second manifesto clearly indicates that P-70 formed in reaction against the *Beton* group, and aimed to throw down the gauntlet of esthetic values. The manifestos soon provoked reactions in the media and a polemic with representatives of the *Beton* group. Saša Ilić spoke on their behalf in "Beton: Same Target, Same Distance" ("Beton: Ista meta, isto odstojanje"),[17] alluding to the group's logo, which also resembles a target, not only the traffic sign limiting the speed by which the prose of the group born after 1970 has been achieving success. Amid fun, on the one hand, and the fear of boredom, on the other, literary activism suddenly sprouted on Serbia's literary scene, accompanied by fierce debates occupying media attention, as was the case with the fe-male bestseller authors. The cult prime-time talk show *Impression of the Week* (led by Olja Bećković), broadcast at 9:00 P.M. on Sundays on the still semiopposition TV B92, featured participants in a round-table discussion (including Vladimir Arsenijević, Vladimir Kecmanović, Boris Dežulović) entitled "Literature and War," organized and published by the daily *Poli-tika* as an introduction to P-70.

Most participants in the literary debates of transitional Serbia agree that "new Serbian literature" should thematically and ideologically focus on transition and postwar traumas that have befallen us: that is to say, trau-mas that we were caught up in, or, perhaps, participated in? All this smacks of the revival of the well-known schism between the "First" and "Second" Serbias in the 1990s. Both schisms—between the two Serbias and the two literary-critical groups—were caused precisely by the confrontation of the two verbs—*caught up in* (passive) and *participated in* (active). A whole polemical discourse developed, focusing on opposing presentations of the wartime, postwar, and transition-era "realities" in Serbia: one camp advocates the notion of being "caught up in" the war, and doesn't insist on "collective" guilt, but rather on the idea of innocent bystanders or victims; the other camp wants a clear determination of "Serbian guilt" in the latest wars, claiming that the transition cannot be overcome unless Serbian culture confronts its own "participation" in the disintegration of Yugoslavia.

In this attempt to reestablish the literary and cultural scene, the participants of the debate have rallied around different concepts of "reality"; this attempt to formulate a literary policy reflects the market values of the transition. It is sobering to consider that many of those who are not participating in the formulation of Serbian literature don't realize that "media reality" is one of the predominant transition-era "realities." "Media reality" is the new arena in which existing esthetics and ideologies clash along the axes of globalism/antiglobalism, and (pseudo)nationalism/(pseudo) internationalism.

Transformation of the Subcultural: Soundtrack, Autobiographical Discourse, and "Nonacceptance"

The market of cultural goods has turned into an ideological and political struggle, in which all participants are equally orthodox and implacable, on the one hand, and corrupted by the idea of success, on the other. It seems impossible to reestablish a cultural community that would generate new values and promote a new, transition-era literature while the myths of perfect writers with politically correct biographies are being revived. Let us, however, ask ourselves whether everything is hopeless and whether media space is crucial for establishing the desired new socio-esthetic communities, for a new experience of the beautiful and useful.

It would not hurt, in this regard, to recall the success of the first genuinely "transition" novel of Serbian literature, Vladimir Arsenijević's first novel, *In the Hold* (*U potpalublju*, 1996), which made Belgrade the background of the war front and defeat. This novel, along with Saša Ilić's *The Berlin Window* (*Berlinsko okno*) and Vladimir Kecmanović's *So Hot Was the Cannon* (*Top je bio vreo*), form the Bermuda triangle of transition, wartime, and postwar Serbian literature. Their points are irreconcilable, their horizons of "reality" totally different. Ilić's novel is constructed in the introspective postmodernist key and depicts a game of detection: the main character searches analytically for the "truth," reinterpreting a series of fragmentary miniatures on the disintegration of communist Yugoslavia. He presents them indirectly, while in temporary exile, on a scholarship in Germany, engrossed in his struggle against the totalitarianism of the symbolic order, which no longer corresponds to the reality in which he lives. Kecmanović's naturalistic narration is structured as multicultural wartime prose, in which the dialogues conceal everything that cannot be expressed by words, everything that is different than it seems. Continuous communication signifies absence of communication, lyrical paragraphs describe the lulls between the killings, and the dialogues are actually the internal monologues of the main character. The protagonist is deprived of choice, caught up in the forces of war which traumatize him, prevent him from laterally viewing war/reality, and condemn him to live in exile, in the darkness of the unutterable real. Arsenijević's novel, on the other hand, is based on urban subcultural communities, depicting Belgrade as a motley scene of people who have come together to survive their own lives: Hari Krishnas, glue sniffers, pot lovers, rock and/or punk addicts, young parents who never thought they would have children, parents who have become grandparents, returnees from the front, and those planning to leave Serbia. They believe their association is good and necessary, and their similar lifestyles endow them with a sense of solidarity even amid the chaos of war. That was the last moment of such a Belgrade: subcultural communities were soon completely restructured and lost the spirit of freedom, individualism, and social resistance inherited from the hippie epoch. But that transformation had not yet occurred at the imaginary moment recorded in Arsenijević's novel, and the characters move painlessly from one minority group to another, in search of refuge: Anđela, the drug dealer, thus turns into a happy housewife. But the transformation of urban subculture is already present, along with a deeper social transformation, looming over the liberal-minded subculture of the 1980s, contaminating the joyous and rebellious spirit of the "urban guerrilla."

Arsenijević's prose and, later, the prose of Srđan Valjarević (*Winter Diary* [*Zimski dnevnik*, 1995]; *Another Winter Diary* [*Dnevnik druge zime*, 2005]; *Komo*, 2006) revived the link between the subcultural community and Serbian literature, revealing the diversity of subcultural communities to which the postmodernist writers once belonged. Writers such as Zoran Ćirić, Zvonko Karanović, and Igor Marojević depict the city not only as a scene of brutal transition and the struggle to survive during wartime, but also as a complex subcultural space. Although they agreed to take part in the detested transition "reality," Zoran Ćirić's, Zvonko Karanović's, and Igor Marojević's antiheroes are at odds with the transition world of war profiteers and fast and dirty money, precisely because they are old-fashioned. They arrived at the transition from earlier eras, from a rich subculture, in which turbo-techno was not the only music style. The rock-and-roll rebellion is the characters' chief credo; they easily agree to unparenthesized reality, and resort to popular culture (movies, comic strips, music mythology), only to clash with it and then withdraw to the world where there was genuine togetherness, or at least an illusion of it. The soundtracks of most of these authors' texts and novels are extremely important: the rebellious tradition of rock and roll interfuses with the melancholy of blues, the passion of world music, and electro mixes, suggesting the merging of different eras within transition "reality." Thus the main character of Igor Marojević's *Ground Floor* (*Parter*, 2009) is a semisuccessful DJ, while the hero of the last part of Karanović's prose trilogy—*Three Faces of Victory* (*Tri slike pobede*, 2009)—used to co-own a CD shop; and the killers and criminals in Ćirić's last novel, *The Night of All Saints* (*Noć svih svetih*, 2009), are connoisseurs of the blues. The soundtrack confirms the antihero's isolation and his fear that there will be no one to hear or remember his life story, his fear that a community of like-minded people is no longer possible. Inclined to viewing the world through the lens of subcultural iconography, the main characters of these novels also realize that other subcultural groups driven by different passions—criminals, forces of law and order, paramilitary formations, agents of corruption and organized prostitution, drivers of jeeps with big golden crosses hanging around their necks—are walking the city streets. The soundtrack thus functions at the level of the symbolic unconscious, addressing the remaining devotees of different subcultural communities; these readers are expected to use the antihero's values to decode the hero's "macho" account, and they feel they are ignored and overrun by the historical and social moment. The authors are attempting to reach the remaining members of the community or (sub)cultural group who have nothing in common with the transition and its gory militarization.

The unexpected transformation of the subcultural context in the 1990s—along with the awareness that such communities are still necessary, although not always tame and harmless—is described by David Albahari in his novel *Leeches* (*Pijavice*, 2006), and then by Vladimir Arsenijević, in his surprisingly poetically radical novel *Predator* (*Predator*, 2008). *Leeches* depicts New Belgrade subcultural urban communities, created by lovers of leisure, unpretentious addicts of rock and roll and marijuana, who mutate into frighteningly ambitious, xenophobic, nationalist-soccer-fan, criminal-led groups, clad in black. This transforms the protagonist's experience of Belgrade; he is yet another of those who leave Serbia forever. In *Predator*, Arsenijević places terrorism and cannibalism in the context of the global "media village," depicting apocalyptic local wars and their media coverage (news) and presentation (Hollywood film production). The main character's esthetic experience, linked to the movie *Predator*, combined with political trauma, becomes more real than life itself, endowing that life with unimaginable, monstrous coordinates of evil. (The event Arsenijević took as the pretext of his novel, unfortunately, really took place: the world press reported for months on a cannibal who openly invited his victims to be eaten, via the internet. The masochism of the victims remains an absolute mystery!) Both novels thematize the transformation of subcultural space into totalitarian trauma, with adverse political consequences. This is in contrast to the 1980s and early 1990s, when, despite terrorist threats by the Red Brigades, subcultural space was a space of social freedom and resistance, which followed the ideals of liberal hippie communes and the revolutionary social views of the 1968 student movement. The transformation of subcultural space mirrors totalitarization at both the global (*Predator*) and local, nationalistic levels (*Leeches*).

Vule Žurić's novel *A Folk Singer's Death: A Melo(s)drama* (*Narodnjakova smrt: Melo(s)drama*, 2009), devoted to the fictional rise and fall of a famous local turbofolk star, also reaffirms the dangerous power of populist-criminal subcultural communities, fully aware of how thin the line is between populist and urban-elitist subcultures. Žurić's work is again grotesque and parodic, a bizarre combination of the postmodernist paradigm (references to masterpieces and popular culture hits), acerbic social criticism (targeting both transition-era Serbia and communist Yugoslavia), and naturalistic descriptions characteristic of his whole opus. He perseveres in his intention to cause the reader's discomfort in the enjoyment of culture. The soundtrack is an extremely important aspect of narration in Žurić's work as well. In the *Folk Singer's Death*, it reveals the protagonist's existential fear; every detail that reveals his nonacceptance of the rules of the subgroup, to which he should belong, may cost him his life. Žurić's soundtrack covers a surprisingly extensive range, given that his character, a turbofolk star, is torn between folk music and an early hit by the Korni Group (the cult rock-and-roll Yugoslav and Belgrade band from the late 1970s and early 1980s), devoted to the death of the communist hero Ivo Lola Ribar. His identification with Ivo Lola Ribar, who died a tragic death under suspicious circumstances (it is believed he was killed on an order of Josip Broz Tito), designates him as a renegade and costs him his life. In his later novel *The Week of the Rats: A Partisan Crime Story* (*Nedelja pacova: Partizanski krimić*, 2010) Žurić continues to explore, with the same passion and intensity, the hybrid identities of postcommunist and post-Yugoslav society in transition.

The novel *Quattro stagioni* (2009), by Slobodan Tišma, a prominent Yugoslav poet and once a rock-and-roll, new-wave star (the frontman for the Luna and La Strada groups during the mid 1980s), is also a showdown with the communist myth, on the one hand, and the transition "reality" of totalitarianism, on the other. The novel's soundtrack is psychotically parodic: contrary to expectations, Tišma evokes not the rock-and-roll subcultural music scene of the 1980s to which he belonged, but the masters of classical music and opera. Written in the manner of a communist gothic novel, it depicts, in the most unusual way, the transformation of the subculture of the 1970s and 1980s. The "commune" functions as a leitmotif, evoking the common experience of Yugoslav artistic and philosophical practice, within which, as Tišma says, "groups of friends"—who usually spoke a mix of Serbian and Croatian, but Slovenian as well—were trying to resist the regime individually and silently, devoting themselves to their own interests and making parallel worlds of values and sense. The commune, as a pacifist utopian project that believes in the individual act, soon proves impossible, and is aggressively destroyed by the system—not without ramifications for the art of the members, who turn to more radical, provocative, and lewder creative actions—provocations (Tišma here evokes several real events in the peaceful life of communist Novi Sad: one of them was the one-year imprisonment of conceptual artist Miroslav Mandić; the other was the first organized gang of thieves, whose leader was sentenced to death for killing two policemen who caught him robbing a newsstand). The main character is a kind of Alice in communist Wonderland, whose memories are full of linguistic burlesques and turnabouts. The playful, absurd language, full of neologisms and word games that are difficult to translate, prevents the reader from establishing logical links between cause and effect, or determining the identity of the heroes and their interrelationships. The simulated narration from a child's perspective at the end of the novel transforms into the horror of internment in death. It turns out that the whole story has been told posthumously, and that the cause of the main character's death is not fully clear. Yet this death finally reveals communist heaven as an eerie, horrible basement in which the grandfather (i.e., stepgrandfather of the main character) keeps jars with formaldehyde containing the fetuses of the babies whose birth he prevented during his secret gynecological practice during communism. *Quattro stagioni* is another novel of radical experimental prose depicting, albeit from a warped, half-autistic perspective, the world following the collapse of the "commune" in the former Yugoslavia. Tišma historically links this to the late 1970s and depicts its grave inability to create or re-create its lost readership-community and its corresponding experience of the (sub) cultural. Tišma's novel is excessive in the best possible way: in terms of language, style, poetics, motivation, and genre.

Mirjana Novaković's queer novelette *Gospel According to Thirsty* (*Jevanđelje po žednoj*, 1996) must also be mentioned here. Her story of a female messiah combines genre aspects of holy scripture, love melodrama, and science fiction. Novaković's anti-utopia illustrates the mutation of subcultural communities into frightening totalitarian groups, which the system fully controls, and which thus can no longer bear the attribute—subcultural.

These novels depict the ephemerality of subcultural communities, the continuous constitution and deconstitution of virtual (cyber) worlds of solidarity and love, but of suffering and hate as well. The members of these communities are critical of but also addicted to (media) society: the offenders but also the victims, the bystanders but also the participants. The selected novels not only thematize the transformation of subcultural communities from pacifist to militant organizations but also target those still believing in the community as a positive, transformative experience. All these authors defend the importance of the community's experience despite the danger posed by the radical, interest-based militarization of transitional and globalist groups. Regardless of who the narrator is and how the narrative is shaped (the allegedly omniscient narrator in Žurić's novel, the combination of first- and third-person narration in Arsenijević's novel, the first-person narrator in Albahari's, Tišma's, Valjarević's, and Novaković's works) these authors skillfully demonstrate the autobiographical account as the dominant discourse of the transition experience of humiliation and helplessness.

Despite that experience, all these novels are similarly associated with those whose "nonacceptance" lies at the core of their artistic practice, which is slowly taking the form of constant, persistent social resistance. Add to this list of antiheroes, the solitary protagonists on the literary stage like the late Judita Šalgo, and Vojislav Despotov; those writing "across the ocean," in exile, like David Albahari, Vladimir Tasić, and Nenad Jovanović; or those always underlining that they are soloists of this mostly male team such as Svetislav Basara, Nemanja Mitrović, and Srđan Valjarević. I think most of them still read comics and believe in the useless Borges-like fantasy without which they would have never written their prose—that those reading the same book for a moment dream the same different dream.

This slow association is not always evident or sufficiently evaluated by critics in the process of mapping the "free creative zones of influence" of Serbian society. But I believe it is of vital significance to the (non)existing Serbian literary stage, which still has not managed to get a grip on itself; the civil war, the collapse of the globalist utopia, and the totalitarianism of the neoliberal market have undermined every positive experience of togetherness. It is precisely this spontaneous association of male and female artists, isolated in their microcreative zones but not divided in teams, that is essential for new strategies of public and artistic action in Serbia, which is caught up in the scandal of transition. Except that these strategies have not been articulated yet—nor are they desirable.

17

Slovene Literature Since 1990

Alojzija Zupan Sosič

George Steiner, a connoisseur of European literature, reflects on contemporary literature in the following words: "I feel that, due to the torrential flow of challenges linked to political barbarism and technocratic slavery, we shall not find our way to the fact of our homeless state, our forced exile from the core of humanity, if we do not reexperience life's meaning in text, music, or art."[1]

Not unlike other European literary scholars, Steiner's observations echo the current state of mankind. My own observations on recent Slovene literature will be similar; because contemporary Slovene literature arose at a time of great sociopolitical change, references to politics and nonliterary qualifiers such as post-Yugoslav, postcommunist, postindependence, and transitional are almost unavoidable. I am well aware of the pitfalls of using a political framework to understand literature, a method that can all too easily confine analysis of post-1990 Slovene literature to historical, sociological, or culturological discussions, rather than literary ones. For this reason, I will place my primary emphasis on literary theory in this chapter, remembering to locate my work in a social and cultural context, both literary and nonliterary.

Slovene literature since the 1990s is part of a larger wave of contemporary literature which was established after 1945, and more critically after 1960. Yet, it can be said that in terms of both quality and quantity, this recent period has seen the greatest development of contemporary Slovene literature. The present discussion will be limited to critically acclaimed works, outlining the specific features that have characterized Slovene literature during this relatively brief time.

The independence struggle in Slovenia, an armed conflict lasting a mere ten days, was not as bloody as it was in some other former Yugoslav republics. Similarly, the change of political system—from socialism to capitalism—was relatively peaceful in Slovenia. There was a gentle break with communism, one might even say a continuity with it, as the former leader of the Communist Party became the head of the new state. If independence and the emergence of an independent Slovenia was the realization of a thousand-year dream, the same cannot be said about NATO, EU membership, and globalization. The restructuring of capital within the global neoliberal system effectively destroyed the Slovene economy and negatively impacted the development of all genres of noncommercial literature. Literary works are now printed in smaller runs of only five hundred and the financial position of authors has similarly deteriorated.[2] Neoliberal capitalism consequently subjected book publishing to market conditions, which limit publishers to printing books that sell in the market, such as cookbooks, travel books, and various New Age guides to personal growth, but rarely noncommercial literary works.

In addition to the new demands of the market, the development of Slovene literature was hindered by its changing role from national-affirmative to one concerned with personal and individual identity. In socialist Yugoslavia, the state financed the production and translation of original literature, thus reinforcing the link between literature and the building of the national identity of Slovenia (and other Yugoslav nations), as well as appurtenance to the Yugoslav multiethnic identity. With the appearance of an independent Slovenia, a paradoxical situation arose: the new state no longer ensured the publication of books in order to strengthen a national or European identity, handing over the responsibility to publishers whose interests were personal rather than collective.[3]

Marko Juvan advanced the following hypothesis to explain the current situation: postcommunist transition, the disintegration of multinational states, and the formation of new states linked with self-regulation of national cultural-artistic systems and a tendency to adapt to global (Western) culture have shaped a literary life marked by commercialization and trivialization of literature and the disappearance of its ideological collective role. In the postindependence period of Slovene literature, the loss of the ideological collective role also undermined the paramount importance that literature had been able to guard in the past, even at the time of greatest political repression.[4] If in the 1980s literature still retained its nation-affirming mission,[5] its role transformed by the 1990s, as it became more concerned with personal rather than collective identity. Although the new state's financial support for literature did not disappear, it shrank substantially. State subsidies, though smaller, continue to be available, as products of cultural policies aimed at preserving Slovene noncommercial literature.

The weakening of the nation-affirming role of literature plays a decisive role not only in the reduction of state subsidies, but in the construction of a new hierarchy of literary themes. With the new state, one would expect "great" themes such as independence, state building, and Europeanization to surface in literature, but, interestingly, "small" or personal topics became prioritized. Strangest of all, "great" themes failed to play a central role even in the novel, a narrative format which lends itself to social issues. Instead, from the late 1980s, "small" stories have prevailed, with a focus on the individual rather than on national identity, themes such as alienation, conflict in love, the encroachment of the public on the private, loss of identity, traumas of turbo-capitalism, and an inability to communicate. The growing interest in the personal over the collective has led to the centrality of themes relating to love, which have invariably privileged certain styles; in the post-1990s, the most common type of novel has become the romantic novel, while in poetry, love and erotic poems have prevailed.

In addition to the replacement of national themes with personal ones, there has also been a change in the hierarchy of literary genre: poetry's longstanding position as the preferred genre has been usurped by the novel. Poetry is still important in Slovenia, but the focus of media attention and reader interest is now on the novel. The 1990s were undoubtedly a decade of the novel; the number of novels published almost tripled since 1990 and the level of interest increased accordingly. A contributing factor was the establishment of the annual Kresnik Award for the best Slovene novel in 1991.[6] Although post-Yugoslav, postcommunist, and postindependence Slovene literature shares transitional traits with the literatures of most new EU member states, it boasts some specific features. Modernism, linked with existentialism, has been the most important aspect of Slovene literature since the 1960s. It remains a constant presence even at the end of the century, when postmodernism has cycled through Slovene literature. The most important representatives of modernism since the 1990s offer a link with pre-1990s literature: the poets Niko Grafenauer, Ifigenija Simonovič, and Dane Zajc; the prose writers Lojze Kovačič, Florjan Lipuš,

Rudi Šeligo, Vladimir Kavčič, Nedeljka Pirjevec, Nina Kokelj, and Vlado Žabot; and the dramatists Emil Filipčič and Peter Božič.

Modernism was replaced by postmodernism, although not completely, as some modernist texts appeared alongside postmodernist ones. This transition was specific to Slovene literature, with postmodernism first making its presence felt in poetry and only gradually appearing in narrative writing and drama (elsewhere, postmodernism is most characteristic of narrative prose). Postmodernism overall had a much smaller influence on Slovene literature in comparison to modernism. In a period of about twenty years, roughly from the mid-1970s to the mid-1990s, a number of collections of postmodern poetry appeared, but very few works of postmodern narrative prose or dramatic texts.

Rather than the appearance of postmodernist texts, postmodernism can be credited with introducing new literary perspectives and approaches. Jameson offered the term *new shallowness* which relates to the establishment of a new society—postindustrial, consumer, media, and information-driven—in which there has been a crucial abandonment of the traditional dichotomy between serious and popular literature. In this new, postmodern society, triviality becomes a popular literary characteristic.[7]

Yet, it should be noted that the growing number of genres characterized by trivial texts is not only a consequence of postmodernism, but also of Slovenia's entry into the European Union and the process of globalization, which—in the name of naïve hedonism or the postmodern conviction that the reading of literature should only be a source of enjoyment—privileges primarily best sellers. Even though postmodernism was already fading in the late 1990s, traces of postmodernist style are still present in Slovene literature: a reliance on traditional (generic) formulas and their modification through allusion, irony, and parody, as well as quotation and self-reference.

The dethronement of postmodernism has raised the question of how to refer to the literature preceding it: whether to use an inclusive sociological label such as postmodern literature, a general literary-analytical term such as post-postmodernism, or a new literary category. The coexistence of different phenomena in the Slovene postmodern is perhaps most successfully encapsulated by the new term literary eclecticism. A closer look shows that it consists of traditional approaches or reliance on tradition literary types, genres, and formulas, reshaped through the addition of new strategies. In contemporary Slovene literature, traditional literary approaches are modified in different ways through modernist, postmodernist, minimalist, or realist techniques.[8] In other words, the new category literary eclecticism suggests a "modified traditional literature"; indeed, the term "modified traditional novel" has already gained some currency.

Slovene literature since 1990 can also be characterized as "new emotionality," a term that embraces common traits shaping personal identity and a new type of emotional subject in literary texts. The subject takes part in a "big story," but, more significantly, strives to assert his or her individuality through "little stories" connected with recognizable generic, stylistic, and formal patterns. In writing about personal rather than social problems, these patterns are best described as a new emotionality, a particular feeling of ennui. In this, it differs from an almost baroque and positivistic excess of postmodernist emotion. New emotionality directs its irony and parody toward extraliterary and intraliterary stereotypes without citing its antecedents or connections. Erasing postmodernist mechanisms of intertextuality also nullifies the impression of contrived and simulated emotion, the most noted characteristic of postmodernist emotionality. It is precisely in the relationship between the sexes and the theme of love where we locate the source of the new emotionality. Along the way, new emotionality poses a number of questions relating to gender roles, (in)flexible identity, and personal predicaments.

In short, a new literary trend preceded postmodernism. Gary Potter and Jose López justify these dialectics by citing the necessity for different intellectual currents to appear, as they demonstrate that postmodernism no longer offers an appropriate response to the exigencies of the time. They suggest that the complexity of form of postmodernist narrative was challenged by critical realism which they posit as a counterpoint to postmodernism.[9] Fredric Jameson, too, identifies the presence of realism in postmodernism, framing it as "remnants of realism" adapted to mass culture.[10]

In Slovenia, alongside postmodernist literature, there also appeared traditional literature with realist tendencies. For this reason the Slovene novel from 1990 to 2010 is often referred to as the modified traditional novel with realist traits, as represented by the novels of Berta Bojetu, Aleš Čar, Mate Dolenc, Franjo Frančič, Nejc Gazvoda, Polona Glavan, Zoran Hočevar, Feri Lainšček, Miha Mazzini, Andrej Morovič, Boris Pahor, Andrej E. Skubic, Marko Sosič, Marjan Tomšič, Suzana Tratnik, and Jani Virk. This kind of novel models itself on the traditional novel, while it has undergone various (post)modernist transformations. The traditionalism of these recent Slovene novels is characterized by a compressed story, motivated relationships between characters, and a recognizable type. The nature of the story is removed from traditionalism by three reshaping factors: genre eclecticism, the revamped role of the narrator, and a larger proportion of spoken fragments.

The common characteristics of modified traditional narratives with realist traits are visible in the predominantly realist techniques aimed at convincing descriptions of reality, the principle of typicality, and differentiation of speech with regard to the social, psychological, and intellectual traits of the characters. These characteristics were fundamental to some earlier forms of realism, but new qualities were added in Slovene literature after the 1990s, such as the influence of different medias, a higher level of idealization and hyperbole, readability of story connected with the aesthetic of identity, and playfulness with regard to established genres, styles, or narrative formulas.

Considering that Slovene narrative since the 1990s is mostly realistic, it is necessary to find an appropriate prefix to add to the base word *realism*. With regard to choosing a prefix for categorizing the new trend after post-modernism, I agree with Mikhail Epstein, who offers *trans-* as the compliment to *realism*.[11] In other words, the phenomena and concepts of the new age, such as reality, objectivity, subjectivity, or sentimentality, are transformed into concepts prefixed by *trans-*: trans-reality, trans-objectivity, trans-subjectivity, and trans-sentimentality. These are comparative and relative concepts, expressed precisely as repetition. Seemingly paradoxical, it is through repetition that these concepts gain authenticity. If *proto-* signals openness and an unresolved future, then *trans-* confirms the continuity of future and past, incorporating alienation, irony, and parody in order to mark its renewed status as the possible, as the possible-reality, and as the possible-objectivity.

The term I propose for the new trend in contemporary Slovene literature is therefore *transrealism*. The prefix links transrealism with the preceding realist trends, but suggests that its repeatability and eclecticism, as well as the new emotional role of the literary subject, take on an added significance. Similar trends of emotionality have been labeled differently in other national literatures: in German, the established term is *new subjectivity*, in Russian *new sincerity*, and in English *supranational subjectivity*. In Slovene, I have labeled the special spiritual-historical and emotional state of the postmodern subject as new emotionality.[12] I understand this as a link between a particular spiritual ennui and the problem of identity in contemporary Slovene literature. The narrative subject, a literary figure and/or narrator, does not participate in the fictional world in order to comment on social problems (as was the case, for example, in realism, neo-realism, social/socialist realism), but feverishly strives to ensure his or her individuality through a readable story. The personal story is part of post-modern ennui, enamored with naïve hedonism and new emotional shifts in the search for identity: (re)evaluating gender and national stereotypes, the establishment of a humorous, cynical, or parodist distance, and the absence of unified aesthetic or philosophical guidelines. The realist principle of typification is aimed primarily at differentiating speech as a mimetic means of characterization, so that in contemporary Slovene narrative the proportion of speech has greatly increased. Transrealism thus has both old and new characteristics, relying on universal realist techniques while incorporating perspectives and methods of new emotionality.

Slovene literature is encompassed by the broad terms post-Yugoslav, postindependence, and postcommunist that suggest a change of political system from communism/socialism to capitalism. Doubtlessly, because Slovenia shares a legacy of political transition with other South Slavic states, most strongly those of the former Yugoslavia, it is often tempting to rely on the umbrella category "transition literature" to understand Slovene works in the last two decades. Yet, while Slovene authors certainly address some themes of political transition such as globalization and Europeanization seen in the literatures of other EU member states, Slovene literature is better understood outside the confines of political demarcations. The most important trend since the 1990s is undoubtedly modernism, which is responsible for the inauguration of contemporary Slovene literature. Modernism remains prominent in Slovene literature even though the Slovene literary scene has taken its leave of postmodernism. Slovene postmodernism can be credited with some new literary perspectives and approaches.

As I have proposed, the most precise definition of Slovene literature since 1990 is achieved by two new categories: literary eclecticism and new emotionality. The first captures the heterogeneous nature of recent Slovene literature, particularly its incorporation of different currents, directions, trends, groups, individuals, and poetics. The second term relates to the common features of texts with regard to personal identity and a new type of feeling. New emotionality is a particular kind of postmodern ennui with an attachment to tradition. In posing numerous questions regarding gender roles, (in)flexible identity, and personal predicaments, new emotionality emanates from somewhere between new seriousness and humorous-ironic-parodist awareness, as well as from the passive boredom and lethargy of the postmodern subject. I have also added to the discussion a new term for this literary trend—*transrealism*—as a possible common denominator for phenomena apparent in Slovene literature since 1990 and combined under the heading of modified traditional literature. As I have defined it, Slovene literature since 1990, or transrealism, exhibits a predominant realist technique and links with former European realist trends, revivified by a new emotionality.

18

The Palimpsests of Nostalgia
Venko Andonovski

There are two critical points in the evolution of Macedonian literature in the twentieth century. The first is in 1945, at the end of the Second World War, when modern Macedonian culture was established and Macedonians were given their own republic as a part of SFR Yugoslavia. The official name Macedonia came into being, with accompanying national and cultural attributes. The second crucial point is around 1990, in the period of the dissolution of the former Yugoslavia. With the acquisition of independent status as the Former Republic of Macedonia, the Macedonian nation came to face a new challenge: the pressure of globalization. For Macedonian literature, this meant the advent of a new—postmodern— manner of writing. Moving away from traditional genres and styles, Macedonian literature started to rely much more on intertextuality, parody, and palimpsest, as modes for redefining the concepts of history and national identity. Although these modes of postmodern writing did, in fact, emerge as early as 1960, reaching their zenith around 1980, they were treated as socially subversive, minor, and ephemeral voices in the homogeneous structure of the dominant artistic (Marxist) ideology before 1990. Literary theory and criticism did not evaluate these voices as facts of regular cultural evolution, but rather as aesthetic caprice, or "imported" Western "decadent" impulses, not worthy of critical attention.

. . .

After the disintegration of Yugoslavia, which started with the secession of Slovenia and Croatia, new political impulses developed as Macedonia entered the age of globalization. This marked the beginning of a new political concept in the Balkans, of independent and democratic states coupled with the rise of nationalism. All of these changes in political discourse were simultaneously evidenced in the radical transformation of literary structures and their functions.

In the first instance, the concept of "truth" was redefined, which implied the redefinition of the notion of "history." After 1990, Macedonian writers became aware of the fact that, as Richard Rorty put it, truth can be constructed despite the traditional belief that it exists per se and waits "to be found."[1] For fifty years, Macedonian writers had lived in a political system which accepted only one incontrovertible truth, namely that of communist ideology. Oddly, none of the literary critics and scholars noticed the "pastoral" dimension of this political "truth," which negates its very status as "truth." The best-known "truth about truth" is that it cannot be pastoral and idyllic, based on romantic exaggeration. The hyperbolic register of discourse cannot be a sample of true discourse, even speaking of political discourse. A case in point is the genesis of the Macedonian novel. The first Macedonian novels (after the Second World War) were written in the spirit of socialist realism, celebrating the birth of a new, heroic, and honorable world, using the form of monologic discourse. This was the world of the communist regime which managed to hide its dictatorship discreetly. In the novel *A Village Beyond the Seven Ashes* (*Selo zad sedumte jaseni*) by Slavko Janevski, this world emerges as an "idyllic chronotope." The plot shows *all* of the villagers overwhelmed with happiness bestowed by communist collectivization, impressed by the tractor and other agricultural machinery, and by the fertility of the soil. This is a monolithic philosophy, with a mythical concept of time that does not contain dissident voices, or an ideological opposition.

Post-Yugoslav literature took on board the notion of "truth as construct." It was obvious that the truth of the communist regime fell apart instantly, with the dissolution of Yugoslavia. But the quest for a new concept of truth began much earlier, during the 1960s, with the emergence of the first generation of "modernists." The first dualistic subversion in the Macedonian novel, as a distant echo of the dissidence of Bogomilism, is found in Georgi Abadjiev's novel *Desert* (*Pustina*, 1961). This novel constructs two points of view for a single narrated event, thus attaining a dialogic structure. The main characters, Gligor and Arso, have two different focalizations (points of view) and, accordingly, two different ideological perspectives about the events that befell them. They are revolutionaries who took part in the well-known diversionary actions of the Thessaloniki assassins (1903), carrying out a series of terrorist attacks in Thessaloniki in order to turn the attention of an indifferent Europe toward Macedonia and its unresolved political status. They are the only two survivors among the saboteurs, caught by the Ottoman empire and sentenced to death. While in prison, their opinions begin to differ. The notion of the one and only truth turns into two personal truths: that both of them swore not to be caught alive, and that by not committing suicide they have not respected the only ideologically allowed truth, expressed by the slogan "freedom or death." While Arso feels he is a traitor to that truth (Cosa Macedonica) and continues to believe in it as the only truth, Gligor constructs a personal truth about the event. His philosophy becomes: "It is not worth dying for any idea or revolution. Life itself is too beautiful, even in prison, to be given up for a cause such as a revolution."

This novel was the first step toward the deconstruction of the notion of a monolithic communist truth. The development of a Macedonian prose idiom (the novel and the short story) has continued to legitimate this polyphonic narrative structure, formerly considered subversive and "dissident." Later modernists, like Branko Varošlija and Dimitar Solev, employed the Freudian concepts of the unconscious, dream-work, and dream censorship, in order to relativize the notion of "one untouchable truth." The unconscious is an inevitable and fruitful source of a variety of symbolic truths for Varošlija and Solev; their fictional characters are dreamers who explore the "black continent" (a synonym for the unconscious) and try to decode the symbols of their dreams. They are interpreters in a literary sense of the word—not interested in interpreting reality, but in interpreting the interpretation of reality (the dreams). That is why they were sharply criticized by the representatives of the "realist" (read: socialist realist) doctrine, such as Dimitar Mitrev. Fortunately, the conflict between Macedonian "modernists" and "realists" did not last long, since the stylistic dominant of "modern" writing quickly superseded the socialist realist structures.

Macedonian modernists prepared the cultural ground for the establishment of the rule of the genre novel. To form the horizon of the genre novel, a stable modern culture is needed, which includes a competent reader ready to accept the epic format of the novel and its dialogic nature, as well as the other conventions of the genre. Macedonian modernists created a competent reader of the novel and short story, who had the ability to recognize the conventions of the genre. More importantly, these authors prepared a kind of reader who refused to accept the "ideological" delivery of a monologic literary discourse reliant on the concept of a "unique truth." It is no coincidence that the first appearance of modern formalist, linguistic, and structural-semiotic studies (associated especially with Bakhtin) in Macedonia appeared along with the first symptoms of the disintegration of the stable "monolithic," "historical" novel:

> Bakhtin develops this view, seeing language not as singular and monolithic, but as plural and multiple; languages inscribed with various evaluative accents become socio-ideological languages intimately bound up with material and social conditions and with the contexts of their production—i.e. their "heteroglossia." Bakhtin applies this to the novel, the form which is exemplary in its ability to represent a dialogic inter-animation of socio-ideological languages. The dialogic nature of the novel can be either open or closed; the author can either let the interplay of languages speak for itself or can impose a privileged authorial metalanguage. For Bakhtin, the dialogic is linked to his concept of carnivalization—i.e. to popular forms that disrupt and relativize meaning in opposition to the "official" discourse.[2]

Postmodern Macedonian writers, starting from 1980, fully exploited not only the dialogic, but also the "polyphonic," intertextual possibilities of modern discourse. Fragments, quoted characters, quoted dialogues, scenes from the Bible and history entered their narratives with an abundance of meanings, code switching, and semantic crossings. As Brian McHale would explain, the "change of a dominant" (from epistemological to ontological) caused a change in perception of the text's *origin*: literary works could be made of other literary texts.[3] Doing so, the author could create alternative meanings, changing the register from pure quotation of the "known" text, to parody and travesty. The ironic effect is obvious, as is illustrated by the short stories and novels by Dragi Mihajlovski, the most prominent Macedonian postmodernist.

Since 1990 the structure of Macedonian literature has changed profoundly, accepting and maintaining all the premises of postmodern writing. It has embraced the inexorable influence of postmodern philosophy, according to which every "historical" discourse is a pure fiction since there is no "objective" approach to historical events. Furthermore, it is impossible to claim that even historians can generate an "objective" proposition about any historical event, because the very procedure of choosing from the chain of events is a subjective, personal act. Giving advantage to one event instead of another is clearly an act of subjective access to history, and retelling (narration) is only a performative mode of telling history. History is more diegesis than mimesis; it is not concerned with events per se but with the *interpretation* of events; it describes not events but testimonies to events. Therefore, a revision of the notion of the "historical novel" is unavoidable, and characterizes the main change in Macedonian literature after 1990: the ironization of history, created through a "game" that skirts between *fiction* and *fact*. This interplay validates the accuracy of one of the most precise definitions of irony: "The basic feature of every irony is a contrast between a reality and an appearance."[4]

It is quite evident that this change from the "historical" to "pseudo-historical" was influenced not only by the reception of "new theories," but also by the bitter experience of the death of Yugoslavia and the war, which involved many Macedonian soldiers who could not escape from the JNA (Yugoslav National Army). It is an extraliterary but very important fact that the first victim of the civil war in Yugoslavia was the Macedonian soldier who was killed in Split, Croatia, by Croatian forces fighting for their own independent state.

This all caused a change not only in the stylistic dominant of literary texts (irony, grotesque, travesty of historical discourse), but also in the thematic field and the level of "political unconsciousness." Recent novels, poems, plays, and short stories are bitter and ironic comments on the "unstable" identity of nations and states in the Balkans. Recent literary works are a satiric critique of the false leaders, prophets, rescuers, and political messiahs. Although the theme of war is not clearly and vividly represented in these literary works that have come into existence since 2001 (when Macedonia experienced a conflict with local Albanians), political lies and hypocrisy usually provide the frameworks for them. It is understandable that allegory is the most exploited register of the altered discourse-meaning. Textual crossings with various intertexts (especially the Bible) produce alternative meanings, but the main semantic pattern functions as a strong allusion to present Macedonian political conditions. Macedonia, after its peaceful secession, was ignored by global politics, forgotten by Europe and the rest of the world (most notably the United States), along with the Balkans' false political prophets. Hannah Arendt points to such specific psycho-sociological phenomena, claiming that "the surest long-term result of brainwashing is a peculiar kind of cynicism—an absolute refusal to believe in the truth of anything, no matter how well this truth may be established."⁵

Dragi Mihajlovski's novel *The Prophet of Diskantrija* (*Prorokot od Diskantrija*, 2001) provides an illustration of Arendt's statement. In one scene in the novel, his protagonist (who has many characteristics of a deceiver or a magician, a man who performs miracles using tricks) wants to make people believe that he is a prophet. He plans to prove this by walking on water. The postmodern manner is patently obvious here: the hypotext-hypertext relationship is revealed in the reference to the biblical story of walking on water. The author elaborates a special intertextual relationship, which in this instance might be called a *travesty of parody* (the parodic intonation of the given scene cannot be overlooked). When a miracle is demonstrated using parody, the miracle is disputable. The parody of the miracle results in realism; if the miracle is a deception (as we are taught by the parody of the miracle), then it is not a miracle at all.

How does Mihajlovski's postmodern prophet walk on water? The "prophet" manages his trick in such a way that he waits for night to come; then he climbs into a boat which is invisible in the dark, and paddles far from the shore. Here he lights a lamp, lifting it up to his face. The invisible boat continues to drift and the people standing on the shore can only see the prophet, moving through the water, as if he were walking on it, without touching it.

The deception is fulfilled; the illusion of reality is complete. Here is proof that truth can be constructed. The prophet proves his identity with a sophisticated deception, of which the reader is aware. The miracle is rationally explained to the reader. Using the vocabulary of Tzvetan Todorov, from his famous book *The Fantastic*, the *miraculous* is transformed into merely the *strange* (the "strange" occurs when an "incredible event" is granted a rational explanation). Here Mihajlovski plays with the theoretical notion of the miraculous, simplifying it to a realistic etymon.

Accordingly, in this scene traces of *metafiction* are also obvious, revealing how miracles are arranged. So, we must agree with Patricia Waugh, when she underlines the importance of self-referential nature of all metafictional narratives.

Each metafictional novel self-consciously sets its individual *parole* against the *langue* (the codes and conventions) of the novel tradition. Ostentatiously "literary" language and conventions are paraded, set against the fragments of various cultural codes, not because there is nothing left to discuss, but because the formal structures of these literary conventions provide a statement about the dissociation between, on the one hand, the genuinely felt sense of crisis, alienation, and oppression in contemporary society, and, on the other, the continuance of traditional literary forms like realism which are no longer adequate vehicles for the mediation of this experience."[6]

So, in revealing the mechanism by which a miracle is happening, *metafiction* becomes not only a method of revealing the *codes of (false) fantastic*, but also a game with the codes that create the fantastic. The codes of the fantastic are abused for pragmatic aims (deception), or for what I term a *call for realism*. The "call for realism" in this novel adds to the layers of meaning, as one of the levels in the story about false prophets. This call for realism literally says: "Wake up, people! You are surrounded by many false prophets!" If so, this episode, although it demonstrates a high level of literary self-consciousness, also adds a semantic layer of active, polemic, and critically oriented statement toward the actual reality. This is clearly shown in the title of the novel: the name of the country (the setting where the story unfolds) is just the written pronunciation of the English "This Country," which is quite a significant signal that the place where the false miracles are happening is Macedonia.

The theme of war is directly addressed in the novels by Blaže Minevski, a novelist and short-story writer primarily interested in the possibilities of "overwriting" historical facts. In his previous novels, Minevski was preoccupied with the fear that somebody had falsified Macedonian history. In a later novel, *Target* (*Nišan*, 2007), he turns to an actual theme, a historical event: the conflict between the Macedonian army and the terrorist groups of Macedonian Albanians, who are purportedly fighting for their human rights. The structure of the novel reveals its "hybrid" orientation, shown as indecisiveness between the poles of the modern and the postmodern. The actual story is set at the front: one sniper becomes aware of being the target of another sniper who turns out to be a woman of exceptional beauty. She does not shoot at her target, because at first she is curious, and later falls in love with him. These elements provide a solid base for a story "in reality," "in the present," which will serve only as a framework for a larger achrony—a long flashback, in which the male sniper, in direct communication with the woman who holds him as a target, will tell the story of his life. The political aspect is evident: the author is describing the confrontation between the Muslim units and the Christian army, fighting on unnamed land, although all the informants (the names of the places and characters) point to Macedonia. Despite the strong political frame of the story, the aesthetic value is preserved because the reader is asking himself questions: Why does this young woman not shoot the narrator, when she knows very well that snipers act spontaneously, immediately at the moment they capture a figure in their optical aim? Why is the victim given a chance to lie down, to take the executioner in his own optical aim? Why, as in a checkmate position, do they then watch one another, studying each other's nearly hypnotized faces? The reason is that the woman, who has the advantage in the situation, desires *the narration*. The male character, using an internal monologue, telepathically transmits his narrative which has the power of an opiate on the woman. His narration exudes a kind of magic that removes the strength she needs to pull the trigger. In this novel, the code of narrative transmission, well known from *A Thousand and One Nights*, in which Scheherazade will stay alive as long as she narrates, is clearly cited in the intertextual relation. In Minevski's novel, the woman listens to the story of an anonymous victim (whose life is in her hands), a pacifist story of a man who has cherished many high ideals, including the desire to become a writer (he had even taken part in a creative-writing workshop in Iowa, where he became friends with many writers of the world, including those from Albania). The story illustrates the absurdity of the war and its power to ruin lives, as well as to make a farce of those things that seem stable—to transform instantly the idealistic writer into the dirty soldier living in the trenches of war.

The metonymy of war is embedded in the title of *Novel About Arms* (*Roman za oružjeto*, 2003), by Ermis Lafaznovski. Exploring the spiritual and material culture of rural Macedonia, the main character incidentally becomes a victim of his own unconventional scientific methodology. Threatened and forced, he starts collecting and documenting bizarre sorts of arms, taking a journey into the unknown and mysterious conditions of the human spirit.

As an opposite current to this group of writers who emphasize the "local" setting, occupied with the present historical Macedonian reality, there is another group of prose-fiction writers, who place their stories *somewhere else*—a definite place, outside Macedonia, including Europe, the United States, and other attractive and exotic, "global" chronotopes. The main characters may be Macedonians but are not necessarily so; they are in contact with the Other, the Stranger, and with different cultural values. This is exemplified by the young and talented novelist Goce Smilevski (*Conversations with Spinoza* [*Razgovor so Spinoza*, 2003] and *The Sister of*

Sigmund Freud [*Sestrata na Sigmund Frojd*, 2007]), and also, the very gifted young woman poet and novelist Lidija Dimkovska, whose "nomadic" novel *Candid Camera* (*Skriena kamera*, 2004) deserves special attention. Of course, it is not a foregone conclusion that these works should receive the highest aesthetic evaluation because of their settings. Just because they try to erase the "local setting" and replace it with a "global" one does not mean that they will be rated more highly by the Macedonian reading public. The opposite tends to be the case: the authors of such works expose themselves to the risk of trivialization and total loss of distinctive stylistic features in their writings, because the Macedonian reader has a wide range of choices of important, world-famous authors in Macedonian bookstores, offering "global" chronotopes. However, this risk does not affect Smilevski and Dimkovska because they masterfully balance the "local" and "global," *deconstructing* that artificially produced binary opposition in the manner of Derrida. There is no stable identity of the local, just as there is no stable identity of the global. There are very important traces of the "global" in the "local" (for instance, European standards of training in schools in Macedonia), just as there are very important "ingredients" of the local in the global: provincial, small-town morals and gossiping in socially allowed forms such as the media and tabloid press, and yellow press. By contrast, the representatives of the "ironic chronotope" are only "local" in appearance, using dialects, colloquial language, and, sometimes, indicators of local recognizable places. The most important thing about all of them is that they always achieve universality, despite the type of setting they use.

. . .

In her representative collection *Ten Modern Macedonian Plays*, Jelena Luzina, the most prominent Macedonian theater historian, has divided the evolution of Macedonian theater into three formations/generations, which implies three different stylistic phases in the development of Macedonian dramatic discourse.[7] Her "third" phase includes five authors, who wrote their best plays just after the breakdown of Yugoslavia: Venko Andonovski, Saško Nasev, Žanina Mirčevska, Jugoslav Petrovski, Dejan Dukovski. Luzina points especially to the works of Dejan Dukovski, referring to a crucial, distinctive feature of theatrical discourse after 1990: *the obsession with evil and aggressiveness*, which are a distant echo (a kind of eternal semiosis) of the Yugoslav civil war and allusion to the congenital evil of humankind. She singles out Dukovski's neonaturalistic play *Powder*

Keg (*Bure barut*, 1994). Although the structure is "fragmented" (according to the principles of postmodern writing),

> by staging this eternal motif in eleven masterfully subversive dramatic situations, set exclusively in a trivial/substandard ambiance (cafes, side streets, trains, buses, life boats, cheap American hotel, prison), Dukovski elicits the *eternal truth* about the *eternity of evil*. The existentialist Sartre may have entrusted us with the powerfully comforting thesis that hell is a product of others, of those around us, but the generations that no longer believe in *eternal values* and *sacrosanct truths*, don't ask to be pardoned for their responsibility for their own actions, and are at the same time sufficiently courageous to admit that they themselves created this hell. Evil resides within us. In Dukovski's play, Europe and the rest of the world recognized and affirmed exactly that eternal *spiral of evil*, and recognized it not only in the Balkans.[8]

These statements are a very precise description of the anatomy of Macedonian theatrical discourse after 1990: the awareness of the "cursed" Balkan area as a geopolitical projection of Western political discourses, as a place of "dirty" and "aggressive" semiotics, projected in order to distinguish Western culture as cultivated in comparison with the dirty Balkans (after the almost "exploited" Orient). The semiotic projection of the Balkans is part of the pragmatic imagology of the West: the West needs such a semiotic and geopolitical project simply because it has to show its "innocence" and disguise its military and economic interest in global domination. It is clear that Macedonian postmodern writers touched on the issue of Otherness and reactualized the generally accepted concept of *balkanism* as an imagological phenomena, first mentioned in Maria Todorova's famous book *Imagining the Balkans* (1997).

It must be underlined here that all these postmodern playwrights have to be seen as successors of two crucial figures from earlier generations: Kole Čašule (the first "modernist" generation) and Goran Stefanovski (the second, modernist-postmodernist generation). In their plays the problem of identity (national or personal) and its unstable nature in relation with the Other was posed for the first time, and became the central dramatic problem for their followers. Stefanovski has even written a play about the war tragedy in Sarajevo (*Sarajevo*) and has been (together with Dukovski) the most famous Macedonian playwright abroad. In Stefanovski's plays written after the breakdown of Yugoslavia, we find correlative themes as a replica of his younger colleagues. Even a brief review of the titles of his plays will show his "compatibility" with the poetics of the "five postmodernists": *The Tower of Babylon* (*Kula Vavilonska*, 1990; an allegory about the former YU and its multicultural and multilingual state, which produced political, ethnic, and national misunderstandings); *Kasabalkan* (1998; a pun composed of the Italian *casa*, "house," and *Balkan*, the Balkans; and an anagram of the famous movie *Casablanca*); *Euralien* (another pun, on the words *EU* and *alien*); *Hotel Europe* (*Hotel Evropa*, 2000; a coproduction of the Interkult, Stockholm, and festivals in Vienna, Bologna, Bonn, and Avignon). Stefanovski is also the only Macedonian winner of the prominent international literary award "Vilenica" (Slovenia).

. . .

This turn in the perception of the World as a Whole is evident not only in prose fiction and drama, but also in the discourse of postmodern Macedonian poets since 1990. Before 1990, the main motifs of Macedonian poets were: the harmony of nature, love, epiphany, and emanations of God on the "surface" world of phenomena. The whole universe was a mysterious and harmonized *text*, full of metaphors which are in accord with each other. Now, with the postmodern vision of fragmentation and the (geopolitically) divided world (which, by definition, includes at least two points of view and at least two cultures and imagologies), a new ironical tone enters the poems. A case in point is Zoran Ančevski's poem "The Balkans" ("Balkan," 1998):

> Cloaca of heresies
> and heretics
> that Europe ignites
> and extinguishes
> on its pyres,
> stretching them out
> on Procrustean beds
> while un-Christian-like
> branding their sin
> on their minds
> A knot of light and dark
> that by definition
> is only resolved with a sword . . .
> From too much past
> neither peace
> nor present.[9]

In his poem "EuropA" (1998), through a mythical perspective (Europa/e was raped by Zeus), we can recognize the stereotype of the Balkans' view of European "ignorance" about the nations on its "margins":

> Ah,
> you more gentle than a goddess
> that our heartless God raped so harshly
> without pardon or mercy
> now you hold a sweet revenge . . .
> . . .
> Ah,
> you Zeus, you most insatiable
> scoundrel of heavenly kind
> you lustful maniac,
> what misery did you bind on our neck
> what sin did you brand on our brain . . .
> . . .
> Ah,
> have mercy you bright-eyed dame,
> we kneel broken before you
> before the gates
> of your mansion of gold
> and kiss humbly your heels
> hear our modest plea
> give us pardon for the ancient sin
> and allow us in for a while
> give us some crusty crumbs
> from your godly table
> and even after
> we'll celebrate your name
> in fearful stutter.[10]

The poet is addressing the goddess Europa, but it is quite clear that it is only a metaphor for Europe today and its authority to decide the fate of "decimal" nations and ethnic groups. The pathetic intonation cannot hide the *fear*, the dominant collective effect of post-Yugoslav nations, about the future of their national and cultural identities. This fear did not exist in any poem by any Macedonian poet before 1990 (except maybe in Slavko Janevski). The last two decades, on the contrary, are marked by that emotion of cultural unreliability and uncertainty, often expressed by the favorite metaphor of native home, as in Katica Kulafkova's poem "Poetics of Laughter" ("Poetika na plačot," 2001):

> For I saw
> at every step in my home
> greed for another home
> passion and then apathy
> dashes in the beginning and in the end
> of history
> (so that one can yell "mine"
> and then pull at them!)
> for I saw
> how people take you in the misery of their neighbors
> and pride insatiably
> mean pride typical for man
> the godly creature, beast, blast![11]

On a formal level, Macedonian postmodern poetry shows a vivid tendency to quote, to overwrite, to parody previous literary works, irrespective of whether they borrow from Macedonian or from other literatures. This poetry is an interplay of signifiers, a complicated net of indices which point to other signifiers, quotations, fragments, and texts. All these changes show that Macedonian poetry made a crucial turn from metaphor to metonymy—it became more *prosaic*, semantically more expressive, and more *polemic*. It is not hard to suppose that the breakdown of Yugoslavia and the ensuing indefinite political status of a new, independent state of Macedonia influenced (at least as a secondary factor) this important change in the dominant style of Macedonian poetry.

Palimpsest is the key word that explains, as a magic, theoretical, descriptive system, the present state of Macedonian literary discourse, which is an effort to overwrite history regarding its unfavorable conditions and unjust decisions affecting Macedonian people. It is an effort to repair the historical damage, to avoid the sin done to Europe by Zeus; an effort to enter the gates of the Goddess Europe (Ančevski); an effort not to be a "dark and dirty place" somewhere in the Balkans (Dukovski, Andonovski); an effort to rewrite the ethnic conflict in Macedonia between the Macedonians and Albanians in a new, love-story code (Minevski); an effort to deconstruct the stereotypes of "local" and "global" cultures (Smilevski,

Dimkovska, Stefanovski, Andonovski, Mihajlovski); an effort to expose and unmask false political prophets who are leading this country ("This countria") and their own people to ruin (Mihajlovski); an effort to accept the Other in order to define, recognize, and understand one's own identity; and an effort to perceive the Other not as an enemy but as a possible friend, because pure difference does not mean "evil" in itself. That is why the postmodern mode of writing has been dominant in the last two decades in Macedonian literature. It is not possible to reach such goals and to fulfill such expectations without *palimpsest* writing.

The palimpsest mode of writing is a quest for identity, because the palimpsest is always grounded in *the previous* text, which undermines in a subversive manner the identity of the new text, with the new text, of course, being a new state—Macedonia. But on the screen of history, as its background, stands the old text, the old history, the old identity, together with the "text" of the old political system. The result is: all traditional values are dead, but the new values have not yet been born. The past has gone (YU), the future (EU) is not yet here, and the present moment is only *waiting* for the future. And when you wait for something, you fill the eternity of the moment, which leads to nostalgia.

Nostalgia is the second keyword. One can be nostalgic in desiring the past or in desiring the future. In Camus' philosophic vocabulary, nostalgia is defined as a desire for Wholeness. Macedonian literature feels nostalgia for the lost Wholeness of the past, and nostalgia for the unfulfilled Wholeness of the future. It is a schizomorphic situation of collective, cultural ambiguity which denies the construction of an (at least) temporary identity. Deprived of the past, not yet endowed with the future, Macedonian literature today is just a nostalgic metonymy of Wholeness.

Part VII

Return to the Provinces

19

The Spirit of the Kakanian Province
Dubravka Ugrešić

An Inner Map

Those provincial train stations with their apricot-hued façades and window boxes of pelargonia (take a train from Zagreb to Budapest!), architecture (hospitals, bureaucratic buildings, schools, and theaters), cuisine (sachertorte, cabbage and noodles, *Kaiserschmarrn*, *Tafelspitz*, dumplings, and poppy-seed noodles), city parks, and the Czech last names sprinkled through the Viennese telephone directory (like poppy seeds on a kaiser roll) are not the only ways to recognize a Kakanian landscape.

I am no expert on the Austro-Hungarian monarchy, I hardly even rank as an amateur, but I have a sense that the monarchy stamped a watermark on the souls of its subjects, an internal landscape, the coordinates of periphery and center. The center became aware of itself thanks to the periphery, the periphery grew to know itself thanks to the center. From the provinces, one went to Vienna to the opera, to Budapest to buy the latest hats. After all, was it not a child of the periphery, a postman's son from Sarajevo, who shot Kakania in the head, and afterward things in Europe were never the same?

The Croatian Kakanian Novel

Croatia lay on the outskirts of Austro-Hungary. I do not know much about the times, but I do recall a few odds and ends from the history of Croatian letters. I remember, for instance, that protagonists of Croatian novels at the turn of the last century studied in Vienna, Prague, or Budapest, and that aside from Croatian, they used German, Hungarian, or Czech. The detail that a person went off to Vienna to study caught my youthful fancy, it seemed so noble, though it is also true that the characters in the novels could barely make ends meet. And if these protagonists were writers, as some were, their poems were occasionally published in Prague, Budapest, or Viennese publications, to the envy of their surroundings. That, too, had a noble ring. The Kakanian metropolises have long since lost their attraction and pizzazz. The center moved elsewhere. I am guessing that today's writers in Prague, Budapest, and Vienna envy the rare compatriot whose name appears as a contributor in—*The New Yorker*.

While I was leafing through a few Croatian Kakanian novels (which I had last cracked in high school), I felt I was working not with literary texts but with genes. It was like discovering something we have always known but failed to attend to, like discovering a birthmark exactly where it was on our parents, children, or grandchildren. At the same time, the literary critic in me grumbled while reading the ongoing episodes of these provincial literary soap operas, which have been going on for a century. Ah, picking up old books again is so often a disappointment.

I will say something about these novels in thumbnail sketches, as befits them, like the episodes of TV soap operas, or teletext. All the examples come from the Croatian literary canon and are required reading in high school. At their center there is invariably a male protagonist, whose life's destiny is told in first or third person. The structure of the novel follows a type, like the window-box pelargonia of Austro-Hungarian railway stations. These literary heroes are distant relatives of Werther and Childe Harold, cousins to the Russian literary heroes, those who would be dubbed "superfluous" by literary critics after Turgenev's *Diary of a Superfluous Man*. The type—the high-strung, oversensitive, educated misfit or outcast—such as Griboedov's Chatsky, Pushkin's Eugene Onegin, Lermontov's Pechorin, Turgenev's heroes (Rudin, Lavretsky, the Kirsanovs, and Bazarov), Goncharov's Oblomov, and others—proliferated throughout Slavic literatures and is exclusively the characteristic of the male literary lineage. The women in these novels belong to one of three varieties: (1) the young, beautiful, noble, and patriotic girl who is abandoned, as a rule, by the hero; (2) the femme fatale (often foreign) who toys with the hero; (3) the unloved, quiet "sufferer" who follows the hero faithfully to the end of her days.

The First Suicide

The novel *Janko Borislavić* by Ksaver Šandor Gjalski was published in 1887 (we are already twenty years into Austro-Hungary at this point). The novel is a belated romantic work on "Faustian problems of the spirit," as Croatian literary criticism of the day deemed it. Janko Borislavić is a Croatian landowner who, while studying abroad, is torn by doubts as to his study, theology, and returns to his estate in the Croatian Zagorje region. Here he falls in love with the charming Dorica, though love, thinks Borislavić, is "fickle," turning a "chaste, holy virgin" into nothing more than a "simple organ for prolonging the species." Possessed by the "intellectualistic" restlessness of the period, steeped in Schopenhauer's philosophy and, of course, a fear of women, Borislavić in his long internal monologues polemicizes passionately with the books he has read. He leaves Dorica and ventures into the world where he spends six years, sinking into greater and greater disappointment. Human "stupidity" is "eternal and absolute," and everywhere:

Ha, ha, for that you, my Diderot, Rousseau and you other unfortunates who were so gifted with human spirit, for this you wrote those volumes of wisdom! In vain your efforts, futile all that work. Ah, so stupid, stupid is the world.

"Compelled by his Faustian nature, his inner fire, to track down the thousands of threads that compose the mysterious source of life," Borislavić travels. He leaves Paris, disappointed ("Eighty years ago you shed so much blood, alas, my Frenchmen!"); he stops briefly in England, where he cannot bear the "stuffiness of human society which lies in wait implacably to thwart all progress and then it serves up peace for the human spirit." From England he goes to America, but there he is put off by the "amalgam of inherited prejudices, the frenzy and struggle of individual wills and desires." Upon his return from America, he disembarks in Germany like "vast barracks of philistine phalanges." Borislavić returns to his native Zagorje, but here, as well, "human malice and stupidity revel in orgy." Again he sets out on his journey, again he returns, he has a "nervous breakdown," slits his wrists, and dies.

A Second Death

A somewhat later novel by Ksaver Šandor Gjalski, *Radmilović* (1894), has a similar plot. Here the hero, Marko Radmilović, is not destroyed by "world anguish" but by the environment of Zagreb, the place where Radmilović comes from the Croatian provinces. Radmilović publishes his poems and short stories in Czech, Polish, Russian, and other Slavic languages; they have even heard of him in Paris, but in Zagreb he is unknown and unrecognized.

It is sad, so sad that such a writer is unknown! . . . Had he been born in France, Russia, or Germany, believe me, the whole world would have known of him. But he is only a Croatian writer, he works on the threshold to the Orient, at the fringes of Europe. . . . This could easily happen here with someone like Bourget, or another more vaunted celebrity. There is no such European or world fame which could so easily surmount our high wall, the wall of pervasive non-reading.

Radmilović is insulted by the "cannabilistic persecutions" of his colleagues, an environment which holds that the literary calling is not worthy of respect and where there is no educated readership.

So, I tell you, were all our literary institutions to collapse, were all our writers to breathe their last, the gentlemen here would not fall silent for so much as an instant, or even notice that something was amiss! But were the German Leipzig Press to stop coming out, heaven forbid, with its *Familienblatters*, its *Buch für Alle*, or its pound-a-novel publications such as *Sibiriens Holle*, these men would be despondent. . . . How many lovely Croatian women know the names of a Gundulić, a Mažuranić, a Preradović, how many of them would blush if you were to catch them unaware of Osman or Čengić? . . . Ah—yet heaven forbid that you come across a single one who knows nothing of German Elise Polko or Marlitt!—for this we struggle, day and night, for this we sacrifice peace of mind and a sure existence, health, everything! Oh, Lord, where do we find the will to keep working?—This work brings us no sustenance, gives us no moral or ethical reward, no fame, no benefit to the people. Why keep working at all?

Radmilović rents a small room in a modest dwelling where a girl named Stanka lives with her ailing mother. Radmilović finds a sympathetic soul in Stanka, but falls in love instead with wealthy, frivolous, beautiful Olga. When Olga becomes engaged to a more profitable life partner, Radmilović plunges into despair. With Stanka's help he completes his novel, *The Sufferers*. Radmilović and Stanka marry, leave Zagreb, and move to a provincial town. Though an attorney by profession, Radmilović finds work at a local attorney's office as an ordinary legal clerk. When a publishing house decides not to bring out his new novel, Radmilović publishes it at his own expense, but the literary critics dismiss the novel with scorn. Radmilović burns his own book in a fit of pique, suffers a nervous breakdown, and soon dies in a madhouse.

The same writer, two of the same endings—a person undone, descending into madness and death. Let us continue on our way and see whether the Kakanian Croatian writers offer us a more cheerful novelistic resolution after the protagonist returns from the metropolis to his native provinces.

Two Worlds

The hero of Vjenceslav Novak's *Dva svijeta* (*Two Worlds*, 1901), Amadej Zlatanić (the Croatian Mozart!), having been left early without parents, finds parental care and support in the local chaplain, Jan Jahoda (a Czech, of course). Jahoda discovers the boy's remarkable musical talent and seeks a scholarship for him through the local authorities so that Zlatanić can attend the Prague conservatory. "Among the smaller peoples—and that means you, Croats—such natural talents are often lost both out of poverty and the lack of understanding by those who should be seeing to their education." The local authorities turn down Jahoda's request. ("Pane Jahoda, our children are not made for such things. We leave this to you Czechs.")

When Jahoda dies, Amadej sells his parental home for a pittance and goes to Prague, where he passes the entrance exam and enrolls at the conservatory. Amadej graduates from the conservatory with success, and his composition entitled "Adelka" (the name of the girl waiting for him at home) is performed at the final student recital. With glowing reviews in the Prague papers and his diploma in his pocket, Amadej returns home full of hope and plans. He is given a modest salary as the local chaplain and marries Adelka. He sends his composition "Adelka" to Zagreb, but its performance receives bad reviews ("A homework assignment, in which the mostly familiar motifs have been reworked"). Amadej plunges into despair, his only solace being the appearance of Irma Leschetizky, the wife of a man involved in a future railway line (see, here are Austro-Hungarian railway lines and foreign women full of understanding!). Amadej spends more and more time with Irma. When Irma leaves, Adelka falls seriously ill. Amadej realizes he has been unfair to Adelka, the one person who is truly dedicated to him.

With the intention of relegating to "the shadows all arrogant talents" in town, the authorities introduce Rakovčić, a tambura player. Rakovčić's tamburitza ensemble is far more draw for everyone than Amadej's classical music. "Mr. Z. played a Chopin piece on the piano which did not warm up the audience. Perhaps this does for the cold north, but in the warm south everything is more lush and heartfelt, even the music." Amadej loses his job, and Rakovčić the tambura player is given it. Faced with poverty, Amadej gives private lessons. Irma Leschetizky speaks for Amadej in Berlin musical circles. Amadej is made an offer to sell his compositions to a Berlin publisher, but he must relinquish the copyright. Amadej refuses, but when Adelka's health worsens, he sells his compositions to the Berlin publisher after all ("I go around the world, nameless, hence no one can see me"). Adelka dies, Amadej loses his bearings, the local authorities lock him up in an asylum, and he soon dies.

Vjenceslav Novak develops a similar theme once more, but this time from the perspective of a theory, popular at the time, of heredity. In the novel *Tito Dorčić* (1906), he describes the sad fate of a fisherman's son. Though all the people in Tito Dorčić's family are fishermen, his father compels the boy to pursue a different path in life. He dispatches him to school in Vienna (again Vienna!), where Tito fritters away his days, utterly disinterested in his surroundings and the study of law. His father's bribes propel him somehow through his studies, and he comes home and finds work as a local judge. The job does not interest him. His father's efforts are finally undone when Tito, out of lack of ability and carelessness, condemns an innocent man to die. Dorčić goes mad and drowns in the sea, returning to where he belongs.

We can add here that the time of mass suicides in Europe came a decade or so later, inspired by the Great Depression and Rezso Seress's hit *Szomoru Vasarnap*. As the story goes, Seress managed to infect not only Central Europeans but Americans with a Central European melancholy. Supposedly, people threw themselves off the Brooklyn Bridge after listening to Seress's doleful hit in New York.

Another Suicide

Milutin Cihlar Nehajev's novel *Bijeg* (*Escape*, 1909) is thought by Croatian critics to be the finest novel of Croatian modernism. Đuro Andrijašević, the protagonist, throws away two years spent studying law in Vienna (Vienna again!), then he returns to Zagreb where he enrolls at the faculty and passes all the exams. All he has left to do is his doctoral dissertation. His uncle, who has been sending him monthly financial support, dies without leaving Đuro the anticipated inheritance. Andrijašević is engaged to Vera Hrabarova, but he fears he will lose her because of his unexpected financial woes. The history of Andrijašević's fall begins the moment he finds a job as a teacher

in a secondary school in Senj. Andrijašević finds everything in the small
costal town boring and strange. "It's not that the people are bad, they are
not repulsive. But they are empty, so horribly empty. And the same—one
is like the next. They have nearly identical habits, they even drink the same
number of glasses of beer." Andrijašević is not interested in the school, and
finds it difficult to write his dissertation. After waiting patiently for several
years, Vera leaves him and becomes engaged to someone else. Andrijašević
falls further and further into debt, spending all his time drinking, quarreling
with a growing number of people, and is ultimately fired. In his last letter,
which he sends to his one remaining friend, he hints at suicide. "The only
thing I feel is: I must put an end to this. I should escape altogether—flee
from this life, so sickening, so disgraceful. . . . Surely you can see that I have
always fled from life and people. I've never resisted—I have stepped aside.
And when I came in contact with the life of our people, a life in poverty
and straightened circumstances, I fled. I fled from myself, not wanting to
see how I was plummeting; drinking, awaiting the end." Andrijašević, who
"carries the tragedy of himself and others," ends his life just as his literary
predecessor Tito Dorčić did, drowning one night in the sea.

Upon hearing these brief statistics, a naïve reader might conclude
that Croats in the late nineteenth and early twentieth centuries used the sea
for nothing but drowning. Fortunately, tourism developed in the meanwhile, which has truly vindicated the deaths of these fictional victims and
reversed the destructive opposition of metropolis-province, at least during
the summer months, to the benefit of the provinces. This, of course, happened in reality, not in literature.

The novels *Povratak Filipa Latinovicza* (*Return of Philip Latinovicz*,
1932) and *Na rubu pameti* (*On the Edge of Reason*, 1937), by Miroslav Krleža,
are the crown of the Croatian Kakanian literary dynasty. The central figure
in *Return of Philip Latinovicz* repeats the trajectory of his predecessors: he is
a painter, forty years old, who returns to his native region, Pannonia, from
Paris after having spent twenty-three years abroad. The hero of *On the Edge
of Reason* describes how he is gradually being destroyed by Zagreb's bourgeois environment just as his literary predecessors were. Krleža's novels can
be read in all the Kakanian languages, and this is the only reason why these
lines about him amount to little more than a footnote. Miroslav Krleža
deprovincialized Croatian literature, imposing exacting literary standards.
These standards were rarely later attained by Krleža's literary progeny,
which is one of the answers to the question of why canonical Krleža is still

a despised writer in Croatia today. In an ideal literary republic, all other Croatian writers, including those mentioned above, would be nothing but a footnote to—Miroslav Krleža.

The Provinces—The Metropolises

Why am I dusting off old books that mean nothing to anyone except high school Croatian literature teachers? Literature is not a reliable aide in detecting the everyday life of a historical era, nor is that its job. Literature plays within its coordinates, its themes, its genres, its language, and even if readers recognize truth in it, this still does not elevate literature to the role of arbiter in questions of what is truth and what is a lie. All the prose examples given so far nevertheless ring with a strikingly similar tone, the same web of motives about the dislocation of the intelligent individual from the environment, and his state of forever being torn between provinces and metropolises. The hero's choice always favors a return to the homeland, the periphery, the provinces.

The stubborn permutation of the theme of a periphery that devours its young is made even more complex if we consider the real historical context, the way Croatia was torn between Austro-Hungary and its dream of independence, a possible alliance of Southern Slavs. Ksaver Šandor Gjalski's now forgotten novel *U noći* (*In the Night*, 1886) is surprisingly close to contemporary Croatian political life. The reader wonders which it was in 1991, just as Croatia was becoming an independent state—did Croatian political life truly regress to Gjalski's nineteenth century, or did it simply fail to move forward?

The self-pitying tone of the provinces resonates to this day. Perhaps the South Slavic states regressed by a century with the collapse of Yugoslavia, as if they were in a session of regressive psychotherapy. Or maybe they simply failed to move. They, too, are torn between options, pro-European versus anti-European positions, the royalist versus the democratic, a willingness to consider stronger alliances versus a more than glaring affiliation with religion, be it Catholicism, Orthodoxy, or Islam.

The colonized mentality has clearly carried on beyond colonial times. Sometimes it seems as if among those living in the former Kakanian provinces there constantly crouches a colonizer-boogeyman, whether in the form of a Turk with fez and saber, or a Hungarian, an Austrian, an Italian, a German, a Bulgarian, fascists and communists, Russians, Serbs, Croats, foreign banks, foreign capital, domestic capital, the Chinese, corrupt politicians, the geographic position, loss in the geopolitical lottery, fate, or celestial constellations. The imaginary acupuncture points on the imaginary national body always seem to respond in the same way. An unending delusion—about independence and freedom, flight from one trap to another, infantilism, immaturity, aggression, passivity, and submissiveness (when choosing between confrontation and comformism, they choose conformism)—all this situates the periphery as the historical victim. Seldom can one remain normal with such a psychogram; the best one can do is to sustain a semblance of normalcy.

The question remains whether socialist Yugoslavia managed to emancipate and deprovincialize the mindset of its citizens. Apparently it did. World War II had ended. Yugoslavia had come out of the war on the winning side, a victor, which was already in and of itself enough to help most citizens repair their self-image. Tito said his historic NO to Stalin. Unlike their communist neighbors, the Yugoslavs had passports in the 1960s, a better standard of living, and open borders. Free schooling, a university education, and self-betterment as fundamental values, a communist faith that knowledge is power, self-management, the nonaligned nations movement, tourism, festivals of international theater and film, a lively publishing industry, a number of cultural centers (Belgrade, Zagreb, Sarajevo, Ljubljana), and the general impression that life was getting better from one year to the next—all this was the praxis of deprovincialization. And yet texts that broach the themes of better and worse worlds, the periphery and the center, kept right on appearing in Yugoslav literatures. And why not add the detail: the passport. In order to contemplate the theme of periphery and center, the author needed a passport that would cut across borders without obstruction. The Yugoslavs had such a passport.

People Who Would Rather Be Sleeping

The novel-essay *Dragi moj, Petroviću* (*My Dear Petrović*, 1986) consists of ten letters, arranged in chronological order, sent by Mihailo Putnik, retired returnee from America, to his friend Steve Petrovich in Cleveland. Putnik writes the letters to help Petrovich, who is wondering whether or not he should return to the old country. The letter writer sits every day in Domovina ("Homeland") Café, and the name of the town is Kopanja. A *kopanja* is a wooden trough for feeding swine.

"Dizzy from the fact that you aren't needed," in a place where "wasteland enters at one door, and boredom sneaks out another," Mihajlo Putnik contemplates civilizations ("You and I no longer live in the same century," writes Putnik to his friend), the backwardness, paralysis, gloom, and lackluster life of the Serbian provinces, claiming that the Earth orbits more slowly where he is from, and that there is a special "delight taken in deadening," a "disease of sleeeping," "relish of neglect and deafness," moments when you "forget where you were headed, what you were after, and you don't want anyone reminding you of it."

Putnik dissuades his friend from returning, claiming that what is drawing him back "is best cherished and held as memory."

There is no real life anywhere for you and me. It is tough there, it is tough here, it is toughest of all with yourself. The trick is chosing the toughness that suits you best right now. As far as I am concerned it would be best if you could stand at the same time in several places, here and there, on your native soil and abroad, in abundance and poverty, in freedom and constraint, and to pass through all that, experiencing the one, while gauging its opposite; to be with your people (because you love them) and yet far away (because you find them disturbing), to serve and be served, to have and have not, never to be in one place with a single, final choice.

Putnik is merciless on the question of emigré illusions of home. He describes his "countrymen" who "seem to enjoy exacerbating their predicament: they aggravate it through laziness and fear, they worsen it by how unaccustomed they are to serious thinking"; their countrymen "would rather have been sleeping, walking in a dream, multiplying and feeding dreamlike for fifty or a hundred years." Putnik is horrified by their stupidity, indifference, stubbornness ("Shout, they don't hear, write, they won't read. They have more pressing things to do. They are working to accomplish what they transcended in the beginning"); their humility and their attachment to authority ("And the ordinary man is always standing with a man who is holding a cudgel"), their coarseness and malevolence.

Putnik furthermore dissects the delusions "our people" cultivate about themselves, tartly describing their traits, their arrogance, from a suppressed "feeling of unimportance." He describes their obsession with death (funerals that, like weddings, last for three days); their penury, how an entire philosophy of impoverishment has grown out of their poverty, troubles and ignorance and "the skills of the poor." The skills of the poor are the "acrobatics of spitting into the wind"; the skill of filching salt shakers, toothpicks, napkins from cafés and toilet paper from public bathrooms; the skill of cursing. Fellow countrymen are suspicious of everything and everybody ("He would rather starve than taste something he has never eaten before"); fearful of the cold ("The poor fear chills"); they have an aversion to "fresh air" ("Drafts are, for them, demonic"); they fear exploitation ("Now that's an idea particular to the poor: to think that it is possible to live without spending life"); they are wasteful and rapacious.

For the holidays, they burst with pork and lamb roasts, stuffed cabbage, and boiled pig's feet. The television and radio programs for those days are like broadcasts from provincial taverns. Truck drivers' songs ring out, hiccupping and burping reverberate, and comedians offer advice for how to get over hangovers. Instead of antacids they recommend brine. Once they've had their fill of food and drink, they strike up a circle dance. The radio and television sets wobble, the kitchen credenza trembles with glasses that are never set out on the table! When Ćira married, he used up a whole tub of lard. For centuries they have been dreaming of a tub of lard, the lard drips down their whiskers, dribbles into their dream.

Putnik holds forth on the servile nature of their "countrymen" and a "terrifying" capacity to adapt to things ("There is nothing they won't learn to live with"). He senses the virulence of hatred ("Their malice has drawn into a clench around their lips, it has settled in their pupils, nestled into their speech"); he is appalled at its force ("Nothing will save you. Not a single public success, no honor, no riches or glory, nothing will give you safe haven"); its longevity ("They have long memories, they are waiting to pay back in kind, they will wait a hundred years for the opportunity. They exact their revenge even from the innocent, only so that they can knock the evil out of themselves"), and the fact that it cannot be rooted out. "The word for hate, *mrzeti*, is too strong. Our people have come up with a word that is more endearing, more heartfelt: *mrzančiti*. I assume you haven't heard it, and I doubt you'll find a true parallel in English. *Mrzančiti* means to exude hatred, to hate in quiet, long, and with determination, in keeping with tradition, for no reason in particular."

The Metaphysical Palanka

The four-hundred-page long philosophical essay *Filozofija palanke* (*The Philosophy of the Palanka*, 1969), by Serbian philosopher Radomir Konstantinović, was and remains a cult book. Konstantinović promoted a new concept; he gave a new, more complex meaning to the old word *palanka*. The *palanka* is not a village or a city, it is somewhere in between the two. The *palanka* is a deterritorialized and decontextualized place, everywhere and nowhere, a state of mind, afloat between "tribal spirit, as ideal-unique, and world spirit, as ideal-open." The *palanka* experiences itself as cast-off, forgotten, time left out of historical time, and then it bemoans its bitter fate, while at the same time turning this accursed destiny into its privilege. Being closed and forgotten means being safe, while beyond, outside the circle of the *palanka*, rules the dangerous chaos of the wide world. Autism, rigidity, petrification, a constant readiness for defense, a strong tribal awareness, infantilism, formulaic patterns of thought, fear of the unknown, fear of change, an apology for purity, innocence and simplicity, the hermetic, a cult of the dead, security, normativity, conservatism, the static, anti-historicism—are only a few of the features typical of the world of the *palanka*. Konstantinović does not see the root of Serbian fascism in imitation of the German fascist model, or of any other for that matter, but instead he sees it in the *palanka*. The *palanka* is the model for Ur-fascism.

The Feast of the Periphery

One of the outcomes of the collapse of Yugoslavia, the wars, and new nationalistic state projects, is the destruction of what had been the shared Yugolsav cultural space, the material destruction of culture (schools, cultural monuments, libraries, books, etc.), vandalism (the demolition of statues), and effacement of cultural segments (for instance, the era of Yugoslav culture). Every state that disappeared from the former Yugoslavia has reconfigured its own national culture. In the tumultuous process of reconfiguration there are creative figures, works, and opuses that have been dropped, some forgotten, some abruptly jettisoned, others degraded, dethroned, yet others overvalued in terms of the current national ideology and interests. There have been bad writers and artists in this time of overinflating national culture who have been elevated to the pedestal of aesthetic values merely because they were Croatian, Serbian, or Bosnian patriots. In the less than twenty years (as of 2012) that the new states have existed on what was the territory of the former Yugoslavia, the cultural landscape has grown grayer, it has narrowed, and become provincial.

The dependent domestic media regurgitate political clichés which they have retrieved from nineteenth-century political dustbins, and the crazed crowd soaks these up as if they are God's own truth. The domestic media and local politicians prattle on in a delirium about the national state, the ethnically pure and impure peoples, patriotism, heroism, defense of the homeland and patriotic honor, the enemy, his crimes against us, and the national identity which had always been suppressed. Meanwhile, at the same time the foreign media exercise their almost knee-jerk colonialism, cranking out colonial clichés which ring true and convincing to their readers. They write of the terrible, wild, abandoned, uncivilized Balkans, communist repression, the consequence of which is a struggle of the little peoples for national identity and independence, while at the same time reinforcing the old mental divisions of Europe into its civilized western part and its wild, uncivilized eastern part. Here, of course, is the primitive, exotic, and bloodthirsty child—the Balkans.

Hence cultural texts are formed. The cultural text is a construct which assumes not only material factual culture but many written pages and miles of celluloid. The cultural text is a sort of metatext. Metropolises create large and productive cultural texts. Vienna is one such cultural text. The Balkans are a cultural text. Kakania is a cultural text. The provinces are a cultural text.

The center is inclusive, the periphery—exclusive, the center communicates, the periphery excommunicates, the center is multinational, the periphery—mononational, the center is like a sponge, the periphery—like stone. Whatever the case, the provinces are an inseparable part of the story of the metropolis, just as the center is an inseparable part of the story of the periphery. Only together do they make sense.

Fluorescent Fishermen

Some ten years ago, I cannot recall precisely when, during a visit to Vienna, I was out strolling along the Donauinsel. The weather was warm, the shore studded with dozens of little restaurants, and the Viennese were out dancing the salsa. The warm summer evening, the swaying bodies, and the sound of South American salsa were nicely incongruous with the image of Vienna on the "beautiful, blue Danube." I saw something unusual on the shore: three figures wearing helmets with beaming flashlights affixed, holding fishing rods and casting flourescent lines into the water. The image of the glowing figures with their glowing fishing rods struck me, especially because I soon learned that these were my countrymen, just as in the old jokes—

a Croat, a Serb, and a Bosnian. It turned out that they lived in Vienna and spent every weekend fishing on the Danube. I nibbled some cheese pastry with them, sipped brandy straight from the bottle (the real homemade stuff, plum brandy). Around us swirled the sensual strains of the salsa.

"Doesn't the noise disturb the fish?" I asked. "Not at all," confirmed the fishermen.

Vienna suddenly shone with the glow of a metropolis. The salsa, the immigrants dancing with the Viennese, my happy countrymen—these flourescent fishermen. The tolerant Danubian fish who were not disturbed by the noise. I remembered that Zagreb is the only city I know which suffers from hydrophobia. While all the other cities I know embrace the shores of their rivers, Zagreb flees from the Sava to the foothills of the nearby hill, Sljeme, which I hope is not being touted as a mountain in all the new Croatian textbooks. As soon as he came into power, Franjo Tuđman proclaimed Zagreb a metropolis. Of course he also proclaimed himself the Croatian George Washington. From his official position, from the mouth of the first Croatian president, poured the language of the provinces with a thundering inferiority complex. Our "little Paris," our "little Vienna," our Croatian "George Washington"—those are the tropes of the provinces. With this rhetorical figure, stuck like a burr to popular references, the provinces do what they can to leap on board the train of history and inscribe themselves on the map.

Culture as Utopia

Most of the culture of Europe came out of the vortex of these fundamental oppositions, from the dynamics of center and periphery, metropolis and the provinces, the *palanka* and the world. Today, at a moment when all the great utopian systems have come tumbling down, when the political and social imagination has been exhausted, when the idea of democracy is spent, when the gray, cold mechanism of money has replaced all else, at a time when the five-hundred-year-old Gutenberg galaxy is dying while the new, young, omnipresent digital galaxy is ascendant, at a time of the barbarization of high technology, culture suddenly looms large as a straw to be grasped at. Culture is suddenly the language, the reason, the goal. Culture has taken the place of the mumbo jumbo of European political lingo and substance—and, hey, the main substance of European unification has suddenly become culture. Culture is the ideological euro, the means of communication. Culture is the diplomatic language and the language of diplomacy. Culture is a field of struggle, an exorcism of superiority. Culture is the legal nursery of chauvinism, rascism, nationalism, otherness, and supremacy (*Dostoevsky vs. Balzac*). Culture is a means of transportation (*Only with culture can we go out into the world*) and a way to export value. Culture is a brand, culture is the vehicle of national identity (*If it weren't for Ivo Pogorelić no one would know a thing about us!*), culture is the tourist industry. Culture is what countries are. Ireland is the land of James Joyce, France is the land of Marcel Proust, Austria is the land of Robert Musil, just as little Klagenfurt is where Musil was born. *These are the people of Ivo Andrić, Miloš Crnjanski*, howled Emir Kusturica at a Belgrade gathering, condemning the proclamation of independence for Kosovo Albanians. And the Kosovars must have separated, of course, only so they could steal culture, *the sacred Serbian monasteries*. James Joyce, who fled from Ireland, was dragged back there after his death and placed on the throne of Irish literature—and Irish tourism. Today his name and face are trapped on souvenir coffee cups. Even little Galway profits from the little house, now a museum, where Nora, Joyce's wife, was born.

So what is culture, then? Culture is a phenomenon that serves for all sorts of things, from money laundering to laundering the collective national conscience, and perhaps a recent event can provide the clearest illustration. Only two days after Joshua Bell, the famous violinist, had performed in Washington at a concert where people paid large sums to come and hear him, he performed the same repertoire at a subway station, except that no one stopped to listen, and he collected barely more than thirty dollars in his hat.

The Kakania Project

In the 1990s, the cultural construct of "Central Europe" surfaced briefly among intellectuals and, for a time, academics and writers such as Milan Kundera, György Konrád, Joseph Brodsky, and others wrote about it. This construct no longer attracts interest, but one occasionally comes across mention of the "Kakania Project," as a half-hearted call for a new republic of writers, or a sense of shared geographical and historical space, or a longing for a new cultural construct. If we play for a moment with the Kakanian literary utopia, we will automatically find ourselves imagining this (and every other) republic of writers as a space of freedom. Why not do the opposite and try to imagine the Kakania republic in other ways: as a space of restriction, or a space of decontamination, or of deprivation—depending, of course, on one's perspective.

So we imagine that at the border of the Republic of Literature of Kakania the imperial officials demand of writers that they leave behind their passports and agree in writing to respect the Kakanian rules of the road. For Kakania is a literary republic, is it not? Are writers not banned, while dwelling there, from strutting the stuff of their nations, their states (they are not literary soccer players after all), their ethnicity, their religious and political conviction? One must be forbidden from speaking of such things. The only visa for entry to the Republic of Letters should be a literary work.

Let us now try to imagine a conversation between two Kakanians, one who is respecting the rules and another who is violating them.

"So, you, too, are a writer?"

"Yes. Aren't we all?"

"We are, we are, we all put pen to paper, we do little else. But some of us are more successful at it than others. It is not the same, if you're English or if you're Macedonian. And, by the way, where are you from?"

"Kakania. Isn't that obvious?"

"Why should it be? I'm betting you're Lithuanian. Come on, admit it."

"No, I am Kakanian."

"OK. Kakanian. I have nothing against it. I am a Czech, my mother is Hungarian, and I'm not ashamed to admit it. From the cultural and historical perspective I have more right to call myself Kakanian than you do. But we aren't splitting hairs here, now are we. What language do you write in?"

"Literary."

"All of us are literate, we wouldn't be here otherwise. But whether you write in the language of Shakespeare or some fellow called Costa Costolopoulus matters. Come on, confess, I won't tell a soul."

"Literary language."

"You are really stuck on that, weren't you baptized? And by the way, do you believe in God?"

"I believe in the muse."

"Jesus, what a stickler! And on top of it you've disguised yourself as a feminist. OK, so that's politically correct. The muses were women after all, so we had to include them in our work. But, do tell, my Kakanian, where do you stand on politics?"

"I believe in humanism."

"Humanism?! Blah, blah, blah . . . I haven't met anyone more boring than you in ages!"

. . .

I am afraid such a utopian Kakania would soon lose its citizens. European writers are too used to lugging with them the baggage of their states, acting as its representatives, espousing its history, its political, national, religious beliefs, its communities and homeland. They are too used to not treating Others, no matter who those others are, as their own. If the Republic of Literature as described above with its rules were to actually exist, it would be a dangerous test for Europe, for its foundations, and its future.

Most writers flourish within their state, religious, political, ethnic, national communities, within their clans, institutions, publishing houses, readers, academies, their honors, and seldom do they toss out all the medals they have received and go out into the world as beggars, relying only on their naked talent. What happens to art when it is stripped of its context is best shown by the example of Joshua Bell. Everyone will spit at you, or even worse, they will not even see you. In any case your hat will be empty.

All in all, writers are only people, and literature is a complex, multifaceted thing, just as the relations of influence and power are complex, interrelations between the periphery and the center, between the metropolis and the provinces, between the *palanka* and the outside world. The well-intentioned creators of European cultural policy and those who are putting it into practice imagine that relationship as if it were part of a fairy tale.

The prince meets a frog. "Kiss me," says the frog, "and I'll turn into a princess." The prince kisses the frog and bingo! it turns into a princess. But the fairy tale could also go like this:

"Kiss me," says the frog, "and I'll turn into a princess."

"No, for the time being you suit me better as a frog," answers the prince.

Or, like this . . .

"I'll kiss you, and you'll turn into a princess!" says the prince to the frog.

"No thanks," says the frog, "for the time being I would rather stay a frog."

Notes

Introduction

1. Arthur C. Danto, "Sitting with Marina," *New York Times*, May 23, 2010, http://opinionator.blogs.nytimes.com/2010/05/23/sitting-with-marina (last accessed September 7, 2012).

2. Pascale Casanova, *The World Republic of Letters*, trans. M. B. DeBevoise (Cambridge, MA: Harvard University Press, 2004), 4.

3. Franco Moretti, *Atlas of the European Novel, 1800–1900* (New York: Verso, 1998); Dudley Andrew, "An Atlas of World Cinema," in *Remapping World Cinema: Identity, Culture and Politics in Film*, ed. Stephanie Dennison and Song Hwee Lim (New York: Wallflower Press, 2006).

4. KPGT is an acronym of the first letters of the four words for theater in Serbo-Croatian, Slovenian, and Macedonian: *kazalište, pozorište, gledališče, teatar*.

5. The Australian-made film *The Ister* (2004) repeats the conceit, pairing a 1942 lecture by Martin Heidegger with a journey up the Danube and past sites of historical tragedy.

6. See, for example, Pavle Levi's *Disintegration in Frames: Aesthetics and Ideology in the Yugoslav and Post-Yugoslav Cinema* (Stanford, CA: Stanford University Press, 2007).

7. Foreign filmmakers were quick to catch on: see, for example, the humiliating and offensive *A New Life* (*La vie nouvelle*, 2002), by Philippe Grandrieux, which stages a nightmarish music video of rape and violence in a fictional Balkan country.

8. Recent international studies of the documentary tendency in literature and film suggest that a shift toward realism, to the document and testimonial, occurs at times when writers and filmmakers feel suspicious of earlier forms. See Birgit Beumers and Mark Lipovetsky, "The Desire for the Real: Documentary Trends in Contemporary Russian Culture," *Russian Review* 69, no. 4 (October 2010): 559–62.

9. *Beton* is a biweekly cultural supplement to the Belgrade daily *Danas* appearing since 2006; see also the electronic archive at www.elektrobeton.net.

Chapter 1. My Yugoslavia

This is a revised version of the keynote address delivered at the conference "*Ex Uno Plures*: Post-Yugoslav Cultural Space and Europe," which took place at Columbia University, New York, March 26–28, 2010.

1. Diana Mishkova, "What Is Balkan History? Spaces and Scales in the Tradition of South-East European Studies," *Southeastern Europe* 34 (2010): 83.

2. Petar Skok and Milan Budimir, "But et signification des études balkaniques," *Revue internationale des études balkaniques* 1 (1934):24.

3. Ibid., 2–3.

4. Ibid., 3.

5. Ibid.

6. Ibid., 4.

7. Ibid., 5.

8. Ibid., 6.

9. Ibid., 13.

10. Ibid., 13–18.

11. Ibid., 7.

12. Ibid., 8.

13. Ibid., 11–13.

14. Ibid., 24.

15. *Balkan Family Structure and the European Pattern: Demographic Developments in Ottoman Bulgaria* (Washington, DC: American University Press, 1993; 2nd. ed., Budapest: Central European University Press, 2006).

16. The detailed elaboration of my thinking on historical legacies can be found in the afterword of the new edition of *Imagining the Balkans* (New York: Oxford University Press, 2009), as well as in *Historische Vermächtnisse zwischen Europa und dem Nahen Osten* (Berlin: Brandenburgische Akademie der Wissenschaften, Wissenschaftskolleg zu Berlin, Fritz Thyssen Stiftung, 2007); repr. in *Europa im Nahen Osten-Der Nahe Osten in Europa*, ed. Angelika Neuwirrth und Guenther Stock (Berlin: Akademie Verlag, 2010).

17. Tomislav Longinović, *Vampires Like Us: Writing Down "the Serbs"* (Belgrade: Belgrade Circle, 2005); *Vampire Nation: Violence as Cultural Imaginary* (Durham, NC: Duke University Press, 2011).

Chapter 3. The Past as Future

Dejan Djokić's last name may also be spelled "Đokić," but because he is better known as "Djokić," the editor decided to keep this spelling here.

1. Stojan Novaković, "Nakon sto godina," in *Srpskohrvatski almanah za godinu 1911*, ed. Milan Ćurčin (Zagreb and Belgrade: n.p., 1911), 9–19; repr., Ivo Tartalja, *Beograd XXI veka: Iz starih utopija i antiutopija* (Belgrade: SKZ, 1989), 252–64. For an English translation see Bojan Aleksov, "One Hundred Years of Yugoslavia: The Vision of Stojan Novaković Revisited," *Nationalities Papers: The Journal of Nationalism and Ethnicity* 39, no. 6 (November 2011): 997–1010. The article was published when this text was in the proofs stage, so the author's argument could not have been incorporated into this analysis.

2. Vidović's surname is appropriate: it means someone who can predict the future (*vidovit*), and it may be also an allusion to St. Vid (Vitus), a saint celebrated on June 28, the anniversary of the Battle of Kosovo in 1389. In the early twentieth century, the Kosovo mythology was part of Yugoslav nationalist discourse, as well as the central Serbian myth. Ironically, only three years after the publication of Novaković's essay the First World War broke out, sparked by the assassination of Austrian Archduke Franz Ferdinand in Sarajevo on June 28, 1914. For an overview of the Kosovo myth and its misuse by modern nationalist ideologies, see Dejan Djokić, "Whose Myth? Which Nation? The Serbian Kosovo Myth Revisited," in *Uses and Abuses of the Middle Ages: 19th–21st Century*, ed. János M. Bak et al. (Munich: Wilhelm Fink, 2009), 215–33.

3. Shkodra, Durrës (Durazzo in Italian), and parts of northern Albania would be indeed occupied by Montenegrin and Serbian troops at the end of the First World War and Shkodra was mentioned in negotiations during the 1919–20 Paris Peace Conference that formally ended the war, but never became part of Yugoslavia, unlike present-day Kosovo and western Macedonia, where ethnic Albanians were in a majority. During Yugoslavia's formative years, ethnic Albanians clashed with the Yugoslav gendarmerie and army. See Dejan Djokić, *Pašić and Trumbić: The Kingdom of Serbs, Croats, and Slovenes* (London: Haus, 2010), 95–97; Andrija Radović et al., *The Question of Scutari* (Paris: Graphique, 1919); the National Archives, Kew, London, FO 608/47, Andrija Radović's memorandum, "Alleged Massacre of Albanians in Old Serbia," Paris, June 25, 1919.

4. See Ljubinka Trgovčević, *Naučnici Srbije i stvaranje Jugoslavije, 1914–20* (Belgrade: SKZ, 1986); and her chapter "South Slav Intellectuals and the Creation of Yugoslavia," in *Yugoslavism: Histories of a Failed Idea, 1918–1992*, ed. Dejan Djokić (London: Hurst, 2003), 222–37.

5. "Izjava kraljevske srpske vlade u Narodnoj skupštini," Niš, December 7 (November 24, O.S.), 1914, in Ferdo Šišić, *Dokumenti o postanku Kraljevine Srba: Hrvata i Slovenaca, 1914–1919* (Zagreb: Matica Hrvatska, 1920), 10. In his proclamation of July 25, 1914, King Nicholas of Montenegro called his people to fight a "holy war for the liberty of Serbdom and Yugoslavdom" ("Proklamacija crnogorskoga kralja Nikole," in ibid., 6–7).

6. R. W. Seton-Watson, *The Southern Slav Question and the Habsburg Monarchy* (London: Constable, 1911), 336. William R. Shepherd's *Historical Atlas* (New York: Henry Holt, 1911) published a map showing the "Distribution of Races in Austria-Hungary," based on the last Austro-Hungarian census, where "Croats and Servians" are shown as a single nation, that is, the population of Croatia-Slavonia, Dalmatia, and Bosnia-Herzegovina. (*Servians* is an archaic form of spelling of *Serbians*, while in this context *race* denotes an ethnic, not a racial group.)

7. Djokić, *Pašić and Trumbić*, esp. chap. 5.

8. A recent study by Vesna Drapac offers a sophisticated analysis of the role of "external factors"—mostly Western intellectuals such as R. W. Seton-Watson—in the "construction" of Yugoslavia, but largely downplays the significance of domestic forces that advocated and eventually created the Yugoslav state at the end of the First World War. See Drapac, *Constructing Yugoslavia: A Transnational History* (Basingstoke: Palgrave Macmillan, 2010).

9. See Ivo Banac, *The National Question in Yugoslavia: Origins, History, Politics* (Ithaca, NY: Cornell University Press, 1984), esp. 70–115; Aleksa Đilas, *The Contested Country: Yugoslav*

Unity and Communist Revolution, 1919–1953 (Cambridge, MA: Harvard University Press, 1991), chap. 1; Elinor Murray Despalatović, *Ljudevit Gaj and the Illyrian Movement* (Boulder, CO: *East European Quarterly*, 1975); Mirjana Gross, "Croatian National-Integrational Ideologies from the End of Illyrism to the Creation of Yugoslavia," *Austrian History Yearbook* 15–16 (1979–80): 3–33; and Dennison Rusinow, "The Yugoslav Idea Before Yugoslavia," in *Yugoslavism*, ed. Djokić, 11–26. The best and most up-to-date general history of former Yugoslavia is John R. Lampe, *Yugoslavia as History: Twice There Was a Country*, 2nd ed. (Cambridge: Cambridge University Press, 2000).

10. For Yugoslavism among Slovenes, see Mitja Velikonja, "Slovenia's Yugoslav Century," in Yugoslavism, ed. Djokić, 84–99.

11. "Idea of Southern Slav Unity," *Southern Slav Library*, no. 5 (London, 1916): 5, 17. For a recent analysis of the Yugoslav Committee's discourse, see Connie Robinson, "Yugoslavism in the Early Twentieth Century: The Politics of the Yugoslav Committee," in *New Perspectives on Yugoslavia: Key Issues and Controversies*, ed. Dejan Djokić and James Ker-Lindsay (London: Routledge, 2011), 10–26.

12. "Krfska deklaracija od 20. (7.) jula 1917," in Šišić, *Dokumenti*, 96–99. The declaration was signed by Ante Trumbić, president of the Yugoslav Committee, and Nikola Pašić, prime minister and foreign minister of Serbia's wartime government. A classic study of the Corfu conference is Dragoslav Janković, *Jugoslovensko pitanje i Krfska deklaracija 1917. godine* (Belgrade: Savremena administracija, 1967). For more on the South Slav lands in the First World War, see Andrej Mitrović, *Serbia's Great War, 1914–1918* (London: Hurst, 2007); Bogdan Krizman, *Hrvatska u Prvom svjetskom ratu: Hrvatsko-srpski politički odnosi* (Zagreb: Globus, 1989); and Mark Cornwall, "The Great War and the Yugoslav Roots: Popular Mobilization in the Habsburg Monarchy," in *New Perspectives on Yugoslavia*, ed. Djokić and Ker-Lindsay, 27–45.

13. According to Bogoljub Kočović's calculations, 11,985,000 people lived in Yugoslavia in 1921; 4,813,000 (40.1 percent) were Serbs (including Montenegrins), 2,797,000 (23.3 percent) Croats, 1,020,000 (8.5 percent) Slovenes, 740,000 (6.2 percent) [Slav] Muslims, and 465,000 (3.9 percent) Macedonians; in total, there were 9,835,000 (82 percent) Yugoslavs. The census that year did not provide for separate ethnic categories among the South Slavs, but only distinguished between language and religion. Kočović, *Etnički i demografski razvoj u Jugoslaviji od 1921. do 1991. godine (po svim zvaničnim a u nekim slučajevima i korigovanim popisima)* (Paris: Dialogue, 1998), 2: 332–33.

14. Stjepan Radić, "Hoćemo u jugoslavenskom jedinstvu svoju hrvatsku državu," in *Politički spisi: Autobiografija, članci, govori, rasprave*, comp. Zvonimir Kulundžić (Zagreb: Znanje, 1971). In his study of Radić, Mark Biondich suggests that during a short period following the unification of Yugoslavia Radić probably harbored separatist ideas, but soon reverted to a "Yugoslav position," where Croatia would enjoy a wide autonomy within a Yugoslav state. Biondich, *Stjepan Radić, the Croat Peasant Party, and the Politics of Mass Mobilization, 1904–1928* (Toronto: Toronto University Press, 2000), 161.

15. *Making a Nation, Breaking a Nation* (Stanford, CA: Stanford University Press, 1998). See also Wachtel, "Ivo Andrić, Ivan Meštrović, and the Synthetic Yugoslav Culture of the Interwar Period," in *Yugoslavism*, ed. Djokić, 238–51.

16. Banac, *National Question in Yugoslavia.*

17. This argument is further elaborated in my book *Elusive Compromise: A History of Interwar Yugoslavia* (New York: Columbia University Press, 2007).

18. See, for example, Hrvatski državni arhiv (Croatian National Archives), Zagreb, XXI-26–1559, Sreski poglavar Grubić, Jastrebarsko, Velikom županu Zagrebačke oblasti, Zagreb, "Proklamacija novog stanja, raspoloženje naroda," Jastrebarsko, January 9, 1929. For Maček's position see Josip Horvat, *Politička povijest Hrvatske* (Zagreb: August Cesarec, 1990; first pub. 1938), 2: 362.

19. Bakhmeteff Archive of Russian and East European Culture, Columbia University, New York, Papers of Prince Paul of Yugoslavia, box 2: Anton Korošec [Interior Minister] to Milan Antić [Minister of the Royal Court], Belgrade, January 16, 1937. The experts were Professors Slobodan Jovanović and Mihajlo Ilić of Belgrade University, Ivo Krbek of Zagreb University, and Laza Kostić of the Law Faculty in Subotica.

20. See Dejan Djokić, "National Mobilization in the 1930s: The Emergence of the 'Serb Question' in the Kingdom of Yugoslavia," in *New Perspectives on Yugoslavia*, ed. Djokić and Ker-Lindsay, 62–81.

21. See Tomislav Dulić, *Utopias of Nation: Local Mass Killing in Bosnia and Herzegovina, 1941–42* (Uppsala: Uppsala University Press, 2005). See also Dulić, "Ethnic Violence in Occupied Yugoslavia: Mass Killing from Above and Below," in *New Perspectives on Yugoslavia*, ed. Djokić and Ker-Lindsay, 82–99.

22. For a recent study that successfully explains the complexity of events in occupied Yugoslavia, see Stevan K. Pavlowitch, *Hitler's New Disorder: The Second World War in Yugoslavia* (New York: Columbia University Press, 2008). See also several works by Jozo Tomasevich, including *War and Revolution in Yugoslavia, 1941–1945: Occupation and Collaboration* (Stanford, CA: Stanford University Press, 2001).

23. Milovan Đilas, *Wartime* (London: Martin Secker and Warburg, 1977), 229–45; Walter R. Roberts, *Tito, Mihailović, and the Allies, 1941–1945* (New Brunswick, NJ: Rutgers University Press, 1973), 106–12.

24. The official figure of war dead in socialist Yugoslavia was 1,709,000. However, the figure has been challenged, most persuasively by Bogoljub Kočović and Vladimir Žerjavić, a Serb and a Croat scholar, respectively, who arrived at a lower figure of around one million war dead independently of each other, using different methodologies. According to Kočović (*Žrtve Drugog svetskog rata u Jugoslaviji* [London: Naše delo, 1985]), a total of 1,014,000 Yugoslavs lost their lives during the 1941–45 period, while Žerjavić (*Gubici stanovništva Jugoslavije u Drugom svjetskom ratu* [Zagreb: Jugoslavensko viktimološko društvo, 1989]) estimates the number of war dead at 1,027,000 (both authors allow for a margin of error of plus/minus 50,000). Kočović estimates the following breakdown according to ethnicity:

> Serbs (including Montenegrins): 537,000 (7.2 percent of all Serbs); Serbs (excluding Montenegrins): 487,000 (6.9 percent); Montenegrins: 50,000 (10.4 percent); Croats: 207,000 (5.4 percent of all Croats); Muslims: 86,000 (6.8 percent of all Muslim Slavs in occupied Yugoslavia); Jews: 60,000 (77.9 percent of all Yugoslav Jews); Slovenes: 32,000 (2.5 percent); Roma: 27,000 (31.4 percent); Yugoslav Germans: 26,000 (4.8 percent); Yugoslav Albanians: 6,000 (1.0 per-

cent); Yugoslav Macedonians: 6,000 (0.9 percent); Yugoslav Hungarians: 5,000 (1.0 percent) (Kočović, *Žrtve*, 111).

25. See Đilas, *Contested Country*; and Dejan Jović, "Reassessing Socialist Yugoslavia, 1945–90: The Case of Croatia," in *New Perspectives on Yugoslavia*, ed. Djokić and Ker-Lindsay. One of the best histories of socialist Yugoslavia is Melissa K. Bokovoy, Carol Lilly, and Jill Irvine, eds., *State-Society Relations in Yugoslavia, 1945–1992* (New York: St. Martin's Press, 1997); while Dennison Rusinow's posthumously published collection of essays offer a valuable insight into the politics and society of Tito's Yugoslavia: *Yugoslavia: Oblique Insights and Observations*, ed. Gale Stokes (Pittsburgh: University of Pittsburgh Press, 2008).

26. This argument has been made by both Stevan K. Pavlowitch and Aleksa Đilas in their numerous writings.

27. Lenard J. Cohen's *Serpent in the Bosom: The Rise and Fall of Slobodan Milošević* (Boulder, CO: Westview Press, 2001) stands out among several biographies of the late Serbian leader. Tuđman and Izetbegović still await serious scholarly biographies, although Croatian journalist Darko Hudelist has written a popular biography of the late Croat president, *Tuđman: Biografija* (Zagreb: Profil, 2004).

28. See a collection of interviews with Mitrović, *Vreme destruktivnih: Intervjui* (Čačak: Čačanski Glas, 1998).

29. Milovan Đilas, *Rise and Fall* (San Diego: Harcourt Brace Jovanovich, 1985); Stephen Clissold, *Djilas: The Progress of a Revolutionary* (Hounslow: Maurice Temple Smith, 1983).

30. A sophisticated critique of Western involvement in the Yugoslav crisis is Stevan K. Pavlowitch, "Who Is 'Balkanizing' Whom? The Misunderstandings Between the Debris of Yugoslavia and an Unprepared West," *Daedalus* 123, no. 4 (Spring 1994): 203–23.

31. The best analyses of the existing explanations of the breakup of Yugoslavia are Dejan Jović, *Yugoslavia: A State That Withered Away* (West Lafayette, IN: Purdue University Press, 2009); and Jasna Dragović-Soso, "Why Did Yugoslavia Disintegrate? An Overview of Contending Explanations," in *State Collapse in South-Eastern Europe: New Perspectives on Yugoslavia's Disintegration*, ed. Lenard J. Cohen and Jasna Dragović-Soso (West Lafayette, IN: Purdue University Press, 2007), 1–39.

32. There is still not a good, book-length study of the Wars of Yugoslav Succession. Lampe provides a useful, brief overview of the 1991–99 period in *Yugoslavia as History*, 2nd ed., chap. 12. See also Steven L. Burg and Paul S. Shoup, *The War in Bosnia-Herzegovina: Ethnic Conflict and International Intervention* (Armonk, NY: M. E. Sharpe, 1999); and Tim Judah, *Kosovo: War and Revenge* (New Haven, CT: Yale University Press, 2000).

33. According to Mirsad Tokača and his team of researchers at the Sarajevo-based Research Documentation Centre (RDC), 80,545 people have been killed or died as a result of war in Bosnia-Herzegovina between 1992 and 1995, while 16,662 are still missing, meaning the total figure of likely casualties is 97,207. Out of this figure, 64,036 of all killed and missing are Bosniaks (65.88 percent of all victims), 24,905 (25.62 percent) Bosnian Serbs and 7,788 (8.01 percent) Bosnian Croats, as well as 478 (0.49 percent) "others." For a detailed analysis see the RDC website: www.idc.org.ba/ (last accessed February 1, 2011).

34. Some 86 percent of Montenegro's 625,000 population voted at the referendum, with just over 55 percent of the vote in favor of independence.

35. For example, when Vida Ognjenović, an eminent author and president of the Serbian PEN, suggested in 2008 that regional PEN centres should consider merging into one, a polemic broke out in Croatia and Serbia. Ognjenović's Croatian counterpart Zvonko Maković strongly rejected the suggestion, on the grounds that it smacked of yet another attempt by Belgrade to establish regional domination. See Milica Jovanović's interview with Maković, "Balkanski PEN kao nova srpska fantazija," *e-novine*, October 15, 2008, www.e-novine.com/sr/kultura/clanak.php?id=17909 (last accessed September 7, 2012); and critical reaction to Maković's view by two eminent Croatian writers: Miljenko Jergović ("Balkanski PEN nije sadnja tikava sa Srbima," *e-novine*, October 14, 2008, www .e-novine.com/sr/kultura/clanak.php?id=17890 [last accessed September 7, 2012]); and Boris Dežulović ("Strah od Jugoslavije," *e-novine*, October 25, 2008, www.e-novine.com/ sr/kultura/clanak.php?id=18293 [last accessed September 7, 2012]).

Even in Novaković's essay there are Yugo-sceptics, such as "a gentleman from Pirot" (in southern Serbia), who complains to Professor Vidović that Yugoslav identity was imposed from above and was detrimental to old, regional identities. Vidović's reply, which revealed Novaković's understanding of the Yugoslav idea, was that Yugoslavism was born not only out of "ethnic and idealistic" motives, but also out of "political and practical necessity," and only by joining their forces together could Serbs and Croats and other South Slavs survive. Novaković, "Nakon sto godina," in Tartalja, *Beograd XXI veka*, 261–62.

36. H. G. Wells, *The Time Machine: An Invention* (London: W. Heinemann, 1895).

37. The majority of political émigrés may have been anti-Yugoslav, but not all of them: the Democratic Alternative, a group of pro-Yugoslav émigrés which included Vane Ivanović among others, advocated a democratic, federal Yugoslavia. In the country itself, the Association for Yugoslav Democratic Initiative (UJDI) emerged just before the disintegration, and included leading intellectuals from across Yugoslavia. For more on their activities see articles by leading members of these organisations: Desimir Tošić, "The Democratic Alternative," and Branko Horvat, "The Association for Yugoslav Democratic Initiative," in *Yugoslavism*, ed. Djokić, 286–97 and 298–303.

38. Should we instead talk of a collective remembrance of Yugoslavia, instead of a post-Yugoslav collective memory? For a convincing argument in favour of the former concept, not necessarily in relation to Yugoslavia, see Jay Winter, *Remembering War: The Great War Between Memory and History in the 20th Century* (New Haven, CT: Yale University Press, 2006).

39. Good examples of "Yugonostalgia" represents the commercial and critical success across former Yugoslavia of two books that deal with popular memory of everyday life, culture, and music during the socialist period. Building on a project started by Dubravka Ugrešić (one of the contributors to the present volume), Iris Adrić, Vladimir Arsenijević, and Đorđe Matić have compiled *Leksikon YU mitologije* (Belgrade and Zagreb: Rende and Postscriptum, 2004), while a leading former-Yugoslav rock critic Petar Janjatović wrote *Ex Yu rock enciklopedija, 1960–2006*, 2nd rev. ed. (Belgrade: Petar Janjatović, 2007). For more on "Yugonostalgia" see Stef Jansen, *Antinacionalizam* (Belgrade: Biblioteka XX vek, 2005), 219–59; Nicole Lindstrom, "Yugonostalgia: Restorative and Reflective Nostalgia in Former Yugoslavia," *East Central Europe* 32, nos. 1–2 (2005): 227–38; Cynthia Simmons, "Miljenko Jergović and (Yugo)nostalgia," *Russian Literature* 66, no. 4 (November 2009): 457–69; and

Zala Volčič, "Yugo-Nostalgia: Cultural Memory and Media in Former Yugoslavia," *Critical Studies in Media Communication* 24, no. 1 (March 2007): 21–38. Nostalgia for President Tito has emerged as a major feature of Yugonostalgia—see Mitja Velikonja, *Titostalgia: A Study of Nostalgia for Josip Broz* (Ljubljana: Mirovni inštitut, 2008); and the "Yugostalgia" exhibition by artists Walter Steinacher and Elena Fajt, www.typotektonik.net/page2/page9/page9.html (accessed February 1, 2011). "Yugonostalgia" is part of a wider phenomenon of nostalgia for socialism across the former Eastern Bloc. See Svetlana Boym, *The Future of Nostalgia* (New York: Basic Books, 2001); and Maria Todorova, ed., *Remembering Communism: Genres of Representation* (New York: Social Science Research Council, 2010).

40. Tim Judah, *Yugoslavia is Dead: Long Live the Yugosphere*, LSEE Papers Series, no. 1 (London: London School of Economics and Political Science, European Institute, Research on South Eastern Europe, 2009). See also [Tim Judah], "Entering the Yugosphere," *Economist* 392, no. 8645 (August 22, 2009): 45–46.

41. As was recently argued by Vuk Perišić in his essay "Jugoslavenski paradoks," *Peščanik*, www.pescanik.net/2011/01/jugoslavenski-paradoks (accessed February 1, 2011).

42. I am grateful for this formulation to Vjekoslav Perica of University of Rijeka. Email correspondence between Vjekoslav Perica and Dejan Djokić (Rijeka–New York, November 2010).

Chapter 4. What Common Yugoslav Culture Was

1. Pascale Casanova, *The World Republic of Letters* (Cambridge, MA: Harvard University Press, 2004).

2. Andrew B. Wachtel, *Making a Nation, Breaking a Nation: Literature and Cultural Politics in Yugoslavia* (Stanford, CA: Stanford University Press, 1998).

3. On the core curriculum see ibid., 184–89; on the same issue, but from the perspective of Slovene nationalism, see Leopoldina Plut-Pregelj, "Slovenia's Concerns About the Proposed Yugoslav Core Curriculum in the 1980s," in *The Repluralization of Slovenia in the 1980s: New Revelations from Archival Records* (Seattle: Henry M. Jackson School of International Studies, University of Washington, 2000), 58–78.

4. On Goethe's concept of *Weltliteratur*, see Fritz Strich, *Goethe und die Weltliteratur* (Bern: Francke, 1957 [1946]).

5. On Mediala, see Miodrag B. Protić, *Srpsko slikarstvo XX veka* (Belgrade: Nolit, 1970), 525–36.

6. KPGT still awaits its historians; there is a brief outline in Petar Marjanović, *Mala istorija srpskog pozorišta. XIII–XXI vek* (Novi Sad: Pozorišni muzej Vojvodine, 2005), 489–90.

7. The best overview of Yugoslav popular music is Petar Janjatović, *Ilustrovana YU Rock enciklopedija, 1960–2000* (Novi Sad: Prometej, 2001).

8. On *Praxis* see Gerson S. Sher, *Praxis: Marxist Criticism and Dissent in Socialist Yugoslavia* (Bloomington: Indiana University Press, 1977); and M. Marković and G. Petrović, eds., *Praxis: Yugoslav Essays in the Philosophy and Methodology of the Social Sciences* (Dordrecht: D. Reidel, 1979). On *Praxis* and nationalism see William L. McBride, *From Yugoslav Praxis to Global Pathos* (Lanham, MD: Rowman and Littlefield, 2001), 19–30.

9. Miroslav Krleža, *Govor na Kongresu književnika u Ljubljani* (Zagreb: Zora, 1952).

10. Jovan Deretić, *Istorija srpske književnosti* (Belgrade: Nolit, 1983).

11. Snježana Kordić has recently contrasted Yugoslav language policy with those of its successor states: although three quarters of Yugoslavs spoke one language, no single language was official on a federal level. Official languages were declared only on the level of constituent republics and provinces, and very generously at that: Vojvodina had five (among them Slovak and Romanian, spoken by 0.5 percent of the population), and Kosovo four (Albanian, Turkish, Romani, and Serbo-Croatian). Newspapers, radio, and television studios used sixteen languages, fourteen were used as languages of education in schools, and nine at universities. See Snježana Kordić, *Jezik i nacionalizam* (Zagreb: Durieux, 2010).

12. Gilles Troude, *Conflits identitaires dans la Yugoslavie de Tito 1960–1980* (Paris: Association Pierre Belon, 2007), 231–38; Marie-Janine Calic, *Geschichte Jugoslawiens im 20. Jahrhundert* (Munich: C. H. Beck, 2010), 247–48.

13. Aleš Debeljak, "Zastarelost jugoslovanstva," *Nova revija* 5, nos. 52–53 (1986): 1390–92.

14. Ibid., 1393–94.

15. Aleš Debeljak, *Twilight of the Idols: Recollections of a Lost Yugoslavia* (New York: White Pine Press, 1994), 35.

16. Ibid., 25.

17. Tim Judah, *Yugoslavia Is Dead: Long Live the Yugosphere*, LSEE Papers Series, no. 1 (London: London School of Economics and Political Science, European Institute, Research on South Eastern Europe, 2009).

Chapter 5. *Discordia Concors*

1. Milan Kundera, "The Tragedy of Central Europe," *New York Review of Books* (April 26, 1984), 33.

2. Ibid., 35.

3. For some of the more prominent contributions to the polemic, see: Peter Vodopivec, ed., *Srednja Evropa* (Ljubljana: Mladinska knjiga, 1991); Marjan Rožanc, "Nekaj iracionalnih razsežnosti," *Nova revija*, no. 57 (1987): 200–210; Slobodan Selenić, "Slovenci i Srbi danas," in *Iskorak u stvarnost* (Belgrade: Prosveta, 1996), 16–26; Milorad Ekmečić, *Srbija između Srednje Evrope i Evrope* (Belgrade: Politika, 1992); Zoran Đinđić, "Jugoslavija na jugoistoku," *Književne novine* 41, no. 771 (1989): 5; Zoran Đinđić, "Hrabrost držača sveće," *Borba* (August 18–19, 1990): 2; Peter Handke, "Abschied des Träumers vom Neunten Land," in *Abschied des Träumers, Winterliche Reise, Sommerlicher Nachtrag* (Frankfurt am Main: Suhrkamp Verlag, 1998), 5–32. For an analysis of the ideological premises and the political context of the debate, see: Milica Bakić-Hayden and Robert Hayden, "Orientalist Variations on the Theme 'Balkans,'" *Slavic Review* 51, no. 1 (Spring 1992): 1–15; Milica Bakić-Hayden, "Nesting Orientalisms: The Case of the Former Yugoslavia," *Slavic Review* 54, no. 4 (Winter 1995): 917–31; Jasna Dragović-Soso, *Saviours of the Nation: Serbia's Intellectual Opposition and the Revival of Nationalism* (London: Hurst, 2002), 162–226; Patrick Hyder Patterson, "On the Edge of Reason: The Boundaries of Balkanism in Slovenian, Austrian, and Italian Discourse," *Slavic Review* 62, no. 1 (Spring 2003): 110–41; Zoran Konstantinović, "Jugosloveni i 'Srednja Evropa,'" *Luča* 9, no. 1 (1992): 90–96; Maria Todorova, *Imagining the Balkans* (New York: Oxford University Press, 1997), 140–60.

4. Danilo Kiš, "Variations on Central European Themes," in *Homo Poeticus* (Manchester: Carcanet, 1996), 95.

5. Ibid., 109.

6. See: Danilo Kiš, "Apatrid," in *Skladište* (Belgrade: BIGZ, 1995), 203–19; and Kiš, "Mirror of the Unknown," in *The Encyclopedia of the Dead* (London: Faber and Faber, 1989), 95–110.

7. László Végel, "Protraćeni: Monodrama na sprovod Danila Kiša," *Književne novine* 62, no. 785 (November 1, 1989): 5.

8. Dragan Velikić, "Srbija, zemlja s one strane ogledala," in *Stanje svari* (Belgrade: Stubovi kulture, 1998), 142. All translations are mine unless otherwise stated.

9. Dragan Velikić, "Granica, identitet, literatura," in *O piscima i gradovima* (Novi Sad: Akademska knjiga, 2010), 32–33.

10. Ibid., 32.

11. Dragan Velikić, "Svi moji prostori ne staju pod jednu zastavu" (speech delivered on receiving the Mitteleuropa Prize, awarded by the Institute for the Danubian Region and Central Europe). For a full version of the speech, see: *Politika*, November 29, 2008.

12. For a similar view of Central Europe as a necessary purgatory on the road to the West, see: Đinđić, "Hrabrost držača sveće," 2.

13. Velikić, "Dozvoliti Drugog," in *O piscima i gradovima*, 48.

14. See Mikhail Bakhtin, "From the Prehistory of Novelistic Discourse," in *The Dialogic Imagination: Four Essays* (Austin: University of Texas Press, 1981), 41–83.

15. László Végel, "Levél szerb barátomhoz," in *Lemondás és megmaradás* (Budapest: Cserépalvi kiadása, 1992), 102.

16. Végel, "Kelet-közép-európai alkímia," in *Lemondás és megmaradás*, 71.

17. Végel, "Koruška utca: albérleti monológ," and "Néphősök utca: bársonyos represszió," in *Peremvidéki élet* (Újvidék: Forum, 2000), 35–40, 51–55.

18. Végel, "Tito marsall sugárút: Képimádók és képrombolók," "Az örmény templom: A történelem porfelhői," "A Dornstädter cukrászda: Közép-európai nosztalgiák," in *Peremvidéki élet*, 79–91.

19. Végel, "Tito marsall sugárút," 89.

20. Végel, "Az örmény templom," 84.

21. Végel, "Néphősök utca," 53.

22. Végel, "Az örmény templom," 84.

23. Ibid., 85–86.

24. G. W. F. Hegel, *Introduction to the Philosophy of History* (Indianapolis, IN: Hackett Publishing, 1988), 32.

25. Drago Jančar, *Terra incognita* (Celovec: Wieser, 1989), 10.

26. Ibid., 10.

27. Ibid., 12–13. Jančar made the same point a few years later, in his conversation with Adam Michnik; see: Jančar and Michnik, *Disput, ali kje smo, kam gremo?* (Celovec: Wieser, 1992), 56–57.

28. Jančar, "Ein neuer Spiegel für Mitteleuropa," in *Errinerungen an Jugoslawien* (Klagenfurt: Hermagoras, 1991), 63.

29. Ibid., 62.

30. Ostensibly a medley of different ideologies and genres, the issue presented a strikingly unified platform on the Slovenian "national question": unrestricted political sovereignty is indispensable for any cultural and linguistic autonomy. Jančar contributed an essay on Slovenian exile, a lament over the demographic and cultural loss that Slovenia incurred through several waves of political emigration and the gradual assimilation of the exiles into different languages and cultures. See: Jančar, "Slovenski eksil," *Nova revija*, no. 57 (1987): 220–28.

31. Jančar, "Vzhodnoevropejci," in *Duša Evrope* (Ljubljana: Slovenska matica, 2006), 46–47.

32. Jančar, "Kupite nas, izkoriščajte nas," in *Duša Evrope*, 62.

33. Végel, "Duna-parti sétány: bábeli habfodrok," in *Peremvidéki élet*, 93, 96.

34. See Angelo Ara and Claudio Magris, *Trieste* (Turin: Einaudi, 1982).

35. Velikić, "Trst: Kulise jednog grada," in *O piscima i gradovima*, 149.

36. Ibid., 150.

37. Ibid., 147.

38. Velikić was by no means the only Serbian novelist to draw on the versatile place and functions of Trieste in Yugoslav discourses. In the 1990s the city's shopper-friendly ethos became a target of acrimonious criticism in Radomir Konstantinović's *Descartes' Death* (*Dekartova smrt*, 1996), while its multicultural makeup served as an apposite area for the historiosophical clash of enlightenment and nationhood in Radoslav Petković's *Fate and Comments* (*Sudbina i komentary*, 1993).

39. Vegel, "Zašto Novi Sad nije postao istočni Trst," *Danas*, April 6, 2008.

40. Ibid.

41. Jančar, *Terra incognita*, 11; "Zemljevidi, pokrajine, ljudje," and "Zgodba, ki jo lahko prespite," in *Duša Evrope*, 72, 80–81.

42. Jančar, "Zakaj smo izdali Srednjo Evropo, ko nam je najbolj potrebna?" in *Duša Evrope*, 182–83.

43. Jančar, "Zemljevidi, pokrajine, ljudje," in *Duša Evrope*, 72.

44. See: Velikić, *Severni zid* (Belgrade: Vreme knjige, 1995); Jančar, "Joyce's Pupil," in *Joyce's Pupil* (London: Brandon, 2006), 7–26.

45. Richard Ellmann, *James Joyce* (New York: Oxford University Press, 1982), 183–406.

46. Ibid., 341.

47. Jančar, "Joyce's Pupil," 11, 16.

48. Ibid., 14, 26.

49. Velikić, *Severni zid*, 117.

50. Ibid., 98.

51. Ellmann, *James Joyce*, 342.

52. Jančar, "Joyce's Pupil," 9.

53. Ibid., 13, 15, 17–18, 26.

Chapter 6. "Something Has Survived . . ."

1. Milica Bakić-Hayden defines the gradation of "Orients" as "nesting Orientalisms," that is as "a pattern of reproduction of the original dichotomy upon which Orientalism is premised, in "Nesting Orientalism: The Case of Former Yugoslavia," *Slavic Review* 54, no. 4 (Winter 1995): 918. See also Bakić-Hayden and Robert Hayden, "Orientalist Variations

on the Theme 'Balkans': Symbolic Geography in Recent Yugoslav Cultural Politics," *Slavic Review* 51, no. 1 (Spring 1992): 1–15.

2. For example, at Slovenian "Balkan parties," only (ex-)Yugoslav pop, rock, alternative, folk, and turbofolk is played, and not Albanian, Greek, or Bulgarian music.

3. Quoted in Vesna Goldsworthy, "The Last Stop on the Orient Express: The Balkans and the Politics of British In(ter)vention," *Balkanologie* 3, no. 2 (1999): 112.

4. Mitja Velikonja, *Eurosis: A Critique of the New Eurocentrism* (Ljubljana: MediaWatch Peace Institute, 2005), http://mediawatch.mirovni-institut.si/eng/eurosis.pdf (last accessed November 27, 2012).

5. Ivan J. Štuhec, "Preprečimo 'privatizacijo' države!" *Družina*, November 7, 2010, 2. Note that *bratstvo i jedinstvo* (brotherhood and unity) was used by Štuhec in Serbo-Croatian and not Slovenian.

6. It is interesting to mention that in less than a year, three different local student journals had published a special issue dedicated completely to Yugo-nostalgia (*RIT Velenje*, *Zapik Kranj*, *Klin Ljubljana*).

7. Niko Toš, *Vrednote v prehodu II* (Ljubljana: Dokumenti SJM, FDV, 1999), 565, 872; Toš, *Vrednote v prehodu III* (Ljubljana: Dokumenti SJM, FDV, 2004), 474.

8. Toš, *Vrednote v prehodu II*, 564, 871; Toš, *Vrednote v prehodu III*, 473.

9. Toš, *Vrednote v prehodu IV* (Ljubljana: Dokumenti SJM, FDV, 2009), 513. According to this document, socialism was associated with "freedom" by 57.2 percent of the respondents (compared to 45.5 percent for capitalism), with "welfare" by 54.3 percent (as compared to 33.1 percent for capitalism) and with "justice" by 53.1 percent (as compared to 22.7 percent for capitalism), while "progress" was associated with capitalism (55.4 percent) more than socialism (41.9 percent).

10. "27 odstotkov bi jih znova živelo v Jugoslaviji," *24UR.com*, January 31, 2010, http://24ur.com/novice/slovenija/27–odstotkov-bi-jih-znova-zivelo-v-Jugoslaviji.html (last accessed September 8, 2012).

11. SHS is the acronym for the state of Serbs, Croats, and Slovenes, or Država Srba, Hrvata, i Slovenaca.

12. The other example is an advertising slogan for Mobitel's new student cell phone plan in 2010, entitled "Džabest," that combines the Serbian-Croatian-Bosnian word *džabe* ("for free") and the English word *best*.

13. Toš, *Vrednote v prehodu III*, 300. According to an opinion poll from 1995, a solid 78.2 percent of respondents "completely disagreed" and "mostly disagreed" with the option that the previous socialist system of self-management under the leadership of the League of Communists should be reinstalled again, while only 11.4 percent "completely agreed" and "mostly agreed" with it. See Toš, *Vrednote v prehodu II*, 615.

14. In Jablanica, Sarajevo, Drvar, and Jajce. This data is from my fieldwork in Bosnia-Herzegovina in 2008 and 2009.

15. Slovenian Yugoslavist discourse goes well in line with another "impossible" attitude and parallels the existence of xenophilia (a fascination with everything that comes from abroad—from the Western world, but particularly from the German part of Europe) and xenophobia (the condemnation of everything that comes from abroad "to spoil our culture

and way of living"—of course, it often comes from the East, not uncommonly referring to the Balkans or Roma populations).

Chapter 7. Vibrant Commonalities and the Yugoslav Legacy

1. This sentence is read aloud as well as written on the screen, in quotes, with the name of Meša Selimović noted under it.

2. This outline of Šerbedžija's life is mostly based on his autobiography. See Rade Šerbedžija, *Do posljednjeg daha: Autobiografski zapisi i refleksije* (Zagreb: Profil, 2005).

3. Muharem Bazdulj, *Travničko trojstvo* (Zagreb: Durieux; Sarajevo: buybook; Cetinje: Otvoreni kulturni forum, 2002).

4. Miroslav Krleža, *On the Edge of Reason*, trans. Zora Depolo (New York: New Directions, 1995), 47.

5. Gordana P. Crnković, *Post-Yugoslav Literature and Film: Fires, Foundations, Flourishes* (New York: Continuum, 2012), 134–35. This quote is slightly edited to fit the present text.

6. Danilo Kiš, *Varia*, ed. Mirjana Miočinović (Belgrade: BIGZ, 1995), 492–93. Krleža becomes more present on the French literary scene a few years after Kiš's interview. All translations are mine unless otherwise noted.

7. Miroslav Krleža, *Mnogopoštovanoj gospodi mravima* (Zagreb: Naklada Ljevak, 2009), 87–88.

8. Predrag Matvejević, *Razgovori s Krležom* (Zagreb: Prometej, 2001), 77–78.

9. Krleža, *Mnogopoštovanoj gospodi mravima*, 71–72.

10. Matvejević, *Razgovori s Krležom*, 124–25.

Chapter 8. *Zenit* Rising

1. Vidosava Golubović and Irina Subotić, eds., *Zenit: 1921–1926 katalog* (Belgrade: Narodna biblioteka Srbije; Institut za književnost i umetnost, 2008), 397–466.

2. The complete set is now available digitally at http://scc.digital.nb.rs/collection/zenit (last accessed September 8, 2012).

3. Miroslav Zec, "Hrvatska ima svoju avangardu"; roundtable in conjunction with the exhibition "Avangardne tendencije u hrvatskoj umjetnosti," *Novi list* (Rijeka, April 25, 2007): 19. The same text has been published in *Glas Istre* (April 25, 2007): 36.

4. Barbara Vujanovic, "Vitalnost avangardne umjetnosti," *Vjesnik* (Zagreb, May 18, 2007): 15.

5. Vaso Milinčević, "Osam i po decenija od nastanka 'Zenita' i zenitizma," *Večernje novosti* (Belgrade), 53, "Kultura" supplement (September 6, 2006), 6.

6. From a conversation with the author, New York, March 9, 2012.

7. *Zenit*, no. 11. Translations mine unless otherwise noted.

8. Miško Šuvaković, "Impossible Histories," in *Impossible Histories: Historical Avant-gardes, Neo-avant-gardes, and Post-avant-gardes in Yugoslavia, 1918–1991*, ed. Dubravka Đurić and Miško Šuvaković (Cambridge, MA: MIT Press, 2003), 3.

9. *Zenit*, 1.

10. Šuvaković, "Impossible Histories," 5. This excellent introduction contextualizes *Zenit* vis-à-vis its political moment and later movements. See also *Zenit i avangarda 20ih godina*

(Belgrade: Narodni muzej-Institut za književnost i umetnost, February–March 1993) for an eloquent summary of *Zenit* chronology, 13–31.

11. Šuvaković, "Impossible Histories," 14.

12. Ibid., 24.

13. Ibid., 20.

14. Sonja Briski Uzelac, "Visual Arts in the Avant-gardes Between the Two Wars," in *Impossible Histories*, 133. See also Irina Subotić, "Vizualna kultura časopisa *Zenit* i Zenitovih izdanja," in *Zenit: 1921–1926 katalog*, 45.

15. Darko Šimičić, "From Zenit to Mental Space: Avant-garde, Neo-avant-garde, and Post-avant-garde Magazines and Books in Yugoslavia, 1921–1987," in *Impossible Histories*, 295.

16. In 2010, the X Initiative in Chelsea put on a provocative exhibit on the subject: "In Numbers: Serial Publications by Artists." For another example, the contemporary magazine *Bidoun* is considered by some to be the most interesting cultural production emerging from and about the Middle East.

17. Walter Benjamin, "The Author as Producer," in *The Work of Art in the Age of Its Technological Reproducibility and Other Writings on Media*, ed. Michael W. Jennings et al., trans. Edmund Jephcott et al. (Cambridge, MA: Harvard University Press, 2008), 83.

18. Ibid., 87.

19. Uzelac, "Visual Arts in the Avant-gardes Between the Two Wars," 145.

20. Walter Benjamin, "The Work of Art in the Age of Its Technological Reproducibility," in *Work of Art*, 38–39. The first version of this famous essay was composed in 1935; the second, on which the translated text is based, is from 1936.

21. Quoted in Dubravka Đurić, "Radical Poetic Practices: Concrete and Visual Poetry in the Avant-garde and Neo-avant-garde," in *Impossible Histories*, 72.

22. Nevena Daković, "The Unfilmable Scenario and Neglected Theory: Yugoslav Avant-garde Film, 1920–1990," in *Impossible Histories*, 470.

23. Ibid., 472.

24. Ibid., 474.

25. Šuvaković, "Impossible Histories," 25.

26. Šimičić, "From *Zenit* to Mental Space," 302.

27. Aleš Erjavec, "The Three Avant-gardes and Their Context," in *Impossible Histories*, 42.

28. Šimičić, "From Zenit to Mental Space," 298.

29. Đurić, "Radical Poetic Practices," 69.

30. As quoted in Pascale Casanova, *The World Republic of Letters*, trans. M. B. De-Bevoise (Cambridge, MA: Harvard University Press, 2007), 220.

31. See the essay by Tomislav Longinović in this volume.

32. Šuvaković, "Impossible Histories," 26.

33. Marjorie Perloff, *21st-Century Modernism: The "New" Poetics* (Oxford: Blackwell Publishing, 2002), 3.

34. Gojko Tešić, "Avangarda kao tradicija," in *Otkrovenje srpske avangarde* (Belgrade: Institut za književnost i umetnost, 2005), 12.

35. Ibid., 17–18.

36. Ibid., 10.

Chapter 9. Post-Yugoslav Emergence and the Creation of Difference

1. Annie Brisset, "Translation and Cultural Identity," in *The Translation Studies Reader*, ed. Lawrence Venuti (New York: Routledge, 2000), 346.

2. Ibid., 353.

3. Sigmund Freud (1930), *The Standard Edition of the Complete Psychological Works*, ed. James Strachey, 24 vols. (London: Hogarth Press, 1953–74), 21: 114.

4. Jacques Derrida, *Monolingualism of the Other; or, The Prosthesis of Origin*, trans. Patrick Mensah (Stanford, CA: Stanford University Press, 1998), 72.

5. Dragan Jurak, "Rane na hrvatskom," *Feral Tribune*, no. 707 (April 5, 1999): 32. All translations are mine unless otherwise stated.

6. Miljenko Jergović, "Marš u sporni organ," *Feral Tribune*, no. 707 (April 5 1999): 23.

7. Basil Hatim and Ian Mason, *Discourse and the Translator* (New York: Longman, 1990), 46.

8. Slobodan Kostić, "Prvi prevod srpskog romana na hrvatski jezik," *Vreme*, no. 456 (October 2, 1999): 17–18.

9. Vinko Brešić, "Lasić i njegovi sugovornici," *Zarez*, no. 183 (June 29, 2006): 122.

10. Kostić, "Prvi prevod srpskog romana na hrvatski jezik," 17–18.

11. For a detailed analysis how translation participates in political and ethnic stereotyping, see Mona Baker, *Translation and Conflict: A Narrative Account* (New York: Routledge, 2006), 122.

12. Francis Jones, "Ethics, Aesthetics, and Decision: Literary Translating in the Wars of the Yugoslav Succession," *Meta* 49, no. 4 (2004): 711–28.

Chapter 10. What Happened to Serbo-Croatian?

1. For details see Rado L. Lenček, "A Few Remarks for the History of the Term 'Serbocroatian' Language," *Zbornik za filologiju i lingvistiku* (Novi Sad) 19, no. 1 (1976): 45–53, a reference particularly apposite here as a tribute to the memory of this former professor in the Slavic Department of Columbia University.

2. For extensive discussion of these and related points, see especially Ranko Bugarski, "One, Two, Three, Four: It's Serbo-Croatian That Counts," in *A Companion in Linguistics: A Festschrift for Anders Ahlqvist on the Occasion of His Sixtieth Birthday*, ed. Bernadette Smelik et al. (Nijmegen: Stichting Uitgeverij de Keltische Draak; Münster: Nodus Publikationen, 2005), 310–23; Bugarski, "Multiple Language Identities in Southeastern Europe (With a Focus on Serbo-Croatian)," in *Europe-Evropa: Cross-Cultural Dialogues Between the West, Russia, and Southeastern Europe*, ed. Maija Könönen and Juhani Nuorluoto (Uppsala: Acta Unversitatis Upsaliensis, Studia Multiethnica Upsaliensia, 2010), 18: 34–49; Bugarski, "Language, Identity and Borders in the Former Serbo-Croatian Area," *Journal of Multilingual and Multicultural Development* 33, no. 3 (2012): 219–35; and Snježana Kordić, *Jezik i nacionalizam* (Zagreb: Durieux, 2010), with further references. Bernhard Gröschel, in *Das Serbokroatische zwischen Linguistik und Politik: Mit einer Bibliographie zum postjugoslavischen Sprachenstreit* (Munich: Lincom Europa, 2009), includes an extremely rich and useful bibliography, and contains a detailed review and assessment of divergent positions on this controversial matter.

3. Ranko Bugarski, "Language in Yugoslavia: Situation, Policy, Planning," in *Language Planning in Yugoslavia*, ed. Ranko Bugarski and Celia Hawkesworth (Columbus, OH: Slavica, 1992), 12.

4. Ranko Bugarski, "Nacionalnost i jezik u popisima stanovništva," chap. 7 in *Jezik i kultura* (Belgrade: Biblioteka XX vek, 2005), 109.

Chapter 11. Language Imprisoned by Identities

Both the first and the second part of this chapter title are possible paraphrases of two claims made by Michel Foucault: the first, that the body can be imprisoned by identity, and the second, that society should be defended. The statement "imprisoned by identity" can be found in many works of Foucault, primarily in *The History of Sexuality*, volume 1. "Why language should be defended" is found in a series of Foucault lectures, "Il faut défendre la société."

1. Hans Georg Gadamer, *Wahrheit und Methode: Grundzüge einer philosophischen Hermeneutik*, 5th ed. (Tübingen: Mohr, 1975).

2. Noam Chomsky, *Language and Problems of Knowledge: The Managua Lectures* (Cambridge, MA: MIT Press, 1991).

3. Karl Kraus, *Die Sprache* (Vienna: Die Fackel, 1937).

4. Dubravko Škiljan, "Sloboda jezika," *SOL, Lingvistički časopis* 7 (1988): 69–78.

5. In several places, after the term *Croatian or Serbian language* went out of use, one can encounter in its place the expression *(new, or general) štokavian*, the term for the most widespread dialect on the basis of which the modern standard language was developed, over a century and a half of its development. In its formative period, which means until the end of the nineteenth century, it developed as a grammar of nation in four countries: two empires (Austro-Hungary, Turkey) and two kingdoms (Serbia and Montenegro).

6. In premodern times debates were carried on about great names like God, Father, Son, and Holy Ghost. Theories of ideologies and discourse theories also involve debates on the phenomenon of great names, such as Freedom, Truth, Justice, Nation, and Class. The semantics of great names still awaits its researcher.

7. Paul Grice speaks of the principle of cooperation, which he uses in a slightly broader sense than the dialogical principle, but it can basically be said that here, in this specific context, we are using a negative version of his principle. See "Logic and Conversation" in *Speech Acts*, vol. 3 of *Syntax and Semantics*, ed. Peter Cole and Jerry L. Morgan (New York: Academic Press, 1975).

8. See Wilhelm von Humboldt, *Über die Verschiedenheit des menschlichen Sprachbaues und ihren Einfluss auf die geistige Entwicklung des Menschengeschlechts* (Stuttgart: Philipp Reclam, 1973).

9. A fine overview can be found in John E. Joseph, *Language and Identity: National, Ethnic, Religious* (New York: Palgrave Macmillan, 2004).

10. I used this expression for the first time in Milorad Pupovac, "The Balkans: Twilight Zone of Civilizations" (working paper, Woodrow Wilson Center for International Scholars, Washington, DC, 1996).

11. Cited after Zlatko Vince, *Putevima hrvatskog književnog jezika: Lingvističko-kulturnopovijesni prikaz filoloških škola i njihovih izvora* (Zagreb: SNL, 1978), 532.

12. Translation by Vasa D. Mihailovich.

13. For more on these concepts see Dubravko Škiljan, *Jezična politika* (Zagreb: Naprijed, 1988).

14. I discussed this term and its meaning for the first time in Milorad Pupovac, "Dva aspekta postmodernog stanja jezične standardizacije," in *Jezik i demokratizacija (Zbornik radova)*, ed. Svein Mønnesland, Posebna izdanja 12 (Sarajevo: Institut za jezik u Sarajevu, 2001).

15. See, for instance, Gradski muzej Virovitrice, www.muzejvirovitica.hr/vijesti/36 (last accessed September 8, 2012).

16. *Večernji list* (February 12, 2010), www.vecernji.hr/vijesti/uhicen-kaznjen-jer-je -policiju-nazvao-milicijom-clanak-95629 (last accessed September 8, 2012).

17. Ibid.

18. In his studies of the literary language, the Zagreb Croatist Ljudevit Jonke often pointed out that the most important rule of the literary language should be: "Write as good writers write."

19. In the Croatian context, but also in the Serbian-Croatian context, an important contribution to increased awareness of this stage was made by Dalibor Brozović's book *Standardni jezik* (Zagreb: Matica Hrvatska, 1970). Before this book, and before the term standard language was introduced into more general usage, Czech and Russian (Soviet) linguists used the term *linguistic technology*, having in mind the many applied linguistics tasks related to the creation or reform of script, literacy programs, and the standardization of the numerous languages of the former Soviet Union. On the issues of standard language and terminology of language planning and language standardization see: Milorad Radovanović, *Sociolingvistika* (Novi Sad: Književna zajednica/Dnevnik, 1986), 186–218; and Radovanović, *Spisi iz kontekstualne lingvistike* (Novi Sad: Izdavačka knjižarnica Zorana Stojanovića Sremski Karlovci, 1997), 17–69.

20. See Dubravko Škiljan, *Javni jezik* (Zagreb: Antibarbarus, 2000).

21. Of course, the terms *language of the people, national language,* or *official language* (*narodni jezik, nacionalni jezik,* or *službeni jezik*) do not belong here, as they denote idioms that have been or can be unstandardized.

22. An interesting attempt at periodizing the process of standardization of the language spoken by Croats, Serbs, Bosnians, and Montenegrins can be found in Radovanović, *Spisi iz kontekstualne lingvistike*, 47.

23. On the relationship between language and the state, see Škiljan, "Sloboda jezika"; and Robert Greenberg, *Jezik i identitet na Balkanu: Raspad hrvatsko-srpskog* (Zagreb: Srednja Europa, 2005); originally published as Robert D. Greenberg, *Language and Identity in the Balkans: Serbo-Croatian and Its Disintegration* (New York: Oxford University Press, 2004).

24. Milenko Perović et al., *Pravopis crnogorskoga jezika* (Montenegro: Ministarstva prosvjete i nauke, Podgorica, 2009), 4; www.gov.me/files/1248442673.pdf (last accessed September 8, 2012).

25. Both the concept of linguistic planning, and its two main forms, status planning and corpus planning, are understood here as defined by Heinz Kloss. One of the first articles on language planning in the area of the former Yugoslavia was published by Ljubiša

Rajić, "Language Planning: Theory and Application," in *Yugoslav General Linguistics*, ed. Milorad Radovanović (Amsterdam: John Benjamins, 1989), 301–19.

26. Perović et al., *Pravopis crnogorskoga jezika*, 5.

27. The phrase *autochthonous Montenegrin citizens* is very unusual, because it suggests that citizenry can be divided into autochthonous and non-autochthonous. It could perhaps be interpreted as indirectly restrictive, for it states that those like eastern Herzegovinians for example, who have the same "remarkable" linguistic features as the speakers of the Montenegrin *koine*, are not included in this language community.

28. Perović et al., *Pravopis crnogorskoga jezika*, 6.

29. Ibid., 4.

30. Mønnesland, ed., *Jezik i demokratizacija*, 39.

31. For lack of anything better, I am introducing here the term *polymorphy*, which should denote the identity domination of fragments of language identity over the whole of the language, on the basis of which language standardization creates a language.

32. On communicability of identity I wrote in Milorad Pupovac, "Language, Identity, and Communication" (unpublished article, written in 1998–99 during a research visit at the Department of Linguistics, Cornell University).

33. I use the term *polyglossia* in the sense developed by Mikhail Bakhtin (V. N. Vološinov), *Marksizam i filozofija jezika* (Belgrade: Nolit, 1980); published in English as V. N. Voloshinov, *Marxism and the Philosophy of Language* (Cambridge, MA: Harvard University Press, 1986). In his view, polyglossia is a characteristic of any type of language reality, from language in general to a particular utterance. Each language and each utterance in it is a result of dialogism, which brings into it elements of another language or of an utterance of the other.

34. *Bosanski kuhar: Tradicionalno kulinarstvo Bosne i Hercegovine*, 5th ed. (Sarajevo: Svjetlost, 1990), 174–75.

35. *Stuffed Turkey*. We use five words to refer to turkey: *tukac*, masculine (*tuka*, fem.), *morac*, masc. (*moruja*, fem.), *bibac*, masc. (*bibica*, fem.), *puran*, masc. (*pura*, fem.) and *ćuran*, masc. (*ćurka*, fem.). This dish had and still has different names: *tukac na pirjanu*, *tukac na tiritu*, *punjeni tukac tiritom*, *nadeveni tukac* (all glossed in English as stewed turkey or stuffed turkey). Ingredients: One whole turkey, young liver (can be also sweetbreads and heart), *majdonos* (leaf and root of parsley), *dereviz* (celery leaf), carrot. Liver and greens should be in sufficient quantity to fill up ½ of the turkey's cavity. One-fourth of this is rice (enough to fill ⅛ of the cavity), salt, pepper, broth, a bit of butter. Clean the turkey. Boil the sweetbreads and heart and throw away the water. Cut in small pieces. Cut the liver as well. Sauté [stew] the rice in butter. Cut the greens. Put salt and pepper and mix all well. Stuff the turkey with this mixture, pour over with the broth and also add some of the grease left from the roast if turkey is not fat. Roast in a deep casserole—*tepsija* [Turkish]. When the turkey is roasted, cut it in half, take out the stuffing and put it on a *pervazija* or *lenger* [oval; Turkish for a copper platter]. Put the split turkey on the top and serve. Serve with *kiselo mleko* [plain yogurt] or other appropriate dishes.

36. This decision was made during presidential elections, with one of the presidential candidates (Dr. Miroslav Tuđman) opposing this decision since that might mean that we recognized that Croatian and Serbian were the same language. If the decision would not

mean that, then he too would agree to the translations being donated to the governments of the neighboring countries.

37. The expression "these spaces" appeared at the end of the 1990s, as a designation for the area of the former Yugoslavia.

Chapter 12. The Vibrant Cinemas in the Post-Yugoslav Space

1. Horton, "Satire and Sympathy: A New Wave of Yugoslav Filmmakers," *Cineaste* 11, no. 2 (1981): 15–17.

2. Director's statement on www.borderpostmovie.com (last accessed November 27, 2012).

3. Rada Šešić, "Bosnia and Herzegovina," in *Variety International Film Guide, 2003* (Los Angeles: Silman-James Press, 2002), 117.

4. Dina Iordinova, *Emir Kusturica* (London: BFI Publishing, 2001), 116.

5. Nika Bohinc, *Slovenski filmi, 2003–2004* (Ljubljana: Slovenian Film Fund, 2004), 13.

6. Ibid., 3.

7. From a personal interview, Sarajevo, August 2003.

Chapter 13. Marking the Trail

1. Patricia White, *Women's Cinema/World Cinema* (Durham, NC: Duke University Press, 2013), p. 3.

2. Maja Weiss has made numerous other films, mostly documentaries. The festival *Crossing Europe*, organized in Linz, dedicated a special section to the work of her and her husband, German filmmaker and musician Peter Braatz.

3. Equally successful was Žbanić's second feature, *Na putu* (*On the Path*, 2010), which, among other things, was nominated for the Golden Bear at the sixtieth Berlin International Film Festival, and won the FIPRESCI (Federation internationale de la presse cinematographique [International Federation of the Cinematographic Press]) Prize at the seventh Yerevan Golden Apricot International Film Festival.

4. *Snijeg* was also the first film directed, written, and produced by a woman in the history of Bosnian cinema.

5. See Dina Iordanova, *Cinema of Flames: Balkan Film, Culture, and the Media* (London: BFI, 2001).

6. Ibid., 56.

7. See Tomislav Longinović, "Playing the Western Eye: Balkan Masculinity and Post-Yugoslav War Cinema," in *Eastern European Cinema*, ed. Anikó Imre (New York: Routledge, 2005), 35–47.

8. This is most frequently achieved by constructing a narrative framework in which the Balkans are represented through the perspective of an outsider, sometimes an expatriate (as in *Before the Rain*) who visits the region and encounters "other" experiences.

9. Iordanova, *Cinema of Flames*, 73.

10. Jurica Pavičić, "Cinema of Normalization: Changes of Stylistic Model in Post-Yugoslav Cinema After the 1990s," *Studies in Eastern European Cinema* 1, no. 1 (2010): 47.

11. Ibid.

12. Ibid., 48.

13. Thomas Elsaesser, "World Cinema: Realism, Evidence, Presence," in *Realism and the Audiovisual Media*, ed. Lucia Nagib (New York: Palgrave Macmillan, 2009), 4.

14. Ibid., 5.

15. Katarzyna Marciniak, Anikó Imre, and Áine O'Healy, eds., *Transnational Feminism in Film and Media* (New York: Palgrave Macmillan, 2007), 4.

16. For example, Marina Abramović, who received a Golden Lion in Venice for her show *Balkan Baroque*, which was turned into a film; short video experiments by Žbanić or *Ecce Homo* by Vesna Ljubić; and the feminist film festival in 1997, in Creteil, where Balkan women showcased their work. This issue is eloquently discussed in Iordanova's *Cinema of Flames*, in a chapter entitled "Representing Women's Concerns."

17. Doro Wiese, "Hallucination: The Entanglement of Race, Gender, and Nationality in *Guardian of the Frontier*," *Identities: Journal for Politics, Gender and Culture* 6, nos. 2–3 (2007–8): 279.

18. Ibid., 280.

19. Ibid., 292.

20. Katarzyna Marciniak, "Palatable Foreignness," in *Transnational Feminism in Film and Media*, ed. Marciniak et. al. (New York: Palgrave Macmillan, 2007), 187–207.

21. Dudley Andrew, "An Atlas of World Cinema," in *Remapping World Cinema: Identity, Culture and Politics in Film*, ed. Stephanie Dannison and Song Hwee Lim (New York: Wallflower Press, 2006), 19, 28.

Chapter 14. Traumatic Experiences

1. Cathy Caruth, *Unclaimed Experience: Trauma, Narrative, and History* (Baltimore: Johns Hopkins University Press, 1996).

2. Sigmund Freud, "Beyond the Pleasure Principle," in *The Standard Edition of Complete Works of Sigmund Freud*, ed. James Strachey, 24 vols. (London: Hogarth Press, 1953–74), 18: 20.

3. Freud, "On the History of the Psychoanalytic Movement," in *Standard Edition*, 14: 243.

4. Ibid., 244.

5. Ibid., 245.

6. Ibid.

7. Riccardo Nicolosi, "Fragmente des Krieges: Die Belagerung Sarajevos in neueren bosnischen Literatur," in *Krieg Sichten: Zur medialen Darstellung der Kriege in Jugoslawien*, ed. Davor Beganović and Peter Braun (Munich: Wilhelm Fink, 2007), 130.

8. Michel Foucault, "Von anderen Räumen," in *Raumtheorie: Grundlagentexte aus Philosophie und Kulturwissenschaften*, ed. Jörg Dünne and Stephan Günzel (Frankfurt am Main: Suhrkamp Verlag, 2006); originally published as "Des espaces autres," in *Dits et écrits* (Paris: Gallimard, 1994), 4: 752–62.

9. Margot Norris, *Writing War in the Twentieth Century* (Charlottesville: University of Virginia Press, 2000), 30.

10. Josip Mlakić, *Kad magle stanu* (Zagreb: Faust Vrančić, 2001), 84; my trans.

11. Faruk Šehić, *Pod pritiskom* (Zagreb: Zoro, 2004), 21.

12. Caruth, *Unclaimed Experience*, 56.

Chapter 15. Culture of Memory or Cultural Amnesia

1. The introductory part of this essay is based on my article on the contemporary Croatian novel, published in the magazine *Eurozine*. See Andrea Zlatar, "Literary Perspectives: Croatia. Posttraumatic Stress Disorder," *Eurozine*, http://eurozine.com/articles/2009-03-31-zlatar-en.html (last accessed October 26, 2012).

2. Part of this was performed within the educational system, especially in primary and secondary schools, where "new" segments of "old" national history entered the curricula, while the period between 1945 and 1990 was suppressed. A sore spot in this conflict is the equating of the antifascist with the communist systems, which only deepened the traditional division between the "left wing" and the "right wing" in Croatia.

3. Dubravka Ugrešić, *Kultura laži* (Zagreb: Arkzin, 1996), 92. All translations in this chapter are my own, with the help of Tomislav Brlek.

4. "I only wonder what happened to the star," Meliha writes ironically and nostalgically at the end of her school paper, a homework assignment about her own memory of the bag with blue, white, and red stripes (Dubravka Ugrešić, *Ministarstvo boli* [Zagreb: Faust Vrančić, 2004], 60).

5. Ibid.

6. Ibid., 64.

7. Maša Kolanović, *Sloboština Barbie* (Zagreb: VBZ, 2008), 19.

8. "If understood in this way, a city's architecture, as the theater-set of memory, is a simulacrum. This gives it the same status as the loci of the buildings, the labyrinths, the parks. Only as a simulacrum, the city, the actual city, receives this fictional dimension that legitimizes it as a site" (Renate Lachmann, *Phantasia, Memoria, Rhetorica* [Zagreb: Matica hrvatska, 2002], 216).

9. The novels of Alen Bović, *Metastases* (*Metastaze*, 2006) and Robert Perišić, *Our Man in the Field* (*Naš čovjek na terenu*, 2007) attest to this, as well as the dramatic texts of Mate Matišić (the postwar trilogy of plays *Nobody's Son* [*Ničiji sin*], *A Woman Without a Body* [*Žena bez tijela*], *Sons Die First* [*Sinovi umiru prvi*]); Ivan Vidić, *White Rabbit* (*Veliki bijeli zec*); and Ivana Sajko, *Woman-Bomb* (*Žena-bomba*) and *Rio Bar* (*Rio bar*).

10. The main character in the novel is the twenty-seven-year-old final-year law student Vjekoslav Modrić, and through his first-person narration we follow the events in the novel. His character as well as his narration are ironic and self-ironic, and he observes and describes reality from a distance. The second protagonist is Hrvoje Modrić, Vjeko's cousin of the same age, whose lifestyle represents the opposing position to Vjeko's worldview. By alternating between the events in the lives of the two protagonists, over a year and a half, we see the reality of Zagreb and Croatia during a period of change not only of the personal but also of collective and cultural identities. The composition of the novel, divided into months (from April to September of the following year), provides a particular rhythm of narration: in a passage of time that seems "natural," Cvetnić condenses the narration of specific moments—important to the characters—into scenes. Vjekoslav Modrić is a modern-day

pícaro of sorts, an urban and intellectual vagabond, who changes jobs several times over the course of several years; thus his own life shows different parts of Croatian reality at the turn of the decade—a meat cooler, an art gallery, the journalistic milieu of the newspaper *Vjesnik*, from the perspective of the basement proofreading office, a company in the process of privatization.

11. A special segment of Ricoeur's reflection on the past is the issue of genocide, especially in terms of responsibility. Ricoeur's reexamination of the philosophy of will, the issues of voluntary, forced, conscious, and unconscious decisions, which started in the 1950s, has in the last decade led him to a radical opinion that contradicts the prevailing notion about the collective character of genocide. Although, in terms of its size, genocide includes thousands and thousands of involved doers, it does not represent a collective act, but is rather a series of individual actions. Therefore, the responsibility and the guilt for the actions of genocide must always be, in the legal sense, processed as individual acts.

Chapter 16. Cheesecakes and Bestsellers

1. Henry A. Giroux, *Beyond the Spectacle of Terrorism* (London: Paradigm Publishers, 2006), 11.

2. Roland Barthes, *The Pleasure of the Text*, trans. Richard Miller (New York: Hill and Wang, 1975), 47–52.

3. Theodor W. Adorno and Max Horkheimer, "The Cultural Industry: Enlightenment as Mass Deception," in *Dialectic of Enlightenment: Philosophical Fragments*, ed. Schmid Noern, trans. Edmund Jephcott (Stanford, CA: Stanford University Press, 2002), 122–27.

4. Hugo Pratt, *Corto Maltese in Siberia*, trans. Elisabeth Bell (orig. pub. in Italian, 1974–75; New York: Nantier-Beall-Minoustchine, 1988).

5. *Poslastičarske priče*, ed. David Albahari and Vladan Mijatović (Belgrade: Arhipelag, 2008).

6. Tihomir Brajović, "Kratka istorija preobilja" [A Short History of Superabundance], Mediacentar Sarajevo, *Sarajevske sveske* [Sarajevo Notebooks] 13 (March 2006): 186–89, www.sveske.ba/bs/content/kratka-istorija-preobilja (accessed February 6, 2011).

7. Vladimir Nabokov, *Lolita*, 2nd ed. (New York: Vintage Books, 1997), 126.

8. Julia Kristeva, "Is There a Feminine Genius?" *Critical Inquiry* 30 (Spring 2004): 493–504.

9. Boris Groys, "The Museum in the Age of Mass Media," 4, Scribd, www.scribd.com/doc/15010876/Boris-Groys-The-Museum-in-the-Age-of-Mass-Media (accessed February 4, 2011).

10. Pierre Bourdieu, *Masculine Domination*, trans. Richard Nice (Stanford, CA: Stanford University Press, 2001), 33–35.

11. Michel Foucault, "What Is an Author?" in *The Foucault Reader*, ed. Paul Rabinow (New York: Pantheon Books, 1984), 118–19.

12. Adorno and Horkheimer, "Cultural Industry," 97.

13. Antonio Gramsci, *Selections from the Prison Notebooks*, ed. and trans. Geoffrey Nowell-Smith (New York: International Publishers, 1971), 102–4.

14. The first "Proza na putu" manifesto, www.prozanaputu.com/index.php/manifest.html (accessed February 12, 2011).

15. The second P-70 manifesto, www.prozanaputu.com (accessed February 12, 2011).

16. Pavle Levi, *Disintegration in Frames: Aesthetic and Ideology in the Yugoslav and Post-Yugoslav Cinema* (Stanford, CA: Stanford University Press, 2007), 135–58.

17. Saša Ilić, "Beton: ista meta, isto odstojanje," *Politika*, December 5, 2009, www.politika.rs/rubrike/Kulturni-dodatak/Ista-meta-isto-odstojanje.lt.html (accessed October 12, 2011).

Chapter 17. Slovene Literature Since 1990

1. George Steiner, *Resnične prisotnosti* (Ljubljana: Literarno-umetniško društvo Literatura, 2003), 49; originally published in English as *Real Presences* (Chicago: University of Chicago Press, 1989).

2. In the past decade, literary production in Slovenia has become large-scale. Slovenia, with a population of two million inhabitants, has a large number of writers, considerably more than in the previous century, but they have been publishing smaller printruns. Whereas before the 1990s an established writer would publish his book in 10,000 copies, today the figure is more likely to be 500. However, it is notable that between 1980 and 1990, 160 novels were published, or 16 per year, while from 1990 to 2000, 370 novels came out, or 37 per year. Over the past decade the average has risen to 100 per year and in 2009 there were as many as 150 novels published.

3. For more on contemporary Slovene literature, see *Antologija sodobne slovenske literature* (Anthology of Contemporary Slovene Literature), published in November 2010 as part of the major project "World Days of Contemporary Slovene Literature" (Ljubljana: Univerza v Ljubljani, Filozofska fakulteta, 2010).

4. Marko Juvan, "Iz slovanskih literatur na koncu 20. stoletja—uvodnik," *Slavistična Revija* 4 (2002): 411.

5. The 1980s were marked by a different kind of engagement by Slovene literary figures, who reacted vocally to political changes and rallied behind ideological groups. The fight for independence was connected with the Slovene Writers Association and the establishment of the journal *Nova revija* (New Review) in 1982, although the "Slovene Spring" was also triggered by some other institutions, such as new social movements and the magazine *Mladina* (Youth). In 1987, issue 57 of *Nove revije* caused quite a stir by publishing "Contributions to a Slovene National Program" in which authors addressed the issue of the organization of Slovene civil society and national politics in a democratic republic. This was built upon by issue 95 of the same publication in 1990, entitled "Independent Slovenia," which argued for a democratic Slovenia with parliamentary elections and territorial independence.

6. Alojzija Zupan Sosič, *Zavetje zgodbe: Sodobni slovenski roman ob koncu stoletja* (Ljubljana: Literarno-umetniško društvo Literatura, 2003), 54.

7. Fredric Jameson, *Postmodernizem* (Ljubljana: Društvo za teoretsko psihoanalizo, 2001), 13; originally published in English as *Postmodernism; or, The Cultural Logic of Late Capitalism* (Durham, NC: Duke University Press, 2001).

8. Slovene literary minimalism is restricted to the short story, while speculation about its presence in the novel has been discredited. The minimalist short story in Slovenia (Polona Glavan, Andrej Blatnik, Dušan Čater) takes American minimalism as a model, not unlike Raymond Carver's prose, for instance.

9. Garry Potter and Jose López, *After Postmodernism: An Introduction to Critical Realism* (New York: Continuum, 2001), 3–16.

10. Fredric Jameson, "A Note on Literary Realism," in *Adventures in Realism*, ed. Matthew Beaumont (Oxford: Blackwell Publishing, 2007), 261–71.

11. Mikhail Epstein (Mihail Epštejn), *Postmodernizam* (Belgrade: Zepter, 1998), 139–42.

12. In my book *Robovi mreže, robovi jaza* (Maribor: Litera, 2006), I describe the new emotionality as a common denominator of novels between 1996 and 2011.

Chapter 18. The Palimpsests of Nostalgia

1. Richard Rorty, "Contingency of Language," in *Contingency, Irony, and Solidarity* (Cambridge: Cambridge University Press, 1989), p. 19.

2. Philip Rice and Patricia Waugh, eds., *Modern Literary Theory* (Oxford: Oxford University Press, 2001), 254.

3. Brian McHale, *Postmodernist Fiction* (New York: Methuen, 1987).

4. Douglas Colin Muecke, *Irony and the Ironic* (New York: Methuen, 1986), 33.

5. Hannah Arendt, "Truth and Politics," in *Between Past and Future: Eight Exercises in Political Thought* (Harmondsworth: Penguin Books, 1993), 257.

6. Patricia Waugh, *Metafiction* (London: Routledge, 1990), 11.

7. Jelena Luzina, *Ten Modern Macedonian Plays* (Skopje: Matica makedonska, 2000).

8. Ibid, 30.

9. Danilo Kocevski, ed., *The End of the Century: Macedonian Poetry in the Last Decade of the Twentieth Century* (Struga: Struga Poetry Evenings, 1999), 97-98.

10. Ibid., 98–99.

11. Ibid., 139.

Index